TRADE
COMPETITIVENESS
DIAGNOSTIC
TOOLKIT

TRADE COMPETITIVENESS DIAGNOSTIC TOOLKIT

José Guilherme Reis
Thomas Farole

THE WORLD BANK
Washington, D.C.

ISBN: 978-0-8213-8937-9
eISBN: 978-0-8213-8938-6
DOI: 10.1596/978-0-8213-8937-9

Library of Congress Cataloging-in-Publication Data

Reis, Jose Guilherme.
   Trade competitiveness diagnostic toolkit / by Jose Guilherme Reis and Thomas Farole.
      p. cm.
   Includes bibliographical references and index.
   ISBN 978-0-8213-8937-9 — ISBN 978-0-8213-8938-6 (electronic)
   1. Foreign trade promotion. 2. Competition, International. I. Farole, Thomas. II. Title.
   HF1417.5.R45 2012
   382'.63—dc23

                                                                                    2011039745

Cover design: Debra Naylor, Naylor Design, Inc.

CONTENTS

Boxes

Figures

Tables

FOREWORD

The pace of global trade integration over the past two decades has been nothing short of extraordinary. Developing countries have been the biggest beneficiaries of trade expansion and the pursuit of "export-led" growth. But leveraging trade for broad-based economic growth is no simple matter—some paths may be better than others, and different countries have had varying degrees of success in achieving this. While the rapid expansion of trade in recent decades was supported by trade policy reforms across the globe, improved market access has not translated into sustainable export growth and diversification for many developing countries. At the same time, in high-income countries that have benefited greatly from an open trading system, trade with developing nations is often viewed more as a threat than as an opportunity.

Clearly, openness to trade and low levels of trade protection, although necessary and important, is not sufficient to ensure sustained export growth and greater diversification. The recent global crises and associated policy responses have shown that most countries remain strongly committed to trade integration, but complementary policies are critical to manage adjustment costs and the effects of volatility. Reflecting this, in recent years the focus of governments has turned toward a broader "trade competitiveness" agenda, aimed at addressing supply-side constraints to investment and trade expansion as well as ensuring an open trade regime. Trade competitiveness is a core pillar of the World Bank's new Trade Strategy, and is also an important dimension of its approach to private sector development. At the operational level, World Bank country teams are increasingly requesting analytical support to understand the factors affecting competitiveness in current traded sectors, along with the prospects for diversification.

But what exactly is "competitiveness?" Where does it begin and end? And how can we assess it and develop policies to shape it? As a concept, competitiveness is intuitively attractive. But it can be frustratingly difficult to pin down and operationalize. Tackling the multifaceted nature of competitiveness requires a deep understanding of the wide range of factors that can contribute to it or constrain it. As these factors are often highly endogenous and interrelated, a piecemeal approach to reform is unlikely to be effective; in practice a comprehensive approach to understanding the determinants of competitiveness is needed.

This *Trade Competitiveness Diagnostic Toolkit* has been developed with the aim of offering guidance to assess an economy's trade competitiveness. The *Toolkit* offers a framework and analytical instruments that can be used to undertake a systematic assessment of a country's position, performance, and capabilities in export markets. Combining quantitative and qualitative tools, the *Trade Competitiveness Diagnostic Toolkit* allows for a rich analysis of a country's trade performance, identification of the main factors that constrain it, and development of targeted policy responses to improve the competitiveness of its firms. The *Toolkit* is designed to be useful both to decision makers as well as for practitioners—it provides a wealth of materials, including policy case studies, tools and indicators, and guidelines for field research, as well as background reading on key policy areas and instruments that affect competitiveness.

Members of the World Bank's Trade Department have worked with country teams to pilot and apply the *Toolkit* in almost a dozen countries, starting in 2010. These countries span most regions of the world. The resulting rich and diverse experience generated important lessons that have been reflected in the present document, and have confirmed that the *Toolkit* can be a very useful instrument to identify specific factors that can contribute to improved competitiveness.

We are confident this *Toolkit* will be a valuable resource for policy makers, practitioners, and analysts who are engaged in policy analysis related to trade, investment, and private sector development.

Otaviano Canuto
Vice President
Poverty Reduction and Economic Management
The World Bank

Bernard Hoekman
Director
International Trade Department
The World Bank

ACKNOWLEDGMENTS

The *Trade Competitiveness Diagnostic Toolkit* was prepared by José Guilherme Reis (task team leader) and Thomas Farole in the International Trade Department of the World Bank (PRMTR), along with a team including Swarnim Waglé (Trade Outcomes and Market Access), Jose Daniel Reyes (Trade Outcomes), Mariem Malouche (Trade and Investment Policy), Michael Friis Jensen (Standards), and Juan Julio Gutierrez (Innovation). The section on Trade Facilitation and Logistics is based heavily on PRMTR's *Trade and Transport Facilitation Assessment Toolkit*, for which the team is indebted to Jean Francois Arvis and Monica Alina Mustra.

The team would also like to thank others who contributed their input and expertise in the development of this *Toolkit*, including: Gladys Lopez-Acevedo, Guillermo Arenas, Olivier Cadot, Leyla Castillo, Ana Paula Cusolito, Ana Margarida Fernandes, Raphael Kaplinsky, Charles Kunaka, Daniel Lederman, Toni Matsudaira, Gerard McLinden, Martha Denisse Pierola, Sebastian Saez, Murat Seker, Cornelia Staritz, and Daria Taglioni.

Thanks also to the peer reviewers and advisers for their valuable input, including Najy Benhassane, Paulo Correa, Jose Luis Guasch, Vincent Palmade, David Rosenblatt, and especially Eric Manes, who was not only a peer reviewer but also a supporter of the *Toolkit* by leading the first pilot Diagnostic. Thanks also to the other task team leaders that supported pilots of the Diagnostic, including Paulo Correa, Julia Devlin, Aurora Ferrari, and Sjamsu Rahardja.

Additionally, thanks to the many others who provided comments and input during the concept and final review meetings as well as throughout the development process, including Kazi Al-Matin, Paul Brenton, Ian Gillson, Harun Onder, Barbara Rippel, and Ravindra Yatawara, and to participants of various seminars including at the World Bank (Latin America and the Caribbean and South Asia Regions) and at the Organisation for Economic Cooperation and Development.

Finally, we are grateful to Cynthia Abidin-Saurman, Shienny S. Lie, Rebecca Martin, and Marinella Yadao for their assistance on administrative issues, and to Stephanie K. Chen who supported the publication process. We also thank the World Bank's Office of the Publisher for efficient management of the publication process, in particular Rick Ludwick, Stephen McGroarty, and Denise Bergeron.

This *Toolkit* was prepared under the direction of Mona Haddad (sector manager) and Bernard Hoekman (director) of the International Trade Department.

ABBREVIATIONS

AAA	Analytical and Advisory Assistance
ACP	African, Caribbean and Pacific
AGOA	African Growth and Opportunity Act
ASEAN	Association of Southeast Asian Nations
ASYCUDA	Automated System for Customs Data
ATC	Agreement on Textiles & Clothing
BACI	*Base pour l'Analyse du Commerce*
BoP	balance of payments
BPO	business process outsourcing
BRIC	Brazil, Russia, India, and China
BTA	bilateral trade agreement
CAN	*Confederazione Nazionale Artigianato*
CEM	Country Economic Memorandum
CEPEX	*Centre de Promotion des Exportations de la Tunisie*
CEPII	*Centre d'études prospectives et d'informations internationales*
CFA	Catfish Farmers of America
CFAD	Sustainably Managed Forest Concessions
CI	CzechInvest
CIF	cost, insurance, freight
CIMO	*Programa de Calidad Integral y Modernización*
CINDE	*La Coalición Costarricense de Iniciativas de Desarrollo*
CMM	capability maturity matrix
COFEMER	*Comisión Federal de Mejora Regulatoria*
COMESA	Common Market for Eastern and Southern Africa
CVD	Countervailing Duty
DB	*Doing Business*
DBP	Development Bank of the Philippines
DEC	Development Economics Unit of the World Bank
DRC	Domestic Resources Cost
DTIS	Diagnostic Trade Integration Study
EBA	Everything But Arms
ECA	Export Credit Agency
ECGA	Export Credit Guarantee Agency
ECOWAS	Economic Community of West African States
EDB	Singapore Economic Development Board
EIA	environmental impact assessment
EICC	Electronic Industry Code of Conduct
EM	extensive margin
EP	entitlement proportion

EPA	Economic Partnership Agreement; also export promotion agency
EPZ	export processing zone
ERP	effective rate of protection
ES	Emergency Safeguard; also Enterprise Survey
ESW	Economic and Sector Work
EU	European Union
EXPY	(Revealed) income content of export basket
FAMEX	*Fonds d' accès aux marchés extérieurs*
FDI	foreign direct investment
FSC	Forestry Stewardship Council
FTZ	free trade zone
FVO	Food and Veterinary Office
GATS	General Agreement on Trade in Services
GATT	General Agreement on Tariffs and Trade
GCI	Global Competitiveness Index
GDP	gross domestic product
GFSME	Guarantee Fund for Small and Medium-Scale Enterprises
GFZB	Ghana Free Zones Board
GIPB	Global Investment Promotion Benchmarking
GLI	Grubel-Lloyd Index
GLOBALGAP	Global Partnership for Good Agricultural Practice
GMP	Good Manufacturing Practice
GNI	gross national income
GSP	Generalized System of Preferences
GSTP	Global System of Trade Preferences
HACCP	Hazards Analysis Critical Control Points
HAI	Human Assets Index
HH(I)	Hirschman-Herfindahl (Index)
HS	Harmonized Commodity Description and Coding System
IAB	*Investing Across Borders*
IAF	International Accreditation Forum
IATA	International Air Transport Association
ICA	Investment Climate Assessment
ICRG	*International Country Risk Guide*
ICS	Investment Climate Survey
ICT(ES)	information and communications technology (enabled services)
IE	International Enterprise Singapore
IEMP	Index of Export Market Penetration
IFC	International Finance Corporation
IFI	international financial institutions
IIA	Investment Incentive Act
ILO	International Labour Organization
IM	intensive margin
IMF	International Monetary Fund
IMO	International Maritime Organization
IMP/IMP2	Industrial Master Plan / Second Industrial Master Plan
I-O	input-output
IP	intellectual property
IPA	investment promotion agency
IPC	*Instituto Politécnico Centroamericano*
IPR	Intellectual Property Rights

ISIC	International Standard Industrial Classification
ISO	International Standards Organization
IT	information technology
ITAF	*Industrial Technical Assistance Fund*
ITC	International Trade Commission
ITU	International Telecommunications Union
KILM	Key Indicators of the Labor Market
JIBC	Japan Export Import Bank
km	kilometer
L/C	letter of credit
LDC	least developed country
LIC	low-income country
LMIC	low- and middle-income countries
LPI	Logistics Performance Index
(MA)OTRI /TTRI	(Market Access) Overall Trade Restrictiveness Index/Tariff Trade Restrictiveness Index
MAS	Modernization and Automation 2 Scheme
MDB	multilateral development bank
MFA	Multifiber Arrangement
MFN	Most Favored Nation
MITI	Ministry of Industry and Trade
MNC/E	multinational company/enterprise
MPIP	Multipurpose Industrial Park
MSC	Marine Stewardship Council
MSTQ	Metrology, Standardization, Testing, and Quality
MUB	manufacturing under bond
N/A	not applicable or not available
NAFIN	*Nacional Financiera*
NAFTA	North American Free Trade Agreement
NAMA	Non-Agricultural Market Access
NCP	National Competition Policy
n.e.s.	not otherwise specified
NGO	nongovernmental organization
NTB/NTM	nontariff barrier/measure
OECD	Organisation for Economic Co-operation and Development
OHSAS	Occupational Health and Safety Accreditation Standard
OLS	ordinary least squares
PIA	Promotion of Investment Act
PIO	Pioneer Industries Ordinance
ppb/ppt	parts per billion/parts per trillion
PPP	purchasing power parity
PREM	Poverty Reduction and Economic Management
PRMTR	International Trade Department (World Bank)
PROCOMER	the Foreign Trade Corporation of Costa Rica
PRODY	(Revealed) income content of product
PROMPEX	Peruvian Commission for Export Promotion
PSDC	Penang Skills Development Council
PTA	preferential trade agreement
R&D	research and development
RCA	Revealed Comparative Advantage
RFI	Revealed Factor Intensity
RHCI	Revealed Human Capital Index

ROO	rules of origin
RPCI	Revealed Physical Capital Index
RTA	Regional Trade Agreement
SAD	Single Administrative Document
SAFTA	South Asian Free Trade Area
SCM	Subsidies and Countervailing Measures
SEI	Software Engineering Institute
SGS	*Societe Generale de Surveillance*
SI(T)C	Standard International (Trade) Classification
SEZ	special economic zone
SMEs	small and medium enterprises
SOE	state-owned enterprise
SPS	sanitary and phytosanitary
SQF	Safe Quality Food
STEM	science, technology, engineering, mathematics
T&C	textiles and clothing
TBS	Tanzania Bureau of Standards
TBT	technical barriers to trade
TCD	Trade Competitiveness Diagnostic
TCI	Trade Complementarities Index
TE	technical efficiency
TEU	twenty-foot equivalent units
TFP	total factor productivity
TII	Trade Intensity Index
TKC	Trans-Kalahari Corridor
TNC	transnational companies
TRAINS	Trade Analysis and Information System
TRQ	Tariff Rate Quota
TSG	Traditional Speciality Guaranteed
TTFA	Trade and Transport Facilitation Assessment
UDE	*Unidad de Desregulacion Economica*
UN	United Nations
UNCTAD	United Nations Conference on Trade and Development
UNESCO	United Nations Educational, Scientific, and Cultural Organization
UNIDO	United Nations Industrial Development Organization
USAID	United States Agency for International Development
VAT	value added tax
VER	voluntary export restraint
WDI	World Development Indicators
WEF	World Economic Forum
WHO	World Health Organization
WIPO	World Intellectual Property Organization
WITS	World Integrated Trade Solution
WTI	World Trade Indicators
WTO	World Trade Organization

INTRODUCTION TO THE TOOLKIT

This *Trade Competitiveness Diagnostic (TCD) Toolkit* provides a framework, guidelines, and practical tools needed to conduct an analysis of trade competitiveness. The toolkit can be used to assess the competitiveness of a country's overall basket of exports, as well as specific traded sectors. It includes guidance on a range of tools and indicators that can be used to analyze trade performance in terms of growth, orientation, diversification, quality, and survival, as well as quantitative and qualitative approaches to analyze the market and supply-side factors that determine competitiveness. The toolkit facilitates the identification of the main constraints to improved trade competitiveness and the policy responses to overcome these constraints.

The output of a TCD initiative can be used for a wide variety of purposes. In the World Bank, it could be a stand-alone product (such as Economic and Sector Work [ESW]) or could contribute to existing World Bank products—for example, it could form a substantial part of a Diagnostic Trade Integration Study (DTIS), a chapter within a Country Economic Memorandum (CEM), or the basis for programs within a Competitiveness Development Policy Loan.

Overall, the TCD is designed to be used in a modular way—full-country diagnostics can be undertaken or various parts of the toolkit can be used to address specific questions of interest to the country team. The output from a TCD will identify issues to be addressed in more detail by technical experts, client-country policy makers and other stakeholders, and development partners. In some cases, it may identify issues that require another level of analysis using existing products from the World Bank or other development partners. In other cases, it will lead to engagement between client countries and specific experts.

The *TCD Toolkit* is intended for policy makers and practitioners involved in analysis of trade performance and design of trade and industrial policy. Although the primary audience is World Bank country and regional staff,

including from Poverty Reduction and Economic Management (PREM), Financial and Private Sector Development (FPD), and other networks, it is also designed for use by donors and development agencies, government ministries and agencies, and academic and policy institutions. Given the diverse objectives and interests of this target group, users are encouraged to make selective use of the *Toolkit* on the basis of their interests, contexts, and capacities.

To make this toolkit useful to different audience needs, it is divided into two main sections:

- **Overview and Guidelines for Conducting a Trade Competitiveness Diagnostic**—summarizes the main issues and offers a step-by-step guideline to conduct a diagnostic of trade competitiveness. This section is appropriate for all audiences, including policy makers and managers overseeing a TCD exercise.
- **Implementation Toolkit**—provides detailed practical information and tools for actually carrying out the TCD. This is appropriate for practitioners conducting the analysis and for task team leaders organizing and managing the exercise. The *Implementation Toolkit* is divided further into three modules:
    - *Module 1: Trade Outcomes Analysis (indicators and tools)*
    - *Module 2: Competitiveness Diagnostics (analytical frameworks, indicators, and interview guides)*
    - *Module 3: Policy Options for Competitiveness and Case Studies*

The modules include a list of references to works cited in the toolkit. In addition, Module 1 offers an annex that describes the two-digit *product classifications* for Harmonized Commodity Description and Coding System (HS) and Standard International Trade Classification (SITC). The book also includes an appendix that summarizes some recent papers on trade competitiveness that contributed to the preparation of the *TCD Toolkit*.

Updates and details on the *TCD Toolkit* are on the World Bank's Trade website at www.worldbank.org/trade.

Box A. The World Bank and the Trade and Competitiveness Agenda

The World Bank and other multilateral organizations have played an important role in promoting trade through support for the adoption of liberal trade and investment policies. In recent years, the agenda to support trade growth has moved beyond trade policy and market access to embrace behind-the-border issues. Indeed, competitiveness lies at the core of the Bank's new Trade Strategy (World Bank, 2011d). At the operational level, country teams are increasingly requesting analytical support to understand the factors affecting competitiveness in current traded sectors, along with the prospects for diversification. This has been reflected in the growing emphasis on trade and competitiveness in the Bank's lending and technical assistance portfolio. Two-thirds of Country Assistance Strategies now recognize trade and competitiveness as a priority and trade-related lending has grown significantly (World Bank 2009d). As of September 2009, more than 250 active Analytical and Advisory Assistance (AAA) projects and 195 active lending products listed competitiveness as a priority. Within World Bank operations, since 2007, a large and active export competitiveness network has facilitated knowledge sharing throughout the World Bank and with clients and development partners.

Although the Bank is in a good position to deploy its expertise across most the issues related to trade competitiveness, it still needs (1) to be able to analyze competitiveness more effectively *ex ante* to respond to competitiveness challenges in a systematic fashion, and (2) to identify the most important constraints to competitiveness in order to prioritize policy responses. This is a particular challenge, given the broad-based, often fuzzy nature of the concept of competitiveness. The *Trade Competitiveness Diagnostic Toolkit* is designed to help address this challenge.

Source: Authors.

Box B. Appropriate Use of the Toolkit

This version of the toolkit is **not** designed to do the following:

- **Pick winning sectors or products:** Although a combination of the analytical tools available in the Trade Outcomes Analysis could be used to identify sectors or products for the purposes of industrial policy intervention, the existing toolkit is designed for diagnostics rather than for opportunity identification *per se.* Thus, no step-by-step guide is provided to conduct product-level analysis and prioritization.
- **Sector-specific diagnostics:** This version of the toolkit is designed primarily to analyze a country's overall export basket. It has the potential to conduct a sector-level analysis as a "lens" through which to view competitiveness of the overall trade sector. Although it is possible to conduct a sector-specific diagnostic using the framework in this toolkit, a version 2.0 of the toolkit will develop a series of tailored modules to analyze specific sectors. In this version, we provide broad guidelines on the types of issues that may be more or less important for specific sectors (light manufacturing, agribusiness, tourism, and business services).
- **Detailed policy prescriptions:** This version of the toolkit includes discussion of broad policy areas and options for consideration in addressing the specific constraints identified through the Diagnostic exercise. It also includes case studies of good practice highlighting policies that were effective in addressing trade competitiveness constraints across a range of countries. Given the highly context-specific and endogenous nature of policy development for competitiveness and the critical importance of taking into account political economy considerations, the toolkit does not provide prescriptive advice on the specific policies that should be adopted.

Source: Authors.

OVERVIEW AND GUIDELINES FOR CONDUCTING A TRADE COMPETITIVENESS DIAGNOSTIC

Understanding Trade Competitiveness: Issues and Current Debates

Trade, Growth, and Convergence

Since the 1980s, when most developing countries abandoned wholesale import substitution models in favor of export-led growth, global trade integration has proceeded at a rapid pace. Trade has arguably been the most important driver of global growth, convergence, and poverty alleviation over the last quarter century. Developing countries in particular have benefited—annual exports from low- and middle-income countries grew 14 percent annually since 1990 compared with only 8 percent from high-income countries. Despite the recent global economic crisis, a consensus remains on the positive relationship between trade and long-run economic growth. This relationship runs in both directions: the richer countries become the more they tend to trade; more importantly, countries that are most open to trade grow richer more quickly. The East Asian experience of export-led growth over the past three decades provides powerful evidence of the role of trade in facilitating growth. However, regions still vary widely in the degree to which they are integrated into global markets as illustrated in figure O.1.[1] Within regions, the variance is even more dramatic—for example, Vietnam's trade is 158 percent of its gross domestic product (GDP), Thailand's trade is 136 percent, and Cambodia's trade is 113 percent, whereas neighboring Lao People's Democratic Republic has a trade share of only 47 percent of GDP.

The economic benefits of exporting have a long-established theoretical basis. Specifically, these include static efficiency gains derived from exploiting comparative advantage and improved allocation of scarce resources, as well as dynamic gains in the more productive export sector engineered by higher competition, greater economies of scale, better capacity utilization, knowledge dissemination, and technological progress. The recent literature on heterogeneous firms also emphasizes that exporters on average are more productive, capital-intensive, larger, and pay higher wages than nonexporters (cf. Bernard et al. 2007). For developing countries, exports are a main source of hard currency necessary to finance the import of capital goods and other inputs. Indeed, the gains to trade are as much derived from imports as from exports—openness to imports also acts as a disciplining force on domestic markets, leading to lower-cost, higher-quality inputs for producers.

The Competitiveness Approach

What are the constraints that prevent countries from exploiting trade potential for long-term economic gain? Traditionally, the focus has been on reducing barriers to market access—through such trade policy measures as reducing tariffs and quotas, granting preferences, and encouraging broader liberalization efforts. But even with the benefit of preferential market access, many developing country exporters are unable to compete in global markets. The barriers they face are many and diverse, including the following: macroeconomic policies that distort efficient market entry and competition; poor factor conditions (cost and skill of labor, cost of capital), infrastructure and backbone services, and transport and logistics inefficiencies that raise production and trade costs; and information and coordination failures and the underprovision of public goods, which prevent the exploitation of intra- and interindustry spillovers. The realization of these enduring barriers to export success has contributed to the emergence of the "behind-the-border" or "competitiveness" agenda, which targets the supply-side constraints to export performance.

Thus, the competitiveness approach seeks to address the *microeconomic environment* that shapes individual firms' capacities and incentives on a daily basis. This competitiveness policy framework can be structured in three pillars, as illustrated in figure O.2.

3

Figure O.1. Evolution of Trade Share of GDP, 1970–2008, and Trade Share of GDP by Region, 2008

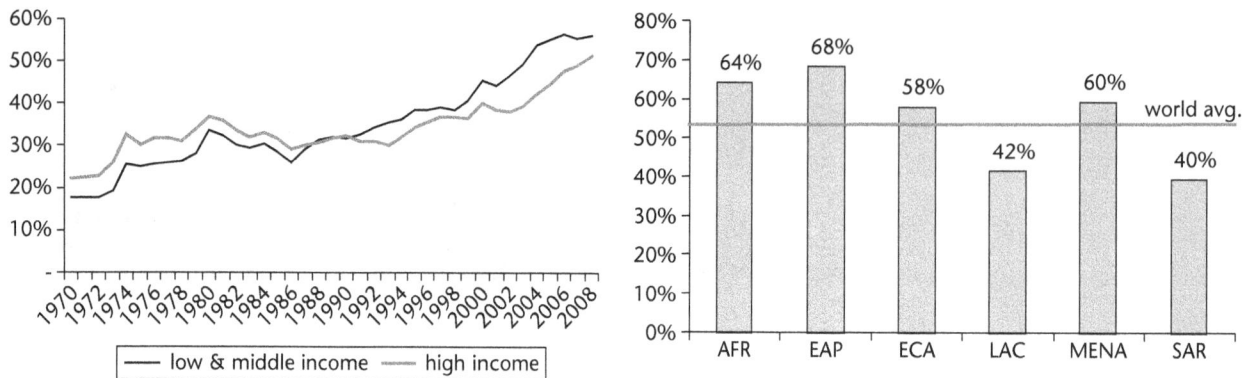

Source: World Bank 2011c.
Note: GDP = gross domestic product.

Figure O.2. The Three Pillars of Trade Competitiveness

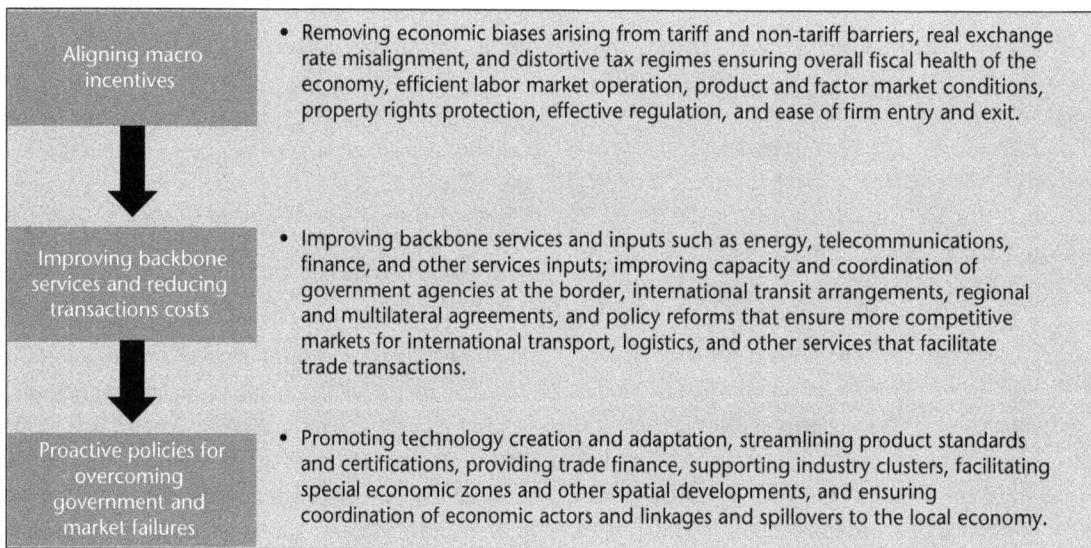

Source: World Bank International Trade Department 2008.

Trade Competitiveness: Issues and Current Debates

For most countries, particularly in middle- and high-income economies, the large majority of export growth takes place at the *intensive margin*—that is, by selling more of the same products to the same markets (Brenton and Newfarmer 2009). This deepening of trade relationships is supported by increasing specialization, which may be across or within products. Within-product specialization can be observed through levels of intra-industry trade, which may derive from specialization in stages of production as well as from specialization at different levels of the quality ladder (what we call the *quality margin*). The former is the source of the trade in components—or intermediate inputs—that characterizes global production

networks. The latter is the source of cross-hauling—or two-way trade in similar end products—that allows for the intense two-way trade within high-income countries in areas like automobiles (for example, Fiats to Germany and BMWs to Italy), clothing (for example, Zara to Sweden and H&M to Spain), and commonplace food items like yogurt, juice, and ice cream. For developing countries, however, growth at the *extensive margin*—including both new product discovery and selling existing products to new markets—remains critical to driving exports and employment. Indeed, the reduced vulnerability to external shocks that results from a diversification of exports is critical to long-run growth. For new trade flows to be sustainable and deliver broad-based growth, however, it is important that a large cross-section of firms is able to take advantage of trade opportunities and that these firms are able to overcome the many constraints that threaten the ***export survival*** of firms in their initial years.

Box O.1 Summarizes some of the key ongoing issues and debates in research and policy in relation to trade competitiveness.

Box O.1. Key Issues and Debates

- ***Trade openness:*** The recent global economic crisis led to a reemergence of the debate over the benefits of openness. Analysis of the crisis suggests that more open economies tended to see their trade and gross domestic product (GDP) levels fall more rapidly than economies who were less integrated in global markets (Eichengreen 2011). On the other hand, the countries and regions (for example, East Asia) that were most integrated into the global economy bounced back more quickly. And despite the concerns that the crisis would lead to a return to protectionism, little evidence indicates that this has been the case. Indeed, most policy makers appear to be convinced of the benefits of openness, while also aware of the risks it brings and the need to adopt policies that can minimize these risks (for a detailed discussion of these issues, see Haddad and Shepherd 2011).
- ***Services trade:*** Trade in services, particularly business services, has become a dynamic component of trade as well as another source of export diversification in developing countries. During 2000–07, trade in services grew as fast as trade in goods, at an average rate of 12 percent per year. India's success is well known: Exports of software and business process services account for approximately 33 percent of India's total exports. Brazil, Costa Rica, and Uruguay export professional and information technology–related services; Mexico exports communication and distribution services; Chile exports distribution and transportation services. African countries are also participating. Morocco, Tunisia, Kenya, and South Africa provide professional services to Europe, and Arab Republic of Egypt has developed a world-class call center sector. Health services are successfully exported by the Philippines and Thailand.
- ***South-South trade:*** Trade among developing countries tripled between 1996 and 2006, and it now accounts for more than 12 percent of all world trade. More than 45 percent of imports in developing countries were supplied by other developing countries in 2008. This trend is driven by the rapid growth in economies like China and India, which is driving trade in both commodities and processed goods. Reductions in the average level and the dispersion of tariffs have been a significant force behind South-South trade. The average tariffs imposed by Brazil, the Russian Federation, India, and China (BRIC) decreased 44 percent during 1996–2008. Tariffs in lower-middle-income countries declined by 31 percent during the same period.
- ***Diversification or reconcentration?*** Imbs and Wacziarg (2003) uncovered an unexpected nonmonotonic relationship between production diversification and GDP per capita. Past a certain level of income (US$9,000 in 1985 purchasing parity power [PPP] dollars), countries appear to reconcentrate their production structure. Klinger and Lederman (2006) as well as Cadot, Carrère, and Strauss-Kahn (2011) analyze the issue from a trade perspective and find the same U-shaped pattern but at higher levels of GDP per capita (more than US$22,000 in 2005 PPP dollars).
- ***The productivity and diversification nexus:*** Although the link between trade and productivity has been long recognized, the direction of its causality has been less clear. The new trade models based on firm heterogeneity (cf. Bernard and Jensen 1999; Melitz 2003; Helpman, Melitz, and Rubinstein 2008) have made important progress in showing how productivity, at the firm level, contributes to export participation. At the same time, this new literature shows that at an aggregate level, export participation contributes to economywide productivity increases.
- ***A natural resource curse?*** The traditional view (cf. Sachs and Warner 1995, 1999) of natural resources (and commodities) as being a "curse," constraining the long-term growth of developing countries, has been challenged by new emprical research and changes in global commodities markets. Evidence suggests it is not natural resources dependence per se that increases risk but rather the concentration of exports (Lederman and Maloney 2007). Indeed, with the demand for commodities rising and likely to be sustained over the medium term, diversification into agriculture and commodities is rising on the agenda of low-income countries.
- ***Sophistication or quality?*** One key debate is whether export competitiveness is best achieved through an evolutionary process of upgrading—selling lower-quality goods to regional markets and building capabilities before moving into more competitive, sophisticated global markets—or leapfrogging immediately to sophisticated goods or rich-country markets. Rodrik (2006) and Hausmann, Hwang, and Rodrik (2007) argue that certain goods provide greater opportunities for growth because of the greater potential to upgrade vertically within the industry (for example, cars versus bananas) and to benefit from interindustry spillovers of knowledge. Coming at it from a different angle, Mattoo and Subraimanian (2009) find that, contrary to conventional wisdom, many of the recent successful emerging economies have grown not only by following comparative advantage but also by using industrial policies to defy it. Others question the premise of "sophistication"—that selling rich-country products is more likely to make you rich—arguing that quality is not ingrained in the product but rather the process (Harrison and Rodrìguez-Clare 2009; Lederman and Maloney 2009; Schott 2004; Xu 2010).
- ***Export discovery or export survival?*** Research by Hausmannn and Rodrik (2002), Klinger and Lederman (2004), and Hausmann, Hwang, and Rodrik (2007) argues that firms in developing economies tend to underinvest in export "discovery," fearing the erosion of their margin by market followers who would not face the same level of sunk costs of investment borne by first movers. On the other hand, recent research on survival (Brenton and Newfarmer 2009) documents extensive experimentation in low income countries and argues that the problem is that these export relationships are short-lived; indeed, in a study of African exporters, Cadot et al. (2011) find that less than 20 percent of export relationships survive the first year. Although the former set of findings suggests policies (for example, subsidies, export promotion) to support the discovery process, the latter indicate the need for greater focus on addressing the constraints to sustaining export flows.
- ***Export agglomeration and spillovers:*** The recent research on export survival suggests that exporting has an element of "learning by doing"—experience with exporting the same product to other markets or different products to the same market are found to strongly increase the chance of export survival. Perhaps more interestingly, export survival appears to be affected by spillovers. For example, Cadot et al. (2011) find that the chances of a firm's exports surviving increase with the number of other firms also exporting a specific product to a specific market (and this effect is stronger for heterogeneous goods that for homogenous ones). These findings suggest the importance of knowledge spillovers across exporters and point to the potentially valuable role of export promotion agencies to facilitate information exchange and collective action.

Source: Authors.

Ultimately, the aim of trade for policy makers is sustainable, broad-based economic growth. Thus, an important question remains: How can a country translate trade into growth and poverty reduction? Not all sectors are equally predisposed to contribute to spillovers and broad-based economic growth.

What matters for competitiveness is not only the capability to be productive in a static or slowly evolving external environment but also the ability to adjust and adapt to structural changes. Being able to remain competitive and adapt to changes requires redeploying resources (capital, labor, institutions) to higher-value activities. Policies that promote entry and exit in both product and factors markets are also important, as inefficient factor and product markets, as well as high costs of entry and exit, may lead firms to incur otherwise-unnecessary adjustment costs whenever a shock hits an economy.[2]

The multifaceted nature of trade competitiveness thus requires a deep understanding of the wide range of factors that may contribute to or constrain it. And as these factors are often highly endogenous, a piecemeal approach to reform is unlikely to be effective. At the very least, a comprehensive approach to understanding the constraints and how they affect the trade sector is necessary.

The TCD Framework

Figure O.3 presents the overall TCD framework, linking explanatory factors to observed trade performance. The figure illustrates two main components: *Trade Outcomes Analysis* and *Competitiveness Diagnostics.*

The **Trade Outcomes Analysis** provides a quantitative and qualitative assessment of historic trade performance using the decomposition of the margins of trade growth as the framework to explore trade competitiveness. Specifically, we define four principal factors on which a country's trade competitiveness performance can be determined: (1) the *level, growth, and market share* performance of existing exports (the intensive margin); (2) *diversification* of products and markets (the extensive margin); (3) the *quality and sophistication* of exports (the quality margin); and (4) the *entry and survival* of new exporters (the sustainability margin).

Understanding a country's relative performance (overall or at a sector level) on these various aspects of trade provides a summary of its competitiveness in global markets. But this is only half the story. To have a chance to improve competitiveness, it is necessary also to understand the main determinants of competitiveness, the factors that are most constraining, and the policy levers that might be pulled to overcome these constraints. This is no simple task, particularly given the broad-based nature of competitiveness.[3] The second component of the TCD, the **Competitiveness Diagnostics,** provides a framework for analyzing determinants of trade competitiveness across three broad areas:

1. **Market access** focuses on the external trade policy environment that may facilitate or constrain exporters from entering and maintaining competitiveness in markets.
2. **Supply-side factors** cover a broad range of determinants, including governance and macrofiscal, trade,

Figure O.3. TCD Framework

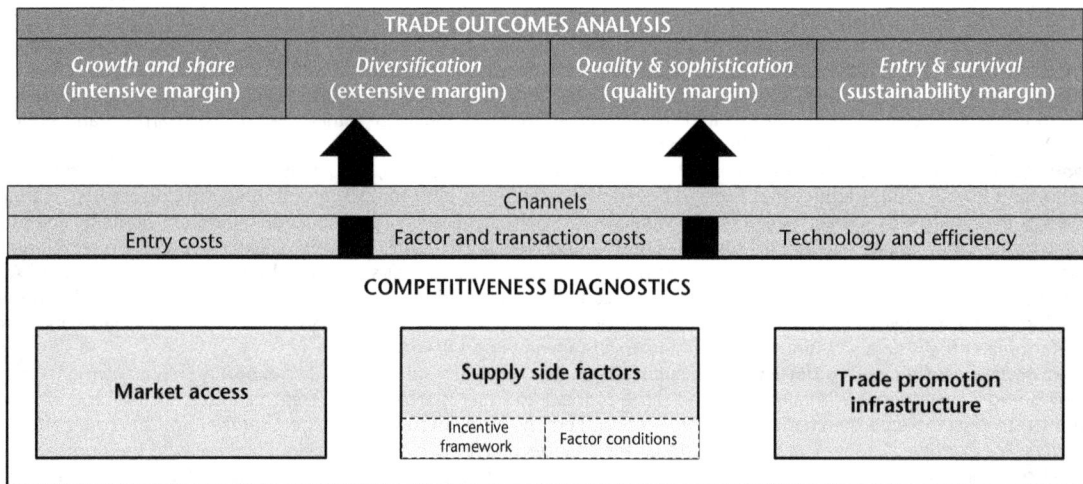

Source: Authors.

and domestic policies that establish the incentive framework faced by the private sector, as well as the factor inputs that determine competitiveness at the factory or farm gate.

3. **Trade promotion infrastructure** covers the range of interventions by government to address market failures (coordination challenges, asymmetric information) and government failures that restrict export participation and performance, including traditional export promotion, special economic zones (SEZs), industry coordination bodies, and standards regimes.

Each of these components shapes observed trade performance through its impact on individual firms in one (or more) of three channels: the *fixed costs* (and risk) of production and export entry, the *factor and transactions costs* that determine factory-gate competitiveness, and the level of *technology and efficiency* at which the sectors and firms operate. In an efficient and a competitive context, capital will be allocated to the most productive firms in the most productive sectors. But in cases in which the policy environment protects certain sectors or firms, it may create an anti-export bias or a gap between areas where capital can appropriate the greatest rents and areas where it is most efficient from an economywide perspective. Equally, in cases in which structural competitiveness gaps exist, firms may underinvest in sectors that should otherwise be a source of comparative advantage.

In practice, the two components—Trade Outcomes Analysis and Competitiveness Diagnostics—are usually conducted separately and sequentially. First, the Trade Outcomes Analysis gives a picture of trade performance, identifies key areas of weakness or risk in trade competitiveness, and raises questions and hypotheses about the contributing factors. This sets the agenda for the Competitiveness Diagnostics that follows, which focuses on understanding the underlying policies, and structural dynamics that shape this observed performance.

Organizing to Conduct a TCD

Establishing the Objectives

The starting point for undertaking a Trade Competitiveness Diagnostic is to define the objectives of the assessment. Objectives will vary from one country to the next, depending on its challenges, its trade and industrial strategy, and the planning and policy processes into which the assessment will contribute. Before undertaking the assessment, at minimum, the issues outlined in table O.1 should be considered.

Because the TCD has been designed in a modular way, the potential scope and output may vary considerably from project to project. Full-country or sector-level diagnostics can be undertaken, and various tools of the TCD can be used to address specific questions of interest. Box O.2 describes one way to use the TCD to develop a series of policy notes on trade competitiveness.

The issues outlined in table O.1 need not be mutually exclusive, and any TCD exercise may pursue multiple objectives. In any case, it is important to start with a clear understanding of what the TCD aims to achieve and how it will be used. This not only will guide and focus the analysis but also will be critical to facilitate communication with stakeholders who will be involved in the project, as well as with internal and external clients who will use its outcomes (and may contribute resources to fund it).

Table O.1. Considerations in Establishing Objectives of the TCD

Objectives of export strategy	• How important has the export sector been and what are the perceptions of recent and future performance? • Is there an emphasis on diversification? Upgrading?
How will the results be used?	• To feed into a national export, trade, or industrial strategy • To inform policy dialogue on opportunities to improve trade performance and remove constraints to export sector • To identify specific projects or programs as part of a wider initiative designed to improve competitiveness
Scope of the assessment	*National versus sectoral* • Is there a need to understand the structure and performance of the overall export portfolio—for example, to assess the economies process of adjustment? • What are the specific sectors—economically critical or potential future opportunities—on which the assessment will focus? *Broad versus focused* • Will the assessment take a comprehensive approach to diagnose "binding constraints" to competitiveness, or are there specific issues (for example, trade promotion, trade logistics, and so on) that will be the main focus?

Source: Authors.

Box O.2. Using Trade Competitiveness Diagnostics to Develop Policy Notes

The Trade Competitiveness Diagnostic (TCD) can provide a useful set of tools with which to engage governments on a broad discussion of competitiveness. One way to organize the TCD to facilitate such a dialogue is to plan for the preparation of a series of policy notes derived from the analysis.

The first stage of the TCD—the Trade Outcomes Analysis—provides a detailed quantitative assessment of trade performance across several measures of competitiveness. This analysis not only can be packaged as a useful note in its own right but also can be used to identify specific sector-level analysis or questions that can guide the TCD efforts and serve as topics for additional policy notes. For example, the Outcomes Analysis might raise important questions like (1) Why has the country been unable to penetrate fast-growing Asian markets with exports that are doing well in Latin America, Europe, and North America? (2) What factors are preventing the country from upgrading in the light-manufacturing sector? and (3) Why are survival rates for exporters particularly low for intraregional trade? The TCD can then be organized around answering those specific questions, giving three clear policy notes as outputs. Finally, the findings from across the three analyses can be brought together to derive overall lessons for trade competitiveness, which could serve as a fifth and final policy note.

Source: Authors.

With the objectives clarified, the next step is to ensure that resources are mobilized to undertake the TCD and that a clear workplan is put in place. A number of project management issuess need to be considered.

Who Should Be Involved?

TCD Team

The TCD is designed to be led by a relatively small core team, most likely including three or four staff members. At least one team member should be a trade economist with an understanding of trade policy and competitiveness issues, as well as technical skills to analyze trade data. The task team leader (TTL) ideally should have some trade experience, but most important, should have in-depth country knowledge and experience. Given that the TCD is not intended to conduct in-depth technical analysis, it should not be necessary to involve technical experts for each component of the diagnostic. If certain topics are seen to be critical from the outset—in particular innovation, skills and productivity, or trade facilitation—it may be useful to bring in specialized technical expertise to lead those components.

To conduct the Trade Outcomes Analysis, it will be important to have a skilled trade data analyst who is familiar with the main data sources used in this *Toolkit* and has some experience using the Stata statistical package. The World Bank International Trade Department has automated much of the process and can provide Stata "do" files that automatically run the analysis and prepare the graphs and figures needed in the Trade Outcomes Analysis. In a second phase of the *Toolkit* implementation, it is expected that fully automated tools will be available online that will enable users to input data and retrieve results.

Counterparts and Stakeholders

In addition to the team leading the data collection and analysis, the success of the TCD will depend on input from a wide variety of stakeholders in the country, including government officials and the private sector. The inclusion of stakeholders is important not only for planning and conducting the TCD, but also and most important for reaching consensus on the priority actions and policies that emerge from the process.

Identification and engagement with stakeholders should begin in the early stages of developing the TCD workplan. This will ensure that key stakeholders agree with the approach and will also facilitate access to information and key contacts. Although consultation will take place through individual and focus group interviews, it may also be useful to organize a steering group to oversee the TCD exercise. Such a steering committee should include both public and private sector members. Its main role would be to advise and intervene at key points in the TCD process, including the following: (1) endorsing the proposed workplan and methodology; (2) reviewing and endorsing the Trade Outcome Analysis Report; (3) reviewing and endorsing of the TCD final report; and (4) preparing and endorsing the proposed policy recommendations and program of action.

Given the broad nature of competitiveness, such a committee may need to draw on members from across a number of different government agencies and industry sectors. A key challenge in this respect will be ensuring inclusivity while avoiding making the committee too large to function efficiently.

How Will the TCD Be Conducted?

The TCD will be conducted in three main steps as outlined in figure O.4. This includes (1) the preparation of the Trade

Figure O.4. Work Stages for the Trade Competitiveness Diagnostic

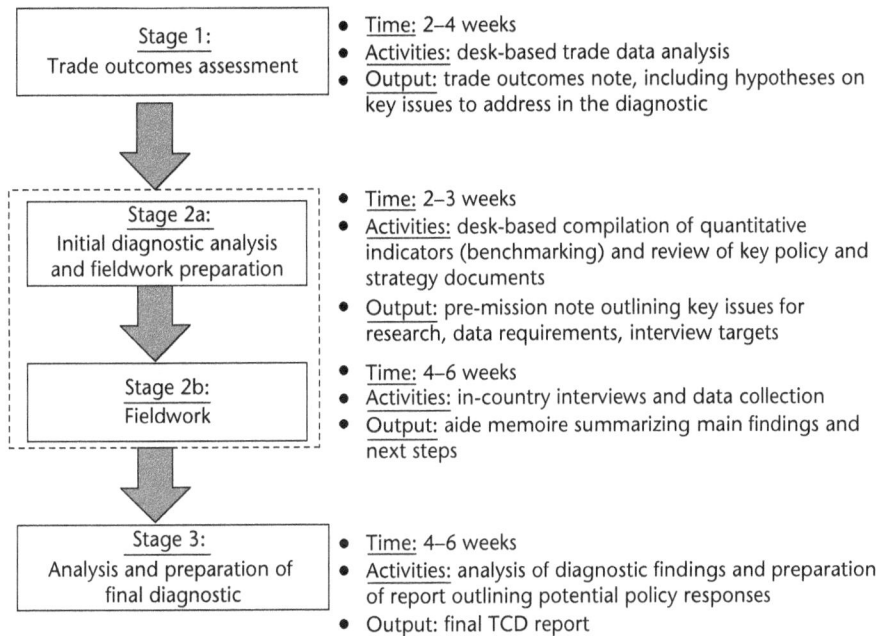

- **Stage 1:** Trade outcomes assessment
  - <u>Time:</u> 2–4 weeks
  - <u>Activities:</u> desk-based trade data analysis
  - <u>Output:</u> trade outcomes note, including hypotheses on key issues to address in the diagnostic

- **Stage 2a:** Initial diagnostic analysis and fieldwork preparation
  - <u>Time:</u> 2–3 weeks
  - <u>Activities:</u> desk-based compilation of quantitative indicators (benchmarking) and review of key policy and strategy documents
  - <u>Output:</u> pre-mission note outlining key issues for research, data requirements, interview targets

- **Stage 2b:** Fieldwork
  - <u>Time:</u> 4–6 weeks
  - <u>Activities:</u> in-country interviews and data collection
  - <u>Output:</u> aide memoire summarizing main findings and next steps

- **Stage 3:** Analysis and preparation of final diagnostic
  - <u>Time:</u> 4–6 weeks
  - <u>Activities:</u> analysis of diagnostic findings and preparation of report outlining potential policy responses
  - <u>Output:</u> final TCD report

Source: Authors.

Outcomes Analysis; (2) initial diagnostics and field preparation, followed by in-country diagnostics field research; and (3) analysis and preparation of the final TCD report.

What Time Will Be Required?

The TCD is designed to be completed within a period of four months. This would include four to six weeks of fieldwork (although it could be as few as two weeks in a small country), as shown in figure O.4.

Module 1 Summary: Conducting the Trade Outcomes Analysis

The Trade Outcomes Analysis guides a systematic generation of hypotheses about a country's export performance, prospects, and challenges by analyzing what it exports, to whom, how much, and for how long. It is designed to not only measure past performance but also assess the likely future trajectory of a country's trade position. The Trade Outcomes Analysis uses the decomposition of the margins of trade growth as a framework for exploring trade competitiveness, as outlined in figure O.5. We define four prinicipal factors on which a country's trade competitiveness performance can be determined: (1) the ***level, growth, and market share*** performance of existing exports (the intensive margin) of exports as well as *market share* performance;

(2) ***diversification*** of products and markets (the extensive margin); (3) the ***quality and sophistication*** of exports (the quality margin); and (4) the ***entry and survival*** of new exporters (the sustainability margin).

Figure O.6 shows the four main steps to conduct a Trade Outcomes Analysis. The Trade Outcomes Analysis is largely a desk-based exercise that involves assessing a series of indicators and analytical tools. The key to a success, however, lies not in the creation of the tables and figures but in their interpretation, and in the conclusions and hypotheses that are drawn from them. Thus, it is important that the analysis is grounded strongly in the country context. This means ensuring that members of the country team are directly involved (if the analysis is being conducted by an anchor unit or a consultant) and, if possible, conducting limited field research. This research will allow for a stronger analysis and will ensure that the quantitative report can be illustrated with relevant examples and anecdotes that shed light on the actual situation. The remainder of this section provides a basic guideline to carrying out each of the four steps.

Step 1: Select Peer Countries

It is important to decide which comparator countries will be included in the analysis. Some of the indicators will focus on country-specific analysis and others on positioning the country of interest in the global landscape; for the majority, however, it will be useful to select peer countries

Figure O.5. Decomposition of Export Growth—a Framework for Measuring Trade Competitiveness

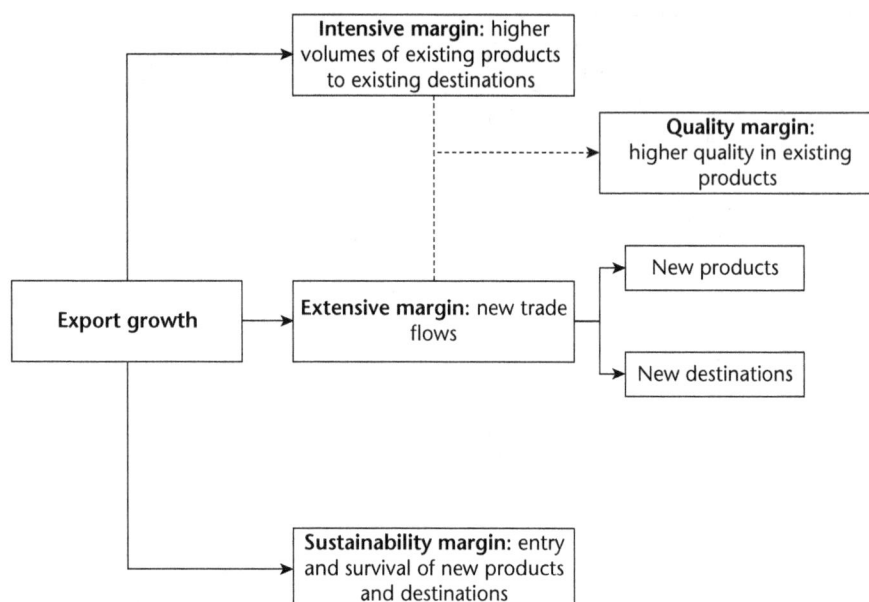

Source: Authors, derived from Carrere, Strauss-Kahn, and Cadot 2011.

Figure O.6. Steps to Conducting the Trade Outcomes Analysis

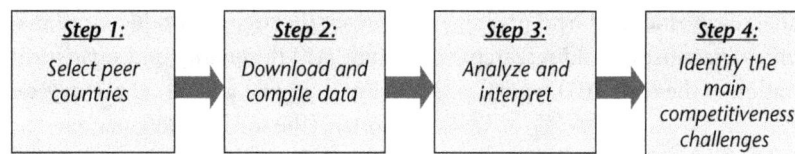

Source: Authors.

for comparison. The purpose of a peer country is to act as a benchmark against which the relative performance of the country can be assessed.

Although stakeholders are often particularly interested in such comparators, the purpose of the peer countries is to set the country's performance in context and not to conduct a comprehensive ranking or benchmarking exercise. Thus, it is not necessary to include the full range of possible comparator countries. Moreover, from a practical perspective, interpreting the accompanying figures and graphs will be difficult if too many comparators are included. Thus, somewhere between four and six peer countries is normally ideal.

Given the sensitivity of many stakeholders to the countries that are considered peers, outlining a clear set of criteria for the selection of the peer countries is important. Indeed, although benchmark comparisons can play a valuable role in engaging in the dialogue with country counterparts, the perception that certain peer countries are deemed inappropriate can undermine a good analysis. Thus, it is

important to reach consensus on the peer countries before any final results are presented. Normally, the selection criteria will include some combination of neighboring countries; countries of similar size, economic development, and economic structure; and possibly countries with whom the country's exporters compete in global markets.

Step 2: Download and Compile Data

Data Sources
The Trade Outcomes Analysis focuses on the assessment of time-series and cross-sectional trade data. Although detailed and useful data may be available from national statistical agencies, comparability across countries and time is critical. As such, the analysis makes use of a few standardized data sources (see table O.2). The majority of measures in the Trade Outcomes Analysis use a single data source—the United Nations Comtrade database that can be accessed via the World Integrated Trade Solution (WITS) website, a software tool developed by the World Bank in collaboration

Table O.2. Main Data Sources for Trade Outcomes Analysis

	Source / Location	Description and main use
World Integrated Trade Solution (WITS)	Available online http://wits.worldbank.org/wits/ (registration required)	Provides detailed time-series data on imports and exports by country and trade partner based on a range of statistical classifications. Primary source of data for almost all indicators used in the Trade Outcomes Analysis.
World Trade Indicators (WTI)	Available online http://info.worldbank.org/etools/wti/1a.asp	Provides precalculated indicators on measures relating to trade growth, services trade, and diversification.
ITC TradeMap	Available online http://www.trademap.org/ (registration required)	Provides a wide range of indicators and tools (for most of which, the TCD uses WITS instead); in TCD used mainly for mapping of growth orientation.
World Development Indicators (WDI)	Available online http://data.worldbank.org/data-catalog/world-development-indicators	Provides a detailed set of time-series socioeconomic data across all countries; used in TCD mainly for • Basic trends in trade growth • Data for context on population, GDP, etc. • Technology content of exports.
World Bank Proprietary data sources	Unit values database (PRMTR)	• Time-series database with unit values at detailed product level for exports to EU countries from all countries; in TCD used for analysis of export quality.
	Customs transactions database (DEC)	• Detailed time-series firm-level data on exporters based on customs transactions; available in approximately 30 countries; in TCD used for analysis of export dynamics, entry and survival.
	Revealed factor intensity database (PRMTR)	• Database mapping factor conditions of all countries (physical capital, human capital endowments) against products to show revealed factor intensity of products; in TCD used to analyze sophistication of exports and comparative advantage.
Other	CEPII—available online http://www.cepii.fr/anglaisgraph/bdd/gravity.htm	• Data set for development of gravity models.
	Product Space Explorer and Product Space Parser—available online www.chidalgo.com	• Tool for analyzing product space.

Source: Authors.
Note: EU = European Union; GDP = gross domestic product; ITC = International Trade Commission; TCD = Trade Competitiveness Diagnostic.

with United Nations Conference on Trade and Development (UNCTAD), International Trade Commission (ITC), World Trade Organization (WTO), and the United Nations Statistical Division.

Module 1 of the toolkit provides details on the data sources for each of the indicators and tools of the Trade Outcome Analysis. Some of these indicators are available precalculated from World Trade Indicators (WTI) or can be calculated using simple online tools from WITS or ITC Trade Map. The World Bank International Trade Department has automated much of the process and can provide Stata "do" files that automatically run the analysis using WITS data and prepare the graphs and figures needed for the Trade Outcomes Analysis. In a second phase of the toolkit implementation, a set of automated tools will be available online, enabling users to input data and retrieve results.

Data Nomenclature, Classification, and Degree of Aggregation

Comtrade's data use two principal classification systems for merchandise trade (data for services trade is much less detailed- see box O.3): (1) Harmonized Commodity

Description and Coding System (HS) and (2) Standard International Trade Classification (SITC). These are summarized in table O.3. SITC has the advantage of a much longer series since 1962 and fewer revisions. For the Trade Outcomes Analysis, the level of aggregation of data is tailored depending on the tool used. For sectoral composition and growth, HS two-digit suffices, whereas for meaningful product-level analysis, either SITC four-digit or HS four-digit are required. HS six-digit data offers the most disaggregation and is the preferred option. Trade data are disaggregated further at the national level, but they cannot be used for comparison or benchmarking because they have not been harmonized across countries.

Use of Mirror Data

The use of different sources and techniques to process raw data could result in trade data varying tremendously across countries. Export data reported by developing countries are often less accurate than the import data reported by high income countries for the same flow. This is because administrative capacities are stronger in industrial countries. Additionally, because import data are needed to calculate tariffs, importers tend to show greater diligence

Box O.3. A Note on Data for the Services Sector

In recent decades, with the advent of new technologies and policy reforms, services are being increasingly traded between countries. In 2009, global trade in merchandise was valued at US$12.1 trillion and trade in commercial services was valued at US$3.3 trillion.[a] There is, however, a severe lack of disaggregated data for services, which prevents analysis of rigor at par with what can be conducted for merchandise trade. This imbalance, driven by data availability, is reflected in this toolkit.

The broadest definition of services includes all activities outside agriculture, mining, and manufacturing that have intangible outcomes. This definition permits a highly heterogeneous inclusion of activities, from banking and insurance, telecommunications and accounting, hotels and architecture, to audio-visuals, education, health, and construction. In 2007, close to 70 percent of the world's gross output was accounted for by value addition in services. Yet, because many of these activities were "untradable" until recently, the share of services in global trade is only around 25 percent. Since the 1980s, however, trade in services has grown faster than trade in goods. Because of policy deregulation and information technology–enabled technologies, some forms of trade in services no longer require a simultaneous presence of both the producer and consumer, which used to be one of the distinguishing characteristics of this trade. Trade in services also subsumes the important subject of direct investment under the logic that services can be provided through "commercial presence" in a foreign market by owners of capital belonging elsewhere. According to the United Nations Conference on Trade and Development (UNCTAD), in 2006, 62 percent of inward stock of foreign direct investment (FDI) was accounted for by services, up from 49 percent in 1990.

Despite growing importance, the quality and availability of data on cross-country trade in services is poor. The main existing source is the International Monetary Fund Balance of Payments statistics. But this does not capture all categories and most likely understates services trade. The World Development Indicators (WDI) provides the same information in a more accessible manner with some disaggregation into insurance and financial services, travel, and transport. UNCTAD has information on FDI flows and stocks as well as sales by affiliates of multinational companies.

Source: Authors.
Note: a. See http://www.wto.org/english/news_e/pres10_e/pr598_e.htm.

Table O.3. Summary of Data Classification Systems

Classification	Degree of disaggregation available	Time period of coverage and revisions
HS	Up to six-digit levels for more than 5,000 products	Available since 1988 with revisions of nomenclature in 1988/92 (HS0), 1996 (HS1), 2002 (HS2) and 2007 (HS3)
SITC	Up to five-digit levels for more than 1,000 products	Available since 1962; third revision (SITC Rev3, from 1988–2007) is widely used because it gives maximum comparability over long sample periods; SITC Rev4 launched in 2007.

Source: Authors.
Note: HS = Harmonized Commodity Description and Coding System; SITC = Standard International Trade Classification.

and regularity in their recordkeeping. For most of the Trade Outcomes Analysis, therefore, mirror data should be used—for example, if calculating exports of Nigeria, instead of using the Comtrade data for Nigeria showing its reported exports to the world, take the data for all countries showing their reported imports from Nigeria.

Firm-Level Data

In addition to the aggregate data sources discussed in table O.2, a much richer analysis of export dynamics, including detailed measurement of entry and survival, can be achieved with access to data about individual firms (see box O.4). It is therefore valuable, wherever possible, to access firm-level microdata. Unfortunately, these data remain difficult to come by and comparability across countries may be limited. Even in individual countries, accessing firm-level data is often difficult (where available) because of concerns over data confidentiality. To conduct the Trade

Outcomes Analysis, two main sources of firm-level data can be considered: (1) an industry census, a registry database (usually including accounts and/or balance sheet data), or enterprise surveys; and (2) a database of customs transactions. These sources are summarized in table O.4.

Step 3: Analysis and Interpretation

Following is a brief summary of each component within the Trade Outcomes Analysis.

Level, Growth, and Market Share: Intensive Margin

An analysis of the basic orientation of trade is crucial to judge whether a country's trade structure is conducive to economic growth. The assessment of level, growth, and market share (the intensive margin) covers a range of issues reflecting the structure and competitiveness of the existing export basket. Table O.5 summarizes the key

---

Box O.4. Why Firm-Level Analysis?

Firms are heterogeneous in characteristics and performance. Moreover, important changes in production models are taking place worldwide, which are deeply affecting the transmission mechanisms of the economies, domestically and internationally. Macro aggregations miss the critical features and effects of firm heterogeneity on the macro-economy. They are not adaptable to changes and innovations in the business landscape within countries and internationally. Hence, at times of structural change they may give a partial or distorted perception of underlying economic realities. This explains why in recent years many macro indicators seem to have lost relevance for explaining trade outcomes and why some policy initiatives do not seem to deliver the expected results in terms of employment, domestic growth, and export performance.

Going deeper in the understanding of firm-level dynamics can improve not only aggregate assessments of competitiveness but also the identification of its drivers and the reaction of the real economy to policy intervention. In short, complementing more aggregate assessments with firm-level data can lead to improved policy toward raising countries' competitiveness. For example, firm-level analysis has distinct advantages when assessing the mechanisms governing the generation of output, the division of production and labor, and the allocation of resources across countries, within countries, and within industries. Drilling down into the various key indicators by detailed firm makes it possible to carry out panel data analysis rich in cross-sectional and time variation data (i.e., it allows controlling for relevant aspects of the activity of businesses).

Source: Authors.

Table O.4. Sources of Firm-Level Data—Benefits and Drawbacks

	Benefits	Drawbacks
World Bank (DEC) Export Growth and Dynamics Project Database or customs transaction data acquired for specific countries on ad hoc basis	Data available from around 30 countries, so possible to create benchmark comparisons Detailed data available on export volumes across time, products, and trade partners make it possible to create a detailed picture of firm dynamics and study patterns of entry, growth, and survival Data available from a number of low-income countries	Lack of data on firm characteristics Only covers exporters, so no data to compare exporters and nonexporters
Census data, Registry data, and Enterprise Surveys	Allow for links between exports (participation and volume) and other characteristics of firms (e.g., size, productivity, and so on) Provide data on both exporters and nonexporters, allowing for comparisons of characteristics	Ad hoc availability and access—varies significantly by country; usually restricted to middle- and upper-income countries Lack of details on exports—usually no data on specific products and markets

Source: Authors.
Note: DEC = Development Economics.

---

issues and indicators covered in this part of the analysis, along with the types of questions that might be answered—or, indeed, raised—by the analysis. It also provides a reference to the page in module 1 of the toolkit where detailed information on the indicator can be found.

Diversification: Extensive Margin

The main argument for diversification of exports is to lessen risk and vulnerability arising from a reliance on too much income from a narrow range of products. Such vulnerability can occur through volatility in international prices and external shocks beyond an exporter's control. Recently, diversification and discovery of new exports have been proven to contribute positive externalities and facilitate higher productivity, ultimately leading to improved long-term growth prospects. This section provides tools to assess the following: (1) the concentration of a country's

exports and the markets they serve; (2) the degree to which the export portfolio is aligned with products and import markets that are growing in the world economy; and (3) the evolution of the market reach of specific exports (successful or unsuccessful) over the past decade (see table 6).

Quality and Sophistication: Quality Margin

What goods countries produce and how they produce them both matter for export-led growth. Products can be disaggregated only by so much, and the quality of products within an internationally harmonized category (such as HS six-digit or SITC five-digit) can vary immensely. All else equal, goods that embody greater value addition in terms of ingenuity, skills, and technology fetch higher prices in world markets. Upgrading product quality, therefore, can be a secure source of both export and economic growth. This section provides tools to analyze (1) the technology,

Table O.5. Summary of Indicators and Issues—Level, Growth, and Market Share

Issue	Indicators	Questions and implicit hypotheses	Page
Trade Openness	Trade-to-GDP ratio Adjusted trade-to-GDP ratio	(1) Relative to countries at comparable levels of income, how integrated is a country in the world? How does the ratio change when it is adjusted to control for population, remoteness, and cost of inland trading? (2) How has the ratio evolved over the past decade?	29
Trend in Trade Growth	Evolution of export volumes of both goods and services, annual growth rates of total exports, and share of merchandise trade in GDP	(3) Has growth of exports of goods and services been steady? Has trade share of GDP grown in tandem with GDP or faster? What explains deviations from the trend, if any?	31
Export Composition, Revealed Comparative Advantage (RCA), and Trade Integration	Total exports (US$) by each (disaggregated) sector, including services, and its share in total exports RCA of each sector Compound annual growth rate in exports over a period of 5 to 10 years Real export per capita Share of manufactured trade in parts and components Grubel-Lloyd Index	(4) How have exports grown at the sector level? Has competitiveness (say, in terms of RCA) evolved differently over time across sectors? Have there been dramatic changes in certain sectors? Why? (5) How has real exports per capita evolved over the past 30 years compared with peer countries? (6) Are export earnings emanating from a diversified economic base? (7) Is the country taking part in global production networks? What is the share of intraindustry trade?	31
Market share	Comparative market share performance in key product	(8) Is a country growing its share in world, regional, or specific country imports in key sectors and products? How are they performing relative to key competitors?	35
Trade Partners	Difference between predicted and actual exports to individual partners obtained from a gravity model Trade Intensity Index Trade Complementarities Index	(9) Does a country "overtrade" or "undertrade" with individual partners, especially those that are rich, large, nearby, or fast growing? (10) What is the role of preferential trade agreements in boosting bilateral or regional trade? (11) Does a country have an unusually high or low level of penetration with partners that could be considered natural trading allies? (12) What is the degree of fit between a country's export profile and a potential partner's import profile?	36
Growth Orientation of Portfolio	Scatter plot of import growth by countries against a country's share in those markets Scatter plot of world growth of products against a country's share in those products	(13) What is the orientation between world growth rate of products and their shares in national portfolio? Are there slow-growing products or markets that a country relies on excessively? (14) What is the experience of exporters in emerging and fast-growing markets? What is inhibiting them (e.g., search costs, market access, competitiveness)?	38

Source: Authors.
Note: GDP = gross domestic product.

income, and factor contents of exports to test whether a country produces sophisticated and high-value products; and (2) the product space to know the sectors in which a country has acquired or lost revealed comparative advantage over time, thereby giving a glimpse of the pace of structural transformation in the economy (see table O.7).

Entry and Survival: Sustainability Margin
The majority of export relationships (at the product-country level) forged by developing countries do not survive for more than a few years. Analysis of firm-level data is critical to improve the understanding of the process of entry, exit, and survival in export markets. Assessing the dynamics of export participation and survival not only is valuable for understanding the competitiveness of a country's trade sector but also provides a critical bridge to the diagnostics stage of the TCD. The nature of firm participation and survival in export sectors helps to identify which broad factors (entry costs, factor costs, technology, and efficiency) may be the biggest constraints to competitiveness.

Table O.6. Summary of Indicators and Issues—Diversification

Issue	Indicators	Questions and implicit hypotheses	Page
Measures of Concentration	Share of top three or five products in exports Share of top three or five markets in exports Hirschman-Herfindahl Index Theil's Entropy Concentration of exports across firms	(1) How concentrated are exports in a narrow range of products, or markets? (2) Is this concentration benign? Does growth in concentrated products generate benefits that outweigh potential cost from vulnerability?	41
Intensive and Extensive Margins	Hummels-Klenow Extensive and Intensive Margins for both products and markets	(3) Over a decade, has a country added economically significant new products to its portfolio? Has it become a bigger player in products that it had a decade ago? In other words, is a country big in what it exports and how much do those exports matter globally? (4) Is a country big in markets it exports to, and how much do those markets matter globally? (5) Who were the entrepreneurs that made those breakthroughs? What is their story?	42
Market Reach of Exports	Index of Export Market Penetration (IEMP)	(6) What were the products that substantially increased the number of markets they served over a 10-year period? (7) Are there many new products or deaths? Which were the notable ones and why? (8) Compared with peer countries, how many of the potential export relationships has a country exploited?	43

Source: Authors.

This section explores (1) the general structure of the export sector; (2) basic descriptive statistics (number, mean, median) of duration of a country's export spells at the product-country level; (3) the decomposition of export growth into intensive and extensive margins, and the survival rate of export relationships; and (4) the extent to which the cause of death of exports is their defiance of comparative advantage derived from relative factor endowments (see table O.8).

Although both aggregate (macro) data and firm-level data can be used to explore these issues, the use of firm-level data gives a much richer and more accurate picture of the dynamics of exporting.

Step 4: Drawing Conclusions from the Analysis— Identifying the Main Competitiveness Challenges

After a thorough assessment of trade performance is undertaken under the four themes, the next step is to home in on the proximate causes of competitive weaknesses that will be the focus of the Diagnostic exercise. In general, the many issues with trade competitiveness can be boiled down to a problem with products, markets, or the general environment for exporters, as illustrated in figure O.7.

Products

Cost competitiveness. In cases in which countries are found to have problems at the intensive margin, particu-

larly where they have been experiencing declining share performance in key export products (across markets), the proximate problems are normally cost-related constraints that affect competitiveness at the factory or farm gate.

Extension (diversification) and upgrading (quality). In cases in which unit price performance has stagnated or declined relative to competitors, or in which the export base remains concentrated with little success in diversification, proximate problems are typically quality and innovation related, including constraints related to technology and efficiency.

Markets

In cases in which countries have been experiencing declining share performance in key export markets (across most products) or in cases in which diversification of existing exporters and products into new markets has been weak, the competitiveness challenges most likely relate to market penetration.

General Export Environment

Finally, if a country has a limited export base, with insufficient creation of new exporters or low survival rates of new exporters, the competitiveness challenges most likely are driven by weaknesses in the general export environment.

In addition to identifying the main issue areas on which to focus in the Diagnostic exercise, it may be useful

Table 0.7. Summary of Indicators and Issues—Quality

Issue	Indicators	Questions and implicit hypotheses	Page
Technological Content	Relative shares of high-, medium-, and low-technology goods in total exports	(1) Over a decade or so, has there been a shift away from the country's dependence on resource and primary exports to medium- and high-technology exports?	44
Unit Values	Cross-country comparison of unit values at the SITC five-digit or HS six-digit level	(2) Given the unconditional nature of unit value convergence, how likely is product upgrading as a strategy to become a secure source of economic growth? (3) What share of a country's exports is in industries that are deemed to be price elastic relative to industries that are quality elastic (revealed quality elasticity)?	45
Sophistication	PRODY and EXPY	(4) What is the income content of a country's exports? Does it produce what rich countries produce? (5) Can a country count on the existing portfolio of exports for future growth, or will it need to augment the process of export discovery? (6) Is sophistication illusory when taking into consideration the share of imported parts and components in final value?	47
Revealed Factor Intensity	RPCI and RHCI	(7) Are the biggest export earners above or below the capital content of the median export? (8) What is the physical and human capital content of exports? What does this imply for efforts to improve long-term national endowments?	49
Product Space	Proximity between products on the product space	(9) How has the economy transformed over the past 20 to 30 years in terms of exports in which a country has (had) a revealed comparative advantage? (10) Are certain products stuck and has there been no movement along the product space (e.g., from garments to machinery)? (11) What new products have emerged? What is the policy narrative behind them? (12) Which products embody latent comparative advantage, and what kind of industrial policy is needed to nurture them? What industries are protected or subsidized? How can they be oriented toward industrial upgrading? How active a coordinating role will the state have to play to nudge the movement of products on the product space?	50

Source: Authors.
Note: EXPY = (Revealed) income content of export basket; HS = Harmonized Commodity Description and Coding System; PRODY = (Revealed) income content of product; RHCI = Revealed Human Capital Index; RPCI = Revealed Physical Capital Index; SITC = Standard International Trade Classification.

Figure 0.7. Linking Trade Outcome Categories to Competitiveness Challenges

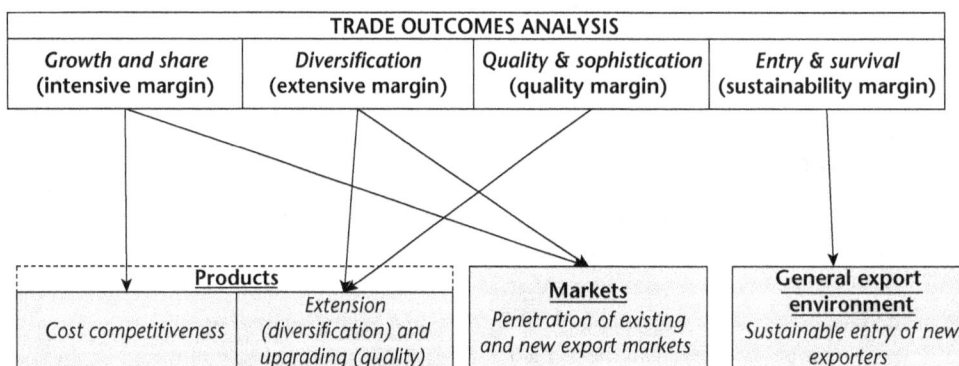

Source: Authors.

to identify the broad questions around which the Diagnostic exercise can be organized (see an example in box O.5). It also will be useful to identify specific questions at the sectoral level that may serve as a proxy to answer broader questions about constraints to competitiveness in the export sector.

Table O.8. Summary of Indicators and Issues—Entry and Survival

Issue	Indicators	Questions and implicit hypotheses	Page
Firm dynamics	Number of firms; number of exporters; nature of exporters (size, FDI share); export share of production	(1) What has been the trend of export participation? Is exporting accessible for most firms? (2) How large are typical exports and how reliant are exporters on domestic v export markets? (3) How important is FDI for the export sector?	54
Longevity	Kaplan-Meier survival function; Nelson-Aalen cumulative hazard function; extended mean graphs	(4) What is the mean and median duration of a country's export relationship? Of the median firm's export relationship? Is this low or high when compared with peer countries? (5) What export relationships were sustained over an extended period? Which sector do they belong to (machinery, electronics)? What types of firms? (6) Which countries had such sustained relationships? What explains this beyond geographical, historical, or linguistic ties? Is there a preferential trade agreement in effect? (7) Of the spells that lasted only one year or so, is there a dominant group of products or countries? Why?	
		(8) Decomposing export growth, which constituent of the intensive and extensive margins contributed most and least to export growth? Was it as expected (i.e., the intensive margin was more robust for well-established exporters, and the extensive margin was more dynamic for start-up developing countries)?	54
Nature of Export Relationships (decomposition of growth and death)	Growth and survival rates of export relationships	(9) Have a country's exports risen when analyzed at the country-product level and not just at the product level? (10) What is the extensive and intensive margin of export relationships, and what is the survival rate? Is survival of relationships associated with trade finance, exchange rates, and so on?	55
Exports Relative to Factor Endowment	Distance between national endowment and the factor intensity of exports	(11) Is the death of exports associated with the products' deviation from the national endowment point? (12) Among new entrants that are ahead of a country's endowment point, is there a case for government support?	57

Source: Authors.
Note: FDI = foreign direct investment; BTA = bilateral trade agreement; RTA = regional trade agreement.

Box O.5. Example Questions

Following are questions that arose from the Trade Outcomes Analysis in Pakistan:
1. What is preventing the extension of existing export products to new markets?
2. What will it take to shift the export basket to more dynamic markets in Asia, Latin America, and other areas (products and competitiveness, market access issues, and so on)?
3. Why are average trade relationships of such low value? What are the constraints to deepening trade relationships?
4. What explains the low rates of export survival outside traditional products and traditional markets?
5. What is preventing Pakistan from expanding exports in more sophisticated export products?
6. What is holding back quality upgrading in traditional sectors?

Source: Authors.

The output of this step—the *Trade Outcomes Analysis Report*—serves not only as a guide to the second-stage Diagnostics, but it should be a valuable output in its own right as a comprehensive assessment of trade performance.

Note: **Module 1 of this *Toolkit* provides an implementation guide to a series of measures and analytical tools that can be used to assess trade performance for each of the components discussed in this section. Each tool is described, the main data sources are identified, a basic description of how to conduct the analysis is provided, and an example is shown.**

Module 2 Summary: Conducting the Competitiveness Diagnostics

Following the Trade Outcomes Analysis, the Competitiveness Diagnostics moves through a logical approach to assess how various factors may contribute to trade performance. The Diagnostic exercise includes three broad areas of assessment, as illustrated in figure O.8:

1. **Market access** focuses on the external trade policy environment that may facilitate or constrain exporters from entering and maintaining competitiveness in markets, including tariffs and quantitative restrictions, preferential agreements, and standards and other technical barriers. These same issues are covered in the incentives section on trade policy. In that section, however, the focus is on how it affects imports; here, the focus is on exports.
2. **Supply-side factors** cover a broad range of determinants in two subcategories:
   i. **The incentive framework** includes factors that establish the broad environment that influences private sector investment and participation in exports, including the macrofiscal environment, exchange rates, trade and investment policy, competition, and the governance and regulatory environment.

ii. **Factor conditions** affect the cost and quality of production; these include access to finance, scale economies, labor regulations and skills, firm-level technical efficiency, land and infrastructure, intermediate inputs, services inputs, and trade facilitation and logistics.
3. **Trade promotion infrastructure** covers the range of interventions by government to address market failures (coordination challenges, asymmetric information) and government failures that restrict export participation and performance, including traditional export promotion and special economic zones (SEZs), industry coordination bodies, standards and certification, and innovation.

Figure O.9 illustrates the four main steps to conduct the Competitiveness Diagnostics. The remainder of this section provides a basic guideline to carry out each of these steps.

Step 1: Identify Primary Areas of Focus for Diagnostics Analysis

The broad-based nature of competitiveness is one of the main challenges for conducting a TCD. The TCD focuses on issues that affect the trade sector directly, in the short

Figure O.8. Competitiveness Diagnostics Components (Shaded Boxes)

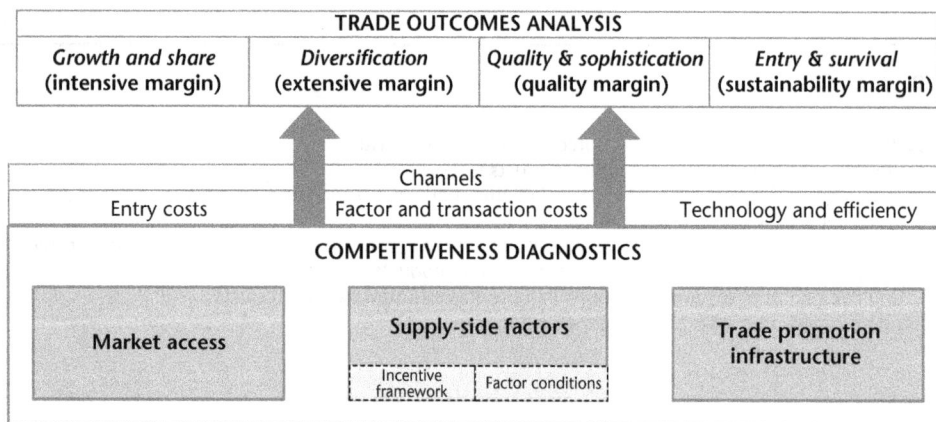

Source: Authors.

Figure O.9. Steps to Conduct the Competitiveness Diagnostics

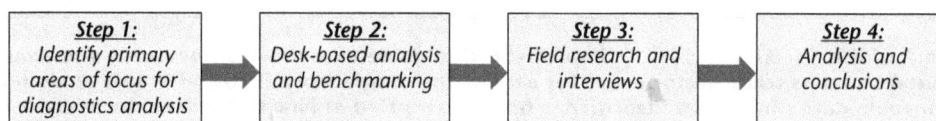

Source: Authors.

to medium term, avoiding detailed assessment of deep determinants such as institutions, basic education, and health that will affect trade outcomes through observable channels like skills, productivity, and the regulatory and governance environment. But even with this focus, the range of issues included in the Competitiveness Diagnostics is wide. Thus, an important first step in the Diagnostics is to review the Trade Outcomes Analysis results and assess the likely candidates for the initial analysis.

The premise of the TCD approach is that trade competitiveness is not determined by any single constraint. Instead, the constraints are likely to be multiple and intertwined and possibly tied to cross-cutting issues for which the trade sector may not have direct policy fixes. The Diagnostic helps prioritize the incremental alleviation of the most binding constraints to export competitiveness in a world characterized by scarce resources and trade-offs among competing choices. For example, trade and investment policies have a bigger role to play if the Trade Outcomes Analysis suggests that the county's openness to trade and structure of production is misaligned with its comparative advantage, whereas the role of technology absorption, innovation, and labor skills is likely to loom large if the country has persistently failed to upgrade the quality of its exports. There is, however, no one-to-one mapping of a symptom to a cause. This is akin to what Sachs (2005) calls clinical economics, in which a range of diagnostic tests and understanding of context need to be employed to home in on the proximate causes of distress.

Table O.9 provides a checklist of the most likely factors affecting competitiveness for each of the broad challenge areas that will be defined from the Trade Outcomes Analysis. As can be seen, in cases in which the main challenges are in export entry and cost competitiveness, a wide set

Table O.9. Checklist of Primary Factors Impacting Competitiveness

		Main challenges identified from the trade outcomes analysis→	General export environment	Cost competitiveness	Product extension and quality	Market penetration	Page
Channels		Fixed entry costs	✓	✓		✓	
		Factor costs	✓	✓	✓	✓	
		Technology and efficiency	✓	✓	✓		
Market access		Tariffs and quantitative restrictions	✓	✓		✓	
		Nontariff barriers	✓	✓	✓		63–74
		Preferential trade arrangements	✓			✓	
Supply-side factors	Incentive framework	Macrofiscal environment	✓				
		Exchange rates	✓	✓		✓	75–87
		Trade and investment policy	✓	✓	✓		
		Competition	✓	✓	✓		88–96
		Regulatory environment and governance	✓	✓	✓		
	Factor conditions	Access to finance	✓		✓		97–99
		Scale economies	✓	✓			
		Labor regulations and skills		✓	✓		100–104
		Firm-level technical efficiency		✓	✓		
		Land and infrastructure		✓			
		Intermediate inputs		✓			105–109
		Services inputs		✓	✓		
		Trade facilitation and logistics				✓	110–118
Trade promotion infrastructure		Export and investment promotion	✓	✓		✓	119–123
		Standards and certification	✓		✓	✓	124–139
		Special customs regimes and SEZs	✓	✓			140–143
		Industry coordination bodies	✓	✓	✓		144–147
		Innovation			✓		148–159

Source: Authors.

of factors may need to be analyzed to identify the main constraints. On the other hand, when market penetration emerges as the main challenge, it may be possible to focus on a much narrower set of issues. The analysis can be taken in stages to ensure a more efficient use of resources. For example, if market diversification is a major problem in a country, a logical point of enquiry is to analyze market access barriers and trade facilitation and logistics. If neither of these is particularly problematic, secondary lines of inquiry may turn to standards and the export promotion infrastructure. Some factors may affect firms in several different ways, and in fact are endogenous with other competitiveness factors. Perhaps most noteworthy in table O.9 is the impact of trade and investment policy not only on the incentive framework that determines whether firms decide to export but also on the cost and quality of goods and services inputs in their production process.

The checklist in table O.9 is based on the broad existing experience of analytical work on trade competitiveness. Although developing a generalized model linking supply-side constraints to trade outcomes is difficult given the endogeneity of many competitiveness factors, some preliminary efforts are under way, through both cross-country and within-country econometrics exercises (see box O.6). As these are refined further, the breadth of analysis that needs to be undertaken in the Competitiveness Diagnostics may be significantly reduced. At the moment, however, they can be taken only as general tools to guide the focus of the analysis.

In addition to identifying the main areas of focus for the Diagnostics, it is also important to consider how the scope and focus of the research and analysis may need to be tailored to take into account the specific context of the country and, if the analysis is being done at the sectoral level, of the focus sector(s). For each of the main competitiveness components, module 2 of this *Toolkit* provides a basic guide for how certain country and sector contexts may require an adjustment to the focus of the research. These categories are shown in table O.10.

Step 2: Desk-Based Analysis and Benchmarking

Taking the econometrics as an initial guide of where to focus, the Diagnostics analysis begins with desk-based research focused on each of the areas identified in table O.9. The purpose of the desk-based research is twofold: to make full use of the existing quantitative and qualitative evidence available to assess how specific factors influence trade competitiveness, and to assist in preparing the field research. This step involves three main types of research: (1) qualitative analysis making use of secondary sources, including recent studies and reports; (2)

Table O.10. Summary of Country and Sector Context Provided in the TCD Toolkit

Country contexts	Sector contexts
• Small (population) and remote/landlocked • Resource rich • Low income, labor abundant • Middle income	• Light manufacturing • Agriculture • Tourism • Business services

Source: Authors.

quantitative analysis based on data from any existing country-specific surveys or census; and (3) quantitative benchmarking comparing performance against a set of peer countries. Table O.11 presents a brief summary of each of these analytical approaches.

The data sources for comparative analysis of Diagnostics are more dispersed than for the Trade Outcomes. However, a number of the most important sources are summarized in table O.12. Specific details on the range of indicators relevant for each topic are included in module 2 of the toolkit. These cover mainly the quantitative data for the benchmarking exercise. The qualitative analysis will necessarily be dependent on what reports have been done in the specific country of interest.

The results from this analytical exercise will indicate which competitiveness factors a country performs particularly well or poorly. This information can establish additional hypotheses to test in the field and questions for further research. The desk research should compile contact information for individuals and organizations to be contacted for meetings as part of the field research. Module 2 of the toolkit includes a list of potential contacts for each component.

Step 3: Field Research and Interviews

Field research is critical to conducting any TCD. This research normally provides the critical insights that connect quantitative benchmarks with observed performance. Depending on the level of detail required and the number of issues being covered, field research can take anywhere from just a few weeks to six weeks or more. Three primary forms of analysis are used in the TCD for conducting field research: semi-structured stakeholder interviews, surveys, and value chain analysis (see table O.13).

Value chain analysis (see box O.7) can provide the most detailed output and, in fact, would normally include interviews and surveys as part of its approach. As such, many Diagnostic exercises may use the value chain approach as their main analytical framework. To obtain specific results, however, the value chain analysis must be done at a level more discrete than even the sector—normally at the level

Box 0.6. Linking Supply-Side Constraints to Trade Outcomes—Econometric Approaches

Cross-country econometric analysis using firm-level data[a]

Based on the stylized facts emerging from the descriptive overview of the firm-level evidence, an econometric model can be designed to link observed trade performance to supply-side determinants. The model starts by organizing the constraints around the three main channels through which they affect exporters: entry costs, factor and transactions costs, and technology and efficiency. The basic specification is based on insights from models of international trade with firm heterogeneity (cf. Melitz and Ottaviano 2008; Del Gatto, Mion, and Ottaviano 2006; and Ottaviano, Taglioni, and di Mauro 2009) and controls for standard trade determinants, including developments in foreign demand, tariffs, preferential trade agreements, exchange rates, and measures correlated with fixed costs to export entry. If data from structural business statistics are available, it is possible to control further for firm-level determinants, which are, however, affected by domestic policy. These include measures of firm performance, measures of financial dependence of the firm (e.g., amount of financing from debt, debt type, debt terms such as interest rate, amount of financing from equity and equity type), measures of intangible capital assets such as investment in R&D and innovation, and measures that allow tracking down foreign sourcing. The analysis can be carried out at the economy-wide, broad-sectoral and broad-regional levels with data broken down by all these dimensions.

Country-specific econometric analysis

In a background paper prepared for the development of the TCD present additional empirical evidence on the relation between total factor productivity, export performance, and foreign direct investment (FDI) inflows in 18 developing countries,[b] based on firm-level data from the World Bank Enterprise Surveys. Of particular value for use in the TCD are the country-level findings on the percentage contribution of groups of investment climate variables to export and FDI performance. This information indicates their relative importance in determining competitiveness. A comparison of the consolidated summary results for African countries and Latin American countries is shown in the chart. Although total factor productivity (TFP) is most important for both sets of countries, beyond that the factors vary considerably, exporting by firms in African countries is affected most by factors like power and internal bureaucracy, and Latin American firms are affected most by informality and bureaucracy at borders.

Percent Absolute Contributions of Investment Climate Groups of Variables to the Probability of Exporting

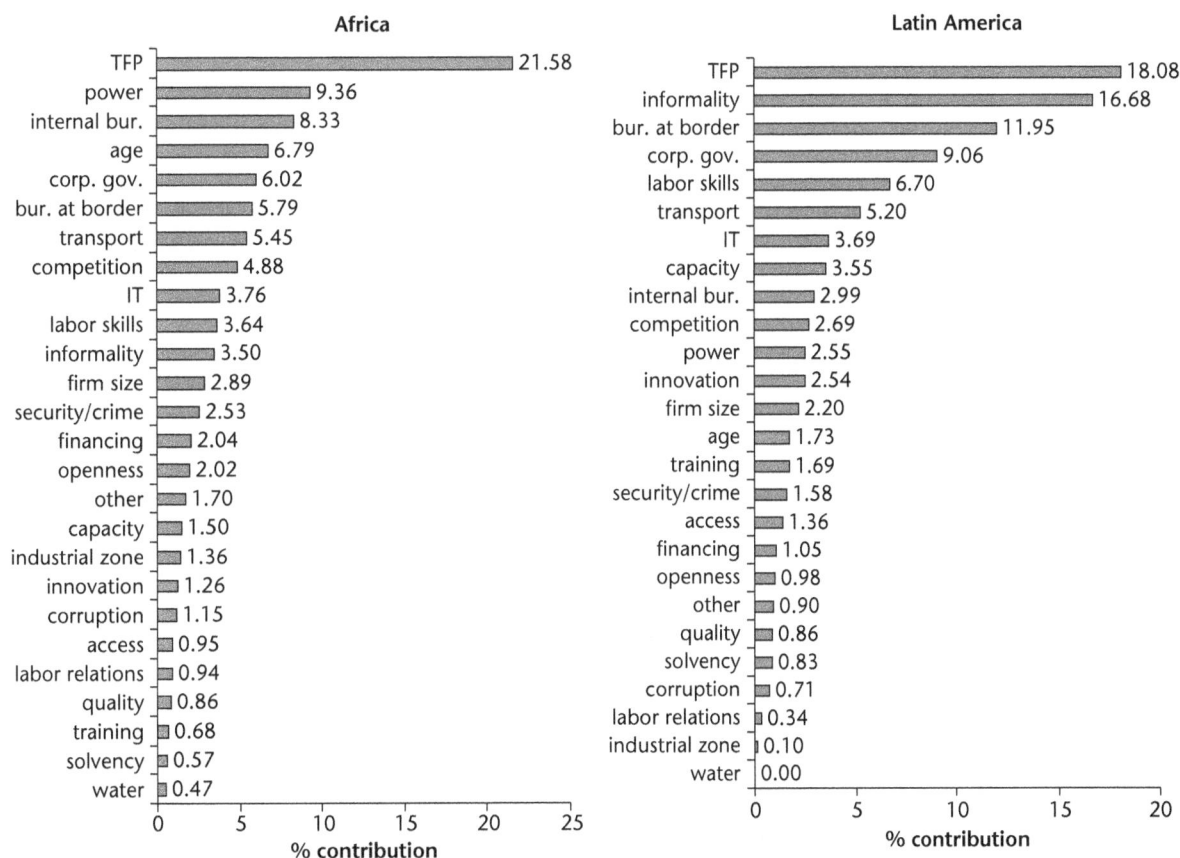

Africa

Variable	% contribution
TFP	21.58
power	9.36
internal bur.	8.33
age	6.79
corp. gov.	6.02
bur. at border	5.79
transport	5.45
competition	4.88
IT	3.76
labor skills	3.64
informality	3.50
firm size	2.89
security/crime	2.53
financing	2.04
openness	2.02
other	1.70
capacity	1.50
industrial zone	1.36
innovation	1.26
corruption	1.15
access	0.95
labor relations	0.94
quality	0.86
training	0.68
solvency	0.57
water	0.47

Latin America

Variable	% contribution
TFP	18.08
informality	16.68
bur. at border	11.95
corp. gov.	9.06
labor skills	6.70
transport	5.20
IT	3.69
capacity	3.55
internal bur.	2.99
competition	2.69
power	2.55
innovation	2.54
firm size	2.20
age	1.73
training	1.69
security/crime	1.58
access	1.36
financing	1.05
openness	0.98
other	0.90
quality	0.86
solvency	0.83
corruption	0.71
labor relations	0.34
industrial zone	0.10
water	0.00

Sources: Authors; Escribano, Pena, and Reis 2010.
Note:
a. Ottaviano, Taglioni, and di Mauro 2007, 2009.
b. Brazil, Chile, Columbia, Costa Rica, Arab Republic of Egypt, Guatemala, Honduras, India, Kenya, Malaysia, Mexico, Morocco, Nicaragua, Pakistan, Peru, Senegal, South Africa, and Turkey.

Table 0.11. Summary of Key Analytical Tools for Desk-Based Analysis

Analytical tools	Role and comments	Risks and shortcomings
Qualitative analysis	• Focus on learning from previous assessment of competitiveness factors • This should draw on secondary sources (Country Strategy reports, CEMs, DTISs, policy analyses, sector studies, etc.) from the World Bank, other IFIs, donors, governments, etc.	• Qualitative analysis of secondary sources should always be confirmed through interviews • Can be biased depending on the sources of information • Risk that information and conclusions become obsolete quickly
Census and survey data	• Detailed firm-level data may be available to provide valuable time-series indications on factors contributing to competitiveness (input costs, factor proportions, productivity, etc.)	• Unlikely to be comparable across countries • Unavailable in most developing countries • Often data problems; require significant care and cleaning of data
Quantitative benchmarking	• Given the relative nature of competitiveness, comparisons are an appropriate analytical tool • Effective way to communicate performance in a nontechnical way • Helps not only to gauge performance but also to give parameters on the potential levels of improvement that are possible	• Of limited use in identifying which constraints are most binding and often fails to identify links across components—treats issues individually • Risk of irrelevant comparisons and risk of jumping to conclusions without controlling properly (critical to have an appropriate peer sample)

Source: Authors.
Note: CEM = Country Economic Memorandum; DTIS = Diagnostic Trade Integration Study; IFI = international financial institutions.

of a product or small group of products. Moreover, the cost and time required to undertake value chain analysis will not always be feasible or practical. In some cases, simply combining detailed interviews of firms and other stakeholders with the desk-based analysis can generate the insights needed to understand how identified constraints affect competitiveness.

Module 2 of this *Toolkit* provides guides for conducting interviews on each of the competitiveness components, including a list of potential interview targets. Following are some suggestions and tips for planning and conducting field interviews:

• *Recognize the crossover in topics:* Particularly in interviews with the private sector, the same individuals may need to be interviewed on more than one topic. Careful planning is needed to ensure that organizations are not contacted twice and that as many of the issues that need to be covered are well integrated into a single interview session.
• *Plan to ensure a balanced sample:* The sample frame for interviews will need to balance public versus private sector versus other stakeholders; mix of sectors; firm sizes; local versus FDI firms; and so on. Ensuring that the sample is relatively balanced is critical to avoid bias in the input received.
• *Different focus and strategy for public v private sector meetings:* Interviews with the public sector should

focus primarily on understanding existing challenges and process, as well as proposed policy changes; private sector interviews should focus on identifying binding constraints and exploring how firms respond to the competitiveness challenges and constraints identified.
• *Communicate effectively in advance of the meeting:* Provide a letter or e-mail outlining clearly the objectives and the issues to be covered in the discussion.
• *Ensure that the interviewee(s) is (are) the right person (people):* It is critical that interviewees are in fact the people who are knowledgeable about the subjects to be discussed; ask specifically in advance communications to ensure that certain people and positions are represented.
• *Number of interview participants:* For the purposes of credibility, it is important to have people with specific experience with and knowledge about the subjects to be discussed. But this needs to be balanced with keeping the team small enough not to overwhelm the interviewee(s) or to make the meeting inefficient. A team of two to three members is usually ideal.
• *Clarify objectives up front:* Restate the context, objectives, and agenda for the meeting up front.
• *Time expectations:* Few interviewees will want to plan for more than one hour. On the other hand, if they are engaged in an interesting discussion, many will be happy to continue. Set some expectations upfront and

Table 0.12. Main Data Sources for Competitiveness Diagnostics Desk Research

	Source/Location	Description	Relevance by component			
			Market access	Incentive framework	Factor inputs	Trade promotion
World Trade Indicators (WTI)	Available online http://info.worldbank.org/ etools/wti/1a.asp	Precalculated indicators on measures relating to tariffs and other trade policy restrictions by country	✓	✓	✓	
WITS – TRAINS database	Available online http://wits.worldbank.org/wits/ (registration required)	Detailed time-series data on tariffs by product and trade partner	✓	✓	✓	
World Bank Doing Business	http://www.doingbusiness.org	Comparative cross-country indicators on investment climate characteristics		✓	✓	
World Bank Enterprise Surveys	http://www.enterprisesurveys .org/ (registration required for microdata)	Detailed firm-level data available across most countries on factors relating to investment climate		✓	✓	
World Economic Forum Global Competitiveness Index	http://gcr.weforum.org/ gcr2010/	Comparative data on measures of competitiveness—includes hard data and perceptions from surveys		✓	✓	
ILO Key Indicators of the Labor Market	http://www.ilo.org/kilm	Time-series data covering 20 indicators of national labor markets			✓	
International Comparison Program Data Set	www.worldbank.org/data/ icp	Cross-country comparative price data on a range of key inputs (at consumer level)			✓	
ITU ICT Indicators Database	http://www.itu.int/ITU-D/ict/ publications/world/world.html	Time-series data across countries for 150 different telecommunication and ICT statistics			✓	
World Bank Logistics Performance Index	http://go.worldbank.org/ 88X6PU5GV0	Comparison of indicators of perceived trade facilitation and logistics environment across 155 countries	✓		✓	
UNCTAD FDI database	http://unctadstat.unctad.org	Time-series data on FDI flows by country and broad sectors				✓
WIPO Patent database	http://www.wipo.int/pctdb/en/	Time-series data on patent filings				✓
WTO Trade Policy Reviews	http://www.wto.org/english/ tratop_e/tpr_e/tp_rep_e .htm#bycountry	Reports (qualitative and quantitative) assessing countries' trade and investment policy environments				✓

Source: Authors.
Note: FDI = foreign direct investment; ICT = information and communications technology; ILO = International Labour Organisation; ITU = International Telecommunications Union; UNCTAD = United Nations Conference on Trade and Development; WIPO = World Intellectual Property Organization; WTO = World Trade Organization.

aim for something in the range of one to one-and-a-half hours.

- **Semi-structured approach:** Use the communicated agenda as a guideline but focus on having an open-ended discussion rather than a question-and-answer session. An open-ended discussion is more likely to keep the interviewee interested and provides greater scope for unscripted issues to be introduced.

Step 4: Analysis and Conclusions

Combining a number of the different quantitative and qualitative tools discussed in this section can allow the practitioner to identify the main elements connecting supply-side factors to trade competitiveness. The specific insights generated by each tool will contribute to increase the accuracy of the Diagnostics, narrowing down the number of candidates to be identified as constraints for

Table 0.13. Summary of Key Analytical Tools for the Assessment

Analytical tools	Comments	Risks and shortcomings
Semi-structured stakeholder interviews	• This should be the core tool used in the data collection process • Selection of interview targets should be broad, covering all key stakeholders • Should draw on a relatively standardized questionnaire or discussion guide, but managed as a semi-structured discussion	• Risk of "camels and hippos" scenario—that is, drawing conclusions from the people who are in the market and excluding those who cannot or choose not to operate • Risk of biased input due to vested interests or biased perceptions (critical to have broad sample) • Risk of obsolescence and volatility of response due to time-specific issues
Surveys	• In most cases, the TCD can take advantage of existing surveys undertaken by the World Bank Group, in particular the enterprise surveys, but additional business surveys may also need to be conducted as needed	• Risk of "camels and hippos" scenario • Risk of obsolescence and volatility of response due to time-specific issues • If undertaking original surveys, sample selection is critical to avoid bias
Value chain analysis	• Provides detailed quantitative and qualitative assessment of competitiveness from the perspective of an investor • Identifies constraints at the sector level, looking at all activities from sourcing through all levels of production, packaging, and delivery to end markets	• Must be done at the product level • Resource-intensive approach • Data often necessarily based on limited number of firms, so cost averages must be viewed cautiously • Risk of obsolescence as conditions and cost structures can change quickly

Source: Authors.

Table 0.14. Illustrative Summary of Diagnostic Results

Trade competitiveness challenges	Primary	Product extension and quality
	Secondary	General export environment
Market access	Tariffs and quantitative restrictions	—
	Preferential tariff arrangements	+
	Standards and TBTs	X
Supply side: Incentive framework for trade	Macrofiscal environment	—
	Exchange rates	—
	Trade and investment policy	X
	Regulatory environment and governance	X
	Competition	—
Supply side: factor inputs	Access to finance	X
	Scale economies	+
	Labor regulations and skills	XX
	Technical efficiency	XX
	Land and infrastructure	—
	Intermediate inputs	—
	Services inputs	—
	Trade facilitation and logistics	X
Trade promotion infrastructure	Standards and certification	XX
	Export and investment promotion	—
	Innovation	XX
	Special customs regimes and SEZs	—
	Industry coordination bodies	—

Source: Authors.
Note: SEZs = special economic zones; TBTs = technical barriers to trade.

+ positive impact on competitiveness

— no major impact on competitiveness

X some negative impact on competitiveness

XX significant negative impact on competitiveness

▨ Typical areas of focus based on primary trade competitiveness challenges

▨ Typical areas of focus based on secondary trade competitiveness challenges

Box O.7. Value Chain Analysis

A value chain describes the full range of activities that brings a product or service from its conception to its end use (and disposal), including design, the sourcing and transformation of raw materials, production, packaging, marketing, and distribution. At an industry level, it combines the industry supply chain with the concept of the value that is added in each step of the process.

The value chain analysis framework centers around three major segments that describe each production link in the value chain: source, make, and deliver. Each activity mapped in the value chain diagram can be represented by a cost breakdown. In addition to mapping the value chain, a value chain analysis typically includes measurement of the chain's performance, establishment of benchmarks (for example, of cost, time, and quality relative to other countries), and, finally, analysis of the performance gaps and the factors that contribute to them.

Example: Apparel Value Chain

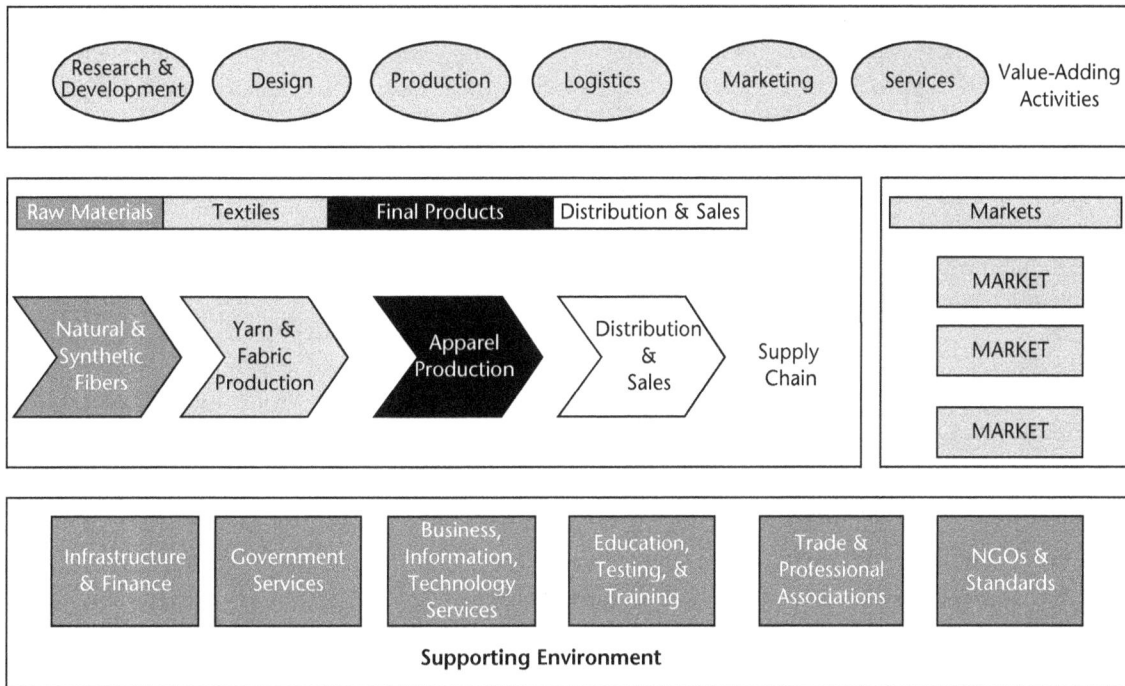

In a diagnostic focusing on a specific sector (for example, apparel as outlined above), value chain analysis could cover core components of the diagnostic, including all aspects of factor inputs and factory-gate competitiveness, transport and trade facilitation, standards and certification, and parts of the internal and external trade policy environment. This would be supported by other tools (for example, standard interviews and textual analysis) to analyze aspects of the incentive framework and the trade promotion environment.

Sources: Gereffi and Frederick 2010; World Bank 2009b.

trade competitiveness. Although the intention is to avoid a laundry list of policy areas to be addressed, it may not be possible to arrive at a simple diagnosis, let alone to identify a single binding constraint. The use of different tools may well suggest different conclusions at some points of diagnostic. This is unavoidable, and the only way to address this problem is through the judgment of the practitioner. Therefore, the team doing the final analysis should include a combination of trade expertise, subject expertise (someone who will have seen it all before in a different context), and most important, country expertise (someone who has an in-depth understanding of the local context).

One way to identify the relative importance of the constraints is to combine the findings from the first and second stages of the TCD to identify areas of weak competitiveness performance in factors that typically matter most for the competitiveness challenges identified in the Trade Outcomes Analysis. In the example shown in table O.14, the Trade Outcomes Analysis identified the primary competitiveness challenge to be product related, particularly in terms of quality upgrading, with a secondary challenge related to the dynamics of export entry and survival. The example country is performing particularly poorly on several components that typically determine competitiveness along these dimensions, specifically in labor regulations and skills, technical efficiency, standards, and innovation.

With the primary issues identified, the practitioner can move on to consider the potential policy responses to the main competitiveness constraints.

Note: **Module 2 of this** *Toolkit* **includes a detailed implementation guide on each component of the Competitiveness Diagnostic, covering its relevance to competitiveness and how to measure it, as well as interview guides.**

Module 3 Summary: Moving from Analysis to Policy Options

Once the main constraints are identified through the Competitiveness Diagnostics, the next step is to translate these constraints into policy and technical assistance projects that address the specific constraints. Policy is complex and almost always context dependent. Therefore, it is not realistic to merely outline a detailed set of prescriptions linked to each of the possible constraints that may be identified through the Diagnostics.

Identifying Policy Remedies and Project Components

Table O.15 presents an overview of broad policy areas linked to each main component of the Competitiveness Diagnostics. The table references the relevant page numbers in module 3 of the of *Toolkit* where the practitioner can find more details on potential policy measures and project components.

Stakeholder Consultation and Workshop

As part of the process of moving to policy recommendations, the team conducting the TCD should consider including some process of stakeholder review and consultation. This may include not only individual consultations with key individuals but also a wider stakeholder workshop. The workshop could be a half-day or one-day meeting during which the main findings are presented and discussed. The stakeholder workshop is designed to test the results from the analysis as well as some the policies and projects being proposed. The stakeholder workshop should ideally be held only after a draft final report has been reviewed and endorsed by the steering committee (if there is one). Results from the stakeholder workshop should then be incorporated into the final report and policy recommendations.

Table O.15. Summary of Broad Policy Areas Linked to Diagnostic Components

Broad policy areas	Market access	Supply side: incentive framework	Supply side: factor inputs	Trade promotion infrastructure	Page
Market access	✓				163
Trade policy	✓	✓	✓	✓	164
Investment policy		✓	✓	✓	164
Business environment, governance and institutional policy		✓			167, 169
Competition policy		✓	✓		167
Labor markets and skills			✓		172
Intermediate inputs			✓		174
Infrastructure and energy			✓		174
Transport and logistics policy			✓		175
Investment and export promotion policy	✓			✓	177
Standards	✓		✓	✓	181
Sector and spatial policy			✓	✓	183, 184
Science and innovation policy				✓	186

Source: Authors.

Note: **Module 3 of the** *Toolkit* **provides more details to assist in thinking about policy options, including the following:**
- *Brief summaries of potential policy remedies and technical assistance project components* **that may be relevant to the specific issues identified; and**
- *Case studies of good policy practice* **from developing countries.**

Notes

1. Trade share is affected significantly by factors unrelated to competitiveness, including natural endowments and, most important, country size and geographic location. This explains, for example, the large gap in traded shares of Germany's economy versus that of the United States.

2. See, among others, Caballero, Engel, and Micco (2004) and Caballero, Cowan, Engel, and Micco (2004) for a discussion of the role of microeconomic flexibility on productivity growth in Latin America and in Chile in the end of the 1990s.

3. For example, the World Economic Forum's *Global Competitiveness Index* (World Economic Forum 2008) covers 12 "pillars" of competitiveness, ranging from microlevel business sophistication to such broad factors as macroeconomic stability and health and primary education. Although these issues no doubt all play a role in determining economy-wide and firm-level competitiveness over the long run, in the case of the TCD, we focus on the issues that affect the trade sector directly and in the short to medium term.

References

Bernard, A., J. Bradford, J. Redding, J. Stephen, and P. Schott. 2007. "Firms in International Trade." CEPR Discussion Papers 6277, Centre for Economic Policy and Research, London.

Bernard, A. B., and J. B. Jensen. 1999. "Exporting and Productivity." NBER Working Paper No. 7135, National Bureau of Economic Research, Cambridge, MA.

Brenton, P., and R. Newfarmer. 2009. "Watching More Than the Discovery Channel to Diversify Exports." In *Breaking into New Markets: Emerging Lesson for Export Diversification,* eds. R. Newfarmer, W. Shaw, and P. Walkenhorst, 111–126. Washington, DC: World Bank.

Caballero, R. J., E. Engel, and A. Micco. 2004. "Microeconomic Flexibility in Latin America." NBER Working Paper No. 10398, National Bureau of Economic Research, Cambridge, MA.

Caballero, R. J., K. N. Cowan, E. Engel, and A. Micco. 2004. "Effective Labor Regulation and Microeconomic Flexibility." NBER Working Papers 10744, National Bureau of Economic Research, Cambridge, MA.

Cadot, O., C. Carrére, and V. Strauss-Kahn. 2011. "Trade Diversification: Drivers and Impacts." In *Trade and Employment: From Myths to Facts,* eds. M. Jansen, R. Peters, and J.M. Salazar-Xirinachs, 253–283. Geneva: ILO.

Cadot, O., L. Iacovone, D. Pierola, and F. Rauch. 2011. "Success and Failure of African Exporters." Policy Research Working Paper Series 5657, World Bank, Washington, DC.

Del Gatto, M., G. Mion, and G. I. P. Ottaviano. 2006. "Trade Integration, Firm Selection and the Costs of non-Europe." CEPR Discussion Papers 5730, Centre for Economic Policy and Research, London.

Eichengreen, B. 2011. "Managing Openness: Lessons from the Crisis for Emerging Markets." In *Managing Openness: Trade and Outward-Oriented Growth After the Crisis,* ed. M. Haddad and B. Shepherd, 11–26. Washington, DC: World Bank.

Escribano, A., J. Pena, and J. G. Reis. 2010. "Trade Competitiveness and the Investment Climate: An International Comparison," Mimeo, World Bank, Washington, DC.

Gereffi, G., and S. Frederick. 2010. "Global Apparel Value China, Trade, and the Crisis: Challenges and Opportunities for Developing Countries." Policy Research Working Paper No. 5281, World Bank, Washington, DC.

Harrison, A., and A. Rodrìguez-Clare. 2009. *Trade, Foreign Investment, and Industrial Policy for Developing Countries.* Cambridge, MA: National Bureau for Economic Research.

Hausmann, R., J. Hwang, and D. Rodrik. 2007. "What You Export Matters." *Journal of Economic Growth* 12: 1–25.

Hausmann, R., and D. Rodrik. 2002. "Economic Development as Self Discovery." CEPR Discussion Papers 3356, Centre for Economic Policy and Research, London.

Imbs, J., and R. Wacziarg. 2003. "Stages of Diversification." *American Economic Review.* 93 (1): 63–86.

Klinger, B., and D. Lederman. 2006. "Diversification, Innovation, and Imitation Inside the Global Technological Frontier." Policy Research Working Paper Series 3872, World Bank, Washington, DC.

Klinger, B., and D. Lederman. 2004. "Discovery and Development: An Empirical Exploration of 'New' Products." World Bank, Washington, DC.

Lederman, D., and W. Maloney. 2007. *Natural Resources: Neither Curse Nor Destiny.* Washington, DC: World Bank and Stanford University Press.

Mattoo, A., and A. Subramanian. 2009. "Criss-Crossing Globalization: Uphill Flows of Skill-Intensive Goods and Foreign Direct Investment." Policy Research Working Paper Series 5047, World Bank, Washington, DC.

Melitz, M. J. 2003. "The Impact of Trade on Intra-Industry Reallocations and Aggregate Industry Productivity." *Econometrica* 71 (6): 1695–1725.

Melitz, M., and G. I. P. Ottaviano. 2008. "Market Size, Trade, and Productivity." *Review of Economic Studies* 75 (1): 295–316.

Ottaviano, G. I. P., D. Taglioni, and F. di Mauro. 2009. "The Euro and the Competitiveness of European Firms." *Economic Policy,* 24 (57): 5–53.

Ottaviano, G. I. P., D. Taglioni, and F. di Mauro. 2007. "Deeper, Wider and More Competitive? Monetary Integration, Eastern Enlargement and Competitiveness in the European Union." ECB Working Paper No. 847, European Central Bank, Frankfurt.

Rodrik, D. 2006. "What's So Special about China's Exports?" *China and World Economy* 14: 1–19.

Sachs, J. D. 2005. *The End of Poverty.* New York: Penguin Press.

Sachs, J. D., and A. Warner. 1999. "The big push, natural resource booms and growth." *Journal of Development Economics* 59 (1): 43–76, June.

Sachs, J. D. and A. Warner. 1995. "Economic Reform and the Process of Global Integration." Brookings Papers on Economic Activity 1995(1): 1–118.

Schott, P. 2004. "Across Product versus Within Product Specialization in International Trade." *Quarterly Journal of Economics* 119, no. 2 (May): 646–677.

WEF (World Economic Forum). 2008. *The Global Competitiveness Report 2008–2009.* www.weforum.org.

World Bank. 2011c. *World Development Indicators.* Washington, DC: World Bank.

World Bank. 2009b. *Clusters for Competitiveness: A Practical Guide and Policy Implications for Developing Cluster Initiatives.* Washington, DC: International Trade Department, World Bank.

World Bank. 2009d. "Lessons for Reformers: How to Launch, Implement, and Sustain Regulatory Reform." World Bank, Washington, DC.

World Bank. 2011d. Leveraging Trade for Development and Inclusive Growth: The World Bank Group Trade Strategy, 2011–2021. June 10, 2011. Washington, DC: World Bank.

Xu, B. 2010. "The sophistication of exports: Is China special?" *China Economic Review* 21: 482–493.

TRADE OUTCOMES ANALYSIS

Growth and Share: The Intensive Margin

Trade Openness

Indicators	Summary of data needs and sources
Trade-to-gross domestic product (GDP) ratio; Adjusted trade-to-GDP ratio	Collect variables as follows for specific years for all countries: total export and import of goods and services, GDP per capita, and population (*World Development Indicators* database); remoteness calculated from GDP and bilateral distance data from *CEPII*; cost of inland trade from *Doing Business* report. Run a cross-country regression.

The *trade-to-gross domestic product (GDP) ratio* is one of the most basic indicators of openness to foreign trade and economic integration. It weighs the combined importance of exports and imports of goods and services in an economy. The ratio gives an indication of the dependence of domestic producers on foreign demand and of domestic consumers and producers on foreign supply. A narrower measure of the ratio of exports to GDP is also used to assess the general acceptability of home commodities at competitive prices and standards in foreign markets. However, because imported inputs can play a big role in the success of exports, a combined look at imports and exports is common. Furthermore, a measure of real outward orientation has been suggested to adjust export-to-trade ratios with the imported input share by industry (UNCTAD 2009). This reflects how secure an export industry is not only to changes in sales prices but also to exchange rate fluctuations. The intensive data requirements, however, mean that this measure is not commonly used.

Figure 1.1, panels A and B, show scatter plots of averaged trade-to-GDP ratios from 1996 to 1998 and from 2006 to 2008 against the log of GDP per capita in purchasing power parity (PPP; constant international dollars). The broken line indicates the world median income, and the

curve is an ordinary least squares (OLS) regression line of the trade-to-GDP ratio on the log of GDP per capita as well as its squared value. This curve reflects a stylized fact that countries tend to trade more, relative to nominal GDP, as their per capita incomes rise, but they do so at a decreasing rate. When trade is divided by real GDP in PPP terms (and not nominal GDP), the relationship is slightly different because real openness corrects for distortions created when nontraded goods are priced differently across countries (Alcala and Ciccone 2004). It can also be valuable to look at the changes in trade openness over time to assess the relative degree to which a country has integrated into global markets. For example, as shown in figure 1.1, panel B, although Pakistan's trade openness has remained stagnant in the past decade, countries like China, India, and Vietnam have experienced remarkable growth in integration.

It is difficult to say whether a country's ratio is low or high without putting other characteristics in context. All else equal, large countries in terms of geography and population tend to have a lower trade-to-GDP ratio than smaller countries because they have the option of undertaking a bigger share of trade within their borders. The large countries to the right of the global median income, such as Brazil and the United States, trade less than what would be predicted for countries at their level of income per person; small-size rich countries, such as Belgium and the Netherlands, trade much more than would be expected for countries at their level of income.

But income is not the only determinant of a country's openness. Structural characteristics such as population and geography greatly matter as well. All else equal, landlocked countries are more disadvantaged to trade than countries with access to the sea. A better measure of what a country can be expected to trade given its structural characteristics can be obtained from a parametric analysis of trade-to-GDP ratios regressed on GDP per capita, population,

Figure 1.1. Openness to Trade

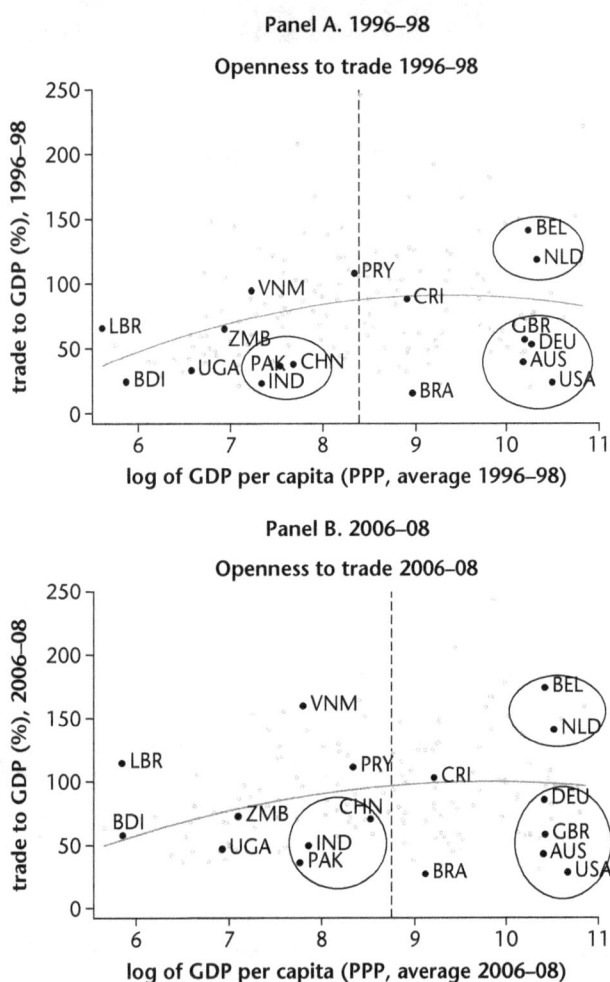

Panel A. 1996–98

Openness to trade 1996–98

x-axis: log of GDP per capita (PPP, average 1996–98)
y-axis: trade to GDP (%), 1996–98

Panel B. 2006–08

Openness to trade 2006–08

x-axis: log of GDP per capita (PPP, average 2006–08)
y-axis: trade to GDP (%), 2006–08

Source: Authors.
Note: GDP = gross domestic product; PPP = purchasing power parity;
CHN = China; IND = India; PAK = Pakistan; VNM = Vietnam; BEL = Belgium;
NLD = Netherlands; DEU = Germany; GBR = Great Britain; AUS = Australia;
USA = United States.

remoteness, and a measure for general cost of trading (which is correlated with being landlocked).

In table 1.1, the predicted trade ratios (columns 2 to 5) differ substantially from the actual trade ratio (column 1) depending on the specification used. Column 2 is a predicted trade ratio when the actual trade ratio is regressed on per capita income. For a country at its level of per capita income, Liberia appears to be much more integrated than its peers. Burundi's actual trade ratio is slightly lower than what is predicted; yet when the square of the log of per capita income is included as an additional regressor (column 3), the predicted trade ratio for Burundi is identical to its observed ratio. When population and the cost of trading[1] are included as additional regressors (column 4), the gap between actual and predicted trade ratios narrows, confirming that large countries like India and the United States rely more on domestic trade. When remoteness is added as a regressor (column 5), the predicted trade ratio of remote[2] countries like Australia is closer to the actual ratio. Even after adjusting the trade ratio to take account of additional characteristics, larger countries tend to trade less than smaller countries relative to the size of their economy.

Figure 1.2 reflects the adjusted openness for some landlocked countries. The ratios are residuals of the regression in column 5 for two time periods 10 years apart (1996–98 and 2006–08). Negative residuals mean that even after controlling for a country's structural characteristics, it trades less than predicted. Figure 1.2 shows that over the past decade, Bolivia and Uganda have both narrowed their "undertrading", while Zambia and Paraguay remain vibrant traders. And while Bhutan has increased its adjusted openness substantially over the past decade, Nepal has seen its level of integration shrink dramatically.

Table 1.1. Adjusted Trade Openness Ratios, 2006–08

	(1)	(2)	(3)	(4)	(5)
	Actual trade/GDP	Potential trade I/GDP	Potential trade II/GDP	Potential trade III/GDP	Potential trade IV/GDP
Liberia	114.5	68.2	57.6	70.4	71.3
Burundi	57.7	68.2	57.7	57.5	54.7
China	70.3	88.4	91.4	55.9	50.9
United States	28.2	104.6	99.5	64.7	52.7
India	49.2	83.4	85.5	50.9	48.4
Australia	42.6	102.6	99.4	88.7	69.0

Source: Values in column 1 from World Bank 2011c; values in columns 2–5 obtained from regression analysis.
Note: GDP = gross domestic product.

Trends in Trade Growth

Indicators	Summary of data needs and sources
Evolution of export volumes, annual growth, and trade share in GDP	Data from *World Development Indicators* database; basic calculations and plots.

One of the first indicators of export orientation is to begin by looking at the broad trend in growth of trade over the past 15 to 20 years. How has total exports (of goods and services) grown? Is growth sustained? In Figure 1.3, panel A, Indonesia's growth of total exports (in nominal US dollars) is seen to have grown from under US$30 billion in 1990 to more than US$150 billion in 2008. Growth has been steady and impressive, except during the aftermath of the 1997–98 Asian financial crisis as well as a smaller dip after 2001.

In figure 1.3, panel B, the share of merchandise exports and imports in GDP are plotted for Indonesia and an aggregate category of lower-middle income countries to which it belongs. As countries become richer over time, they trade more. This is confirmed by the lower-middle-income country aggregate whose volume of goods trade, relative to the economy, rose from 35 percent in 1990 to 60 percent in 2008. The corresponding share of goods trade for Indonesia falls within this range, between 41 to 52 percent over the period but GDP shrank during the Asian crisis elevating the share of goods trade to "abnormal" levels between 1998 and 2001. The growth of constituent product categories within goods exports is covered in the next subsection (composition of exports); notably, many low-income countries depend on a narrow range of commodity exports. In such cases, the analyst should decompose the extent to which

Figure 1.3. Analyzing Broad Trends in Trade Growth, Indonesia, 1990–2008

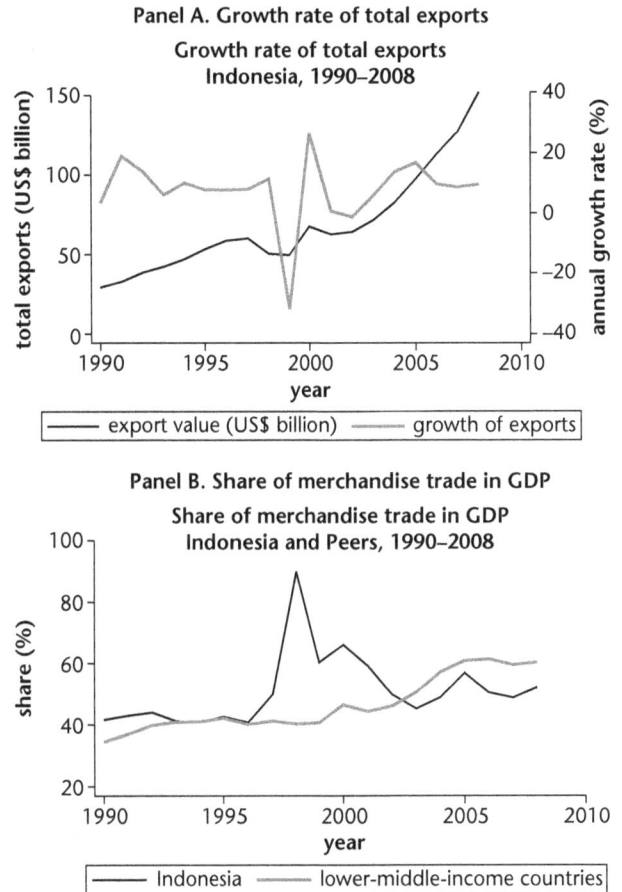

Panel A. Growth rate of total exports

Panel B. Share of merchandise trade in GDP

Source: Authors.

export growth is driven by rising world prices for such commodities versus an increase in output.

Composition of Exports (Goods and Services), Revealed Comparative Advantage, and Trade Integration

Indicators	Summary of data needs and sources
Total exports (U.S. dollars) by each (disaggregated) sector, and its share in total exports Revealed comparative advantage (RCA) of each sector Compound annual growth rate in exports over a period of 5 to 10 years Real export per capita Share of parts and components in manufactured exports Grubel-Lloyd Index	Disaggregate overall export figures (from WITS) into meaningful categories, such as that proposed by Hanson (2010) or Leamer (1984); calculate RCA and changes for comparison between two time periods; share of trade in parts and components can be calculated by coding Comtrade categories as being either 'final goods' or 'parts and components' as per Athukorala and Menon (2010).

Figure 1.2. Adjusted Trade Openness—Examples

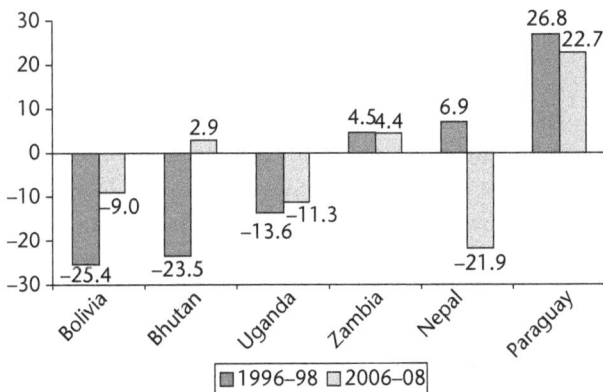

Source: Authors.

Table 1.2. Annual Growth Rates and Share of Services Exports, 1998–2008

	Average growth rate in services exports, 1998–08	Average growth rate in goods exports, 1998–08	Share of services in total exports, 2008	Share of services in total exports, 1998
East Asia and Pacific	17.31	17.73	11.44	11.80
Europe and Central Asia	9.58	19.92	13.84	28.37
Latin America and Caribbean	7.88	12.08	11.86	16.47
South Asia	17.29	15.66	27.61	24.91
Sub-Saharan Africa	8.92	16.58	11.26	20.02

Source: Computed from data in WDI (World Bank 2011c).

Export Composition

To assess how a country's exports have performed, it is useful to compare the changing shares of export by industries over time. Ideally, this is to be done for both goods and services. Reliability of cross-country data for export of services is poor, however. For an indicative exercise, table 1.2 computes the compound annual growth rate of exports in both services and goods between 1998 and 2008 for five developing regions of the world as well as selected countries. The data on services exports are calculated by subtracting merchandise exports from combined export of goods and services in the *World Development Indicators* (WDI) database.[3] However, the export-related data in WDI reflect figures reported by the exporting countries themselves—that is, they are not based on mirror data. Therefore, the quality of the data must be viewed with some suspicion.

Figure 1.4 illustrates the growth rate in nominal US dollars of the expansion in the exports of merchandise goods and services for some countries. India's annual growth rate in services between 1998 and 2008 was higher than its growth rate for goods, whereas the reverse is true for China.

Figure 1.4. Compound Annual Growth Rate (%) of Goods and Services Exports, 1998–2008

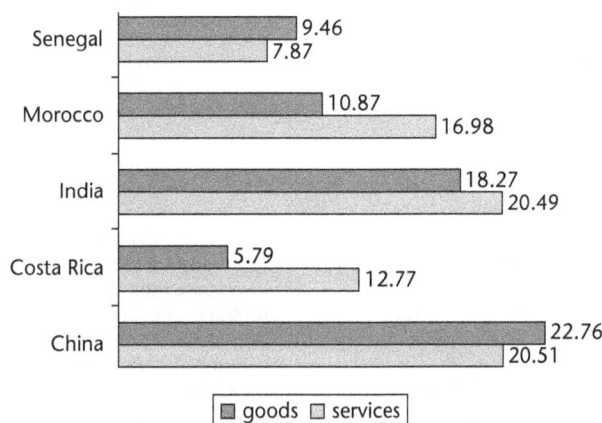

Senegal: goods 9.46, services 7.87
Morocco: goods 10.87, services 16.98
India: goods 18.27, services 20.49
Costa Rica: goods 5.79, services 12.77
China: goods 22.76, services 20.51

goods ▦   services ☐

Source: Authors.

Table 1.2 reports similar growth rates as well as the share of services exports in total exports for five developing regions of the world.

In table 1.3, merchandise exports are clustered across industries, following Hanson (2010), that share similar factor intensities and are likely to rely on similar technological or institutional foundations as a basis for production. For example, the first sector includes land-intensive activities surrounding agricultural production; the second includes manufacturing activities that use agriculture, forestry, and other land-intensive inputs.[4]

Revealed Comparative Advantage

In table 1.3, columns 1 and 4 state the total value of exports by sector (in nominal terms) across two periods (2000 and 2008, for Costa Rica in this example). When divided by population and expressed in real terms, exports per capita can be a good indicator to judge how successful a country has been in facing international competition. Columns 2 and 5 indicate the share of those export sectors in the two time periods that, when divided by the world share of those sectors in total world exports, gives the RCA in columns 3 and 6.[5]

$$RCA_{ik} = \frac{\dfrac{x_{ik}}{X_i}}{\dfrac{x_{wk}}{X_w}} \qquad (1.1)$$

An RCA index above 1.0 indicates that a country's share of exports in a sector exceeds the global export share of the same product. Because high export volumes can result from subsidies or other incentives provided, including undervalued exchange rates, RCAs have been argued to be a misnomer in the sense that they are a better measure of competitiveness than comparative advantage (Siggel 2006). Table 1.3, column 7, shows the annual average of the growth rate of export sectors. Column 8 captures the change in Costa Rica's share of each sector in the world

Table 1.3. Change in Costa Rica's Shares of Exports, 2000–08

Panel A. Shares of goods exports

		(1)	(2)	(3)	(4)	(5)	(6)	(7)	(8)
	Sectors	Exports 2000 (US$ '000)	Share 2000 (%)	RCA 2000	Exports 2008 (US$ '000)	Share 2008 (%)	RCA 2008	Aggregate (%)	Competitiveness
1	Agriculture, meat and dairy, seafood (HS 1–10, 12–14)	2,110,849	29.55	7.05	4,164,910	24.4	6.05	7.03	−0.0056
2	Food, beverages, tobacco, wood, paper (HS 11, 15–24, 44-48)	538,538	7.54	1.18	1,261,659	7.38	1.31	8.89	0.0007
3	Extractive industries (HS 25–27, 68–71)	117,777	1.65	0.12	213,379	1.25	0.06	6.12	−0.0010
4	Chemicals, plastics, rubber (HS 28–36, 38–40)	365,840	5.12	0.44	867,462	5.07	0.39	9.02	−0.0008
5	Textiles, apparel, leather, footwear (HS 41–42, 50–65)	943,280	13.21	1.77	426,861	2.50	0.50	−7.62	−0.0111
6	Iron, steel, and other metals (HS 26, 72–83)	118,069	1.65	0.24	391,492	2.29	0.23	12.74	−0.0001
7	Machinery, electronics, transportation equipment (HS 84–89)	2,693,129	37.70	0.90	8,566,144	50.09	1.46	12.27	0.0256
8	Other industries (HS 37, 43, 49, 66–67, 90–97)	255,563	3.58	0.51	1,219,026	7.13	1.20	16.91	0.0054

Source: Computed using mirror data in Comtrade.

Panel B. Shares of services exports

		(1)	(2)	(3)	(4)	(5)	(6)	(7)	(8)
	Sector	Exports 2000 (US$ '000)	Share 2000 (%)	RCA 2000	Exports 2008 (US$ '000)	Share 2008 (%)	RCA 2008	Aggregate (%)	Competitiveness
1	Services	1,940,271	25	1.28	4,034,862	29.66	1.43	9.58	—

Source: Computed using data in WDI (World Bank 2011c).
Note: — = not available.

MODULE 1

Figure 1.5. Change in Costa Rica's RCA, 2000–08

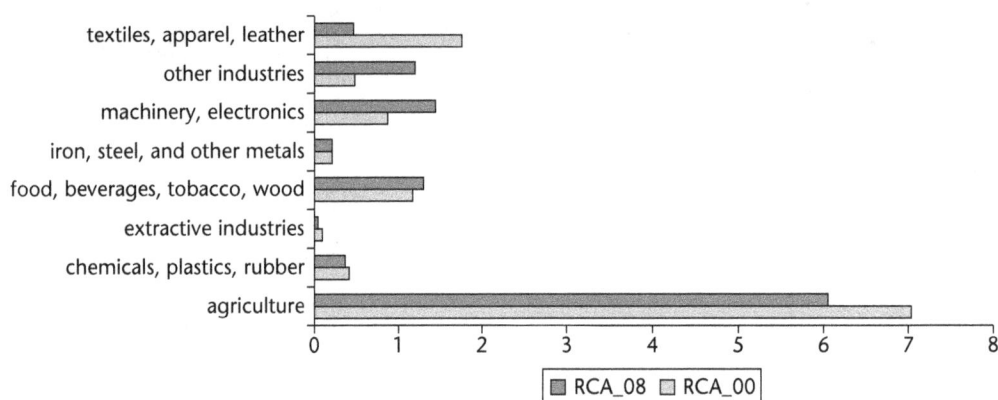

Source: Authors.

multiplied by the share of world exports for each sector in total world exports in the initial year (2000). This is one of several ways to measure competitiveness.

Ideally, table 1.3, panels A and B, would be merged to treat goods and services exports (as well as their constituents) in a comparable manner so that a shift in the economy from goods to services or vice versa could be tracked. When sources of data are different, however, they will not be comparable with precision. Here, goods data is collected from mirrored statistics in Comtrade, whereas services data is from balance of payments statistics in WDI. Despite this caveat, it is not difficult to see that services exports are becoming more important in Costa Rica, with an increase in revealed comparative advantage (RCA) over eight years.

In goods exports between 2000 and 2008, we note two major structural changes: (1) the absolute value as well as the national and global share of textiles, apparel, leather, and footwear (sector 5) dropped significantly; and (2) the share of machinery, electronics, and related manufacturing (sectors 7 and 8) expanded significantly. These changes are confirmed by the changing values of RCA (see figure 1.5). The country remains competitive in the agricultural sector as well as agribusiness (sectors 1 and 2). It therefore appears to have a dual competitive presence in sophisticated goods, such as electronics and some machinery, as well as in primary goods.

Trade Integration

When analyzing export composition of manufactured trade, it is now increasingly important to distinguish between trade in final goods and trade in parts and components. The expansion of global production sharing over the past two decades, especially in the SITC categories 7 (machinery and transport equipment) and 8 (miscellaneous manufacturing), requires a much-detailed analysis at the country level. To trace the pattern of trade flow between countries, Athukorala and Menon (2010) and Athukorala (2010) extract products at the SITC five-digit level that are "parts and components" and not final manufactured goods. They reach a policy conclusion that trade in parts and components is less sensitive to relative price changes; therefore, the exchange rate is likely to be less effective in balance of payments adjustment in countries that rely heavily on trade of parts and components.[6]

To explore the extent to which countries play a role in global production networks, trade data could be regrouped into components and final goods, and the evolution of export and import shares charted over time. An assessment of **parts and components** is also important to determine whether the level of sophistication of a country's export basket as judged by looking at final goods is illusory. In 2006–08, according to WDI, countries with the largest share of high-tech goods in total manufactured exports included the China, Costa Rica, Côte d'Ivoire, Cuba, Gabon, the Philippines, and Thailand alongside Ireland, the Republic of Korea, the Netherlands, Singapore, and the United States. Some of these countries contribute only to the final assembly of high-value intermediate inputs made in other countries. When it is difficult to trace and assign value added to different phases of production, it is instructive to look at the share of parts and components in exports and imports. Rising imports of parts and components indicate a country's increased assembly activity, whereas a rise in their export suggests its growing importance in the global supply chain. Trade in components offers opportunities to less-developed countries to specialize in niches rather than an entire production chain. But competitiveness in this form of trade requires a mix of policy openness, low wages, and good infrastructure, what Golub, Jones, and Kierzkowski (2007) term "service links".

As shown in figure 1.6, the share of parts and components in total manufactured exports at the HS six-digit level (excluding agricultural and extractive industries) for China rose from 19 percent to nearly 32 percent between 1998 and 2008. China remains a big consumer of parts and components as it continues to have a large role in the final assembly of goods, but it is also increasing its share of the production of intermediate parts and components, which usually have high capital content. Despite the suggestion that Vietnam has been a laggard in global production sharing, unlike other East Asian countries, its share has improved because of distorted foreign direct investment (FDI) priorities in the 1990s.[7] Its share of parts and components in nonagricultural goods exports more than doubled from 5 percent to almost 11 percent in a decade. India's export of parts and components is also rising, albeit from a lower base than China's.

In the absence of detailed data on parts and components, one could also compute the **Grubel-Lloyd Index (GLI)** to measure the scale of intra-industry trade. In sector i, E and M are values of exports and imports, respectively. A GLI of one indicates maximum intra-industry trade and a GLI of zero indicates the presence of only interindustry trade. This index is relevant for countries seeking to diversify exports not across industries but rather within an industry. One purpose of bilateral or regional trade agreements (BTAs or RTAs) is to enhance competitiveness by taking advantage of regional markets and supply chains. In

this, the Southeast Asian trade bloc (the Association of Southeast Asian Nations [ASEAN]) performs a much higher share of intraregional intraindustry trade than any other trade bloc in the developing world (Brülhart 2008).

$$GLI = 1 - \frac{\sum_i |E_i - M_i|}{\sum_i |E_i + M_i|} \qquad (1.2)$$

Market Share

Indicators	Summary of data needs and sources
Overall market share; relative share growth	Data from Comtrade (WITS) on market shares of key importers by relevant market at disaggregated product level (six digit); scatterplots on Stata.

A standard definition of export competitiveness, popularized by the OECD, is the degree to which, under open market conditions, a country can produce goods and services that meet the test of foreign competition while simultaneously maintaining and expanding domestic real income. One way to measure this is a **country's share in world exports** over time. In 2002, China's exports constituted 4.9 percent of the world total compared with the United States' 10.2 percent. In 2008, China's share had risen to 8.8 percent whereas that of the United States had fallen to 7.7 percent. In absolute terms, the exports of the United States did not fall, but China's expanded rapidly. These ratios portray a country's depth of integration in the world economy, but to know what products constitute those trade baskets, the figures need to be disaggregated by sector.

Indeed, measuring market share by specific sectors and specific products provides a good measure of performance of a country's exports over time. This must be taken in context with growth, however. For example, many countries have experienced fairly robust growth in exports in manufacturing sectors but still show declining market share performance over the past decade, as a result of the huge growth in China's market share. Figure 1.7 illustrates one way to analyze a country's market share performance—that is, by looking at **relative performance against a specific competitor** (in this example, analyzing Indonesia's market share performance versus China in the European Union, for a range of manufacturing products). The graph in figure 1.7 is split in four quadrants: those in the upper right indicate market share gains for both Indonesia and China over the decade; those in the lower right indicate gains for Indonesia and losses for China; the upper left shows gains for China and losses for Indonesia; the lower left shows

Figure 1.6. Share of Parts and Components in Manufacturing Exports[a] for Selected Countries

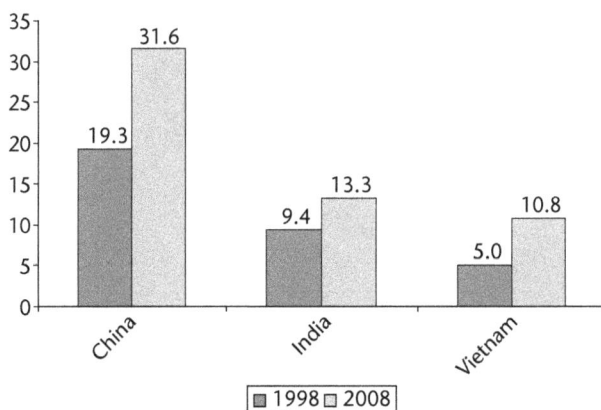

Source: Computed from data in Comtrade and coding of parts and components from Athukorala (2010).
Note: a. Excludes HS chapters 1–24, 44–48, 25–27, 68–69 and 71.

MODULE 1

Figure 1.7. Market Share for Selected Manufacturing Products: Indonesia versus China in the European Union, 2000–08

Sectoral growth of EU-25 import share, 2000–08 (% pt)

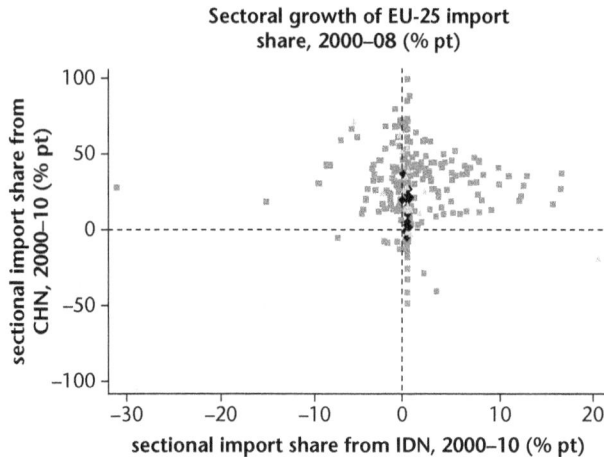

Source: Authors.
Note: IDN = Indonesia.

losses for both. As the figure illustrates, the majority of products show market share gains for China and losses for Indonesia.

Trade partners

Indicators	Summary of data needs and sources
Difference between predicted and actual exports to individual partners obtained from a theory-grounded gravity model	Trade data from WITS; gross domestic product–related variables from *World Development Indicators*; gravity-related variables from *CEPII*; regression run on Stata following precise technical steps as per Helpman, Melitz, and Rubinstein (2008).
Trade Intensity Index	
Trade Complementarities Index	

Where do a country's exports go? How has the share of exports in a particular market changed over time? A simple analysis of change in market share of a country's total exports by destination can reveal trends in the country's dynamism in its ability to reorient or diversify exports. In figure 1.8 for Morocco, it can be seen that the European Union remains the most important trading partner. The share, however, has declined from 75 to 59 percent over eight years. Exports have been reoriented substantially toward higher growth markets, like BRIC (Brazil, Russia, India, and China), whose share grew from 6 percent to 14 percent between 2000 and 2008. Other major growth destinations have included Mexico, Pakistan, and Saudi Arabia. The increase in the US market is modest despite the presence of a bilateral trade agreement.

Gravity models can be used for a more disaggregated analysis of areas where more exports ought to be going, for example, destinations that are large or rich or growing, or

simply nearby. Figure 1.9 applies a gravity model for Senegal to assess if Senegal trades as would be predicted with potentially important partners. It plots actual export amounts (divided by 1,000 and then converted to log)[8] earned in those markets against amounts that were predicted by a regression model described in box 1.1. It is apparent that Senegal trades less than would be expected with notably large countries like the Brazil, China, Germany, and the United States (located above the 45-degree line), and has a stronger export relationship with India, Italy, Mali, and Spain. Its trade with Côte d'Ivoire and France is inline with predictions of the gravity model.

Figure 1.8. Change in Morocco's Exports by Destination, 2000–08

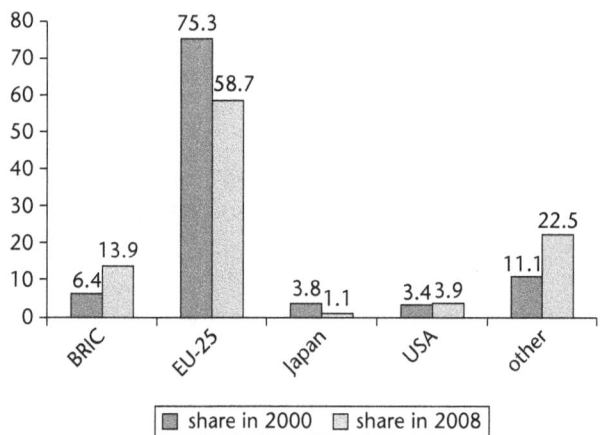

Source: Authors.
Note: BRIC = Brazil, Russia, India, and China.

Figure 1.9. Example of Gravity Model Analysis of Senegal's Bilateral Trade

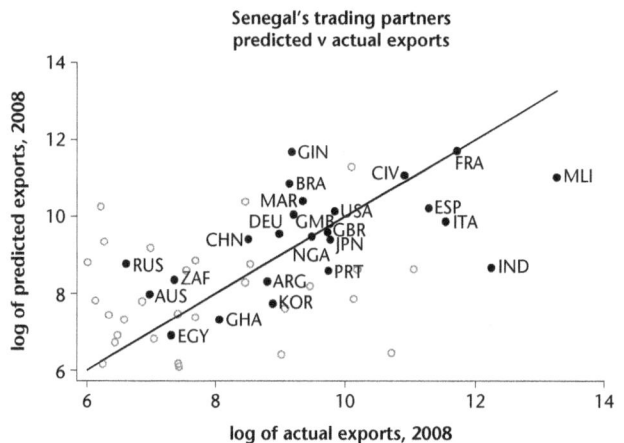

Source: Authors.
Note: AUS = Australia; ARG = Argentina; BRA = Brazil; CHN = China; CIV = Cote d'ivoire; DEU = Germany; EGY = Egypt; ESP = Spain; FRA = France; GBR = United Kingdom; GHA = Ghana; GIN = Guinea; GMB = Gambia; IND = India; ITA = Italy; JPN = Japan; KOR = Korea, Republic of; MAR = Morocco; MLI = Mali; NGA = Nigeria; PRT = Portugal; RUS = Russian Federation; USA = United States; ZAF = South Africa.

Box 1.1. Gravity Models

Gravity in economics is one of the field's most successful empirical models. First applied by Dutch economist and Nobel Laureate Jan Tinbergen (1962), it asserts that two large economic clusters interact more with each other than smaller ones, and nearby clusters attract each other more than far-off ones.[a] In trade, the gravity model presumes that *distance* (proxying for actual shipping cost, policy barriers, and informational asymmetry) and *mass* (gross domestic products [GDPs] of exporting and importing countries) explain a large share of bilateral trade. One can gauge whether a country is "underexporting" to a destination country of interest by comparing actual export values in a given year with a predicted export value obtained from a regression that controls for the standard gravity variables, such as absolute bilateral distance, GDP, and per capita incomes. Because two countries are likely to trade more if they share a common language, a common border, and similar legal systems (and possibly the same colonial relationships), gravity equations also include dummy variables for these shared characteristics.[b]

Furthermore, gravity models ought to incorporate three recent innovations. *First*, as suggested by Anderson and van Wincoop (2003), "multi-lateral resistance terms" should be incorporated in regressions because bilateral trade depends not only on absolute trade costs or distances between pairs of countries but also on relative distances. *Second*, instead of dropping observations when bilateral flow is not recorded, the Heckman sample selection correction method should be used to add the probability of being included in the sample as an explanatory variable, that is, having a nonzero trade flow. When observations with nonexistent bilateral trade are dropped, as an ordinary least squares (OLS) method does in a log-linearized model, the dependent variable is not really measuring bilateral trade, but one *contingent* on a relationship existing. Therefore this technique corrects for a potential bias in regression estimates when the probability of selection is correlated with GDP or distance. *Third*, following Helpman, Melitz, and Rubinstein (2008), the model could control for firm heterogeneity (without using firm-level data). This decomposes trade flows into intensive and extensive margins to take note of the fact that firms vary in terms of productivity, and it is usually the more productive firms that export. This may require making assumptions about how firm productivity is distributed. With these steps, the gravity results of whether a country "overtrades" or "undertrades" with particular partners are better grounded on trade theory.[c]

Source: Authors.
Note:
a. See Brakman and van Bergeijk (2010) for details and recent theoretical advances on the gravity model.
b. It is also common to include a dummy variable to indicate whether the two countries are members of the same preferential trade agreement. If importer and exporter fixed effects are used, one can drop country-specific information such as GDP, GDP per capita, and remoteness.
c. Econometrically, this involves a two-step estimation process. First, a probit estimation is run to obtain predicted probabilities. These are then used to construct controls for sample selection bias and firm heterogeneity bias. These controls are then included in the second-stage regression, which can be estimated parametrically or semiparametrically. See Helpman, Melitz, and Rubinstein (2008) for details.

When discussing bilateral or regional trading partners, another measure of interest is the **Trade Intensity Index (TII)**. This index is similar to the RCA index introduced earlier, but it applies to export markets and not to products. It is measured as country i's exports to country j relative to its total exports divided by the world's exports to country j relative to the world's total exports. For example, in 2008, Senegal's TII with France was 2.93, indicating that its exports to France represent a much greater share of its total exports than the share of the world's export to France. In contrast, Kenya's TII with France in 2008 was less than 0.61. This indicates that Senegal's export presence in an important EU member nation is stronger than Kenya's presence. With Germany, however, Kenya's TII was 0.38, higher than Senegal's 0.15.

$$TII_{ij} = \frac{\dfrac{x_{ij}}{X_i}}{\dfrac{x_{wj}}{X_w}} \qquad (1.3)$$

To judge whether there's a good fit between what a country exports and what a potential partner imports, the **Trade Complementarities Index (TCI)** is a useful measure. Cadot, Carrère, and Strauss-Kahn (2011) describe it as a correlation between a country's exports to the world and another country's imports from the world, implying that the two countries stand to gain by trading more with each other when one has a comparative advantage in products in which the partner has a comparative disadvantage. Algebraically, TCI is expressed as follows: m_k^i is product k's share in country i's total imports, x_k^j is product k's share in country j's exports to the world. A maximum score of 100 indicates that the two countries are ideal trading partners. A lower score indicates that the two countries export similar products and there may not be much scope in expanding one's exports to the other.

$$TCI_{ij} = 100\left[1 - \sum_k \frac{\left|m_k^i - x_k^j\right|}{2}\right] \qquad (1.4)$$

TCI can be particularly useful when analyzing the potential gains from a bilateral or regional trade agreement, as well as when determining which countries stand to gain the most from lower trade barriers. Figure 1.10 shows an example of the trade complementarity indexes for each Economic Community of West African States (ECOWAS) member country as measured against the trade basket for ECOWAS as a whole. It shows relatively low levels of complementarity overall but suggests that Senegal has the greatest potential to gain from ECOWAS trade, whereas Guinea, Guinea-Bissau, and Liberia have trade structures that are

Figure 1.10. Trade Complementarities Index for ECOWAS Countries, 2007

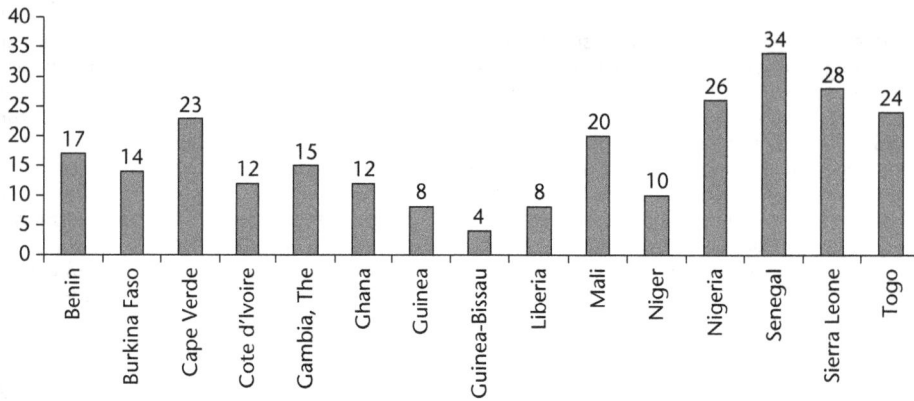

Bar chart values: Benin 17, Burkina Faso 14, Cape Verde 23, Cote d'Ivoire 12, Gambia, The 15, Ghana 12, Guinea 8, Guinea-Bissau 4, Liberia 8, Mali 20, Niger 10, Nigeria 26, Senegal 34, Sierra Leone 28, Togo 24.

Source: Authors.
Note: ECOWAS = Economic Community of West African States.

poorly aligned with the intraregional opportunities. From a policy perspective, an analysis showing low complementarity may suggest a search for new partners and a heightened role for export promotion agencies.

Growth Orientation

Indicators	Summary of data needs and sources
Scatterplot of import growth by countries against a country's share in those markets	Trade and growth data computed from WITS; ITC Trade Map also has data at the HS four-digit level.
Scatterplot of world growth of products against a country's share in those products	

One measure often used as an indicator of export competitiveness is **exports per capita**, which tests the degree of presence in foreign markets (Wignaraja and Taylor 2003). Figure 1.11, panel A, gives an example of this indicator. Just as income per capita is not always a good measure of human well-being, however, export dollars per capita is also not an adequate measure of export success. It matters whether countries earn high export dollars from a domestic production base that is well diversified and not from a narrow range of sectors, such as oil, gas, and minerals. The former can expect a more sustainable growth pattern. As in figure 1.11, panel B, it will be useful to draw real exports per capita against a measure of economic diversification indicated by the combined share of manufacturing and services in GDP. McKinsey (2010b) argues that, as countries develop, they tend to meet both the objectives of earning

Figure 1.11. Macro Analyses of Export Competitiveness

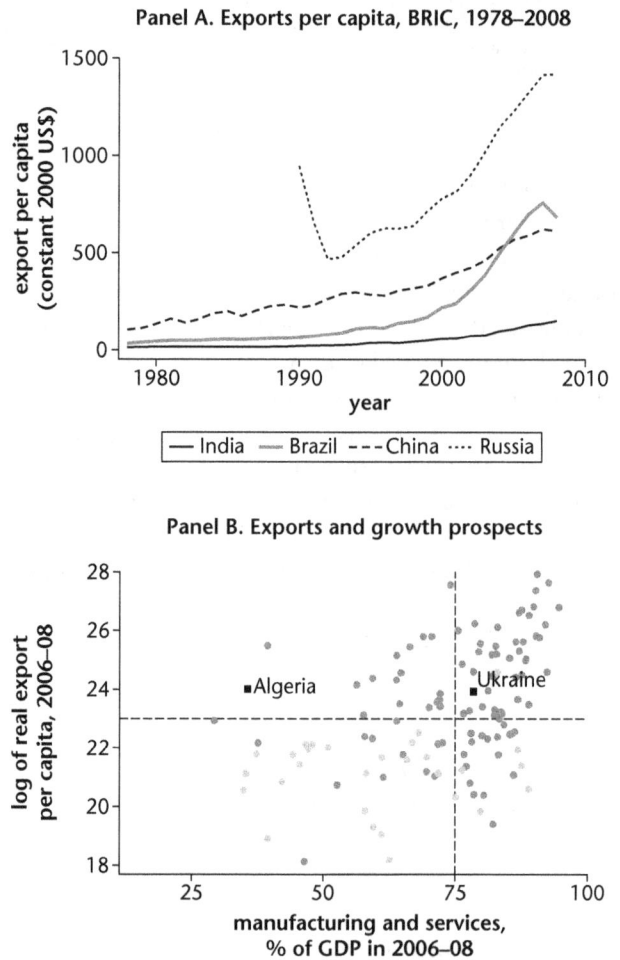

Panel A. Exports per capita, BRIC, 1978–2008

Legend: India, Brazil, China, Russia

Panel B. Exports and growth prospects

Scatterplot with labeled points Algeria and Ukraine; x-axis: manufacturing and services, % of GDP in 2006–08; y-axis: log of real export per capita, 2006–08.

Source: Authors.
Note: BRIC = Brazil, Russia, India, and China; GDP = gross domestic product.

foreign exchange to finance capital imports needed for investment (real export per capita) and developing a diverse source of growth away from natural resources and agriculture.

In Figure 1.11, panel B, countries in the first and second quadrants have a diversified economy.[9] Those in the first and fourth quadrants earn above-average export income, but in an economy that is less diversified. As an example, both Algeria and Ukraine have comparable export earnings per person, but Algeria derives that income from an economic base that is half the share of manufacturing and services in Ukraine's GDP. All Sub-Saharan African countries, except South Africa, are in the low-exports-per-capita and less-diversified quadrants. Generally, countries in the second and third quadrants are in transition, and the role of public policy is to nudge them toward the first.

Openness to trade often goes hand in hand with openness to FDI. Like the trade-to-GDP ratio, the outcome of openness to FDI can be assessed by looking at the ratio of the inflow of FDI (or stock of FDI) relative to GDP. Unlike tariffs in trade, however, no summary statistic is universally accepted to measure policies directly related to openness of FDI.

Looking at how a country's current export basket and competitiveness may shape future performance is a critical part of the analysis of the intensive margin. Plots of **export shares against the world growth rate** of products and countries can give a portfolio view of one's exports: Is the country exporting products that are growing in demand in the world? Is one exporting to countries that are not only large and rich, but also growing fast?

As the examples in figure 1.12, panels A and B, show, a weak, positive correlation exists between Pakistan's top exports—cotton, apparel, leather, and cereals—and their rate of growth in the world market. But for Pakistan's exports to be "pulled" further by the world growth of products that it exports, that relationship ideally has to be stronger. In terms of destinations, Pakistan relies heavily on Europe and the United States, but it has not made breakthroughs in countries that are growing fast and that have the potential to be richer in the future. With the exception of China, and to a lesser extent Turkey, Pakistan's partners are not among those that have seen the highest rates of import growth between 2000 and 2008. Because the richest economies of the world (the European Union, Japan, and the United States) are slow growing,[10] countries that trade the most with them will have a downward growth orientation for their destinations. This is likely to be the case for an overwhelming majority of countries. This kind of analysis, therefore, could exclude rich countries and be used to analyze a country's relationship only with emerging economies.

Figure 1.12. Orientation of Exports and Destinations, Pakistan, 2008

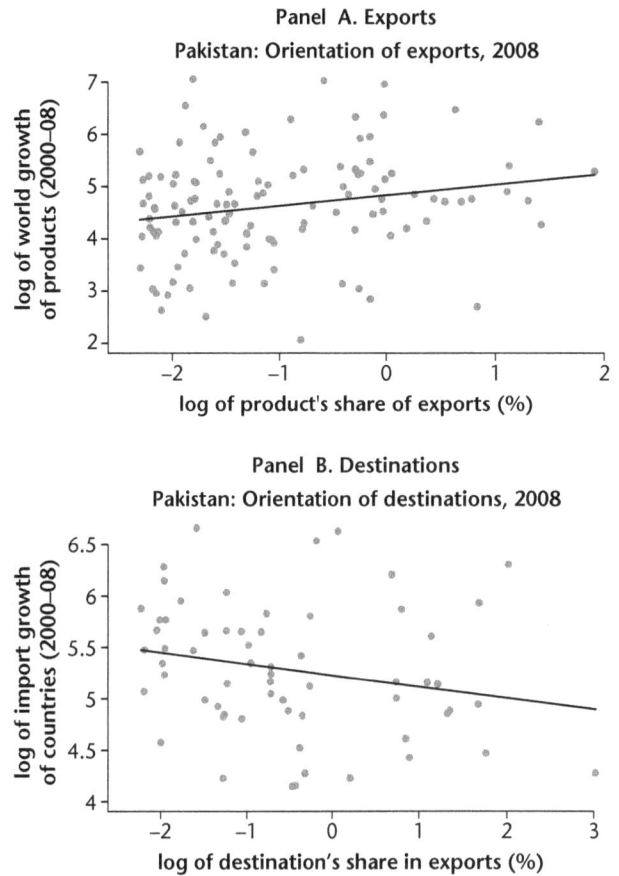

Panel A. Exports
Pakistan: Orientation of exports, 2008

Panel B. Destinations
Pakistan: Orientation of destinations, 2008

Source: Authors.

It would be important to learn what the experience of Pakistani exporters has been in trying to break into the newer fast-growing markets. What enabled those that have been successful? To those that have not, what factors have been the biggest hindrance? If it is search costs or lack of information, export promotion might have a role to play; if it is policy barriers in foreign markets, trade agreements will have a role; and if it is lack of competitiveness, the onus is on the domestic productivity agenda.

In terms of products, some of Pakistan's most important exports like cotton and leather have not been growing as fast as other sectors (for example, fruits, grain, oil seeds, cereals, chemicals, cement, and plastic) in which Pakistan has a decent production base. What would it take to augment the performance of some of these promising sectors? Figure 1.13, created by the ITC TradeMap, essentially confirms the previous result, but it names countries and products and shows the growth orientation for a more recent period (that is, 2004–08).

MODULE 1

Figure 1.13. Alternative Assessment of Product-Market Orientation, Pakistan, 2008

Panel A. Prospects for market diversification
Product : Total all products

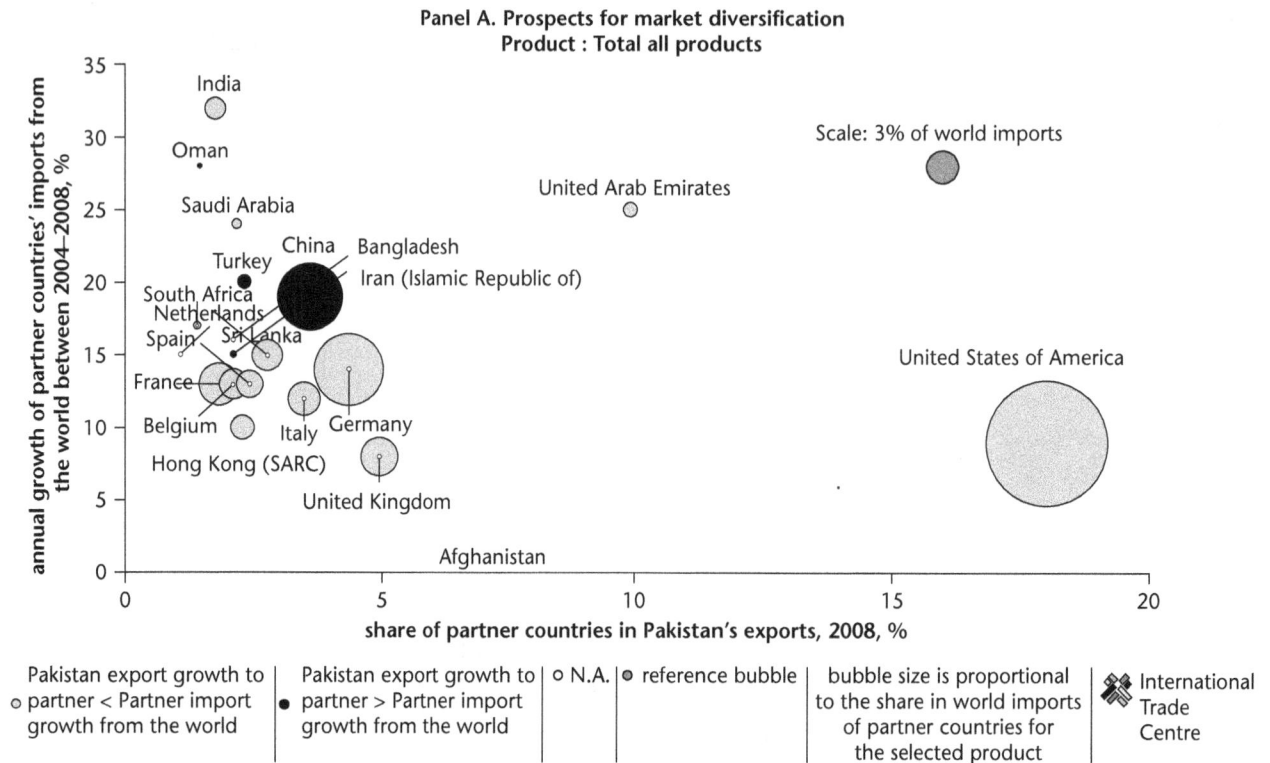

Pakistan export growth to partner < Partner import growth from the world | Pakistan export growth to partner > Partner import growth from the world | o N.A. | ● reference bubble | bubble size is proportional to the share in world imports of partner countries for the selected product | International Trade Centre

Panel B. Size of national supply and growth of international demand
for export products of Pakistan - 2008

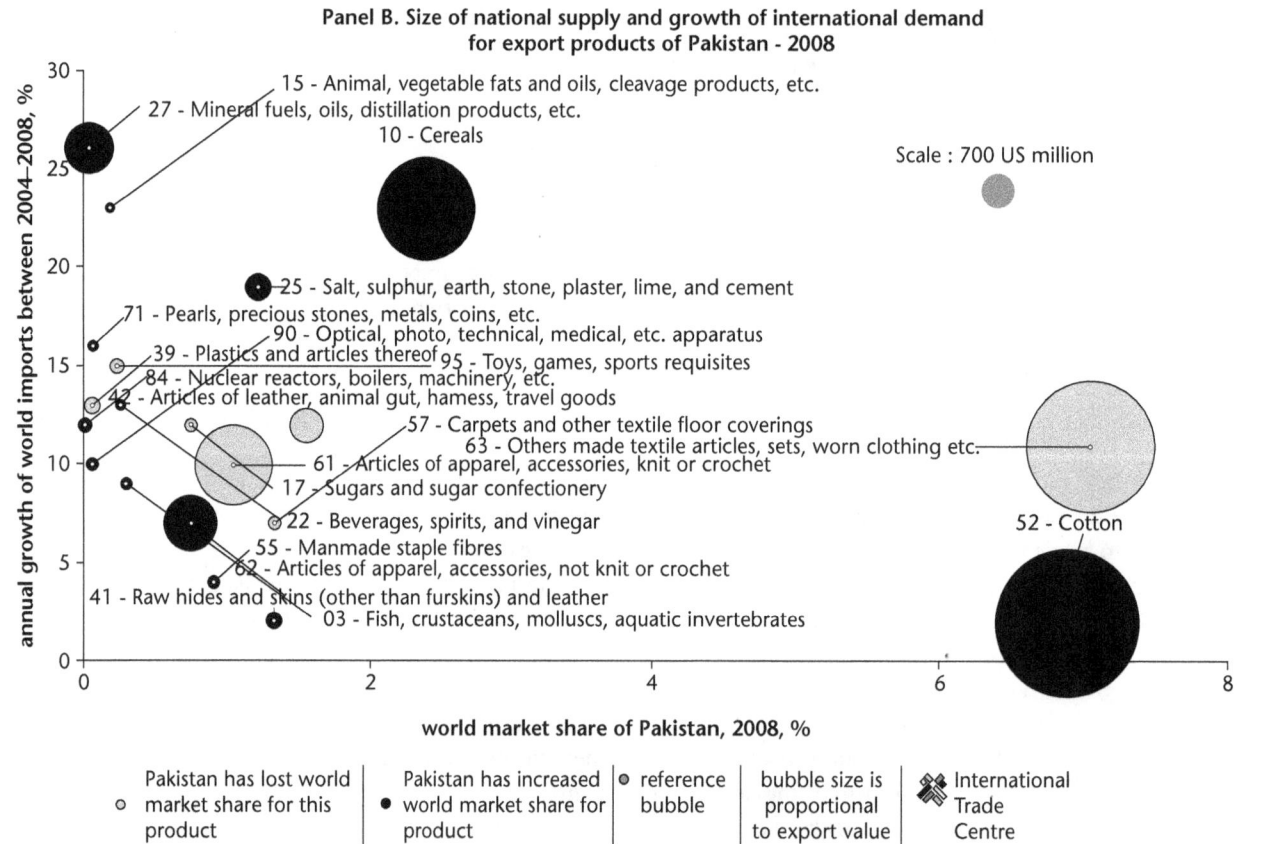

Pakistan has lost world market share for this product | Pakistan has increased world market share for product | ● reference bubble | bubble size is proportional to export value | International Trade Centre

Source: ITC 2011.

Diversification: The Extensive Margin

Measures of Concentration

Indicators	Summary of data needs and sources
Share of top three or five products in exports	Trade data from WITS; alternatively, the ITC Trade Competitiveness Map displays precomputed data as does the World Trade Indicators.
Share of top three or five markets in exports	
Hirschman-Herfindahl Index	
Theil's Entropy	

All else equal, a more diversified structure of production is in most cases preferable to one that relies on a few goods, especially primary commodities. It may also be better to rely on a greater number of export destinations than fewer. Two questions to answer when measuring product or market concentration are as follows:

- In a given year (or over the past few years), what share of total exports has been accounted for by the top three or five products (at a suitable level of disaggregation, such as HS six-digit or SITC four-digit levels)?
- What share of the country's total exports is sold in the top three or five markets?

For example, according to the ITC's Trade Competitiveness Map, in 2008, at the HS four-digit level, only 12.5 percent of Germany's exports were accounted for by its top three products, whereas in Nigeria, the top three exports accounted for 94 percent of total. In terms of markets, three top partners buy 23.3 percent of Germany's exports whereas for Nigeria, the share of its top three destinations is close to 60 percent. Formally, the **Hirschman-Herfindahl Index (HHI)** can be used to estimate export concentration.[11] S is the share of export j in the total exports of country i. A country with a perfectly diversified export portfolio will have an index close to zero, whereas a country which exports only one export will have a value of one (least diversified).

$$H_i = \sum_i (S_{ij})^2 \qquad (1.5)$$

Another measure of export concentration is the **Theil's Entropy.** High entropy values indicate a diversified export portfolio. If one good is all that a country exports, the entropy is zero. If n goods have an equal share, the maximum value is the log of n. Theil's Entropy can be computed for subgroups of exports and decomposed additively to measure concentration within and among groups of exports. The most concentrated subgroups have the highest weights. A portfolio with high concentration of specific subgroups of goods produces an HHI closer to one and an entropy value closer to zero. Table 1.4 calculates concentration indexes for six countries in 2000 and 2008. It shows that the two measures (HHI and entropy) both indicate changes in concentration in the same direction.

$$E_i = -\sum_i S_{ij} \log(S_{ij}) \qquad (1.6)$$

In manufacturing, Easterly, Reshef, and Schwenkenberg (2009) show that for every country they assessed, exports are dominated by a few "big hits." They find that success in exports, and specialization, is driven by a narrow range of specific exports to specific markets. Although this appears to undercut the argument for export diversification, Imbs and Wacziarg (2003) find that economies tend to diversify over most of their development path. Only after reaching a relatively high threshold of income is further growth associated with specialization. Klinger and Lederman (2004) find a similar inverted U relationship between income and export activity. Diversification is important for developing countries because it allows them to develop competence over a broader range of manufactured goods. Countries develop by learning to make new things, and through entrepreneurial dynamism and growth, not by relying only on what they have traditionally done well.

Table 1.4. Concentration of Goods at HS Two-Digit Level, 2000–08

	HHI 2000	HHI 2008	Concentration	Entropy 2000	Entropy 2008	Concentration
Chile	0.29	0.41	Increased	1.49	1.23	Increased
Costa Rica	0.25	0.19	Decreased	1.66	1.81	Decreased
Morocco	0.21	0.17	Decreased	1.77	1.86	Decreased
Senegal	0.24	0.20	Decreased	1.61	1.78	Decreased
Vietnam	0.23	0.18	Decreased	1.65	1.88	Decreased
South Africa	0.18	0.22	Increased	1.87	1.69	Increased

Source: Authors.

MODULE 1

Intensive and Extensive Margins

Indicators	Summary of data needs vand sources
Hummels-Klenow extensive and intensive margins for both products and markets	Trade data from WITS: country exports, global imports trade-weighted by product and by market.

Export growth can take place at the *intensive margin* (selling existing products to existing markets) or at the *extensive margin* (selling existing products to new markets, new products to new markets, and new products to existing markets). There are multiple definitions of the intensive and extensive margins. In this *Toolkit* the concepts are invoked in the context of diversification as well as survival of exports. In the former, the attempt is to explore to what extent countries have been able to add new products and new markets—that are economically significant—to their portfolios. When the two margins are discussed in the context of export survival, the attempt is to decompose export growth into constituents capturing growth of old products in old markets versus the rest.

In the context of diversification, how has a country performed on the intensive margin (*IM*) and the extensive margin (*EM*) of exports, say, over the past decade? Drawing on Hummels and Klenow (2005), it is possible to infer (1) how big a player a country is in what it exports (*IM*), and (2) how important what it exports is to the world (*EM*). This approach improves on the method of simply counting how many new export items have been introduced by weighing the new products by their share in world trade. So, adding pencils to the export portfolio is not the same as adding high-value chemicals. If K^i is the set

of products exported by country i, X_k^i the dollar value of i's exports of product k to the world, and X_k^w the dollar value of world exports of product k, then the intensive margin (*IM*) below calculates a country's share in its representative products. The extensive margin (*EM*) calculates the *breadth* of one's export portfolio relative to all exports that exist in the world.

$$IM_i = \frac{\sum_{k^i} X_k^i}{\sum_{k^i} X_k^w} \qquad EM_i = \frac{\sum_{k^i} X_k^w}{\sum_{k^w} X_k^w} \qquad (1.7)$$

In figure 1.14, panels A and B, the **Hummels-Klenow intensive and extensive margins** are plotted jointly on an intensive–extensive margin space for Costa Rica and Vietnam, first with respect to products and second with respect to markets. Costa Rica's share in exports that the rest of the world also exports (intensive margin) has increased slightly over the last 10 years, but the global importance of export items it has a foothold in has dropped. The intensive margin as measured here indicates how big Costa Rica is in what it exports, and the extensive margin measures how globally important is *what* it exports. This is probably driven by its improved performance in semiconductors. Had Costa Rica not exported any semiconducters in 1998, the extensive margin would have significantly increased. Furthermore, several textile and apparel items, which remain a major export globally, are no longer produced in Costa Rica. In contrast, Vietnam managed to increase its share of export in goods that the rest of the world produces (intensive margin) as well as the breadth of its export portfolio relative to all exportable products (extensive margin).

Figure 1.14. Intensive and Extensive Margins

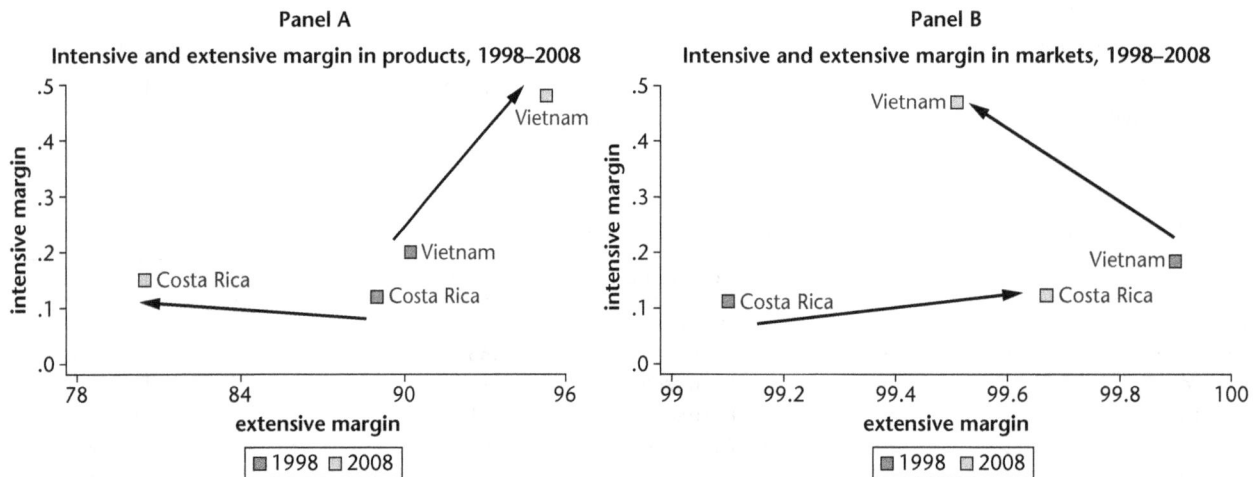

Panel A
Intensive and extensive margin in products, 1998–2008

Panel B
Intensive and extensive margin in markets, 1998–2008

Source: Authors.

Extending this to analyze destination markets, Costa Rica's export share in countries to which it currently exports (intensive margin) has increased, as has its reach to markets that cumulatively are larger relative to the world in 2008 than in 1998 (extensive margin). In contrast, Vietnam increased its existing share of exports to existing markets, but it did not add new markets that are globally significant to its portfolio of destinations.[12]

Market Reach of Exports

Indicators	Summary of data needs and sources
Index of Export Market Penetration (IEMP)	Trade data from WITS: target country exports; sum of all country nonzero imports of product (as described below).
Scatterplot of the value of specific exports against the number of markets reached	

How successful are a country's individual exports? How many markets do they reach and how much do they earn in aggregate? In this section we review two ways of looking at the future potential for market expansion.

One measure is the **Index of Export Market Penetration (IEMP)**. This index looks at a country's total number of exports, and the number of markets that each of those products reaches. Then, the number of countries in the rest of the world that import each of the products (which the country of interest exports) is counted. Pairing products and countries this way, we obtain the maximum potential number of export relationships that a country can establish given its export portfolio at present. The actual number of export relationships is then divided by the potential

number to assess how much export opportunities a country is exploiting. As an example, Brenton and Newfarmer (2009) compare Albania's IEMP with that of the Czech Republic. In 2004, Albania exported 955 products and the Czechs exported 2,863 products (using a common level of commodity classification). At the extreme, if Albania exported all its exports to all the countries that import what Albania exports, it would have formed 90,350 export relationships. In reality, it only exploited 2.27 percent of the potential. In contrast, the Czech Republic exploited around 20 percent of the potential. No country ever exports all its exports to all the countries that import them. In fact, one of the world's most successful exporting nations, Germany, exploits only around 50 percent of its potential, and this can serve as a best-case benchmark.

Brenton and Newfarmer (2009) calculate the IEMP as follows, where exporter j, for whom I_{ij} is the set of products (i) in which positive exports are observed, $Y_{ijk} = 1$ for $X_{ijk} = 1$, else $Y_{ijk} = 0$ and $Z_{ik} = 1$ for $M_{ik} > 0$, else $Z_{ik} = 0$, where X_{ijk} is the value of exports of product i from exporter j to importer k, and M_{ik} is the value of imports of product i by importer k.

$$IEMP_i = \frac{\sum_{i \in I_{ij}} \sum_k Y_{ijk}}{\sum_{i \in I_{ii}} \sum_k Z_{ik}} \qquad (1.8)$$

Figure 1.15 gives an example of the IEMP for several low- and lower-middle-income countries, including Germany as a global benchmark. It is clear from the data

Figure 1.15. Examples of IEMP in Selected LIC and LMIC versus Germany, 1999 and 2008

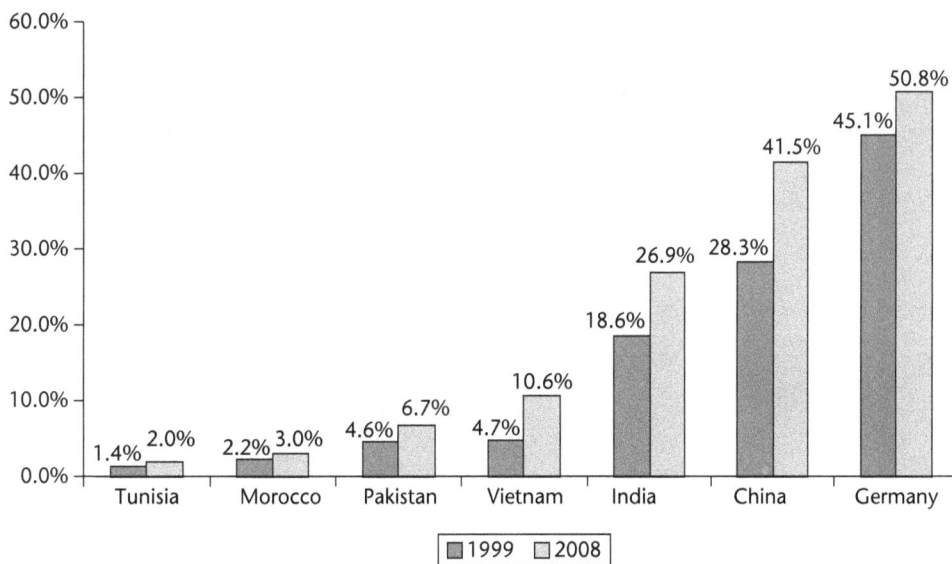

Source: Authors.
Note: LIC = low-income countries; LMIC = lower-middle-income countries.

that penetration of export markets by most of these countries is far below not only that of Germany but also of China, which has substantially increased its market penetration over the past decade.

One major limitation of the IEMP is that unlike the Hummels-Klenow indexes explained earlier, it does not weigh exports by their relative importance. Therefore an insignificant export to a small economy counts the same as a major export breakthrough in a large economy. Like all the indicators discussed in this *Toolkit*, this index should not be used in isolation but rather in conjunction with other indicators to portray a more complete trade picture. Nonetheless, a country whose IEMP is inexplicably low could generate, for example, a hypothesis regarding product quality or the efficacy of its export promotion agencies.

A second measure is the **number of export destinations** reached per product. Figure 1.16, panels A and B, illustrate the success of individual Russian exports. Over the eight-year period, 2000–08, Russia expanded the number of export markets that at least one of its products (at the HS six-digit level) serves from around 80 to more than 100. In both 2000 and 2008, 1,396 products reached at least 10 markets. In this subgroup, 975 products reached a higher number of markets than in 2000, and 348 products reached a smaller number. The value of individual export products has also grown. The most prolific products are vodka and oil. The total value of Russia's existing products (gray) in the newly expanded or existing markets has increased. The light gray dots indicate products that were not exported in 2000 but were in exported 2008, which proxy for new discoveries. The black dots are products that were exported in 2000, but not in 2008, possibly indicating death or suspension. Some new exports in 2008 have already reached around 25 markets. The analysis identifies particular prod-

uct stories that may be worth further analysis to understand, for example, why a new product managed to so quickly reach a large number of countries (was it the nature of the product? specific trade promotion efforts? or other factors?) or why an established product across many countries is no longer being exported to any. These findings may be valuable at the product level and also may be generalizable cases for the wider export sector.

Quality and Sophistication: The Quality Margin

Technology Content

Indicators	Summary of data needs and sources
Radar graph of the share of high-tech, medium-tech, low-tech, primary and resource-based exports	Data. available up to 2006 at http://info.worldbank.org/etools/prmed/; the *World Development Indicators* database also has indicators of the share of high-tech exports in manufactured exports, together with the share of fuel or minerals and ores exports.

Although deciding which exports embody high-level technology, or which country is engaged in the most technology-intensive phase of production, can be controversial in an era of global production sharing, a basic classification of final exports into broad categories of high, medium, and low technology—and whether exports are primary and resource based—gives an indication of how a country's export basket has transformed over a period. In figure 1.17, the **technological content**[13] of Morocco's exports is gradually improving, but its sophistication of goods exports remains relatively low. Comparing figures across a decade from 1996 to 2006, Morocco's exports exhibited some diversification away from agriculture and

Figure 1.16. Market Reach of Exports

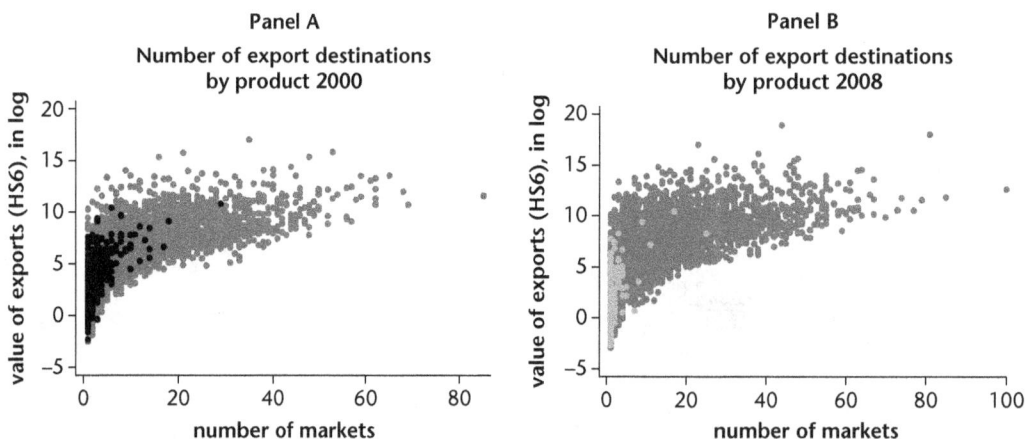

Panel A

Number of export destinations by product 2000

Panel B

Number of export destinations by product 2008

Figure 1.17. Technological Content of Morocco's Exports

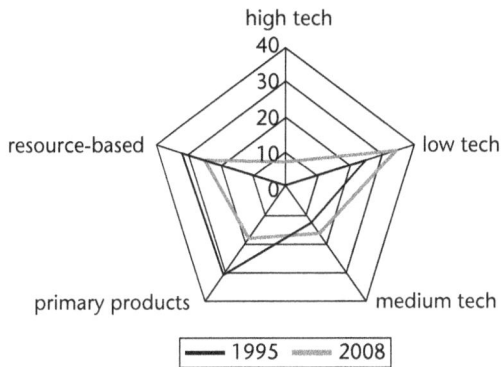

Source: Authors.

fertilizers toward manufacturing with moderate technological content. Apparel was one such new industry as was trade in parts and components related to automobiles. In terms of share of high-tech products in its overall exports basket, Morocco's ratio is less than 10 percent, but this marks a significant improvement from a decade earlier.

Unit Values

Indicators	Summary of data needs and sources
Cross-country comparison of unit values and quality at the SITC five- or HS six-digit level **Quality ladders** **Co-mapping of quality and market share performance**	Unit values computed from trade data in WITS; World Bank International Trade Department database developed for EU imports based on the COMEXT database from EUROSTAT; quality measured by unit prices relative to 90th percentile of the unit value distribution across countries exporting the product to the market.

Goods in the same product category vary widely in quality, proxied by **unit values** (nominal sales divided by quantity). When supply is competitive, higher prices are generally associated with higher quality and greater product differentiation.[14] One way to increase the absolute amount of export per capita is to increase the value of export per unit. Hwang (2006) finds strong evidence of convergence in product quality: When countries introduce a new product, they are usually low in quality, but their unit prices tend to converge to the global frontier at a rate of about 5 percent per year. The variance in the unit price of goods signals opportunities for countries to upgrade quality and to grow faster. Because upgrading of quality is potentially a secure avenue to boost growth, it is imperative to assess not only what a country produces but also what the quality of exports looks like.

Table 1.5 gives an example of how unit values of seemingly similar products (at the SITC five-digit level) differ.[15] The table includes unit values of imports into the United States in 2008 of selected goods from a range of developing countries, as well as Germany. Some products command an identical unit price (for example, dry or crushed capsicum), suggesting that prices are dictated internationally and little room exists for within-product upgrading. Unit values of some goods vary marginally (for example, basketwork, printing press parts, cutting blades for machines) whereas those of others vary widely (for example, frozen tuna, locks and keys, motor car bodies).

Hwang (2006) suggests that because convergence of unit values occurs unconditionally, low-income countries need to produce goods within a category in which the global frontier of productivity is high and is possibly dominated by rich countries. Learning and catch-up is highest in those categories. If a country's portfolio consists of a small share of differentiated goods in which upgrading possibilities are limited, the need for diversification becomes more urgent.

Decomposing exports into value and volume contributions can tell an important story about competitiveness. For example, figure 1.18 illustrates that in Mongolia, the rapid growth in minerals exports in recent years is explained almost fully by rising world prices, a factor over which the country has little control. By contrast, in many other key products, like meat and cashmere garments, in

Table 1.5. Examples of Unit Values of Exports to the United States, 2008

SITC 5	Product	China	India	Costa Rica	Senegal	Vietnam	Pakistan	Germany
07513	Capsicum dry and crushed	3.070	3.070	3.070		3.070	3.070	3.070
89971	Basketwork, wickerwork, etc.	4.698	4.736	4.868	4.468	4.570	4.852	4.716
72699	Printing press parts	57.020	57.020	57.025		57.016	57.044	57.020
69561	Cutting blades for machines	12.304	12.049	10.816		12.898	12.901	13.747
69911	Locks/keys/clasps/parts	9.227	18.305	133.196		5.846	42.371	26.477
03414	Tuna/skipjack/bonito		14.686	10.310	6.242	13.342		
78421	Motor car bodies	495.27	170.997	123.23				10,522.75

Source: Computed using mirror data in Comtrade.

Figure 1.18. Decomposition of Export Growth across Key Products, Mongolia, 2002–07

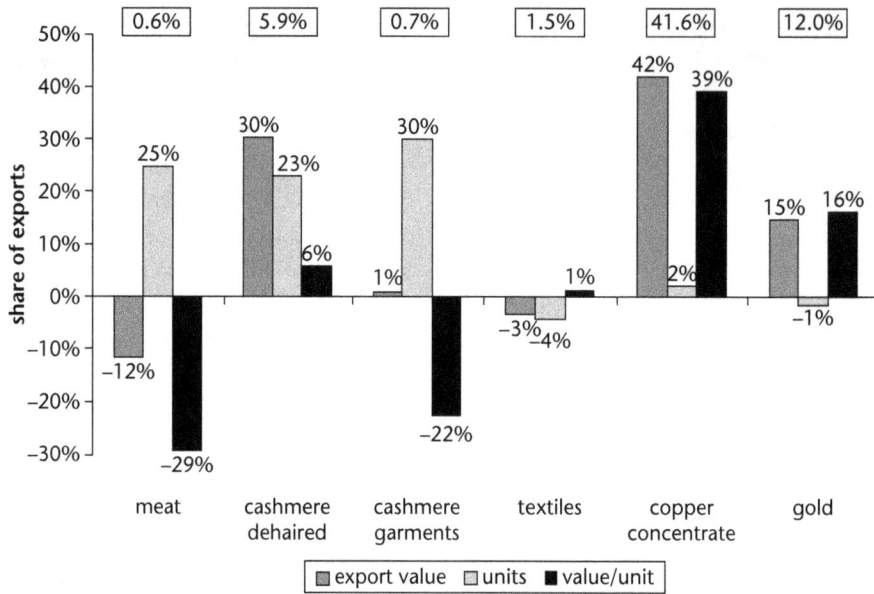

Source: Authors.

which prices are more dependent on producer competitiveness, Mongolia has experienced substantial declines in the unit value of production, suggesting poor quality competitiveness.

Analyzing data on unit prices of important export products against key competitors can provide a valuable assessment of the trends in a country's quality competitiveness. We rely on the COMEXT database from EUROSTAT to characterize the relative unit values of import in each EU member country. As in Schott (2004), unit values were calculated simply as the quotient of general import values and quantities. Within any product (eight-digit Combined Nomenclature code) for any given year, we then have a distribution of unit values of imports from the different source countries. For each good i and exporting country c, in time year t, we generate a measure of relative quality R as follows:

$$R_{itc} = \frac{uv_{itc}}{uv_{it}^{90}} \qquad (1.9)$$

Where u_{itc} denotes the unit value of the good and u_{it}^{90} denotes the value at the 90th percentile of the unit value distribution across countries for that product. R_{itc} denotes the relative quality of the country's export of that good, that is, quality relative to other countries exporting the same good. Figure 1.19, for example, shows price per unit trends for Indonesia's top five garment export products to Europe, against its main competitors. In this case, it high-

Figure 1.19. Analysis of Indonesia's Unit Price Trends for Top Five Garment Exports to the European Union Relative to Main Competitor, 1988–2008

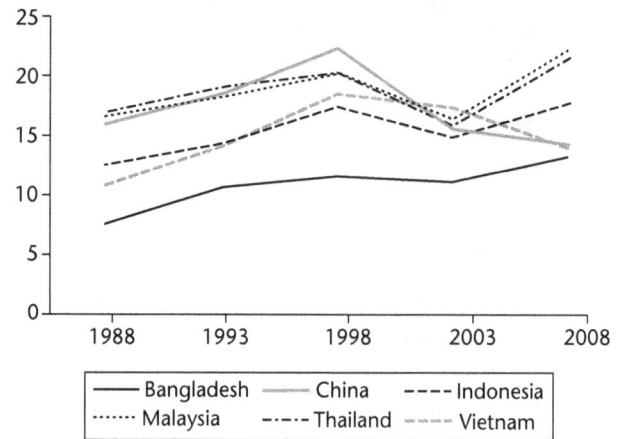

Source: Authors.

lights the fact that Indonesia might be getting caught in the middle in terms of competition in garment export markets—it struggles to compete on price with low-cost producers like Bangladesh and China, but it is not yet able to reach the quality levels of Malaysia and Thailand.

Using data on unit prices it is also possible to develop analyses of **quality ladders**, measuring the relative quality of a country's exports against all other countries that export a specific product (worldwide or to a specific

Figure 1.20. Quality Ladder for Women's Cotton Blouses and Shirts Imports to the European Union, 1998 and 2008

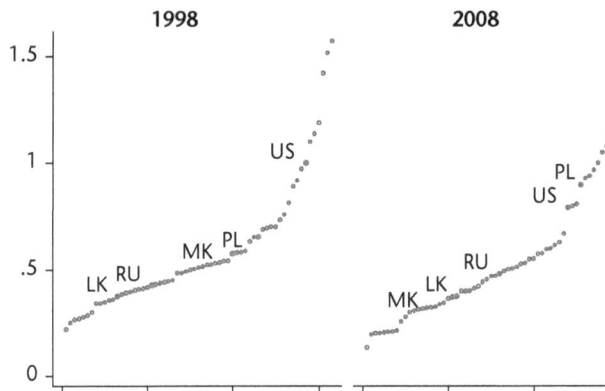

Source: Authors.

market). As illustrated in figure 1.20, the plot of all countries on the basis of their rank in quality and their relative pricing creates a "ladder" or a long tail. Figure 1.20 highlights the declining quality performance of Macedonia in one of its most important export products—between 1998 and 2008, the quality of its exports declined and it was overtaken in quality by countries like Sri Lanka and Russia.

The next step in the analysis is to look at the relation between changes in the relative quality measure and changes in market shares—it is one thing to increase quality; but if it comes at the expense of market share, it may be a trade-off not worth having. Similarly, improving market share in the context of declining quality may actually represent an increase in cost competitiveness rather than a decline in quality per se. Figure 1.21 plots these results for three products (defined by an eight-digit Combined Nomenclature code) for Senegal in the European Union. The x-axis shows the growth rate of market share (log difference of market shares) between 1996–2008 and 2006–08. The y-axis represents the growth rate of the average quality measure between the same periods of time. The size of each bubble is the importance of each product in Senegal's export basket.

Sophistication

Indicators	Summary of data needs and sources
PRODY and EXPY	Data obtained from Comtrade (WITS); PRODY and EXPY calculation plotted against gross domestic product per capita.

The foundational trade models like Hecksher-Ohlin or Ricardo attribute trade to differences in factor endowments or technology across countries. Economists seldom

analyze the growth of countries explicitly from the perspective of actual goods produced. Instead of predetermining the classification of products (for example, technology-intensive or not), Hausmann, Hwang, and Rodrik (2006) estimate the sophistication of products on the basis of the income levels of countries that produce them. If a product, say, internal combustion engine, is largely produced by rich countries, that product would be revealed to be "rich" and sophisticated. This outcome-based measure of sophistication for each product, called PRODY, is a weighted average of the per capita GDP of countries producing that good, with weights derived from RCA. Similarly, PRODY of coffee beans would be much lower because the countries that dominate its production are generally low income.

$$PRODY_k = \sum_j \frac{\left(\dfrac{x_{jk}}{X_j}\right)}{\sum_j \dfrac{x_{jk}}{X_j}} Y_j \text{ and}$$

$$EXPY_i = \sum_k \left(\frac{x_{ik}}{X_i}\right) PRODY_k \tag{1.10}$$

PRODY values of all products that a country exports are then weighted by the product's share in the country's total export basket and summed to derive a country's level of GDP per capita as inferred from the sophistication of its export basket. Called **EXPY**, this measures the income content of a country's export basket. It is regarded as a more inclusive measure of sophistication than intensity in technology or R&D. It captures the wages supported by production of a good. Hausmann, Hwang, and Rodrik (2006) show that countries with high EXPY tend to have higher growth rates in the future. Countries "become" what they export by converging to the income level implied by their export baskets.

For each country in figure 1.22, one can ask whether the products it is currently exporting are more sophisticated than would be suggested by that country's level of income. This information can then inform an agenda aimed at gauging the urgency with which the country ought to be promoting or discovering new export activities. According to Klinger (2010), for incumbent products, many of the conventional competitiveness variables matter (the broadest set is the 12 pillars covered by the World Economic Forum's *Global Competitiveness Report*). For "new products," however, they may not be sufficient, as countries need to deal with distinct market failures related to informational externality and coordination problems. On the basis of the measure of export sophistication (EXPY), countries like China, India, Indonesia, the Philippines, and

MODULE 1

MODULE 1

Figure 1.21. Change in Senegal's Market Shares and Relative Quality in the Food, Textiles and Clothing, and Footwear Products in the European Union

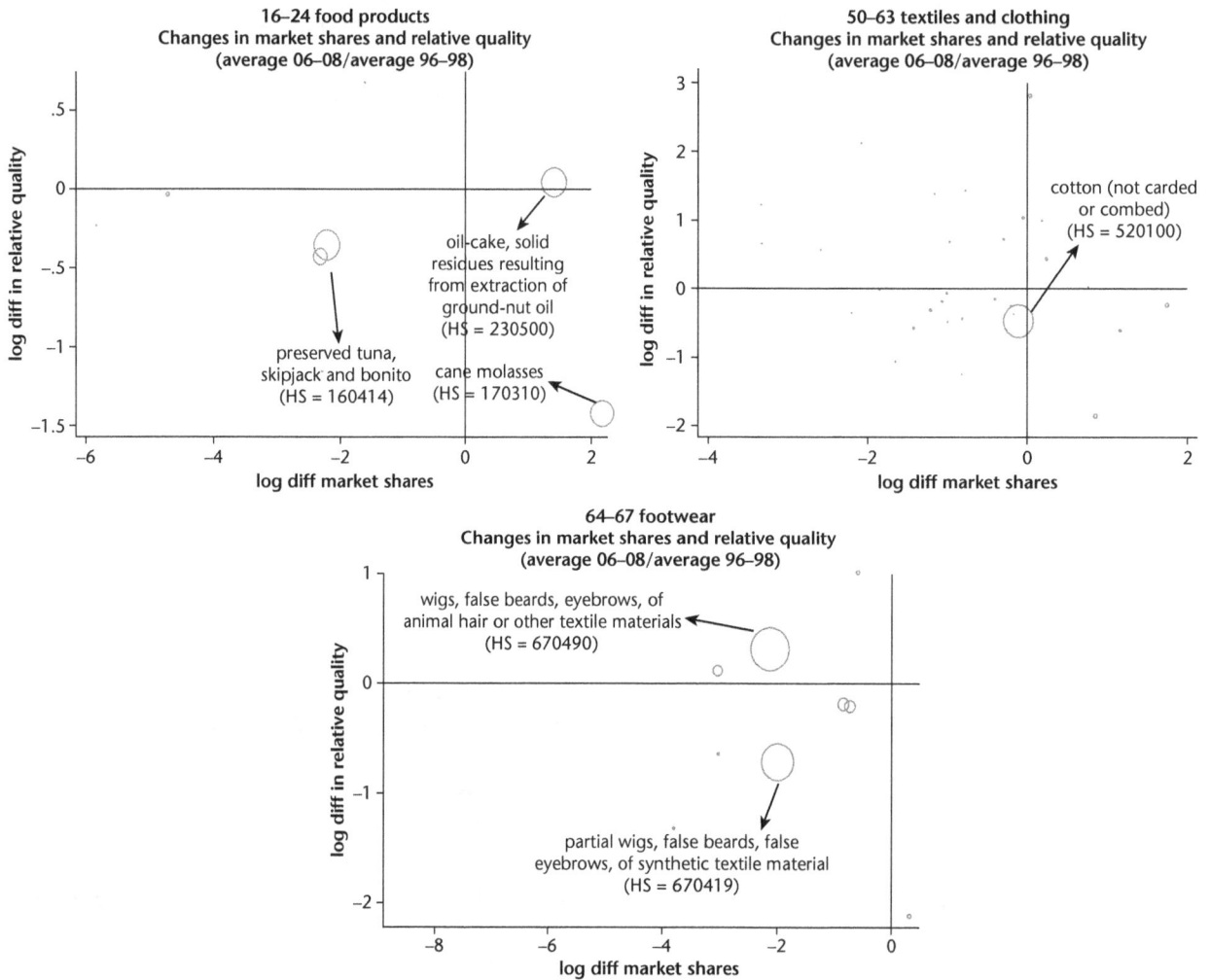

16–24 food products
Changes in market shares and relative quality
(average 06–08/average 96–98)

y-axis: log diff in relative quality
x-axis: log diff market shares

oil-cake, solid residues resulting from extraction of ground-nut oil (HS = 230500)

preserved tuna, skipjack and bonito (HS = 160414)

cane molasses (HS = 170310)

50–63 textiles and clothing
Changes in market shares and relative quality
(average 06–08/average 96–98)

y-axis: log diff in relative quality
x-axis: log diff market shares

cotton (not carded or combed) (HS = 520100)

64–67 footwear
Changes in market shares and relative quality
(average 06–08/average 96–98)

y-axis: log diff in relative quality
x-axis: log diff market shares

wigs, false beards, eyebrows, of animal hair or other textile materials (HS = 670490)

partial wigs, false beards, false eyebrows, of synthetic textile material (HS = 670419)

Source: Authors.

Thailand are above the line, which implies that their export basket is "richer" than they are. Developing new products is much more important for countries below the line, such as resource-rich countries like Qatar and Russia. Countries above the line can expect to see growth from existing exports.

As with many measures presented in this toolkit, EXPY has its drawbacks (see box 1.2). Despite this, measuring EXPY or another indicator of sophistication over time can give an important indication of the relative growth in sophistication of the export basket and the degree to which this is affecting growth of per capita income. As figure 1.23, panel A, shows, over the past two decades, sophistication of China's export basket has increased every biennium (each dot represents two years), and this has been associated with rising per capita income. India's exports are also becoming

more sophisticated but not as fast as China's. Vietnam resembles the trajectory of India. Starting from a very low base around the time it began its reforms under *Doi Moi* in the late 1980s, it has since caught up with many low-income countries like Pakistan, whose export sophistication has not undergone as stark an improvement as its Asian peers. From this figure alone, we cannot say whether rising export sophistication pulled up per capita incomes or whether countries moved into production of more sophisticated exports after average incomes rose. However, Hausmann and Klinger (2007), using a large pool of countries, have shown that current export sophistication is a good predictor of economic growth in the future. Felipe (2010) estimates that a 10 percent increase in EXPY at the beginning of a period raises growth by about half a percentage point. Figure 1.23, panel B, provides an additional

Figure 1.22. The Relationship between Income and Export Sophistication, 2003–05

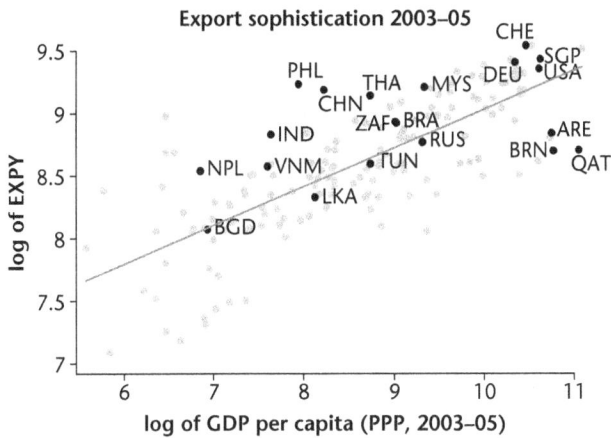

Source: Authors.
Note: ARE = United Arab Emirates; BGD = Bangladesh; BRA = Brazil; BRN = Brunei Darussalam; CHE = Switzerland; CHN = China; DEU = Germany; IND = India; LKA = Sri Lanka; MYS = Malaysia; NPL = Nepal; PHL = Philippines; QAT = Qatar; RUS = Russian Federation; SGP = Singapore; THA = Thailand; TUN = Tunisia; USA = United States; VNM = Vietnam; ZAF = South Africa.

explanatory element by adding dates to each dot on the graph—this helps us see more clearly the consistent trajectory of China (upward) and Russia (downward) and the more ambiguous picture in Brazil.

Revealed Factor Intensity (RFI)

Indicators	Summary of data needs and sources
Revealed Physical Capital Index (RPCI) and Revealed Human Capital Index (RHCI)	Indexes available from UNCTAD (http://r0.unctad.org/ditc/tab/index .shtm) and World Bank International Trade Department database.

Figure 1.23. Evolution of Export Sophistication

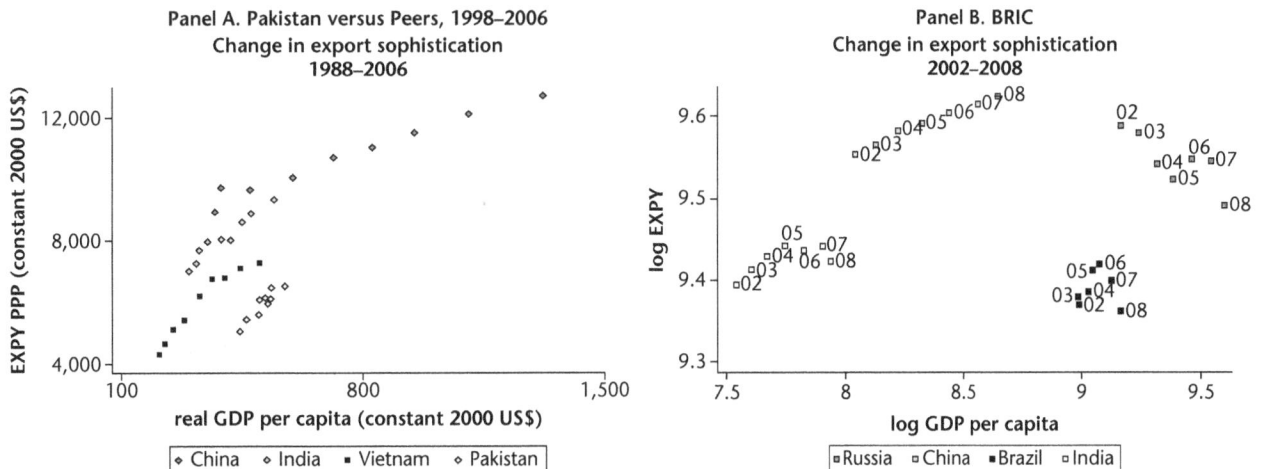

If PRODY and EXPY reflect the income content of exports, the **revealed factor intensities** of traded goods reflect the human and physical capital content of exports. They are computed in a similar manner to PRODY, but they arguably have a stronger theoretical linkage to comparative advantage derived from factor endowments. Goods that are predominantly exported by countries rich in human capital and physical capital are revealed to be intensive in human capital and physical capital, respectively. The indexes are computed by weighting the factor endowments of all countries exporting a particular product; weights are derived from a modified version of the RCA. Human capital is estimated by the average years of schooling, and physical capital stock is estimated by the perpetual inventory method, which reconstructs capital stock estimates from investment flows by recursively adding up current investments to a previous period's capital stock with appropriate depreciation. The database of factor intensities (human, physical, land, and natural resources) of all products at the SITC four-digit and HS six-digit level are made available by United Nations Conference on Trade and Development (UNCTAD).[16]

$$RPCI_k = \sum_j \frac{\left(\dfrac{x_{jk}}{X_j}\right)}{\sum_j \dfrac{x_{jk}}{X_j}} * \frac{K_j}{L_j} \quad and$$

$$RHCI_k = \sum_j \frac{\left(\dfrac{x_{jk}}{X_j}\right)}{\sum_j \dfrac{x_{jk}}{X_j}} * H_j$$

(1.11)

Source: Authors.

MODULE 1

Box 1.2. The Drawbacks of PRODY and EXPY

The concepts of PRODY and EXPY are not free of criticism. The PRODY of some products is counterintuitively high, suggesting sophistication in products merely because rich countries produce them: bacon and ham, for example, have a higher PRODY than internal combustion engines. Furthermore, the quality of products varies (even if they all have an identical code at the HS six-digit level)—cars from country X may not be the same quality as cars from country Y. When product quality is not taken into account, EXPY overestimates the importance of sophisticated products from low-income countries. Xu (2006) shows that once products at the HS six-digit level are further divided by relative unit values, the structure of China's exports is consistent with its level of development. This has led authors like Lederman and Maloney (2009) to conclude that how a country produces an export matters more than what it produces. Seemingly high-tech products like computers can be produced in low-tech ways and vice versa.

Furthermore, because of fragmentation of production, while the final export of a sophisticated product might be from a low-income country, its contribution might have just been in the final assembly of high-value intermediate inputs made elsewhere. One should not, therefore, lose sight of the entire value chain and explore which stage of production creates and captures the greatest value. Even if computers are deemed not to be sophisticated because the final assembled package is exported from a low-income country, the parts and components could be highly skill-intensive and possibly imported from richer countries. According to Dean, Fung, and Wang (2007), imported inputs accounted for 57 percent of Chinese computer exports in 2002. Koopman, Wang, and Wei (2008) estimate the foreign content in China's exports to be about 50 percent overall, and 80 percent in sophisticated products like electronic devices. In the well-known example of the iPod, an overwhelming share of the final assembled value of an iPod exported from China is captured by the creators of intellectual property and not in the form of wages earned by the assemblers.

Krugman (2008) discusses this issue in the context of a paradox that increased trade of the United States with developing countries appears to be in skill-intensive products, contrary to trade theory. Much of this increase is due to aggregation bias, where only the labor-intensive final stages of production could be from developing countries, yet they give the illusory impression that the entire production of the finished good occurred within the borders of that country. To the extent possible, total exports net of components imports could reveal a country's place in global production sharing. For example, in 2006–07, nearly 75 percent of components imported for machinery and transport equipment (SITC 7) by China were from the rest of East Asia (Athukorala and Menon 2010).

Source: Authors.

Figure 1.24, panels A and B, plot the physical *and* human capital content of exports on the same graph for Pakistan and the Republic of Korea, with dots weighted by export value in 2003. The quadrants are formed by the median human and physical capital contents of each country's exports that year. The Korean space appears more dense, indicating that it exports many more goods (at the HS six-digit level) than Pakistan. Most notable, however, is the fact that some of the biggest-earning Pakistani exports (indicated by bubble size) embody human and physical capital content that is below the median of its portfolio. In contrast, Korea's big export earners embody capital content that is above the median of its overall export portfolio. Pakistan's most important exports in terms of value are those that need few machines, little capital equipment, and little schooling. Its exports that are capital intensive are yet to be scaled up.

Figure 1.24, panels C and D, compare only the revealed human capital intensity of the exports of Qatar and Singapore. The quadrants in both graphs are formed by the median of Qatar's export earnings and human capital content of its exports in 2003. Singapore exports 20 times more products (it has a much bigger native population than Qatar's, but the workforce is not more than five times larger). The human capital content of a large share of those exports are higher than the median content of

human capital of Qatar's exports. Despite the large number of goods, the human capital content of the median export is almost identical (Singapore's 7.7 to Qatar's 7.8). The human capital content and economies of scale of existing exports have implications for the human resources policies of Qatar if it seeks to diversify away from its reliance on natural resource–based exports into knowledge-based industries and services.

Upgrading: Analyzing Product Space

Indicators	Summary of data needs and sources
Proximity between products and product densities	Tools like Product Space Explorer and Product Space Parser downloadable from www.chidalgo.com; Cytoscape (open-source bioinformatics software) downloadable from www.cytoscape.com; revealed comparative advantage data to be computed from WITS.

When structural transformation or economic growth is studied as being determined by broad aggregates, such as human and physical capital, analysts and policy makers risk underappreciating the complexity of sector-specific ingredients needed for economies to adapt, experiment, and evolve. Hausmann and Klinger (2007) argue that every product requires capabilities that are specific to that activity, from labor training and physical assets to regulatory requirements, property rights, and infrastructure.

Figure 1.24. Revealed Factor Intensity

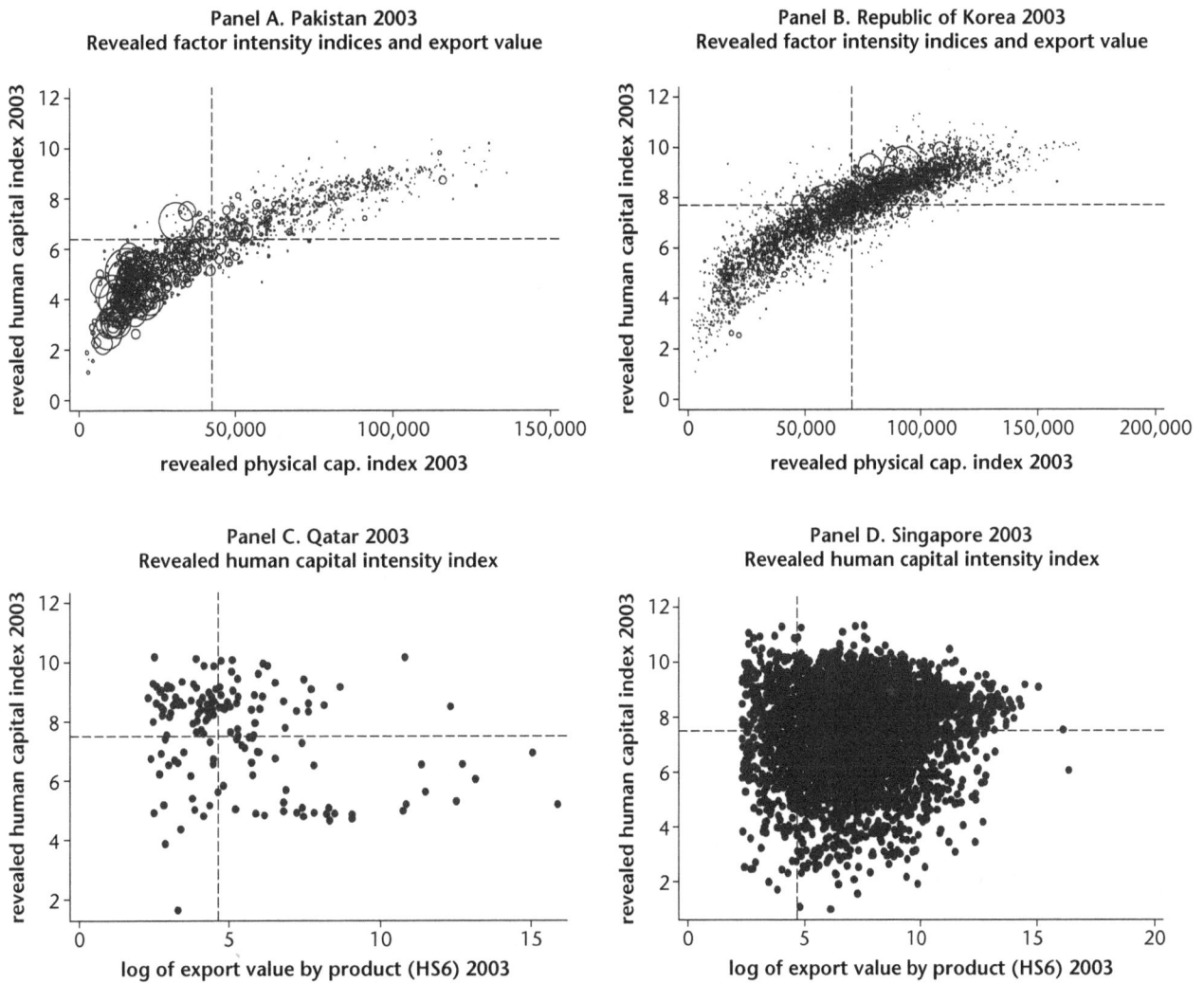

Panel A. Pakistan 2003
Revealed factor intensity indices and export value

Panel B. Republic of Korea 2003
Revealed factor intensity indices and export value

Panel C. Qatar 2003
Revealed human capital intensity index

Panel D. Singapore 2003
Revealed human capital intensity index

Source: Authors.

Exporting mangoes requires different capabilities (such as a decent sanitary and phytosanitary regime) than producing synthetic apparel, but the capabilities for producing mangoes are likely to be similar to exporting vegetables. Similarly, gold mining or even extraction of forest products may require a higher level of property rights enforced than, say, assembly of electronic parts. The ease with which an economy can move to producing new exports depends on what its installed capability looks like. The hypothesis is that countries that build up competence in producing a certain good can redeploy their human, physical, and institutional capital more easily if they seek to produce goods that are "nearby" those that they currently are producing.

Proximity between products in the **product space** is computed from the pairwise likelihood that a country

exports a product given that it also exports another product.[17] Proximity between any two goods (m and n) is the minimum of the pairwise conditional probabilities of having comparative advantage.

$$\varphi_{m,n} = \min\left\{ P\left(\frac{RCA_m}{RCA_n} \right), P\left(\frac{RCA_n}{RCA_m} \right) \right\} \qquad (1.12)$$

In the product space map presented in figure 1.25, the southeast part of the map has a lot of products that are clustered together, particularly related to industries such as chemicals, machinery, and metals. Peripheral products include petroleum, agriculture, cereals, and labor-intensive products. Whether a country's exports in which it has comparative advantage are located in the denser part of the product space or in the periphery can predict the ease with which that country transforms itself economically. Structural

MODULE 1

MODULE 1

Figure 1.25. Product Space Maps of Pakistan—Overview

Panel A. 1993

Panel B. 2008

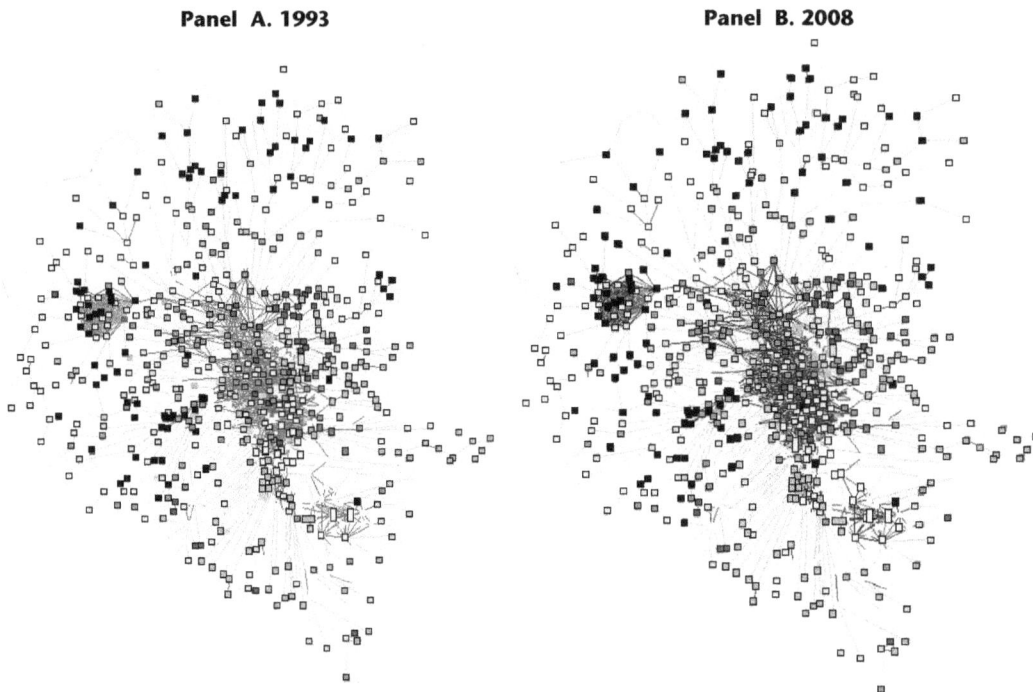

Source: Authors.

transformations are not smooth movements along a continuum but rather a messy process beset by market failures. When such market failures are binding, it is harder for firms to hop longer distances without government coordination and support. Because products do not evolve in sequence, that is, having iron ore deposits does not necessarily make a country an efficient steel producer, lateral linkages are as or more important than forward linkages with downstream industries.

Using the tools pioneered by Hidalgo, Klinger, Barabasi, and Hausmann (2007), the product space maps indicate all tradable products at the SITC four-digit level. The black dots are those with RCA. Other shades indicate the category of goods to which they belong, such as resource based, raw materials, labor- and capital-intensive manufactures, and so on. In their analogy, the product dots are trees that group themselves to form dense and sparse parts of a forest. Location of firms in the denser parts of the forest creates more opportunities for diversification and technological upgrading because market failures are less binding when firms have to make smaller adjustments to move to produce nearby goods that require similar capacities.

The center of the product space, for example, is quite dense with better connectedness among industries related to metallurgy, vehicles, and machinery. To the bottom right of the product space lie the more sophisticated electronics

and chemical industries. The scattered industries on the upper half are largely agricultural and resource based. Countries that succeed in transforming themselves over time from producing unprocessed natural or agricultural goods and labor-intensive manufactures (such as footwear and garments) to more sophisticated manufactured products like machinery and chemicals tend to see higher rates of economic growth. Over the past 40 years, countries like China, Indonesia, the Republic of Korea, Malaysia, Singapore, Thailand, and Turkey have undergone the most dramatic transformation and have seen some of the fastest rates of economic growth.

In Figure 1.25, panels A and B, the product space maps for Pakistan are shown. The cluster on the top where Pakistan had several products in both years with RCA (greater than 1) represents garments. It has also performed well in textiles, which incidentally is closer to industries that are more capital intensive and generally produced by rich countries. Between 1993 and 2008, during which time Pakistan increased the number of agricultural and labor-intensive products in which it had comparative advantage, it had not had a major breakthrough in more sophisticated products.

Figure 1.26, panels A to D, classify Pakistan's exports (valued above US$10,000) into four categories. The first is a group of products in which Pakistan has consistently

Figure 1.26. Pakistan's Exports, Mapped in Product Space, 1993–2008

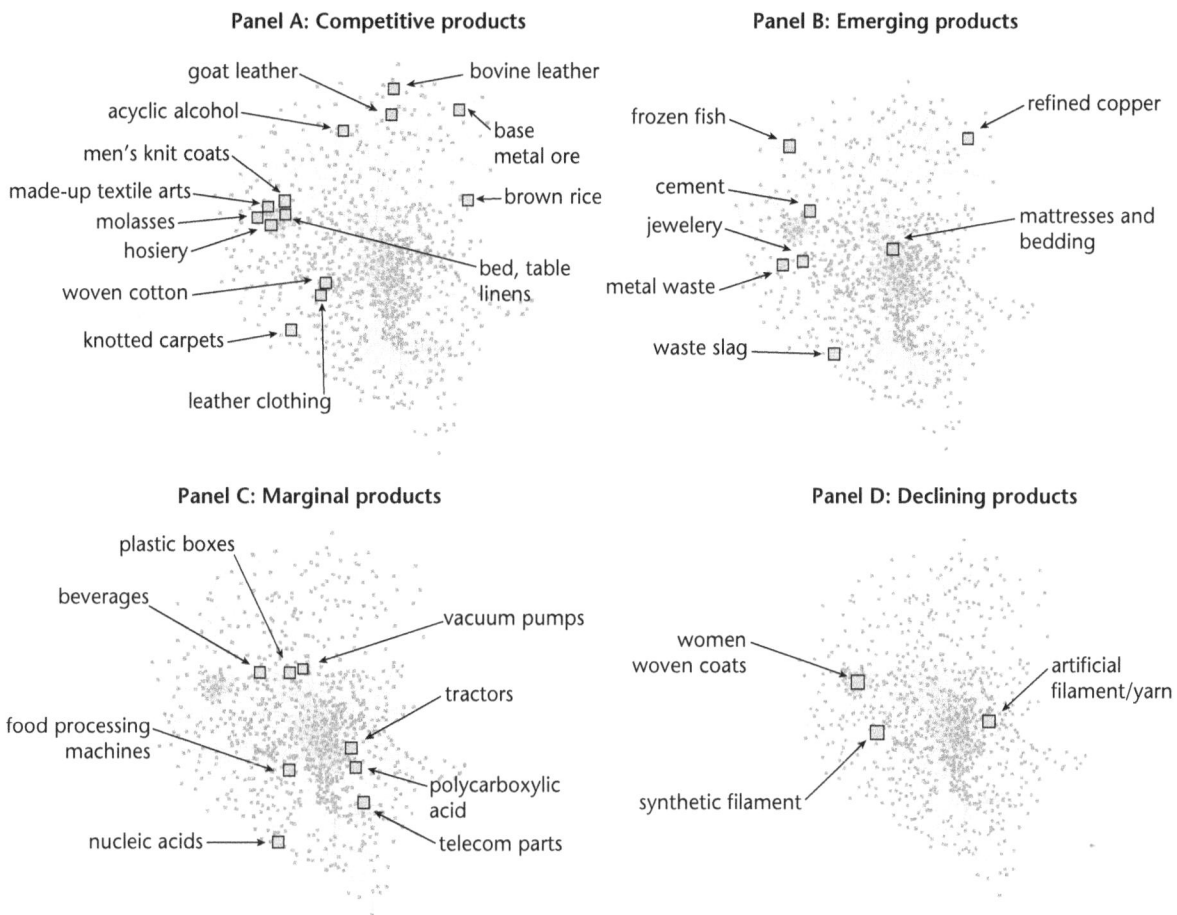

Panel A: Competitive products

goat leather
bovine leather
acyclic alcohol
base metal ore
men's knit coats
made-up textile arts
brown rice
molasses
hosiery
woven cotton
bed, table linens
knotted carpets
leather clothing

Panel B: Emerging products

frozen fish
refined copper
cement
jewelery
mattresses and bedding
metal waste
waste slag

Panel C: Marginal products

plastic boxes
beverages
vacuum pumps
tractors
food processing machines
polycarboxylic acid
nucleic acids
telecom parts

Panel D: Declining products

women woven coats
artificial filament/yarn
synthetic filament

Source: Authors.

been competitive. In 1993 and 2008, 103 products had an RCA greater than 1. These products are mainly textiles and garment items, such as linen, cotton, curtains, carpets, men's coats, and leather clothing. Figure 1.26, panel A, shows some of the top products from this category with at least 0.5 percent share in Pakistan's total exports in 2008. On the product space map, the textile cluster comes closest to the denser, high-value manufacturing industries. No Pakistani export (with RCA > 1) is firmly embedded in this part of the product space.

Thirty-eight major products did not have an RCA greater than 1 in 1993 but did in 2008. Figure 1.26, panel B, shows some of these "emerging" products with at least 0.2 percent share of national exports in 2008.[18] These products include potentially high-value exports like bedding and mattresses, frozen fish, jewelry, cement, and metal waste. The shipping-dependent heavier products are likely to be more competitive in regional markets.

The third category includes "marginal" products that Pakistan exported both in 1993 and 2008, but that had an

RCA of less than 1. There were more than 400 of such marginal exports. Figure 1.26, panel C, illustrates a few of these with national export share in 2008 of at least 0.05 percent. With external facilitation, some of these marginal products could be upgraded and made more competitive. They include vacuum pumps, chemicals (acids), wheeled tractors, telecommunications parts, and food-processing machines. These products indicate that Pakistan has installed capacity to move readily into fairly sophisticated manufacturing industries. Why it has not succeeded in becoming a major player in any of these products would be one major line of policy inquiry.

The fourth category includes goods that were competitive in 1993 but no longer in 2008. More than 20 major products were in the declining products category. In figure 1.26, panel D, three of the products that had an export share of at least 0.05 percent in 1993 are illustrated. These declining products include textile and garment products that were no longer able to withstand competition from countries producing similar items.

MODULE 1

Figure 1.27. Characteristics of Exporting Firms in Selected Indonesian Manufacturing Sectors, 2004

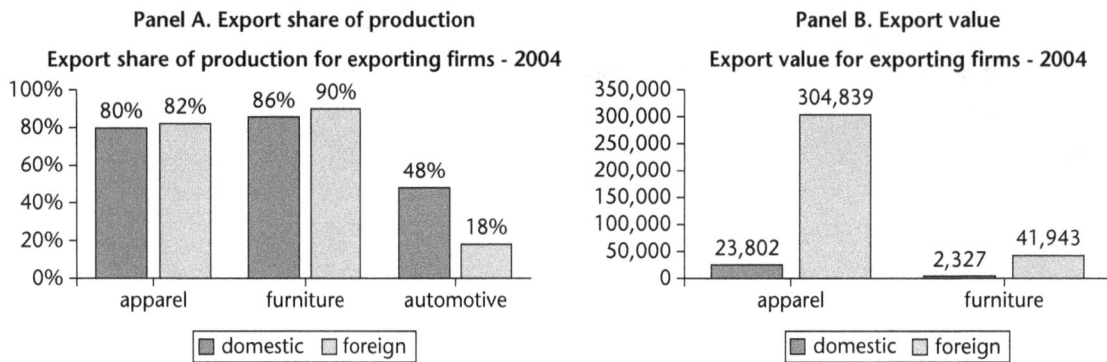

Panel A. Export share of production

Export share of production for exporting firms - 2004

Panel B. Export value

Export value for exporting firms - 2004

Source: Authors.

Entry and Survival: The Sustainability Margin

Structure of the Export Sector

Indicators	Summary of data needs and sources
Number and nature of firms participating in trade	Data from Enterprise, Manufacturing or Industrial Census (country-specific), or from Customs Transactions Database

One important determinant of trade performance and sustainability is the **structure of the trade sector** itself—specifically, understanding the degree to which a significant share of firms are participating in trade, the average and distribution of size of exporters, and the role of FDI in the export sector. Analyzing this performance requires substantial firm-level data, which are not likely to be available to the analyst in every country. Normally, the analysis will rely on access to census data—for example, from a manufacturing, industrial, or establishment census. Figure 1.27, panel A, shows that the apparel and furniture sectors in Indonesia are bifurcated—although most firms do not export, those that do export tend to export the large majority of their production. Figure 1.27, panel B, highlights the dramatic difference between domestic and FDI exporters in these sectors, with FDI firms producing and exporting 15 to 20 times (on average) that of domestic exporters.

Longevity of Export Episodes

Indicators	Summary of data needs and sources
Kaplan-Meier survival function; Nelson-Aalen cumulative hazard function; extended mean graphs	Trade data from WITS; regression run in Stata using commands designed for survival analysis.

Attempts by developing countries to introduce new exports in new or incumbent markets are fraught with challenges. Exploring why countries succeed in penetrating

foreign markets but fail to sustain those flows can help explain the varying export performance across countries. Empirical exercises with firm-level data could shed light on whether firm characteristics such as age, size, and type of ownership can influence **export longevity**. At a more aggregate level, Brenton, Pierola, and von Uexkull (2009) find that the size of the initial export flow explains subsequent duration of flows, as do search and information costs and exchange rate volatility.

In figure 1.28, panels A and B, the survival rates of Qatari and Singaporean exports at the SITC four-digit level are assessed for the 10-year period from 1999 to 2008. Qatar has 9,387 country-product pairs (excluding petroleum and gas). For many of these pairs, trade takes place just once or for a single spurt of consecutive years. Some pairs die and are then revived. So, the total number of export spells is 22,534. The median duration of the export spell is only 1 year, and the mean duration is 2.3 years.

The first graph (Kaplan-Meier survival function) shows that the probability of a Qatari export relationship surviving until the second year is less than 50 percent, and maintaining a relationship for more than two years is less than 25 percent. In comparison, the survival rate of Singapore's export relationships is much higher. It has 76,429 export relationships. The probability of a Singaporean export relationship surviving beyond the first year is 70 percent. Singaporean exports also have a much higher probability of survival in countries with which it shares a border (namely Malaysia, indicated by the red line). This is marginally true for Qatar's exports to countries with which it shares a border (Saudi Arabia and the United Arab Emirates), but the increased chance of survival is not as stark as for Singapore.[19] Geographic location is not a trade policy variable, but for almost all

Figure 1.28. 10-Year Export Survival Plots, 1998–2008

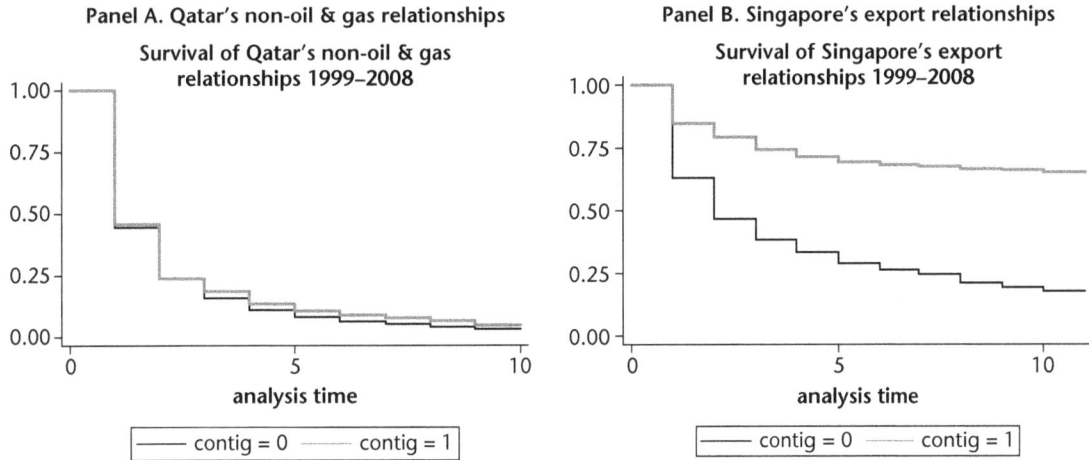

Panel A. Qatar's non-oil & gas relationships

Survival of Qatar's non-oil & gas relationships 1999–2008

Panel B. Singapore's export relationships

Survival of Singapore's export relationships 1999–2008

Source: Authors.

MODULE 1

countries, proximity matters, highlighting the importance of logistics, business organization, and infrastructure that reduce trading time and cost.

Decomposition of Export Growth and Death

Indicators	Summary of data needs and sources
Growth and survival rates of export relationships; breakdown of the intensive and extensive margins into their constituents	Trade data from WITS; computations in either Excel or Stata.

This section complements the earlier discussion on the intensive and extensive margins by looking at export *relationships* at the level of country-product pairs. This exercise has the advantage of exposing better the relationships along the intensive margin (*existing exports to existing markets*) and extensive margin (*new exports to existing markets, new exports to new markets*, and *existing exports to new markets*), as illustrated in figure 1.29. This can also reveal the scale of decline and death of major exports in specific markets.

For mature exporters, growth generally occurs at the intensive margin. The share of export growth contributed by existing flows to existing markets is usually dominant. This growth contribution can be tempered by the extinction of products or decline in export value of existing products in existing markets. On the extensive margin, expansion of existing products to new markets is more commonplace.[20] In figure 1.30, panels A and B, export growth is decomposed for India and Senegal between 2001 and 2008. In India, existing flows to existing countries accounted for nearly 100 percent of the growth, but this growth was offset by exports that fell to existing markets

Figure 1.29. Export Relationships: Intensive and Extensive Margins

	old market	new market
old product	intensive margin	extensive margin
new product	extensive margin	extensive margin

Source: Authors.

(5.8 percent). A modest 6 percent of export growth was explained by existing products to new markets. Although the categories can be sensitive to the thresholds and cutoffs used, overall, in poorer countries, growth at the extensive margin can play a bigger role than it does in higher-income countries, as can the decline and extinction of existing flows (low survival rates). This is illustrated by the decomposition of export growth for Senegal, which saw a bigger percentage increase in exports of existing products into existing markets (110 percent) as well as a bigger percentage decline in the same category (42 percent). Growth at the extensive margin (both of new products to new makets and of old products to new markets) was much higher for Senegal than India.[21]

Going further, one can analyze whether a pattern can be identified in the *death of exports.* Are exports becoming extinct more frequently in particular markets? Do declining exports belong disproportionately to a particular industry cluster like animal products or labor-intensive industries? In the Senegal example, 305 export relationships (out of 9,720 country-product pairs) had at least one

Figure 1.30. Decomposition of Export Growth

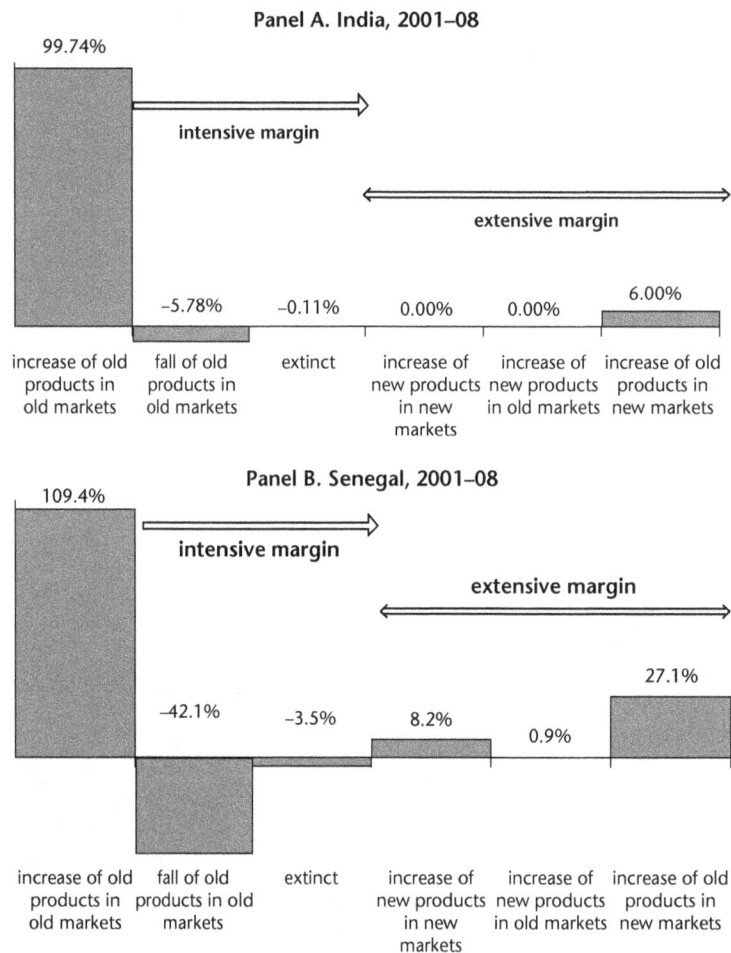

Panel A. India, 2001–08

99.74%		intensive margin →			
			extensive margin ↔		6.00%
	−5.78%	−0.11%	0.00%	0.00%	
increase of old products in old markets	fall of old products in old markets	extinct	increase of new products in new markets	increase of new products in old markets	increase of old products in new markets

Panel B. Senegal, 2001–08

109.4%		intensive margin →			
			extensive margin ↔		27.1%
	−42.1%	−3.5%	8.2%	0.9%	
increase of old products in old markets	fall of old products in old markets	extinct	increase of new products in new markets	increase of new products in old markets	increase of old products in new markets

Source: Authors.

nonzero value between 2001 to 2006 but had a zero export value in both 2007 and 2008 (see table 1.6). In terms of markets, the maximum number as well as cumulative value (from 2001 to 2006) of export relationships that failed to survive were destined mainly to neighboring countries like The Gambia, Guinea, Guinea-Bissau, Mali, and Sierra Leone. The three notable non-African markets were France, India, and the Netherlands. In terms of products, the dominant industry groups to which export deaths belonged were petroleum and cereals. For India, during the same period, the major markets in which its exports disappeared were Indonesia, Japan, Oman, and the Syrian Arab Republic. As for products, the main ones that disappeared in 2007 and 2008; were all related to petroleum (motor spirit and light oil) (see table 1.7).

A related anlaysis is a more explicit accounting of export relationships by product and country. In table 1.8, for the period 2004–08: (1) German exports are the most versatile with the maximum number of goods reaching the most number of countries, covering half of all relationships that could exist; (2) India exported three times more than Vietnam in 2008, but the average value of each relationship was similar, at US$3.8 million; (3) the annual growth rate of exports is many times higher than the annual growth rate of export relationships, indicating that it is easier to expand existing exports to existing markets than to connect new products with incumbent or new markets, or to expand old products to new markets; and (4) if the intensive margin is defined as the export of old products to old markets (that is, defined as relationships that existed at the beginning and the end of the five-year sample period), most trade occurs at the intensive margin. In 2008, 99 percent of German exports were in products that went to countries that already existed in 2004. This ratio was 98 percent for China, 94 percent for India, and 93 percent for Vietnam.

Table 1.6. Destinations of Declining Exports of Senegal

Code	Country	Region	Cumulative value (US$ '000) 2001–06	Number of relationships
MLI	Mali	Sub-Saharan Africa	92,257	23
GMB	Gambia, The	Sub-Saharan Africa	19,066	21
GNB	Guinea-Bissau	Sub-Saharan Africa	16,764	18
GIN	Guinea	Sub-Saharan Africa	9,875	15
FRA	France	Western Europe	9,137	38
NLD	Netherlands	Western Europe	8,304	5
LBR	Liberia	Sub-Saharan Africa	5,780	2
SLE	Sierra Leone	Sub-Saharan Africa	4,931	5
TGO	Togo	Sub-Saharan Africa	4,795	5
IND	India	South Asia	4,385	3
CPV	Cape Verde	Sub-Saharan Africa	4,354	5

Source: Authors.

Table 1.7. Declining Exports of Senegal

SITC	Product name	Industry	Cumulative value (US$ '000), 2001–06	Number of relationships
3330	Petroleum oil, crude	Petroleum	246,743	15
3342	Kerosene/medium oils	Petroleum	111,475	14
2634	Cotton, carded/combed	Cereals	45,200	25
3345	Lubricants (high petroleum content) etc.	Petroleum	9,077	20
3341	Motor spirit/light oils	Petroleum	8,913	7
3344	Fuel oils, n.e.s.	Petroleum	4,197	3
812	Fodder bran/by-products	Cereals	2,395	2
422	Rice husked (brown)	Cereals	2,329	3
2633	Cotton waste	Cereals	2,142	8

Source: Authors.

Exports Relative to Factor Endowment

Indicators	Summary of data needs and sources
Distance between national endowment and the factor intensity of exports	Trade data from WITS; endowment data from United Nations Conference on Trade and Development.

To explain why a country's exports cannot be sustained, one of several areas to investigate is whether the exports that die represent attempts to produce goods that require a different mix of factor endowments than supported by the economy. If a nation's endowment point is represented by the intersection of its average stock of physical and human capital, we can see how far or close to the average endowment point are the factor intensities of exports. By construction, most low-capital countries will be seen to produce exports that have capital content exceeding their endowment point (to the northeast). If the goods they produce are also produced by capital-rich countries, then the average

capital content of the export will be higher, reflecting the capital stock of all countries that produce those goods. Similarly, for capital-rich countries, their exports are likely to be to the southwest of their national endowment points. This occurs when goods produced by capital-rich countries are also produced by countries with lower physical and human capital stock. Because of aggregation bias even at the HS six-digit level, this is a pervasive problem in trade data. The insight, therefore, is obtained not by looking at the share of products that exceed the endowment point but by looking at the share of products that are *distant* from the national endowment point regardless of whether the endowment point is on the lower or the higher ends of the axes.

Take the example of Nepal. With no exception, the most significant exports of Nepal in 1993 were in line with the country's factor endowments, with some embodying capital greater than the national average. By 2003, Nepal's endowments had increased, and it produced an increasing

Table 1.8. Export Performance across Products and Markets, 2004–08

	China	India	Vietnam	Germany	Tunisia	Costa Rica
No. of export relationships in 2004	82,186	50,825	15,770	99,307	4,715	6,455
Realized (global) potential 2004 (%)	41.09	25.41	7.89	49.65	2.36	3.23
Average value of a relationship (US$ million)	11.48	1.97	2.20	16.75	1.51	1.80
Export value in 2004 (US$ million)	943,852	100,310	34,668	1,663,440	7,135	11,683
No. of export relationships in 2008	82,992	53,820	21,123	10,1542	4,047	7,316
Realized (global) potential 2008 (%)	41.50	26.91	10.56	50.77	2.02	3.66
Average value of a relationship (US$ million)	22.94	3.82	3.85	26.09	2.29	2.32
Export value in 2008 (US$ million)	1,903,742	205,808	77,507	2,648,773	9,261	17,039
Annual growth in export (2004–08, %)	19.17	19.68	22.28	12.33	6.73	9.89
Annual growth in exp. relation (2004–08, %)	0.24	1.44	7.58	0.56	−3.75	3.18
No. of new exports, 2004–08, two-year cutoff[a]	3,389	2,316	1,149	2,328	244	1,249
No. of relationships from Year 1 through Year 5	60,027	31,938	9,592	76,552	936	2,160
Survival rate over 5 years (2004–08)	73.04	62.84	60.82	77.09	19.85	33.46
Export value of relationships existing in Year 1 and Year 5 (US$ million)	1,864,135	193,837	72,263	2,623,793	5,398	16,264
Intensive margin, 2004–08	97.92	94.18	93.23	99.06	58.29	95.45
Extensive margin, 2004–08	2.08	5.82	6.77	0.94	41.71	4.55

Source: Authors; Computed using data in Comtrade.
Note:
a. Judging a "new product" using a two-year cutoff means that the export relationship did not exist in years $n – 2$ and $n – 1$, but it did exist in years n, $n + 1$, and $n + 2$.

share of exports with a higher level of physical and human factor requirements. The major exports, however, remained close to the endowment point (see figure 1.31).

In figure 1.31, panel C, the darkest dots show exports that existed in 1993 but not in 2003. The majority of such exports were those that required a relatively high level of physical and human capital. Of the 608 exports in 1993, 143 had disappeared by 2003. In the subsample of Nepal's exports with revealed physical capital index greater than 50,000, the death rate by 2003 was 37 percent (87 dead among 236 exports). In the subsample with revealed physical capital index less than 50,000, the death rate was 15 percent (56 dead among 372 exports). It can be hypothesized that, all else equal, ambitious ventures that defy a country's comparative advantage probably have a higher rate of failure. At the same time, by 2003, export activity had increased substantially (see figure 1.31, panel D). By that time, Nepal exported 1,510 products, of which only 465 were also exported in 1993. The majority of these new

exports that were active in 2003 (darkest dots), but not a decade earlier, were moderately capital intensive.

Success of exports depends on an array of factors, including accumulated national capabilities, search and information costs related to the business of exporting, and exchange rate volatility. Deviation from generalized comparative advantage is neither necessary nor sufficient for exports to die. In fact, many successful exporting countries in Asia used policies to push the limits posed by static comparative advantage to move into products exported by rich countries. If a country suffers from high rates of export death, however, this metric ought to be examined. The analysis of comparative advantage may be more relevant for smaller developing countries than large ones. The average capital endowments of large developing countries like Brazil and India may not be comparable to that of rich countries, but they are known to produce sophisticated, capital-intensive products such as helicopters and light aeroplanes.

Figure 1.31. Export Flows and Factor Endowments, Nepal

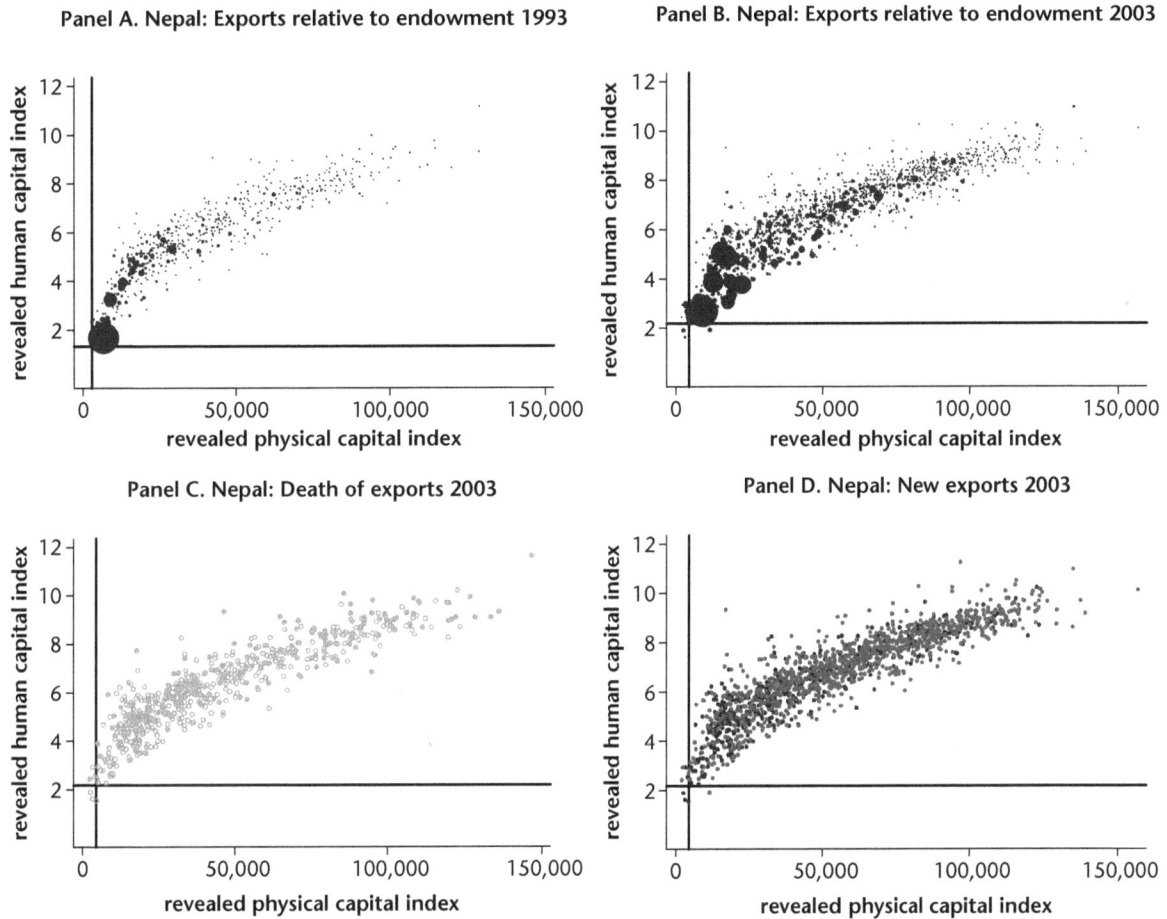

Panel A. Nepal: Exports relative to endowment 1993

Panel B. Nepal: Exports relative to endowment 2003

Panel C. Nepal: Death of exports 2003

Panel D. Nepal: New exports 2003

Source: Authors.

Annex A. Product Classifications

Classification of Products (HS two-digit)
(*Harmonized Commodity Description and Coding System*)
These eight categories are adapted from Hanson (2010).

1. **Agriculture, meat and dairy, seafood** (HS 1–10, 12–14): land-intensive activities surrounding agriculture production
2. **Food, beverages, tobacco, wood, paper** (HS 11, 15–24, 44–48): manufacturing activities that use agriculture, forestry, and other land-intensive inputs
3. **Extractive industries** (HS 25–27, 68–71): nonmetallic minerals, ores, petroleum, precious stones, precious metals, and other industries based on subsoil resources
4. **Chemicals, plastics, rubber** (HS 28–36, 38–40): manufacture of chemicals and other petroleum-based products
5. **Textiles, apparel, leather, footwear** (HS 41–42, 50–65): the production of labor-intensive clothing and apparel items and the inputs for these goods (textiles and leather)

6. **Iron, steel, and other metals** (HS 26, 72–83): production of iron, steel, and other metals
7. **Machinery, electronics, transportation equipment** (HS 84–89): production of skill and capital-intensive machinery, electrical materials, electronics, and transport equipment
8. **Other industries** (HS 37, 43, 49, 66–67, 90–97): collection of remaining manufacturing industries (photographic material and equipment, fur, printed material, umbrellas, hats, musical instruments, arms, furniture, toys, and miscellaneous items)

Classification of Products (SITC two-digit)
(*Standard International Trade Classification, Rev. 2*)
These 10 categories are adapted from Leamer (1984) and Felipe, Kumar, and Abdon (2010).

1. **Petroleum:** petroleum and petroleum products (33)
2. **Raw materials:** crude fertilizers and crude minerals (27); metalliferous ores (28); coal, coke, briquettes

(32); gas (34); electric energy (35); nonferrous metals (68)

3. **Forest products:** wood, lumber, cork (24); pulp, waste paper (25); wood, cork, manufactures (63); paper paperboard (64)

4. **Tropical agriculture:** fruits, vegetables (05); sugar (06); coffee, tea, cocoa, spices (07); beverages (11); crude rubber (23)

5. **Animal products:** live animals (00); meat (01); dairy (02); fish (03); hides, skins, furskins (21); crude animal and vegetable minerals (29); animal, vegetable oils and fats (43); animal, live not otherwise specified (n.e.s.) (94)

6. **Cereals:** cereals (04); feeds for animals (08); miscellaneous food preparations (09); tobacco (12); oil seeds, oil nuts, oil kernels (22); textile fibers (26); animal oils, fats (41); fixed vegetable oils (42)

7. **Labor intensive:** nonmetallic mineral manufactures (66); furniture (82); travel goods, handbags (83); clothing (84); footwear (85); miscellaneous manufactured articles, n.e.s. (89); postal packages (91); special transactions (93); nongold coins (96)

8. **Capital intensive:** leather (61); rubber (62); textile, yarn, fabrics (65); iron and steel (67); manufactures of metal (69), sanitary fixtures, fittings (81)

9. **Machinery:** power generating (71); specialized for particular industries (72); metalworking (73); general industrial (74); office and data processing (75); telecommunications (76); electrical (77); road vehicles (78); other transport equipment (79); professional and scientific instruments (87); photographic equipment (88); armored vehicles, firearms and ammunition (95)

10. **Chemicals:** organic (51); inorganic (52); dyeing and tanning (53); medicinal and pharmaceutical (54); oils and perfume (55); fertilizers (56); explosives (57); artificial resins and plastic (58); chemical materials, n.e.s. (59).

Notes

1. Population is the log of a country's total population, averaged between 2006 and 2008. The cost of exporting is proxied by a subindicator from the *Doing Business* indicators (see, for example, World Bank 2008), which measures fees levied on a 20-foot container for documents, customs clearance and broker fees, terminal handling charges, and inland transport. The cost does not include customs tariffs and duties, costs related to ocean transport, or bribes.

2. A country's remoteness measure is a GDP-weighted average distance between a country and all its trading partners. Weights are calculated by dividing the GDP (current US dollars) of each partner by an estimated World GDP of US$55 trillion, for the years 2006–08.

3. Exports of goods and services in the WDI database (World Bank 2011c) represent the value of all merchandise, freight, insurance, transport, travel, royalties, license fees, and other services, such as communication, construction, financial, information, business, personal, and government services. They exclude compensation of employees and investment income (formerly called factor services) and transfer payments.

4. Hanson (2010) classifies products in the Harmonized Commodity Description and Coding System (HS). An alternative is suggested by Leamer (1984) for products following the Standard International Trade Classification (SITC). See Annex A.

5. RCA of product k in country i is the export of product k relative to the country's total exports divided by the world's export of product k relative to total world exports.

6. Athukorala and Menon (2010) also use these disaggregated data to debunk the so-called decoupling thesis that argues that East Asia can maintain its own economic dynamism: They show that China's reliance on the import of components from other East Asian countries has grown at the same time its share of final exports of manufactured goods to this region has declined, suggesting that China links East Asia to the developed markets of the European Union and the United States through global production networks.

7. Leung (2010) singles out Vietnam as a conspicuous laggard in East Asia in terms of both assembly and manufacturing of components, attributes the slow entry of Vietnam into the global supply chain to the protection of the state sector in the 1990s, and notes the orientation of FDI to joint ventures with state-owned enterprises in heavy industries. Only after 2000 have reforms been undertaken to propel Vietnam into being a player in global production networks in light manufacturing.

8. Log value of 13.35, for example, is a US dollar amount equivalent to exp(13.35) * 1,000, which is approximately US$632 million.

9. Quadrants are formed by the global median values of log of export per capita (y-axis) and the share of manufacturing and services sectors in GDP (x-axis).

10. The US nominal GDP is nearly US$15 trillion. Even a 1 percent annual growth of this economy creates economic value of around US$150 billion, which is equivalent to a 10 percent growth in a US$1.5 trillion economy (such as Brazil, Canada, or Spain). All else equal, however, a sustained growth rate of 1 percent every year doubles present income every 35 years, whereas a sustained growth rate of 10 percent doubles present income every seven years or so. It is this power of compound growth that has transformed China after its reforms and opening-up process (*Gaige Kaifang*) began three decades ago.

11. This index was initially developed to test the market power of firms, but it has since had wider applicability.

12. These calculations are sensitive to the thresholds set for minimum export values. If any export above US$0 is included in the sample, the calculations are less informative than when a sharper cutoff of, say, US$10,000, is used, below which exports are defined as insignificant or equivalent to zero.

13. Classified by the World Bank's Poverty Reduction and Economic Management (PREM) Network using data from Comtrade. Data available at http://info.worldbank.org/etools/prmed/. High-technology exports generally include products with high research and development intensity, such as in aerospace, computers, pharmaceuticals, scientific instruments, and electrical machinery.

14. There are caveats, as explained in Racine (2010), when (mirror) export values are measured inclusive of cost, insurance, and freight, larger distances introduce larger biases. Products like oil, whose prices are set internationally, have a weaker association between unit values and quality. High unit values could reflect high costs or market power in specific locations. They may also vary with the processing stage of production, with downstream industries typically having higher unit values than upstream.

15. Rauch (1999) classifies commodities into the following categories: (1) those traded in organized exchanges (homogenous products), (2) those with reference prices (for which the brand of producers is not important), and (3) differentiated products. Special links between countries (common language and colonial ties) are found to be more important for trade in differentiated products because they lower search and matching costs between sellers and buyers.

MODULE 1

16. Cadot, Tumurchudur, and Shirotori (2009) describe the methodology of the computation of the indexes; database available at http://r0.unctad.org/ditc/tab/index.shtm.

17. The minimum of the two probabilities is taken to avoid the problem that originates when the number of exporters of a product falls. If good A is produced only by one country, the conditional probability of all other products being produced given that A is produced by that country is 1, reflecting the uniqueness of the country not the similarity between goods. The reverse probability is not the same. See Hausmann and Klinger (2007) for methodological details.

18. The product space maps include 775 products, whereas medium- to large-size countries typically export more than this number. Several products that Pakistan exports cannot be mapped on the product space.

19. According to the log rank test, the difference between survival rates to countries with and without a shared border is statistically insignificant.

20. Brenton and Newfarmer (2009) find in their study of 99 developing countries that the increase in exports of existing products to existing markets accounted for 105 percent of total export growth between 1995 and 2005.

21. This analysis for the period 2001 to 2008 assumed the following: (1) products that were exported to at least one country either in 2001 or 2002 were classified as existing products, and those not exported anywhere in 2001 and 2002 were new products; and (2) markets that were reached with any product in either 2001 or 2002 or 2003 were classified as existing markets, and the rest were new markets. Products that were not exported to any country in 2007 and 2008 were deemed "dead." Alternative time periods should be considered to check for robustness.

References

Alcala, F., and A. Ciccone. 2004. "Trade and Productivity." *Quarterly Journal of Economics* 119 (2): 612–645.

Anderson, J. E., and E. van Wincoop. 2003. "Gravity with Gravitas: A Solution to the Border Puzzle." *American Economic Review* 93: 170–192.

Athukorala, P. 2010. "Production Networks and Trade Patterns in East Asia: Regionalization or Globalization?" Working Papers on Regional Economic Integration 56, Asian Development Bank.

Athukorala, P., and J. Menon. 2010. "Global Production Sharing, Trade Patterns, and Determinants of Trade Flows in East Asia." ADB Working Paper Series on Regional Economic Integration No. 41, Asian Development Bank, Manila.

Brakman, S., and P. A. G. van Bergeijk. 2010. *The Gravity Model in International Trade: Advances and Applications.* Cambridge: Cambridge University Press.

Brenton, P., and R. Newfarmer. 2009. "Watching More Than the Discovery Channel to Diversify Exports." In *Breaking into New Markets: Emerging Lessons for Export Diversification,* eds. R. Newfarmer, W. Shaw, and P. Walkenhorst, 111-126. Washington, DC: World Bank.

Brenton, P., M. Pierola, and E. von Uexkull. 2009. "The Life and Death of Trade Flows: Understanding the Survival Rates of Developing-Country Exporters." In *Breaking Into Markets: Emerging Lessons for Export Diversification,* eds. R. Newfarmer, W. Shaw, and P. Walkenhorst, 127–144. Washington, DC: World Bank.

Brülhart, M. 2008. "An Account of Global Intra-Industry Trade, 1962–2006." http://ssrn.com/abstract=110344.

Cadot, O., V. Strauss-Kahn., and Céline Carrère. 2011. "Trade Diversification: Drivers and Impacts." World Bank, Washington, DC.

Cadot, O., B. Tumurchudur, B., and M. Shirotori. 2009. "Revealed Factor Intensity Indices at the Product Level." UNCTAD mimeo.

Dean, J., Fung, K. C., and Z. Wang. 2007. "Measuring the Vertical Specialization in Chinese Trade." USITC Working Paper, United States International Trade Commission, Washington, DC.

Easterly, W., A. Reshef, and J. Schwenkenberg. 2009. "The Power of Exports." Policy Research Working Paper No. 5081, World Bank, Washington, DC.

Felipe, J. 2010. *Inclusive Growth, Full Employment, and Structural Change: Implications and Policies for Developing Asia.* London: Anthem Press.

Golub, S. S., R. W. Jones, and H. Kierzkowski. 2007. "Globalization and Country-Specific Service Links." *Journal of Economic Policy Reforms* 10 (2): 63-88.

Hanson, G. 2010. "Sources of Export Growth in Developing Countries." University of California–San Diego.

Hausmann, R., and B. Klinger. 2007. "The Structure of the Product Space and the Evolution of Comparative Advantage." CID Working Paper No. 146, Center for International Development, Harvard University, Cambridge, MA.

Hausmann, R., J. Hwang, and D. Rodrik. 2006. "What You Export Matters." CEPR Discussion Papers 5444, Centre for Economic Policy and Research, London.

Helpman, E., M. Melitz, and Y. Rubinstein. 2008. "Estimating Trade Flows: Trading Partners and Trading Volumes." *Quarterly Journal of Economics* 123 (2): 441–487.

C. A. Hidalgo, B. Klinger, A.-L. Barabási, R. Hausmann, 2007, "The Product Space Conditions the Development of Nations", Science, 317: 482–487.

Hummels, D., and P. Klenow. 2005. "The Variety and Quality of a Nation's Exports." *American Economic Review* 95 (3): 704–723.

Hwang, J. 2006. "Introduction of New Goods, Convergence and Growth." Job Market Paper, Department of Economics, Harvard University, Cambridge, MA.

Imbs, J., and R. Wacziarg. 2003. "Stages of Diversification." *American Economic Review.* 93 (1): 63–86.

Klinger, B. 2010. "(New) Export Competitiveness." Center for International Development, Harvard University, Cambridge, MA.

Klinger, B., and D. Lederman. 2004. "Discovery and Development: An Empirical Exploration of 'New' Products." World Bank, Washington, DC.

Koopman, R., Z. Wang, and S. Wei. 2008. "How Much of Chinese Exports Is Really Made in China? Assessing Domestic Value-Added When Processing Trade Is Pervasive." NBER Working Paper No. 14109, National Bureau of Economic Research, Cambridge, MA.

Krugman, P. 2008. "Trade and Wages, Reconsidered." *Brookings Papers on Economic Activity 1: Macroeconomics,* 103–138.

Leamer, E. 1984. *Sources of International Comparative Advantage: Theory and Evidence.* Cambridge, MA: MIT Press.

Lederman, D., and W. Maloney. 2009. *Trade Quality, Regional Study (LCR).* Washington, DC: World Bank.

Leung, S. E. 2010. "Vietnam: An Economic Survey." Crawford School of Economics and Government, ANU, Canberra.

McKinsey Global Institute. 2010b. "Lions on the Move: The Progress and Potential of African Economies." McKinsey Global Institute, Washington, DC.

Racine, J.-L., ed. 2010. "Harnessing Quality for Global Competitiveness: Upgrading Eastern Europe and Central Asia's Quality and Standards." World Bank, Washington, DC.

Rauch, J. E. 1999. "Networks versus Markets in International Trade." *Journal of International Economics* 48: 7–35.

Schott, P. 2004. "Across Product versus Within Product Specialization in International Trade." *Quarterly Journal of Economics* 119 (2) (May): 646–677.

Siggel, E. 2006. "International Competitiveness and Comparative Advantage: A Survey and a Proposal for Measurement." *Journal of Industry, Competition and Trade* 6: 137–159.

Tinbergen, J. 1962. *Shaping the World Economy: Suggestions for an International Economic Policy.* New York: The Twentieth Century Fund.

UNCTAD (United Nations Conference on Trade and Development). 2009. "Training Package on Trade Policy Analysis: Module 1 Descriptive Statistics." UNCTAD Virtual Institute, Geneva.

Wacziarg, R., and K. H. Welch. 2008. "Trade Liberalization and Growth: New Evidence." *World Bank Economic Review* 22 (2): 187–231.

Wignaraja, G., and A. Taylor. 2003. "Benchmarking Competitiveness Performance in Developing Countries: A First Look At The Manufactured

Export Competitiveness Index." In *Competitiveness Strategy in Developing Countries*, ed. G. Wignaraja, 61–88. London: Routledge.

World Bank. 2011a. *Border Management Modernization,* eds. Gerard McLinden, Enrique Fanta, David Widdowson, and Tom Doyle. Washington, DC: The World Bank.

World Bank. 2011b. "The Russian Federation: Export Diversification through Competition and Innovation—A Policy Agenda." World Bank, Washington, DC.

World Bank. 2011c. *World Development Indicators.* Washington, DC: World Bank.

World Bank. 2008. *Doing Business.* www.doingbusiness.org.

WTO (World Trade Organization). 2005. *Ministerial Declaration,* Geneva: WTO, WT/MIN(05)/DEC, available at: www.wto.org/english/ thewto_e/minist_e/min05_e/final_text_e.htm.

Xu, B. 2010. "The sophistication of exports: Is China special?" *China Economic Review* 21: 482–493.

COMPETITIVENESS DIAGNOSTICS

Market Access

Link with Competitiveness Challenges Identified in Trade Outcomes

	Competitiveness challenge areas			
Main components of market access	General export environment	Cost competitiveness	Product extension and quality	Market penetration
Tariffs and quantitative restrictions	✓	✓		✓
Nontariff barriers (NTBs)	✓	✓	✓	✓
Preferential trade arrangements (PTAs)	✓			✓

Quantitative Analysis: Indicators and Data Sources

Indicators	Source
General restrictions • ROW average applied tariff, MA-TTRI, MA-OTRI • Tariff escalation ratio • Nontariff coverage ratio **Zero or preferential tariff** • MFN[a] zero-duty exports (percent of total) • Exports to PTA partners • Preferences utilization rate (percent) and actual value (percent of exports) in the United States and European Union **Product-specific access** • Applied tariffs and NTMs faced by the country's *key exports*, compared with what peer exporters face in the world's major markets in the North and South (matrix) • Number of major export products (HS six digit) that face tariff peaks (MFN > 15 percent) in the world's top 10 major markets • Share of export value rejected from border in the past 12–18 months	World Trade Indicators (WTIs, which draw on TRAINS, Comtrade, ITC MacMap); World Trade Organization (WTO) Trade Policy Reviews Note that some of these data is now available via World Development Indicators.

Descriptions of key indicators

Tariff average, simple and weighted: The extent to which a foreign market restricts imports can be measured by the arithmetic average of tariffs on goods (at an appropriate level of classification, such as the Harmonized Commodity Description and Coding System [HS] at the six- or eight-digit level). A simple average includes statutory tariffs on goods in which trade flow is zero. The weighted average takes into account the tariff rate and the volume of imports. For very high rates of tariff, however, the weighted tariff underreports trade restrictiveness: A rate of zero and a prohibitively high tariff rate receive similar weights. Because no measure is perfect, it is common practice to report tariffs in all their forms: simple and weighted average, minimum, maximum, and standard deviation (UNCTAD 2009).

Rest-of-the-world (ROW) applied tariff: Following above, the ROW applied tariff average are rates imposed by a country's export partners at the HS six-digit level and can be reported either in simple or weighted form.

Tariff escalation ratios: Are calculated as the percentage change between the applied tariff for fully processed goods and applied tariffs for raw materials (or primary products). If tariffs are higher on finished products than on raw materials, they implicitly encourage the export of primary products. Because tariff escalation acts as a tax on value addition, developing countries face reduced incentives for industrial upgrading required to produce processed goods.

Market Access–Overall Tariff Restrictiveness Index (MA-OTRI): Although measures of simple and trade-weighted tariff averages, as well as tariff dispersion, are widely used, they are without theoretical foundation. Building on the work of Anderson and Neary (1994), World Bank economists have created indexes summarizing all forms of trade restrictions—tariffs, quotas, licenses, and so on—into a common metric by estimating the ad valorem equivalent of NTBs at the tariff-line level. They are then aggregated to produce a single tariff rate imposed by all trading partners on exports of a country in a manner that maintains the current level of exports. This uniform tariff is called MA-OTRI (Kee, Nicita, and Olarreaga 2008).

Market Access–Trade Tariff Restrictiveness Index (MA-TTRI): This is computed in the same manner as the OTRI but only for tariffs (including preferences) imposed by trading partners on a country's exports.

Nontariff measure coverage ratio: Is calculated by coding products (with a zero or one) within a category that is affected by at least one NTB, then multiplying the binary variable with the share of imports or exports, and summing to produce a coverage ratio. This ratio is only indicative of the prevalence of NTBs and is silent on the restrictiveness. This weakness is similar to the one discussed for weighted average of tariffs in which case a highly restrictive barrier acquires a low weight by reducing trade flows (UNCTAD 2009).

Antidumping and countervailing duties: In practice, antidumping duties are almost identical to tariffs, and are generally expressed ad valorem. As discussed, however, the process of determining these duties can be highly distortionary and interruptive. Active use of antidumping measures by a country can lower export of unconcerned products and aggregate exports to that country.[b] Ideally, all these effects should be accounted for, but there is no common technique available to do so. The tariff equivalent of a dumping duty is expected to be slightly larger on the domestic price of imports because part of the ordinary tariff is normally absorbed by exporters. With antidumping duties, however, exporters have no incentive to lower the price (Deardorff and Stern 1997). Countervailing duties are also levied like tariffs, but their purpose is to offset any subsidies given by foreign governments.

Note: Vandenbussche and Zanardi (2010) found that in India and Mexico, both active users of antidumping measures, aggregate annual imports decreased by around 7 percent.

a. MFN (most favored nation) refers to a nondiscriminatory trade policy commitment whereby countries agree to apply to each other the lowest level of import duties and quota restrictions which they apply on similar imports from other trade partners.

Qualitative Analysis: Interview Targets and Issues for Discussion

Senior policy makers at the Ministry of Trade or Foreign Affairs	• Do exporters make use of negotiated tariff preferences? Or, do they instead opt to pay for the MFN rate because the costs associated with meeting the rules of origin (ROO) or preparing official documents to qualify for reduced duties are onerous?
	• What explains the country's low penetration in x market despite having a PTA? Are ROOs too restrictive to be eligible for preference; or are exports uncompetitive to the extent that the tariff margin does not compensate for higher productivity of competitors?
	• Is there correlation between recent surges in exports and increased stringency in the application of sanitary and phytosanitary (SPS) measures and technical barriers to trade (TBT), or in the number of antidumping and CVD investigations initiated against their exports? Is there also a correlation between recent cuts in the importing country's tariffs, and its shift toward increased use of trade remedy laws?
Chambers of commerce	• What is the experience of major exporters in complying with NTBs, especially those related to sanitary and phytosanitary, technical, and security/terrorism standards? How much do these compliance costs typically add in terms of tariff equivalents?
	• How readily do policy makers or staff in embassies take up concerns in bilateral negotiations, or at the WTO on behalf of exporters?
Major exporters	• Are tariffs so high that they drive exporters out of competition despite enjoying lower input costs or higher productivity than in countries that enjoy tariff preferences? Are PTAs signed by the export destinations leading to trade diversion?
	• Have there been costly rejections of exports in the past 12–18 months? List products (for example, nuts, shrimp, honey) and countries that rejected them? What were the grounds? The SPS agreement requires that regulation be based on scientific principles and not maintained without sufficient scientific evidence except in cases of scientific uncertainty. Was this complied with or were they arbitrary, excessive, and a form of disguised protection? What was the cost incurred by the exporter? Could export tragedies be avoided with better information?
Export promotion agencies	• When the SPS and TBT concerns on the part of the importer are genuine, what kind of capacity building initiatives are needed for exporters? How is the service and capacity of domestic institutions to facilitate exports regarding testing standards, preshipment inspections, and so on?

Analytical Approach

For a rapid Diagnostics aimed at understanding the major trade policy barriers a country's exports face, following is a simple two-stage analytical process that can be followed.

Step 1: Understand the Structure of Tariffs Affecting Key Exports

• *High or peak tariffs.* Is Country B a major export market for County A in terms of existing size (for example,

Germany or the United States) or growth potential (for example, Brazil, China, or India)? Does Country B have high tariffs (or peaks) on major exports from Country A? Does it escalate tariffs to deter import of value-added goods? Are there tariff-rate quotas (TRQs)? As an example, the United States has high MFN applied duties against the import of HS 240120 (tobacco, partly or wholly stemmed/stripped). The average tariff for least developed countries (LDCs) is more than 77 percent. However, an African LDC like Malawi qualifies for a zero tariff, but a non-African developing country can face a specific tariff of US$5,480 per ton, or a tariff equivalent of 158 percent. It would be highly difficult to compete in an identical product when a competitor has a substantial margin of tariff preference, which is the case in many agricultural and labor-intensive manufactured exports.

- *Penetration of markets.* Because the tariff rates faced by a country as well as its competition determine the depth of one's market access, it is crucial to know about other competing countries that export similar products as Country A. In the example in table 2.1, exports in 2008 of product category HS 6204 (women's suits, jackets, and so on) to the world's four major importers are shown. China, Romania, Turkey, and Vietnam are large exporters of the product. In Bangladesh and Morocco, both products were important, accounting for 8.8 and 4.6 percent of their total exports. In the United States, Morocco's exports are substantially less than that of Bangladesh, despite the fact that Morocco has a free trade agreement with the United States, and qualifies for reduced tariffs. In HS 6204, the MFN tariff that Bangladesh pays is 14 percent. Morocco is eligible for the preferential rate of 2.8 percent. Although its focus on the EU market is understandable given the geographic proximity, the underpenetration of the US market is worth exploring. Why are preferences being underutilized in a lucrative market? Although the rate of utilization can be calculated quantitatively, the reasons will have to be gathered through qualitative assessments and interviews.

- *Margin of preferences.* Does one or more of the competitors receive a preferential tariff either through a regional, bilateral, or unilateral arrangement from a major importing country? What is the margin of preference? Does this margin received by competing countries outweigh any cost and price advantage that Country A enjoys? If Country A receives preferences itself, are they negated by compliance criteria such as tight ROO? For small LDCs, concessions on market access appear to be more important than for larger exporters that rely on scale and cost advantages to be competitive despite having to face negative preferential margins on tariff.

Step 2: Find Out about the Main Nontariff Barriers Faced by Exporters

In addition to tariffs, several trade instruments can potentially be invoked to restrict market access, including quotas, antidumping and countervailing duties, and safeguards. Other provisions can also be applied with restrictive intent, such as technical safety and sanitary requirements, and compliance with intellectual property rights (IPR). Major questions to ask regarding NTBs are as follows:

- *Technical regulations.* To what extent do SPS and TBT measures represent prominent restrictions to exports? Are these measures perceived as justified or used to restrict trade? Is compliance difficult and expensive? Are procedures cumbersome? Is the information publicly available and accessible? Are the problems related to the measure itself or the inspection at the border? Are these measures applied on an MFN basis? Are there any mutual recognition agreements for standards with key partners and at the regional level?

- *Incidences of trade remedy action.* Is a particular export part of an industry that is a frequent target for trade remedy actions? Has there been an antidumping investigation against the country's export, in the past 18 months?[1] By which country in which product and industry? Did the investigation lead to an actual imposition of duty? Has there been a CVD investigation, and

MODULE 2

Table 2.1. Market Shares of Major Exporters of HS 6204 (Women's Suits) in 2008 in Selected Markets

	World (US$)	Bangladesh	China	Morocco	Romania	Turkey	Vietnam
Canada	1,144,146	4.49	58.11	0.48	0.94	1.75	2.14
European Union	13,007,403	4.36	41.80	7.62	—	14.12	2.06
Japan	3,388,246	0.06	82.04	0.39	0.48	0.22	2.85
United States	12,411,131	4.73	38.63	0.32	0.25	0.49	7.84

Source: ITC 2011.
Note: — = not relevant.

was the duty imposed? Has there been a safeguard measure applied? Were exports restricted? How did those actions affect exports?

- *Quotas and other NTMs.* Do exporters face tariff-rate quotas on some key export products? Are surtaxes, beyond tariff, common?

Although tariff and nontariff barriers are explicit policy-induced barriers to foreign market access, several other factors affect market access, such as geographic distance and cost of transport; colonial, linguistic, or cultural affinity; exchange rate misalignment; and costs related to search and information as well as contract enforcement. These are, however, not related to direct trade policy measures in the sense that they are hard to change through unilateral action, or bilateral, regional, and multilateral negotiations.

Tailoring the Diagnostics to Country and Sector Characteristics

Access to foreign markets is either granted on concessional terms to specific partners, or negotiated multilaterally, regionally, and bilaterally. Generally, preferential schemes applying to developing countries depend on the stage of development, geographic or cultural proximity, and any specific terms and conditions negotiated between governments. All country Diagnostics need to know the conditions under which foreign markets are accessible to a

country's products on preferential terms. Table 2.2 illustrates for a sample product (HS 610120) how tariffs can vary widely in the world's three major economies—Japan, Europe, and the United States—depending on an array of criteria, such as the following: developing countries; LDCs; African, Caribbean, and Pacific Countries (ACPs); trade agreement partners; nonagricultural goods; agricultural goods; and services.

Developing Countries

Since the 1960s, industrial economies like Japan, the European Union, and the United States and at least 10 other countries have provided preferential access to exports from more than 100 developing countries unilaterally under the Generalized System of Preferences (GSP). National programs vary, however. The United States, for example, does not include textiles and clothing exports in its GSP program. Developing countries like China, Pakistan, and Sri Lanka pay the MFN tariff rate on their apparel exports to the United States (see table 2.2). The European Union, however, includes textiles and clothing in its GSP scheme from which countries like Pakistan benefit. Chinese exports were disqualified for tariff preferences in the European Union after 2004. The European Union also offers duty-free access to a distinct subgroup of developing countries: under its GSP-plus program, beneficiary countries have to demonstrate that their economies are vulnerable and have to have ratified and implemented the 16 core conventions of human and labor rights and at least 7 out of the

Table 2.2. How Tariffs Differ across Trade Partners
Illustration of HS 610120 (Men's or boys' overcoats, cloaks, anoraks)

	Kenya	Sri Lanka	Lesotho	Bangladesh	Pakistan	China
UNITED STATES: Gives zero tariffs to SSA, NAFTA, Central American, and Caribbean, and Andean countries.	0 AGOA preference	15.9 Not an LDC; and apparel not included in U.S. GSP for developing countries	0 AGOA preference	15.9 An LDC, but receives no preference	15.9 Full applied MFN duty; bill proposed in U.S. Congress to grant preference to Pakistan	15.9 Applied MFN duty
EUROPEAN UNION: Gives zero tariffs to LDCs, EPA, and GSP+ countries.	0 Preference received as a trade partner (EPA), but not an LDC	0 Neither an LDC nor an EPA partner, but receives preference as an incentive for sustainable development	0 Preference received as an LDC, but also as a trade partner (EPA)	0 Preference received as an LDC, but not an EPA partner	9.6 Preference received as part of GSP	12 Applied MFN duty
JAPAN: Gives zero tariffs only to LDCs.	10.9 Applied MFN duty	10.9 Applied MFN duty	0 LDC preference	0 LDC preference	10.9 Applied MFN duty	10.9 Applied MFN duty

Source: Compiled from ITC MacMap (2010).

11 conventions on good governance and protection of the environment. Sri Lanka was among such countries benefiting from GSP-plus, until it was suspended in 2010 for governance-related issues. In general, ROOs under the EU GSP require two significant value-adding processes (often referred to as "double transformation") to be performed within the beneficiary country.

Least Developed Countries

The acronym LDC is often used generically to refer to any less developed country. In the United Nations as well as the WTO agreements, however, LDC refers to a distinct group of low-income countries classified by the United Nation to include those with (1) gross national income (GNI) per capita under US$905; (2) poor Human Assets Index (HAI) based on indicators of nutrition, infant mortality rate, education, and the literacy rate; and (3) economic vulnerability in terms of population size, remoteness, export concentration, homelessness from natural disasters, and so on. There are 48 LDCs as of November 2011.

The most favorable arrangement under the EU GSP is reserved for LDCs. The Everything But Arms (EBA) amendment, which became effective in March 2001, extended duty- and quota-free access to all products originating in LDCs, except arms and ammunition. Lesotho and Bangladesh benefit from zero tariffs in the European Union as LDCs (see table 2.2).

The Japanese and Canadian programs are simpler and cover almost all products except, for example, eggs, poultry, and dairy in Canada, and rice and sugar in Japan. To qualify for preferences in textiles and clothing, exporters generally have to satisfy double transformation ROOs (for example, fabric and clothing). In recent years, large developing countries like China and India have also unilaterally begun to grant preferences to LDCs on a negotiated list of products. The preferences granted by China, for example, include both natural resources like minerals and agricultural products as well as manufactured goods, including some processed foods, light manufactures, and textiles.

Importantly, one of the pending items in the unfinished Doha Development Agenda is the pledge by WTO members in 2005 to make it compulsory for industrial countries, and voluntary for developing countries, to give duty- and quota-free market access to all exports from LDCs. The flipside of this pledge was that 3 percent of tariff lines could be exempted from receiving zero tariff rates. Because LDC exports tend to cover a narrow range of products, this clause could negate any meaningful access the LDCs could receive.

African, Caribbean, and Pacific Countries

The group of ACP countries, now numbering 77 (excluding South Africa), has traditionally received more generous tariff preferences on a broad range of products than those covered under the EU GSP (Staritz 2011). Kenya, for example, benefits from this scheme (see table 2.2). The United States does not have a specific program for LDCs, but it provides duty-free treatment on approximately 83 percent of tariff lines from 15 Asian LDCs, 88 percent of tariff lines from selected Caribbean and Andean countries, and 98 percent of tariff lines for several low-income countries under the African Growth and Opportunity Act (AGOA). Kenya and Lesotho benefit from AGOA preferences in the United States, but LDCs from elsewhere (like Bangladesh) do not benefit on apparel-related exports, and they pay the same MFN tariff as larger developing countries like China (see table 2.2). Under AGOA, however, ROOs required at least 35 percent value addition, which many potential beneficiary countries found hard to meet, resulting in very low utilization of the preferences. These rules were later relaxed for apparel exports, giving the option to source inputs from third countries.

Trade Agreement Partners

The third type of countries that benefit from preferential market access are those that have signed BTAs or RTAs with the major importing countries. This includes the EU's Economic Partnership Agreement (EPA)—a web of BTAs. To qualify for preferences, exporters have to satisfy ROOs, such as minimum value addition or change of tariff heading. The latter requires that the value addition should be sufficient to change the tariff classification of a product either at the HS four- or six-digit level. The United States also grants favorable market access to partners in its RTAs like the North American Free Trade Agreement (NAFTA), and nearly 20 other agreements with specific countries. To qualify for preferences in textiles and clothing, exporters generally have to satisfy triple transformation ROO (yarn, fabric, and clothing); however, less developed countries from Africa may source inputs (yarn and fabric) from third countries and undergo a single transformation.

China is the only exporter that receives no tariff preference in any of the markets. Yet, in 2008, it was the largest exporter of the above product (HS 610120) in all three markets (Japan, the European Union, and the United States). This suggests that it is able to offset the higher tariff with productivity that results in either lower cost or higher quality of the product. But tariff preferences are important to many exporters. Lesotho has no market presence in Japan and almost none in the European Union, but for a country of its size, it is a major exporter to the United States, taking advantage of the AGOA preference and lenient ROO requirements. Both in Japan and in the European Union, Lesotho enjoys preferences, but the ROOs are harder to comply with, which explains its negligible presence.

Market access in terms of tariffs and NTBs varies widely by sector. In particular, there are significant differences in tariff levels, dispersion, and in the nature and importance of NTBs between agricultural and nonagricultural (or manufactured) goods. The Diagnostics should therefore analyze market access issues separately by sector, bearing in mind that, within sectors, specific products can be subject to distinctly high measures of tariff and nontariff restrictions.

Nonagricultural Goods

In high-income countries, tariffs and NTBs against imports are generally low. The Overall Trade Restrictiveness Index (OTRI), which summarizes the trade restrictiveness of tariffs as well as nontariff measures in Japan, the European Union, and the United States ranged between 5 and 6.1 percent in 2006–09, according to the WTIs. This is historically very low, even though the average does conceal tariff peaks in specific items, such as labor-intensive manufacturing goods like footwear and apparel, as shown in table 2.2. The emerging developing countries like India, who argue that they are still in the process of industrialization, maintain higher trade restrictions in nonagricultural goods.

As seen in figure 2.1, the OTRI of India is 17 percent. China's restrictions came down substantially during the course of its negotiated accession to the WTO in 2001.

Tariffs aside, nonagricultural goods are less susceptible to sanitary and technical barriers,[2] but these goods are perhaps more vulnerable to antidumping petitions and other contingent measures.

Agricultural Goods

In contrast to restrictions in industrial goods, the richest countries of the world continue to maintain high levels of tariff and nontariff restrictions in agriculture. In Japan and the European Union, the OTRI for agricultural goods is more than 50 percent. In the United States, it is nearly 20 percent. Developing countries like China and India also restrict agricultural goods, primarily to safeguard the interests of small farmers. Agricultural goods are also more sensitive to sanitary and phytosanitary conditions, increasing their vulnerability to rejections and other costly precautionary non-tariff measures.

Services

The WTO's General Agreement on Trade in Services (GATS) envisions four modes through which trade in services occurs:

1. *Mode 1: Cross-border supply*—a user in one country receives service from a provider abroad (for example, financial, accounting and other professional services, information technology (IT)-enabled medical diagnostics and advice, online energy trading)
2. *Mode 2: Consumption abroad*—a user moves abroad to consume a service (for example, tourists, health patients)

Figure 2.1. Overall Trade Restrictiveness Index, 2006–09
(*Applied MFN tariffs and nontariff measures in selected countries*)

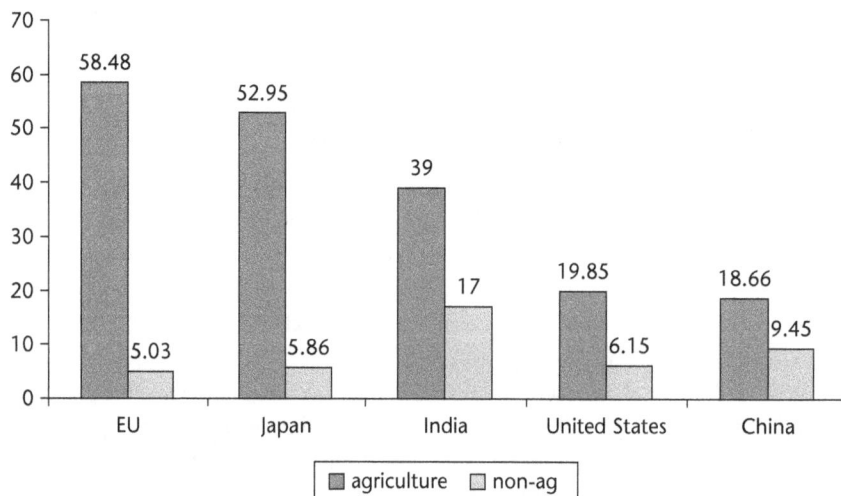

Source: Authors.

3. *Mode 3: Commercial presence*—a user is offered service by entities owned by foreign providers (for example, foreign-owned subsidiary in insurance, telecom, or electricity)
4. *Mode 4: Movement of natural persons*—a service provider moves abroad to supply a service (for example, doctors, construction workers)

Market access in services overwhelmingly focuses on modes 3 and 4. Mode 3 is essentially FDI in services (for example, South African telecom services based in other African countries). An importing country could restrict this form of trade by imposing screening requirements, limiting the number of service suppliers, limiting the value of transactions, restricting the number of persons employed, and so on. The most common restriction, however, is to cap the ownership of equity in firms by foreigners.[3] Mode 4 is even more contentious. Although it is about temporary movement of service suppliers, it is easily tied to threats of permanent movement or immigration if managed ineffectively. This is why most countries have liberalized more the movement of skilled and corporate personnel than low-skilled labor, in which poor countries have an export interest. Remittance sent by temporary service suppliers (for example, Bangladeshi or Nepali construction or factory workers in Gulf countries) has become a major source of national income in developing countries.

In modes 1 and 2, market access is much more in the control of exporting countries, as their competitiveness is highly dependent on domestic regulations and capacity. For mode 1, the presence of a technical or professional talent pool and decent infrastructure (especially telecom and Internet connectivity) are prerequisites. Take IT services: In 2008, the global market for outsourced IT services was valued at US$250 billion and expected to grow by up to 9 percent per year until 2013; India and Israel were the top two developing country exporters with US$23.1 billion (Engman 2010). Other countries like Argentina, Costa Rica, Malaysia, the Russian Federation, and Sri Lanka are seeing rising exports. In addition to IT, professional services such as medical diagnosis, architectural design and consultancy, accounting, and distance learning can also be traded through mode 1.

For mode 2, infrastructure is key, not only for tourism, but especially for health care. In 2008, more than 400,000 nonresidents purchased health services in the United States, 450,000 in India, 300,000 in Malaysia, 410,000 in Singapore, and 1.2 million in Thailand (Cattaneo 2010). Thailand, in fact, established the Long-stay Management Corporation in 2002 to encourage elderly foreigners to visit the country for long periods and take advantage of diverse care packages. Because portability of insurance is important, it requested Japan to allow health insurance coverage for treatment of Japanese patients in Thailand. Countries could, in fact, specialize in different segments of health care. While the United States offers highly sophisticated services that are costly, other countries have developed capacities to provide different services at affordable prices. Health care can also be provided through other modes, for example, telemedicine (mode 1), hospitals established overseas (mode 3), and doctors and nurses moving to provide services overseas (mode 4).

Beyond infrastructure and human resources, evolution and coordination of new regulations is critical to facilitate market access for services trade through modes 1 and 2. These issues include privacy and protection of data, recognition and harmonization of regulatory standards across borders, jurisdictions regarding taxation and indemnity, and rules governing government procurement (Chanda 2006).

Background Reading: Relationship Between Market Access and Trade Competitiveness

Trade policies adopted by trading partners, as well as those implemented at home, affect how competitive a country's exports are in world markets. In commercial diplomacy, "market access" is a broad concept referring to all measures that restrict a country's exports in foreign markets. These restrictions are a subset of overall trade costs. All else equal, access to a foreign market can be hindered by a partner's use of *tariffs* (taxes on imports) and nontariff measures, such as *quantitative restrictions* (quotas, licenses, voluntary export restraints), *contingent protection* (antidumping measures, countervailing duties, safeguards), and *technical barriers* involving safety and sanitary standards.

Increased market access is important to realize the gains from trade. Access to world markets allows firms to exploit scale economies, reduce unit costs, and specialize. Some measures act as an absolute barrier to access (for example, quotas, technical bans), but in general, the main channels through which barriers in foreign markets hurt export competitiveness are (1) *by increasing the fixed costs of entry*—that is by raising prices of goods in the importing country through increased cost of compliance and add-on taxes (and if the tariff-imposing country is particularly large in terms of its share of the global market, the world price of the affected good could fall, hurting exports even in third markets); and (2) *raising risk*—while tariffs are at least predictable, technical barriers raise significant risks for exporters, who may invest in

MODULE 2

product development, production, and transport only to find their goods rejected at the border. Box 2.1 summarizes some of the important current issues and debates around market access.

Figure 2.2 illustrates the main component factors that shape market access from a policy perspective. Each of these components is then discussed in the remainder of this section.

Tariffs

Tariffs are taxes levied on imports mainly with the dual objective of protecting domestically produced goods from foreign competition, and raising revenue to finance public expenditure. They can be expressed either *ad valorem*, that is, a fixed percentage of the declared import value, or as a *specific* tax, which is a fixed amount per specified quantity, size, or weight. Some tariffs can be expressed in both a

---

Box 2.1. Key Issues and Debates—External Market Access

Are LDCs taking advantage of market access? Although market access has long been a concern on the trade agenda for developing countries, and it remains so in key areas like agriculture, most LDCs now have preferential market access to industrial countries for an extensive range of manufactured products as well as many important commodities. But many developing countries struggle to take advantage of this market access. This not only is a function of nontariff measures (particularly around technical standards) but also more broadly reflects behind-the-border constraints in home markets that continue to render producers uncompetitive.

South-South trade and market access: With the growing importance of South-South trade, market access among developing countries is becoming an increasing priority. Yet, tariff barriers among developing countries remain much higher than between industrial and developing countries. Moreover, evidence from the recent global crisis suggests that developing countries are quicker to raise barriers against each other. On the other hand, technical standards tend to be less of a barrier to South-South trade.

Implementation of RTAs: Perhaps because of the failure of multilateralism in Doha, the number of regional preferential agreements is growing rapidly. More new RTA agreements were concluded in 2009 than in any previous year. But implementation of RTAs has been slow. In fact, only 313 of the 505 RTAs notified to the WTO as of November 2011 are actually in force.

Source: Authors.

Figure 2.2. The Main Components of Market Access

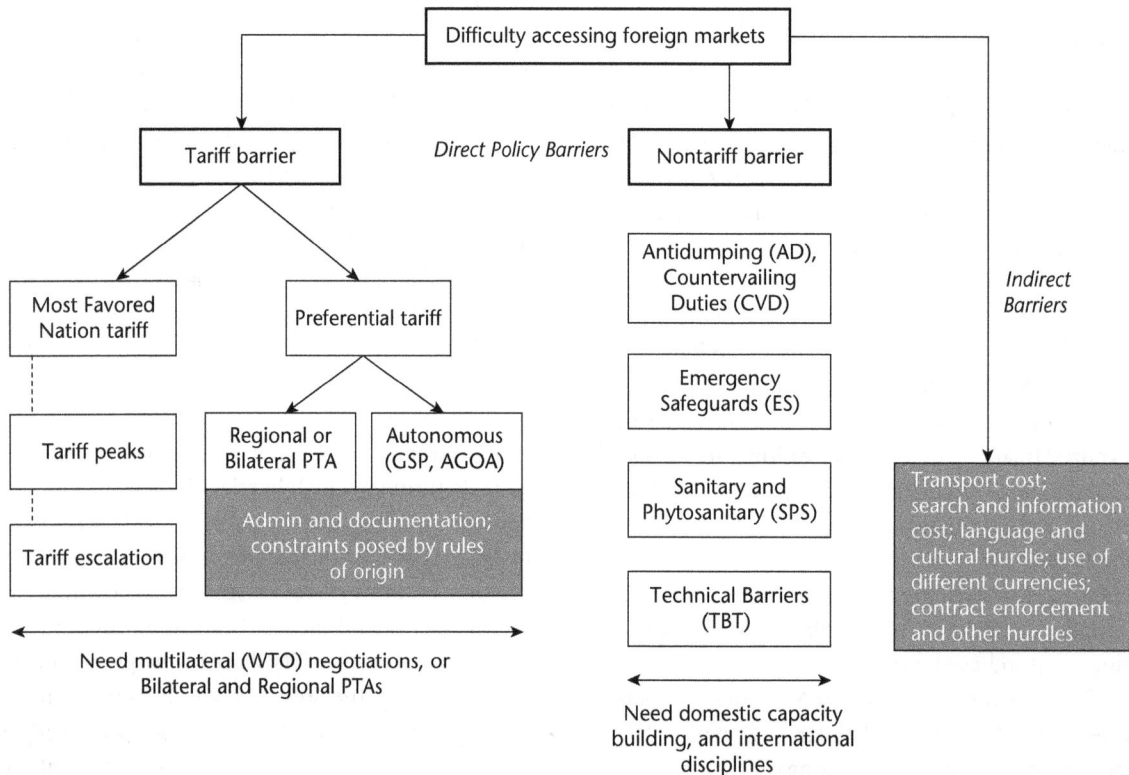

Source: Authors.

specific and ad valorem form. The level of tariff a country's goods are charged by its trading partner may well depend on whether the two countries have a PTA, are members of the WTO, or neither. Tariffs that are levied in a nondiscriminatory manner on goods irrespective of their country of origin are called MFN tariffs. Tariffs that have been negotiated bilaterally or regionally to be less than the MFN level are known as preferential tariffs. To qualify for preferential tariff rates, countries normally have to meet ROO criteria (see box 2.2).

Nontariff Measures

As import tariffs have been reduced worldwide, NTMs have risen in prominence and have become a major trade policy tool with important implications for exporters and importers. NTMs include a wide category of instruments such as SPS, TBT, quotas, subsidies, anticompetitive measures, import or export licenses, export restrictions, custom surcharges, financial measures, and contingent measures. It is, however, necessary to make a distinction between NTMs and NTBs. Although NTMs may have a clear domestic goal of preventing unfair trade or protecting the health of citizens, they become NTBs when used with clear protectionist intent to stop imports. NTMs are therefore considered NTBs when they restrict trade. Quotas,

prohibitions, nontariff charges, licenses, SPS and TBTs, and contingent measures are among the most prominent NTMs. Exporters should identify whether their export products face any of these barriers and analyze the impact on their competitiveness, in particular, compared with competitors.

Quotas, Prohibitions, Licenses, and Nontariff Surcharges

An import quota is a type of protectionist trade restriction that sets a physical limit on the quantity of a good that can be imported into a country in a given period of time. Above a certain quantitative threshold, no imports are permitted into the country. Through negotiations at the WTO, most quotas have now been converted to tariffs, or have taken the form of tariff-rate quotas (TRQs),[4] in particular, for agricultural products. In a competitive setting, quotas and tariffs are alike in that just like a quota truncates excess demand for an imported good, an equivalent level of tariff can be found that reduces imports by the same amount with identical effect on domestic prices. Although tariff revenues accrue to the government, rents from quotas can be captured by either domestic license holders, the government if it auctions off quotas, or foreign suppliers in the case of a voluntary export restraint (VER).

MODULE 2

Box 2.2. Tariffs, Preferences, and ROOs

When Country X applies a tariff of 19.7 percent, say, on men's or boys' cotton shirt not knitted or crocheted (HS 62052020) from Country Y, but exempts a tariff on the same import from Country Z with which it has a PTA, all else equal, exporters from Country Z have a substantial *price* advantage over exporters from Country Y. If domestic firms in Country X also produce such items, they benefit too by making imports from Country Y less competitive. Even if exporters from Country Y are the world's most efficient, they may still not be able to compete on price when tariffs are high. For exports from Country Z to qualify to enter Country X duty-free, it may need to fulfill agreed criteria on ROOs and other NTMs, which can present a *cost* disadvantage in a manner that negates partly its positive margin on tariff.

As explained in Staritz (2011), in the early 2000s, Bangladesh was the top supplier of cotton t-shirts in the European Union, but it did not figure among the top t-shirt suppliers in the United States. One of the reasons for this is that the European Union grants Bangladeshi clothing exports duty-free entry as an LDC and Bangladesh is able to meet the EU's double transformation ROO. In the United States, by contrast, Honduras was the top supplier of t-shirts followed by Mexico, El Salvador, and the Dominican Republic—all countries that have preferential access to the United States. Similarly, until 2000, nearly three-quarters of clothing exports from Sub-Saharan Africa (SSA) were directed to the European Union where SSA countries enjoyed duty- and quota-free access under the Lomé Convention. Only South Africa and Mauritius were important exporters, however, because preferential market access required fulfilling double transformation ROO. These export patterns have changed dramatically since 2000–01 when the United States introduced AGOA. Exports to the United States more than doubled, whereas those to the European Union stagnated. Kenya, Lesotho, Madagascar, and Swaziland became large clothing exporters to the United States because AGOA allowed quota- and duty-free access by requiring only single transformation ROO.

A tight ROO regime favors countries with an "integrated" industry (such as manufacture of fabric and sewing of apparel). Those that only seek to add value mostly through labor fail to meet this requirement. Therefore, preferences programs that relax ROO, by requiring less value addition to qualify, or permit the sourcing of inputs from abroad are utilized more. At the same time, the rules ought not be relaxed too much so that it encourages transshipment from third-country exporters who merely use the preference-receiving country as a port and contribute little to the economy. The debate continues on what constitutes an appropriate balance between the goal of preventing transshipment to encourage integrated production structure in poor countries, on the one hand, and the goal of offering preferential market access conditions on terms that can be fulfilled and used by poor countries, on the other.

Source: Authors.

When the domestic industry is not perfectly competitive, however, quotas and tariffs that permit the same volume of imports into a country can have different effects on domestic prices. Prices that consumers pay under a quota are higher than with a tariff because a quota caps imports and leaves the monopolist facing an imperfectly elastic demand curve. With tariffs, if the domestic monopolist raises its price, imports can increase. Quotas choke off a supply response, and restore a monopolist's market power in a way tariffs do not. This is illustrated in figure 2.3.

From the perspective of export competitiveness, quotas are more burdensome because irrespective of the price competitiveness of an export, or quality, goods may not be permitted to enter a foreign market after a certain threshold is reached. This is one of the reasons why, barring

exceptional circumstances (see, for example, box 2.3 on the Multi-Fibre Arrangement), the WTO prohibits the use of quantitative restrictions. With the gradual elimination of quantitative restrictions, and cuts in tariff, the focus of trade negotiations has increasingly turned to the reduction of NTMs. NTMs in Country A affect exports from the rest of the world. But these could also hurt the competitiveness of Country A firms by limiting their options to source the cheapest inputs.

Export markets may also prohibit the import of some products. Moreover, both quotas and bans are usually subject to licenses that may be granted automatically or that may be given more restrictively on a nonautomatic basis. Charges, taxes, and other paratariffs may also increase the cost of the exported product and hurt its competitiveness

Figure 2.3. Quotas and Tariffs under Different Market Conditions

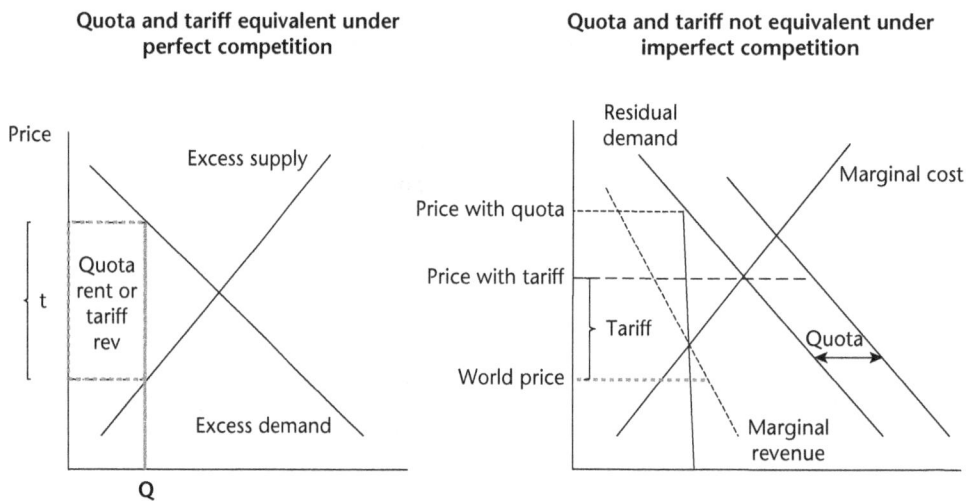

Source: Authors.

Box 2.3. Quotas in Textiles and Clothing

The global trade in textiles and clothing (T&C) was distorted by an elaborate system of quotas for more than 40 years until they were removed on December 31, 2004. The Multi-Fibre Arrangement (MFA), in violation of the fundamental GATT principle of nondiscrimination, enabled industrial importing countries to impose quotas, applied as negotiated "voluntary" export restraints against those imports from individual countries ("low-cost suppliers") deemed to cause or threaten market disruption in the importing country. The MFA, renewed several times between 1974 and 1994, continued and expanded the product and country coverage of two earlier regimes of protection: the 1962 Long Term Arrangement Regarding International Trade in Cotton Textiles and the 1961 Short Term Arrangement. These were ended by the Agreement on Textiles and Clothing (ATC), an outcome of the GATT Uruguay Round. The ATC froze the number of quotas in place in 1994 and set an irrevocable schedule for their elimination over a 10-year transitional period (1995–2004). Although the purpose of the MFA was to restrain trade, it did result in some "benign" outcomes. As manufacturers/and exporters shifted production from countries that faced a binding quota restraint to those that were less restrained by bilateral quotas, T&C industries sprung up in poor countries like Bangladesh and Sri Lanka that have remained competitive even in the postquota era (Waglé 2005a).

Source: Authors.

on the export market. These may include customs surcharge and services charges.

Contingent Protection

Contingent protection measures are applied as temporary deviations from a normal import policy and include antidumping measures, countervailing duties, or emergency safeguards.[5] Antidumping duties are levied against imports that are believed to be sold at prices below those in the good's country of origin or other countries. Such practices on the part of foreign exporters could be sporadic, persistent, or predatory, the last of which provides the strongest economic justification for antidumping duties. Countervailing duties are levied on imports from countries that subsidize exports. Safeguard measures are applied when surges in imports temporarily disrupt a domestic industry. Antidumping and countervailing duties are normally an issue that affects only large developing countries, like Brazil, China, and India. Smaller countries seldom have the scale of production to actually engage in dumping or to do it on sufficient scale to affect the domestic markets of trading partners.

Contingent protection may be used as a disguised protectionist measure. Although antidumping duties were almost exclusively levied by industrial countries in the 1990s, developing countries are now active users. In the last quarter of 2009, 26 WTO members initiated 26 product-level investigations under national trade remedy laws. More than three-fourths of the cases were brought by developing countries, of which 71 percent targeted exports from China. In the same quarter, 30 measures were imposed following prior investigations, of which 25 were initiated by developing countries and only five by industrial countries (Bown 2010).

The process of establishing antidumping and countervailing duties is also an important cause of distortion of behavior and export flows. Antidumping petitions are particularly disruptive, because in certain sectors such as textiles and clothing that are frequently targeted, back-to-back investigations could be initiated over many years (see box 2.4). By the time a verdict is reached, trade flows could be severely curtailed. Often the exporters affected are SMEs in poorer countries, whose ability to "dump" products is questionable in the first place. For example, a series of antidumping actions were imposed by the European Union against bed linen exports from India, Pakistan, Thailand, and Turkey in the 1990s. By the time the imposition by the European Union of antidumping duties on Indian bed linen imports was settled at the WTO in India's favor in 2001, the disruption was such that exports had fallen from US$127 million in 1998 to US$91 million. This led to job losses for 1,000 workers in the southern city of Pondicherry, where one of the targeted firms was based. Even after the WTO verdict of 2001, the terms of the complaint were altered slightly, and new antidumping duties were applied. This illustrates that trade remedy measures can take a long time to resolve and the cost of arbitration is high (Oxfam 2004).

Sanitary and Phytosanitary Requirements and Technical Barriers to Trade

SPS measures are applied by governments to protect human, animal, or plant life or health from risks arising from the entry or spread of pests, from plant- or animal-borne pests or diseases, or from additives, contaminants, toxins, or disease-causing organisms in foods, beverages, or foodstuffs.[6] This includes checking for pesticide residue in food, or subjecting animals to veterinary examination.

Box 2.4. Catfish and the Politics of Antidumping

In the late 1990s, the United States became a major export market for Vietnamese exporters of catfish. Their inroads hurt the domestic producers, represented by the Catfish Farmers of America (CFA). The CFA argued that the Vietnamese catfish were not catfish and lobbied the US Congress to include language in the 2002 Agriculture Appropriations Act that barred Vietnamese exporters from labeling their fish as catfish. The Act stipulated that only catfish of the species *Ictalurus Punctatus* can accurately be labeled catfish; the Vietnamese fish is of the family *Pangasius*. The Vietnamese complied by renaming their fish "basa" or "tra." The change in name, however, had little effect on Vietnamese catfish sales in the United States. The CFA then filed an antidumping petition alleging that the Vietnamese fish were being sold in US markets at unfair prices. The CFA petitioned for the low prices to be redressed with a dumping margin (tax) of 191 percent. The Vietnamese argued that their export prices were competitive because of the attributes of the Mekong River, low labor and feed costs, and traditional knowledge, as well as the fact that state subsidies were not involved. During the investigation, the United States treated Vietnam as a "nonmarket economy" and used prices from surrogate markets (Bangladesh and India). In January 2003, the US Department of Commerce announced a preliminary determination that imports of frozen basa and tra fish fillets were indeed being dumped and that the margins against their imports had to be levied in the range of 38 to 62 percent. Duties on catfish before this investigation were less than 5 percent.

Source: Waglé 2003.

For example, the United States mandates Hazard Analysis and Critical Control Point (HACCP) certification (which requires processes to reduce the risk of contamination in food production) for imports of juice and meat, and the European Union has adopted a suite of standards governing the "farm-to-table" chain, targeting a series of linked product and process standards governing food safety, animal health, animal welfare, and plant health. Similarly, TBTs refer to all technical regulations and standards applied to industrial products and aimed at ensuring consumers' health and safety.

Although both measures aim to achieve legitimate policy objectives, they may be used to restrict trade and serve as an NTB (see box 2.5). The WTO SPS Agreement contains a number of provisions to ensure that adopted SPS measures are not a camouflage for protectionism, such as, among other things, the obligation of any country wishing to introduce an SPS measure to conduct a scientific risk assessment, to demonstrate consistency in its SPS actions, and to reduce negative trade effects, when

designing and adopting its SPS measures. Trade regulations can be WTO compatible and still be discriminatory or even create obstacles to trade because of their implementation.

Under the SPS Agreement, countries may depart from international standards if there is a scientific justification or if a member determines that a higher level of protection is appropriate after conducting a risk assessment. Although the SPS Agreement obliges countries to accept the SPS measures of other WTO members as equivalent if the exporting country can demonstrate that its measures are adequate, the TBT agreement is softer in that countries can give a "positive consideration" to accepting as equivalent the technical regulations of other countries, but they are not obliged to accept them. As Staiger and Sykes (2009) argue, it is these kinds of provisions that give countries freedom to select their own level of risk without much regard for the costs of achieving the regulatory target or the incidence of those costs on exporters or importers (see box 2.6)

Box 2.5. The Increasing Importance of Standards

As tariffs are being lowered, a new family of potential barriers has become prominent—standards over products and processes. The ability to meet these standards has become central for market access, particularly in high-income markets. Standards create both a threat and an opportunity for producers: generally the process is costly and can act as a barrier to enter, particularly for small-scale producers; alternatively, they provide the potential to enter high-margin markets and improve capabilities of producers. Three characteristics of standards as a barrier to global trade differentiate them from tariffs and quotas: (1) standards are not just established by governments but also involve a range of private actors, particularly firms, international industry bodies, and civil society organizations; (2) unlike tariffs and quotas, which are publicly codified, standards that producers have to meet often are not widely publicized or stable and consistent; (3) unlike tariffs and quotas for which there are established mechanisms to resolve conflicts (for example, the dispute resolution procedures under the WTO), the determination of performance with respect to standards is generally an asymmetric process, determined solely by the buying party or country, with the producer having little capacity to challenge decisions on conformance. A detailed discussion on standards and certification is included in the section "Trade-Promotion Infrastructure: Standards and Certification" in this module.

Source: Kaplinsky 2010.

Box 2.6. Sanitary and Environmental Concerns as an NTB

Sanitary and environmental issues that appear alternately as food-safety and eco-labeling requirements have acted as NTBs. The European Union, for example, has adopted a policy of "zero tolerance" to fish products containing the residual antibiotic chloramphenicol. The standards have led to a plunge in shrimp imports from major Asian exporters. Advances in the technology of seafood analyses have been made to the point that pesticide and pharmaceutical residues can be detected at the parts per billion (ppb), and in some cases, at the parts per trillion (ppt) levels. When zero tolerances are established on the basis of the ability of a test to detect ppm, the increase in sensitivity to ppb or ppt can turn a "safe" product into an "unsafe" one. Regulations that draw on HACCP have made fish inspection programs tough; absence of such food-safety guidelines at home means that standards of the richest importing markets are applied to imports from poorer exporters. In cases in which sanitary requirements are scientifically justifiable, the appropriate course is not to lower those standards but to help exporting countries meet the standards.

Source: Mathew 2003.

Incentive Framework: Trade and Investment Policy

> **Note to the Practitioner:** Many of the issues for analysis and the quantitative measures with regard to trade policy in this section are much the same as in the section "Market Access." In this section, the emphasis is on the import side—understanding how trade policy facilitates or creates barriers to accessing quality and cost-effective inputs. In "Market Access," the emphasis is on the export side—how these same trade policies, imposed by current or potential trade partners, affects the competitiveness of exporters.

Link with Competitiveness Challenges Identified in Trade Outcomes

Main components of trade and investment policy	Competitiveness challenge areas			
	General export environment	Cost competitiveness	Product extension and quality	Market penetration
Trade policy	✓	✓		✓
Export restrictions	✓		✓	
Investment policy		✓	✓	
Exchange rates	✓	✓		✓

Quantitative Analysis: Indicators and Data Sources

	Indicator	Source
Import restrictions: Tariffs and NTMs	MFN tariff all products, manufactures, and primary goods—simple, weighted, maximum, dispersion	WDI/WITS-TRAINS
	MFN zero-duty imports (percent of imports)	
	Share of MFN tariff lines with international peaks, all products, manufactures, and primary goods (percent)	WDI/WITS-TRAINS
	Share of MFN tariff lines with domestic tariff peaks all products, manufactures, and primary goods (percent)	WDI/WITS-TRAINS
	Share of MFN tariff lines with specific rates, total, manufactures, and primary products (percent)	WDI
	Applied tariff rate, all products, manufactures, and primary goods—simple and weighted average	WDI
	Tariff rate with key PTA partners, all products, manufactures and primary goods–simple and weighted average	WITS-TRAINS
	Customs and other import duties, total and in key products (percent imports)	WDI
	Customs and other import duties (percent tax revenues)	WDI
	NTMs frequency ratio	WITS-TRAINS/WTI
Export restrictions	Export taxes, total, and in key products (percent total exports)	WDI
	Export taxes, total, and in key products (percent tax revenues)	WDI
	Export subsidies and presence of export processing zones (EPZs)	
	Export surrender requirements, Yes/No	WTI
	Export repatriation requirements, Yes/No	WTI
	Requirement for licenses, Yes/No	WTI
Exchange rate	Nominal exchange rate volatility (standard deviation)	WDI
	Real effective exchange rate (percent change)	WDI
FDI policy	Foreign equity ownership index	Investing across Borders
	Foreign equity ownership index—sector specific	Investing across Borders
	Starting a foreign business—ease of establishment index	Investing across Borders

MODULE 2

Qualitative Analysis: Interview Targets and Issues for Discussion

The analysis outlined in this section can be mostly undertaken as desk research. For most countries, data on tariffs and exchange rate are quickly available. Moreover, significant existing research is likely to have been conducted in recent years by the World Bank and other development partners such as the WTO (for example, see the WTO's *Trade Policy Review* series of country reports). The analysis could be completed in a couple of days. Issues that may be covered during interviews are outlined in this section. Depending on the size of the economy, fieldwork could be conducted in 10 to 14 days.

- *Policy makers*: Interviews with director-level or higher official staff is important to understand the vision and policy objectives the government has been pursuing, including some background on past policies and new directions. For example, the discussion should help shed light on the political-economic forces explaining the country's existing structure of trade protection, markets, and choice of exchange rate regime.
- *Exporters and business groups*: How do major export-oriented firms rate their experience of sourcing inputs from abroad? Which of the factors do they find most constraining: (1) tariff on intermediate inputs, (2) over-

valued exchange rate, (3) burdensome trade-related measures, (4) export taxes, or (5) other? The challenge is to interview exporters that may offer different views depending on their sector and size. The sample should include large firms and SMEs, successful exporters and some of their competitors, and if possible unsuccessful exporters. To identify these players, first locate market leaders and ask them about their competition. Business groups, sectoral chambers, and export promotion agencies could provide information on potential candidates, including producers that face difficulties to export.

- *Academia*: In many countries, local scholars have studied development and could offer insightful views on the role of the domestic trade policy on export competitiveness.

Interviews with Government

	Interview targets	Key issues for discussion
Tariffs	• Ministry of Trade • Ministry of Industry • Ministry of Finance • Customs • Export and investment promotion agencies	• Government trade policy objectives (for example, export growth, export diversification, domestic protection, regional integration, industrial policy, and so on) • Applied MFN tariff structure: tariff bands and peaks; publication and frequency of tariff changes • Preferential trade agreements • Export restrictions
NTMs	• Ministry of Trade • Ministry of Industry • Ministry of Agriculture • Other agencies responsible for issuing permits and licenses • Customs/Single Window	• Find out which ministries and agencies set up trade-related regulations • Potential overlap/coordination among ministries and agencies • Barriers to export • Simplification of procedures and Single Window • Use of risk management by customs and other border agencies
Exchange rate	• Central Bank • Ministry of Trade	• Government policy on exchange rate • Role of exchange rate to promote exports or protect industries
FDI policy	• Ministry of Trade • Ministry of Industry • Ministry of Finance • Investment promotion agency	• Overall strategy with respect to FDI—sector-specific targets • Sectors restricting foreign ownership • Other specific requirements for FDI over and above what is required for domestic investors • Incentives available for foreign investors—terms, requirements (for example, only in special economic zones)

Interviews with Private Sector and Other Institutions

General Issues	• How do they perceive the government's trade policy (for example, supporting an open trade regime and exports or protecting domestic production)? • Do they perceive the government's trade policy as business friendly, transparent, and predictable? • How do they perceive the government's preferential trade policy (for example, did they materialize in important market access)? • What are the most binding domestic policies for their export competitiveness? • Have they benefited or are they benefiting from any specific incentives? • Discuss specific issues relative to the firm size (in particular small versus large). • Discuss the top-three recommended actions the government should take to help them improve their export competitiveness.

Tariffs	• Do they pay tariffs on their imports (which goods and what rates)?
	• Do they feel that import tariffs are a burden for their export competitiveness?
	• Can they provide an estimate of the share of import duties in their cost structure?
	• Are PTA tariff schedules implemented effectively?
	• Is access to information on tariffs transparent?
	• Do they face obstacles at customs with identification of the right tariff schedule?
	• Is corruption prevalent at customs and is it hindering their competitiveness?
NTMs	• Are NTMs implemented by their own country perceived as hurting their competitiveness?
	• Is compliance with NTMs perceived as an obstacle in terms of number of requirements, bureaucracy, overlap and lack of coordination among agencies?
	• Are associated fees moderate or high, and what is their approximate share in cost structure?
	• What is the time to clear goods (specify import and export regime)?
	• Are there procedures to challenge decisions made by customs and other border agencies not to clear imported merchandise?
	• Is risk management used by customs and other border agencies?
	• What is the impact from state-trading enterprises on their business?
Exchange rate	• How is the exchange rate seem to be helping or hurting their exports?
	• How does the exchange rate affect their use of imported inputs/and integration into global and regional value chains?
	• Is the government's exchange rate policy transparent and predictable?
	• Are there any issues they have with accessing foreign exchange?
	• What is the availability of hedging markets and instruments?
	• What are the requirements for hedging due to volatility?
	• Discuss links with access to finance and availability of loans in local currency versus the US dollar or other international currencies.
FDI policy	• Is the government open to foreign investment in key input sectors (transport, ICT, energy)?
	• Are there any restrictions put on foreign investors outside what is clear in the law (for example, through limited licenses, capping the number of transactions, and so on)?
	• Are there any restrictions on foreign exchange availability?
	• What incentives are available to foreign investors?
Interviews with business groups (across all issues)	• Address the questions asked above but at the sectoral and industry level.
	• Are there initiatives to alert the government about binding constraints and the government's responsiveness/actions?
	• Is the government open and responsive to their concerns and suggestions?
	• Discuss examples of failures (for example, lost export opportunities, nonsurvival of new exporters).
	• Discuss key factors for success (in general and sectoral).
	• Discuss specific issues relevant to some firms by size or new firms.

MODULE 2

Analytical Approach: Key Issues to Understand

Component	Main issues
TRADE POLICY: TARIFFS, NTMs, EXPORT RESTRICTIONS	
MFN tariff regime	**1. Complexity of import tariff regime**
	• Trend in the simple and weighted average level
	• Summary statistics: Minimum, maximum, tariff dispersion (coefficient of variation in tariff rates, computed as 100 times the ratio of the standard deviation to the mean), tariff bands, frequency distribution of tariff rates
	• International comparison
	2. Sectoral differences in import tariff regime
	• Distribution of tariff rates across products, sectors, and industries
	• Tariff escalation (imposing higher tariffs with each stage of processing) by product: for example, look at tariffs imposed on first stage, semifinished, and fully processed light manufacturing) as an indication in effective protection
Preferential tariff rates	**1. Complexity of PTAs**
	• Number of PTAs, their coverage, and implementation phase
	2. Wedges between preferential and nonpreferential trade partners

Customs duties	**1. Revenue impact of import tariffs**
	• Implicit tariff rates, that is, the rates implied by actual tariff collections: (a) customs duties collected as a percentage share of the total value of imports and; (b) custom duties collected as a share of only dutiable imports
	• Implicit tariff rates by industry and by processing stage (first stage, semifinished, and final) to see whether customs exemptions attenuate the escalation of statutory tariff rates
	• Specific tariffs (duties levied on the monetary value of imports): identify tariff lines with specific duties; infer ad valorem duties by calculating implicit tariff rates (duties actually collected as a share of import values)
	• Tariff revenues as a share of government revenues
	2. Export taxes
NTMs	**1. Existence of quantitative import restrictions**
	2. Complexity and transparency of trade-related regulations
	• Number of import licenses and permits
	• TBTs and SPS
	3. Import and export customs procedures
	• Differences between general and export regimes, if any
	4. Identify any state-trading enterprises and collect information on their import and export practices
EXCHANGE RATE	
Exchange rate	**1. Nominal exchange rate policy**
	• Volatility
	2. Real effective exchange rate
	• Trend
	• Any misalignment with long-run equilibrium exchange rate
	• International comparison with comparators and competitors
INVESTMENT POLICY	
FDI policy	**1. Foreign equity ownership restrictions**
	• Local ownership requirements
	• Other barriers (licensing, concessioning)
	2. Other practical restrictions on FDI
	• Setting up a foreign business
	• Arbitration procedures
	3. Incentives to promote FDI
	• General incentives—for example, tax breaks
	• Sector-specific issues

Tailoring the Diagnostics to Country and Sector Characteristics
Summary of Specific Considerations by Country Type

Country type	Relative priorities and issues for consideration
Small (population) and remote/landlocked	• Likely to be heavily dependent on imports—pressure to use trade policy for import substitution, but import restriction would be a significant barrier to upgrading
Resource rich	• Exchange rate policies will be critical—potential for overvalued exchange rate and volatility
	• Issue of export restrictions may arise from policies that discourage commodity exports and increase value addition from domestic producers
	• State trading may be an issue
	• FDI policy with respect to resources sectors (for example, the Mining Code) will be critical
Low income, labor abundant	• Likely to be reliant on imported inputs in light-manufacturing sectors—focus on effective rates of protection and any policies that protect local monopolies
	• Check on use of FDI incentives in export sectors (for example, light manufacturing) versus input sectors (which are often more protected)
Middle income	• NTBs often are a bigger issue
	• Protection of the services sector (mainly through investment policies) is an issue to check

Summary of Specific Considerations by Sector

Sector	Relative priorities	Other issues for consideration
Light manufacturing	• High reliance on imported inputs and intermediates in most light-manufacturing sectors requiring a focus on import tariffs and effective rate of protection (ERP) • TBTs can become a disguised way to restrict imports • State trading may arise as a by-product of the nationalization of an ailing industry or as a means to pursue government policies on products or industries considered to have strategic importance	• Many sectors will have special import regimes for imported inputs designed for export manufacture (for example, textiles and clothing) • Countries may extend preferential access in some sectors through PTAs • Trade facilitation • Cost and efficiency of key services
Agriculture	• Heavily protected sector with a prominent use of high tariffs and quotas • SPS can become a masked way to restrict imports • State trading is common in many economies in which agriculture is an important sector of trade, in industrial countries as well as in agriculturally based developing countries, to provide price support for important agricultural products or to ensure food security • Export duties are mostly used for agricultural products	• Countries may extend preferential access in some goods through PTAs
Services	• Investment restrictions are critical given that many services are nontradable in a traditional sense • Export services such as transportation, tourism, professional services, and IT	• Regulatory barriers to entry • Competition

Background Reading: Relationship Between Trade and Investment Policy and Trade Competitiveness

Countries raise barriers against imports for a number of reasons. On the one hand, tariffs are a revenue source for governments (increasingly less so in most countries but still important in many developing countries with limited alternative sources of revenue). At the other end of the spectrum, NTMs, particularly technical restrictions, often are raised at least nominally to protect the health and safety of consumers. But perhaps most important, tariffs, quotas, and NTMs, as well as exchange rate policies, all are employed as part of industrial policies designed at best to support domestic "infant industries" and at worst to protect long-entrenched special interests. In an environment of increasingly integrated global production, trade in inputs and components plays a critical role in the competitiveness of most exporters. A country's barriers against imports to support the development and growth of domestic economy can deter its own export competitiveness, mainly by increasing the cost of inputs and final goods and by reducing the availability of imports.

Trade barriers distort production and consumption prices and choices, which often translates into the misallocation of resources and protection of inefficient local industries. As such, import protection acts as a tax on a country's export sector, and export-tax equivalents of import tariffs can be large for some developing countries (Tokarick 2006). An anti-export bias arises, for example, when imported inputs that are used in production are restricted (through high tariffs or other barriers), making it more difficult for such exports to compete with similar products from other countries. Trade policy barriers against imports hurt the export competitiveness of domestically produced goods and deter private sector incentives to increase productivity, innovate, and enhance export potential. Potential efficiency losses are greater when the domestic market is small and in industries intensive in intermediate products, such as light manufacturing. From a policy point of view, reducing import barriers would serve as an export-promotion strategy.

Trade policy has for a long time been designed with a mercantilist worldview, in which exports are good, imports are bad, and the protection of domestic producers is a priority. Governments put in place import-substitution policies to develop and support a domestic industry and provide jobs. But with the emergence and proliferation of disaggregated production processes, transnational supply chains, and cross-border investment, trade policy is playing an increasingly greater role in supporting a competitive export sector and cross-border integration. In addition to reducing tariffs, developing countries' development programs aim to minimize trade-related regulations and administrative frictions and to facilitate the movement of goods. Services trade liberalization has become a pillar of countries' export competitiveness agenda. Governments' strategy is not only to increase services exports but also to make services, as input to the industry, more efficient and cost effective.

MODULE 2

Many developing countries have used trade and investment openness, together with sound domestic policies, as a key driver for their development and have seen significant reductions in poverty and increases in welfare. The literature provides strong evidence that an increase in the import of intermediate goods boosts productivity and economic growth (Lee 1995; Eaton and Kortum 2001; Miroudot, Lanz, and Ragoussis 2009) (see figure 2.4). Empirical analyses also indicate that exporting firms are the most productive (Wagner 2005; Park et al. 2009). This growth in productivity is a direct consequence of the rise in the number of varieties of imported inputs through better complementarity with domestic varieties and the learning effect of foreign technology. The increased diversification in imported inputs also entails an increase in the number of domestic varieties produced and exported (Carrère, Cadot, and Strauss-Kahn 2011).

Services also can be intermediate inputs when they are used to produce goods. Given the domestic regulatory nature of barriers to trade in services and the lack of information on these restrictions (for example, in the form of databases, as in the case of tariffs), services trade policy deserves special attention and differentiated treatment. The analysis of these barriers to trade must be undertaken on a sector-by-sector basis, relying on government documents and the expertise of sector specialists. Global integration of the world economy is calling for increasingly efficient services sectors, from the development of transport and telecommunication sectors and efficient banking and insurance to professional business services to help exporters better compete in international markets. With low trade costs and efficient services, countries may gain a comparative advantage for services-intensive manufactured goods, an advantage that is enhanced if the country also produces intermediate services more effectively or has lower barriers to entry for services suppliers.

Some countries seek to benefit from international trade by promoting a dual economy, protecting a domestic industry, while supporting exporting firms through tax privileges and subsidies to grant duty-free access to imported inputs, thus removing or reducing price distortions and correcting the anti-export bias. Exporters often also benefit from other measures that remove or reduce high transactions costs through efficient streamlined admissions of imports and customs clearance.

Export restriction measures penalize exporters of restricted products. By affecting the price and quantity of trade, export restrictions produce trade-distorting effects in the same way as import restrictions. Export duties raise the cost of exported products, resulting in decreased export volumes, which may then divert some supply to the domestic market, leading to a downward pressure on domestic prices and reducing incentives for the suppliers to increase their production and investment. Moreover, price volatility and unstable supplies contribute to an insecure business environment.

Governments may apply different types of export restrictions (for example, export bans, taxes, quotas, or restrictive licensing) in pursuit of various public policy objectives (such as security, social, health, and safety) or to control inflationary pressures and maintain adequate supply of essential goods. The relative ease of implementing tax regulations through customs procedures makes export duties an attractive option for governments, especially when international prices are high (see box 2.7). Globally, export controls are more frequently imposed on primary commodities or scarce agricultural goods to control their domestic price, and are mostly imposed by developing countries.

Export restrictions also can act as an implicit subsidy when they promote downstream industries by providing them with an artificial competitive advantage. Such measures create a differential between the price available to domestic processors and the price charged to foreign buyers, and thus these measures provide domestic-processing industries using the concerned products with an advantage.

Figure 2.4. The Trade-TFP Relationship

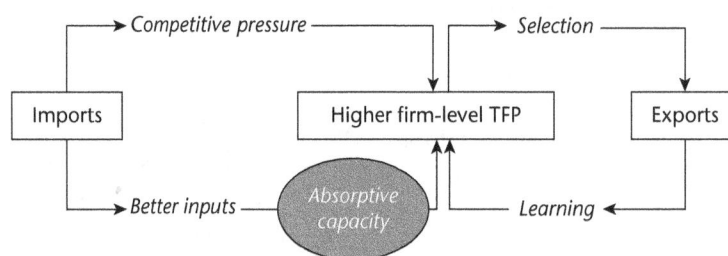

Source: Carrère, Cadot, and Strauss-Kahn 2011.
Note: TFP = total factor productivity.

Box 2.7. Use of Export Restrictions by Developing Countries

In recent years, export restrictions have continued to attract the attention of trade policy makers, both as a perceived means to achieve certain objectives (for example, value addition) and because of perceived gaps in international disciplines on their use. For example, following the peso devaluation in 2002, Argentina applied export duties to all exports to cushion the effects of exchange rate fluctuations on domestic products and to counter the sharp fall in tax revenue. After successive increases in rates, the applicable duties were 5, 20, 15, 20, 25, and 45 percent (depending on products) as of mid-2006. In 2007, China eliminated value-added tax (VAT) rebates on exports for 553 items to restrain the export of products regarded as highly energy consuming, highly polluting, and consuming large amount of raw materials. Since 1999, Cameroon has gradually prohibited exports of logs to promote the processing industry. From 1999 until the prohibition of log exports in 2004, a certificate of registration had to be obtained to export timber; this was intended to ensure that 70 percent of production is processed locally and only 30 percent of the annual harvest exported as logs.

In 2007–08, the world experienced a period of high food prices, which was aggravated by export controls being imposed by some food-exporting countries on major food exports. Such controls were undertaken to mitigate the impact on domestic prices; however, by reducing international supply, they exacerbated the increase of international prices. A study based on data for Argentina, a country with a long record of substantial export taxes and quantitative restrictions on food exports, showed that that such policies have in fact harmed the competitiveness of Argentina's agricultural sector more than tariff and nontariff barriers imposed by its trading partners. Elimination of export restrictions prevailing in mid-2007 in Argentina would increase production and employment levels of primary agriculture.

To increase value added, Mongolia imposed an export ban on raw cashmere between 1994 and 1996 and then imposed an export tax from 1997 to 2009. Experience shows, however, that unless a country has market power (which is clearly not the case in Mongolia, where neighboring China is also a major producer), the impact of export restrictions is to reduce domestic prices received by local producers encourage inefficient value addition, and promote the use of substitute inputs. In Mongolia, 15 years of export restrictions had no impact on industry value addition but instead shifted more of the power and profits in the industry from the herders to the processers.

Sources: World Bank 2003; Nogués 2008; Jeonghoi 2010.

Production distortions result from the fact that too much is produced in the exporting country's downstream industry, whereas too little is produced in the importing country's downstream industry. This production efficiency loss is sometimes justified by the "infant industry" argument. It is not clear, however, whether this infant industry strategy leads to successful results.

The real *exchange rate* also plays an important role in countries' export competitiveness. The emphasis should be on the real exchange rate rather than the nominal rate because what matters for private-sector profitability is the ratio of unit price over unit costs. In general, exchange rate policy should target the (hypothetical) equilibrium real exchange rate, which should reflect long-run fundamentals of the country, in terms of relative prices in domestic markets. Directed policies to support either an overvalued or undervalued exchange rate can affect relative competitiveness. Both can be detrimental over the long term.

An overvalued real exchange rate, defined as the ratio of global prices expressed in domestic currency over the domestic prices and often defined as the ratio of tradable goods prices over nontradable prices, can hurt export competitiveness in several ways:

- First, an overvaluation of the real exchange rate makes exporters' goods expensive in foreign markets by raising the prices of exported goods and services in foreign

currency terms through two potential channels. On the one hand, if the real exchange rate is overvalued because of a nominal appreciation, the foreign currency price of exports is excessively high, thus reducing foreign demand for exports. On the other hand, if the overvaluation is due to excessively high domestic inflation relative to global inflation, then domestic costs of production would be artificially high, thus reducing profits from exporting, or firms would be forced to raise their prices, thus reducing foreign demand.

- Second, although an overvalued exchange rate makes imports cheaper, political economic pressures build up to increase trade protectionism to support import-competing firms that find it more difficult to compete against cheaper imports, hurting the export competitiveness of export-oriented industries. An overvalued exchange rate can divert government resources to less efficient production in the domestic market.

According to this analysis, exchange rate depreciation to bring the real exchange rate closer to equilibrium (driven by the relative productivity of the economy) would stimulate exports and curtail imports, whereas exchange rate appreciation would be detrimental to exports and encourage imports. In the presence of high import content or in countries that are substantial net oil importers, however, exports are less adversely affected by currency

MODULE 2

appreciation. The lower import prices due to appreciation reduce the cost of export production and generate productivity improvements. Service exports, nevertheless, with very low import content, tend to suffer from currency real appreciation.

Undervaluation cannot be an optimal or long-term policy. Although undervalued exchange rates, subsidies, and suppressed wages can boost exports in the short term, this is not the same as securing competitiveness through productivity growth. According to Porter, Ketels, and Delgado-Garcia (2006), competitiveness has to enhance an economy's productivity measured by the value of goods and services produced per unit of a nation's human, capital, and natural resources. Indeed, a number of countries—including Austria and more recently the former Yugoslav Republic of Macedonia—have used a rigid exchange rate to force exporters to improve competitiveness rather than rely on devaluation. Evidence from both countries suggests it can be highly effective over the medium term.

Furthermore, the maintenance of an undervalued real exchange rate can be costly and unsustainable over long periods of time because it requires sterilized intervention in foreign exchange markets, usually by the monetary policy authority. As capital flows in, the monetary authority buys foreign exchange with domestic currency, which can be inflationary. To reduce inflationary pressures from the growth of the monetary base, the monetary authority usually engages in open market transactions by issuing public bonds (either central bank or federal government paper) in exchange for domestic currency, which is withdrawn from the market. As the supply of domestic bonds increases, however, domestic interest rates must rise for market agents to hold the additional bonds denominated in domestic currency. Consequently, capital inflows tend to rise as domestic interest rates rise, thus requiring another round of sterilized intervention. In some instances, the government can force domestic economic agents to hold additional domestic bonds at a constant interest rate, but this requires an additional distortion. For instance, in some countries, state-owned banks can be forced to accept additional bonds at an artificially low interest rate. This requirement would imply that depositors are forced to accept artificially low deposit interest rates. Other policy instruments, such as financial transactions or capital inflow taxes, could be implemented to reduce pressures on the real exchange rate while also raising public revenues. Finally, a fiscal contraction (for example, a reduction of the primary fiscal deficit or an increase of a surplus) could reduce real exchange rate appreciation by reducing domestic interest rates (thus reducing incentives for capital inflows) and reducing domestic inflationary pressures.

In addition, volatility of exchange rates raises uncertainty and may force exporters to shift to less risky activities (products or markets), which could raise costs through adjustment as well as contribute to a suboptimal allocation of resources. The negative impact, however, depends on access to information, attitudes toward risk, and market structures. These impacts will be most acute in financially underdeveloped countries and economies that do not provide hedging instruments and opportunities that enable firms to guard against this risk (Eichengreen 2008).

Finally, *investment policy*—specifically policy with respect to FDI—can support competitiveness of a country's exporters. This role is important because foreign investors tend to be overrepresented in the export sector, particularly in countries with relatively limited home markets. Research on FDI shows not only that they tend to be more productive than firms in the domestic market but also, and most important, that they generate spillovers to domestic firms in the backward-linked supplying industries (Javorcik 2004), thus contributing to wider productivity growth. Foreign investors can play a critical role in introducing greater competition in local markets and breaking down the local monopolies that can be a source of poor input competitiveness and anti-export bias.

Main Components of Trade and Investment Policy Analysis

Trade policy is more conducive to economic growth and business friendly when it is open, transparent, and predictable. Governments may use various instruments to control trade flows, generate revenues, and protect domestic production and employment. Analyzing a country's trade policy and its implications for competitiveness requires an assessment of several instruments, including (1) tariff policy, (2) NTMs, (3) restrictions on exports, (4) exchange rate policy, and (5) investment policy. These instruments are outlined in figure 2.5.

Tariff Policy

Several trade and competitiveness issues are related to import tariffs:

- Import tariffs increase the cost of inputs and intermediate goods, increasing the domestic production cost. They tend to restrict the variety of goods affordable to producers that seek to be competitive in international markets.
- Relatively high average tariffs introduce an anti-export bias into the trade regime because they make it more attractive for companies to produce for the protected domestic market rather than to sell overseas.

Figure 2.5. Framework on the Relationship between Trade Policy and Competitiveness

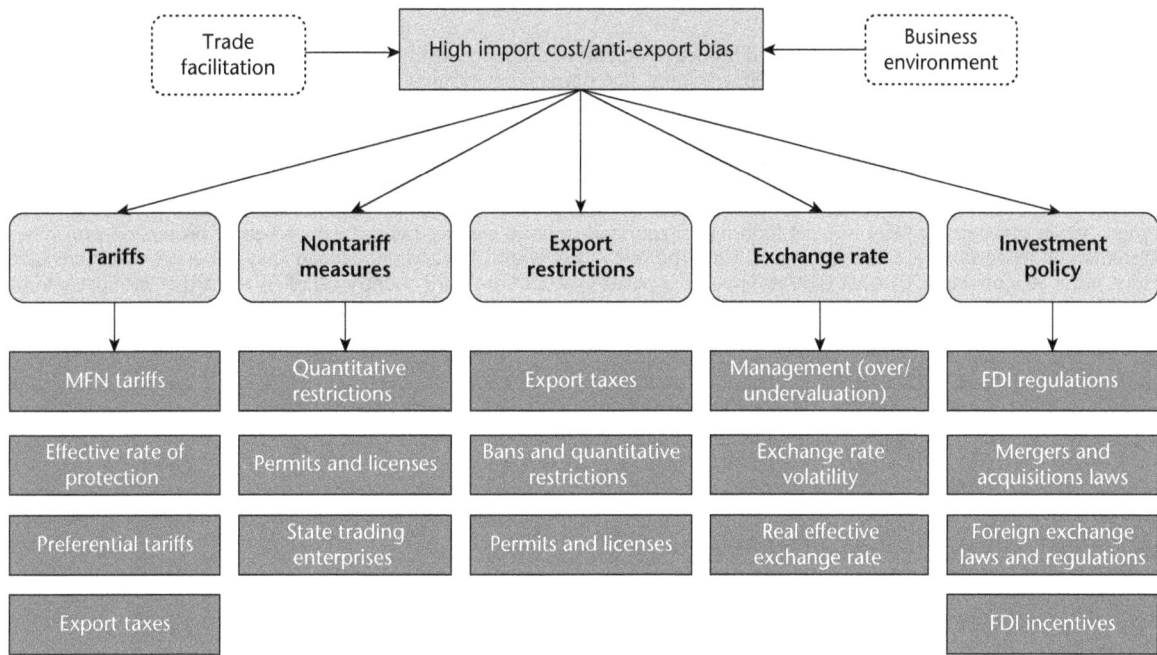

Source: Authors.

Duty-drawback and import-under-bond systems only partially offset this anti-export bias, while at the same time introducing additional administrative burdens on enterprises. Reducing prohibitively high tariffs also provides benefits in the form of increased tariff revenues and reduced incentives for fraud, corruption, and smuggling.

- High levels of tariff dispersion—the degree to which different sectors or products within a sector face different tariff levels—can introduce significant distortions. Dispersion often results from the use of excessive exemptions and tariff escalations. Countries with significant tariff dispersion often show a large number of tariff bands, with certain sectors being protected through particularly high rates of protection. This protection has a distorting effect on resource allocation within the economy.
- Higher tariffs on final products than on inputs increase the ERP. By taking into account protection on both outputs and inputs, ERPs provide a better representation of tariff-generated transfers to producers than nominal rates of protection, which only protect outputs. High effective rates of protection shield inefficient producers from adjusting to changing needs.
- Although tariff reduction through PTAs has become widespread, lack of implementation of PTAs and

overlapping commitments may complicate business operations and access to information. Although PTAs often lead to trade expansion among members, by making imports from other PTA members cheaper, these agreements may hurt export competitiveness, particularly when countries keep high MFN import tariffs with the rest of the world. In that case, PTAs may lead to trade diversion away from more competitive nonmember countries, and hence hurt firms' efficiency and competitiveness.

Economists and policy makers might not agree on the optimal level for tariffs, but establishing a uniform tariff presents several advantages, including the fact that (1) effective protection is the same for all sectors and equals the nominal protection rate; (2) it is simple, clear, and transparent, and therefore reduces business costs; (3) it reduces the cost of the customs administration; and (4) it reduces discretion (corruption). Moreover the manner in which countries reduce tariffs has important implications in terms of export incentives. Tariff-reduction schemes that exempt high tariffs or sensitive sectors could leave countries out by creating more distortions (see box 2.8). A strategy to reduce all tariffs—in which high tariffs are cut more than low ones—would do the most to improve export incentives and real income (Tokarick 2006).

MODULE 2

> **Box 2.8.** Avenues to Reduce Tariffs
>
> The WTO multilateral trade rounds have helped reduce bound tariffs on goods, which are the maximum tariff rates WTO member countries can apply to imports from other WTO members. Autonomous or unilateral liberalization of trade barriers has accounted for most of the trade liberalization in developing countries over the past two decades. Hence, applied tariff rates globally are well below their bound rates. Countries may reduce their tariffs through PTAs or RTAs. This option could lead to deeper integration, including some traditionally sensitive sectors such as agriculture and services. Regional trade liberalization may be even more central for trade in intermediates, which are more sensitive to trade barriers and have an important regional dimension. Trade liberalization can go further, and investment and trade in services are also likely to be liberalized. Liberalization toward selected partners, while maintaining MFN rates at high levels, can lead to large wedges between the levels of protection provided by preferential tariffs and those levied on imports from the rest of the world. These discrepancies may generate distortions across sectors in the economy and losses of tariff revenue as importers switch from third-country suppliers to partner producers to take advantage of tariff preferences.
>
> *Source:* Authors.

Nontariff Measures

As import tariffs have been reduced worldwide and locked in under the twin pressures of multilateral rounds and preferential agreements, NTMs have grown significantly and now represent one of the most important areas of concern in trade policy. Between one-third and two-thirds of traded goods are affected by one or more NTMs, with technical standards being the most prevalent. Unlike tariffs that directly increase the price of imports and indirectly increase import quantities, NTMs tend to directly limit import quantities and indirectly limit the cost of imports. NTMs tend to have a significant trade-reducing affect that is on par with tariffs. Estimates by Hoekman and Nicita (2008) suggest that cutting the ad valorem equivalent of NTMs in half (from around 10 to 5 percent) would boost trade by 2 to 3 percent. Some NTMs intentionally restrict trade, such as import quotas that limit the quantity of some goods that may be imported, however the WTO forbids such quantitative restrictions. NTMs are typically trade-related regulations, such as TBTs (for example, product standards or labeling requirements) that may be imposed for legitimate purposes, such as protecting public health or the environment, but that may restrict trade either intentionally or unnecessarily. Governments may twist normal health and safety standards or custom procedures to place additional costs on foreign exporters, thereby limiting imports. UNCTAD developed the following standard nomenclature for the categories of NTMs, which provides perhaps the most comprehensive definition of NTMs:

- SPS (sanitary and phytosanitary) measures
- TBT (technical barriers to trade)
- Preshipment inspection and other formalities
- Price control measures
- Licenses, quotas, prohibitions, and other quantity control measures
- Charges, taxes, and other paratariff measures
- Finance measures
- Anticompetitive measures
- Trade-related investment measures
- Distribution restrictions
- Restrictions on postsales service
- Subsidies (excluding certain export subsidies included under export-related measures)
- Government procurement restrictions
- Rules of origin
- Export-related measures

When poorly designed and adopted with little consultation with the private sector, NTMs may hurt competitiveness by constraining the ability of companies to outsource key inputs, putting them at a competitive disadvantage on international markets. NTMs often complicate day-to-day business and distract managerial attention. Firm surveys highlight private-sector demands for more transparency in the adoption and application of NTMs across countries. In many countries, the need to streamline cost-raising NTMs is now recognized as a key component of national competitiveness agendas.

With the prominence of NTMs and their relatively opaque impact on imports (and hence on exports that rely on imported inputs), streamlining NTMs has become an important component of any competitiveness agenda. Because governments can use NTMs to pursue different policy objectives and may be implemented by various government agencies, it is crucial that they be transparent, consistent, efficient, nondiscriminatory, and the least trade-distorting. In reality, NTMs habitually lead to excessive, complex, costly, and redundant procedures that dampen the competitiveness of importers and exporters, even when implemented for legitimate public policy objectives. Below are key principles required by the WTO for regulations:

- Measures should not discriminate between countries and between domestic and foreign producers.
- Measures should be transparent so that all parties have access to the information.
- Measures should be formed on a scientific basis in the case of SPS measures.
- There is no less trade-impeding alternative. Governments should use regulations that are not more trade and investment restrictive than necessary to fulfill legitimate public policy objectives. Creating such regulations requires careful assessment of their impact to ensure that in both design and implementation they do not create unjustified difficulties for the free flow of goods, services, and investment.

State-trading enterprises (STEs) may be used to implement a number of trade policy measures that are not consistent with WTO provisions. The most common is a violation of market access obligations. For example, an STE might be used to provide protection for the domestic market in a given product by setting resale prices of imports at very high levels, thus negating tariff concessions bound in WTO schedules. The provision of subsidies to STEs which mainly are involved in exporting may run afoul of export subsidy disciplines. Even in cases in which the objective of the government acting through the STE does not intentionally distort trade, the STE operations nevertheless may do so. For example, the protection of public health, which is a frequently stated rationale for the maintenance of monopolies on alcohol and alcoholic beverages, may seriously distort trade in those products. It is only when the activities of the STE are examined and their impact on trade is analyzed that more effective rules can be developed. WTO provisions seek to make the STEs behave as private competitive traders and thus remove the potential for trade distortion offered by government involvement in an enterprise's decisions and activities.

Export Restrictions

Some governments impose export taxes on exported goods. These taxes most commonly are imposed with unprocessed products, with one or both of the following objectives: (1) to maintain a large supply of a product (particularly a staple food crop) in the country to control price escalation, and (2) to promote increased value addition within the country (for example, for food products, wood, minerals, and so on). Export restrictions take various forms, such as prominently export duties, but also include quantitative restrictions and licensing requirements. Although quantitative export restrictions are, in principle, prohibited by WTO rules, there is no substantive discipline on export duties, only efforts to revise this at the multilateral and bilateral levels. A recent OECD study shows that the number of countries applying export duties over the period of 2003–09 has increased compared with previous years and that such duties were introduced primarily by middle-income developing countries and LDCs (Jeonghoi 2010).

When designing export restrictions, several factors should be carefully considered: (1) whether the measures are effective in achieving intended policy objectives; (2) whether the benefit of the measures outweighs the cost (not only in the target sector but also on other sectors in the economy); and (3) whether the measures achieve the objectives in the least trade-distorting ways. Some governments responded to high food prices in 2007–08 with an increase in the international price of a commodity to limit inflationary pressures. An export restriction, by increasing domestic supply, reduces the domestic price of the product, thus partially offsetting the inflationary pressures coming from higher prices abroad. Such measures, however, prevent exporters from benefiting from high international prices. Also, when applied by large countries that can influence world prices, these measures can have a negative impact on the welfare of trading partners, especially those of small countries, by reducing the supply to the world market and thus amplifying the negative aspects of the initial high price. To address inflation in food prices, some governments have responded with more trade-friendly policy options, such as reducing or suspending import tariffs on food products. Another response has been to provide targeted cash transfers to vulnerable groups. To promote value addition, some governments have included positive incentives—for example, measures to promote targeted investment, including subsidized credit and accelerated depreciation—for investment in downstream sectors.

Exchange Rate

The nominal exchange rate is the price of one currency expressed in terms of another, and it is crucial to exporters. When the exchange rate rises, goods priced in local currency become more expensive in foreign currency—so demand for these dearer exports drops, reducing overall demand. Imports become cheaper in local currency, putting downward pressure on inflation and interest rates. Conversely, a lower exchange rate typically boosts export demand and increases the cost of imports, putting upward pressure on inflation and interest rates.

The real exchange rate can be expressed as the nominal exchange rate relative to the price of nontradables. Being the relative price of nontraded goods, it cannot be controlled by policy makers directly. Rather, it is the outcome of other policies and processes influencing supply and demand.

Some researchers have advocated for consciously maintaining undervalued exchange rates in developing countries intent on boosting exports. Rodrik (2008) articulates two stories in which real exchange depreciations expanded the tradable sector. In one, tradables are special because they suffer disproportionately from the institutional weakness and contracting incompleteness that characterize low-income environments. In the other, tradables are special because they suffer disproportionately from the market failures (information and coordination externalities) that block structural transformation and economic diversification. In both cases, an increase in the relative price of tradables acts as a second-best mechanism. Indeed, Rodrik (2008) shows that growth over the medium term is much higher in countries with more undervalued exchange rates. This result is confirmed by Miao and Berg (2010) and implicitly suggested by Freund and Pierola (2008), who find that a change in relative prices due to a real exchange rate depreciation leads to entry in new export industries and the discovery of new markets.

An important caveat regarding the use of the exchange rate as a policy instrument to boost exports and growth is that it suffers from a fallacy of composition—that is, the tool would be ineffective if many developing countries were to employ it because of competition among them. It would also hurt both domestic consumption and export-oriented industries with high import content.

Foreign Investment Policy   Investment policy includes the various laws and regulations that determine whether and how a foreign entity may invest in firms, infrastructure, or other economic activities in a country. At the heart of FDI policy is the existence of restrictions or regulations on the nature or level of investment in certain sectors or in certain types of firms—this might include, for example, the requirement for some local shareholding or even majority local holding in any investment (or it might bar FDI completely in certain sectors). Beyond this, foreign investors can face restrictions to investment through the following:

- Limitations or caps on the availability of licenses or concessions in certain sectors
- Laws related to mergers and acquisitions
- Foreign exchange laws, which may make it practically difficult to operate
- Regulations and processes involved in company registration
- Other industry-specific regulations

FDI openness varies considerably across sectors, with services sectors—particularly the critical input services like telecommunications, energy, and transport—often most restrictive in terms of FDI access. Box 2.9 provides a summary of good practices with respect to various aspects of cross-border investment policy.

Box 2.9. Investing Across Borders—Reviewing Good Practices

Most research and empirical evidence finds that, on balance, FDI helps foster development in recipient economies (Nair-Reichert and Weinhold 2001). These benefits are particularly increased in countries with good governance, well-functioning institutions, and a transparent, predicable legal environment. Foreign investors and governments concerned about the competitiveness of their economy's business environment have a broad range of resources at their disposal. The most recent resource is the World Bank's *Investing across Borders 2010*, which includes up-to-date indicators that measure FDI regulation in four specific policy areas: (1) investing across sectors, (2) starting a foreign business, (3) accessing industrial land, and (4) arbitrating commercial disputes. Countries can improve their FDI competitiveness by looking for lessons and good practices of other countries that scored well on *Investing across Borders* indicators, summarized as follows:

Investing Across Sectors
- ***Allowing foreign ownership in the primary, manufacturing, and services sectors.*** The global trend has been to liberalize a growing range of economic sectors. In many countries, the benefits of openness to foreign capital participation have overcome the reasons for restricting certain sectors from foreign ownership.

(continued on next page)

Box 2.9. *(continued)*

Starting a Foreign Business

- *Equal treatment of foreign and domestic investors.* The start-up process should be governed by the same rules for all companies regardless of their ownership. Any differences in treatment should be due to companies' size, legal form, or commercial activity, and not the nationality of its shareholders.
- *Simple and transparent establishment process.* Countries should consolidate start-up procedures and abolish unnecessary ones (that is, investment approvals for small projects). In addition, countries can enable investors to register business online. Fast-track alternatives, even if they entail higher processing fees, are usually valuable to foreign investors. Countries should not require foreign companies to go through a local third party (lawyer, notary, public entity).

Accessing Industrial Land[a]

- *Clear laws providing fair and equal treatment for foreign and domestic companies.* Laws should provide security to investors—foreign and domestic—so that they feel comfortable operating and expanding their businesses and should not limit their ability to develop, renew, transfer, mortgage, or sublease land.
- *Accessible land information and efficient acquisition procedures.* Law records should be current, centralized, integrated, and easily accessible, and should provide information useful to investors and the general public. There should be clear rules for acquiring private and public land, avoiding unnecessary and cumbersome procedures.

Arbitrating Commercial Disputes

- *Strong arbitration laws in line with arbitration practice.* Ideally, arbitration laws should be consolidated in one law or a chapter in civil code; these laws should be coherent, current, and easily accessible. A strong legal framework should be associated with effective arbitration practices and greater awareness of the benefits of arbitration.
- *Autonomy to tailor arbitration proceedings.* Good arbitration regimes provide a flexible choice for commercial dispute resolution.
- *Supportive local courts.* There should be strong support from local courts for arbitration proceedings and consistent, efficient enforcement of arbitration awards.
- *Adherence to international conventions.* Adherence to and implementation of international and regional conventions on arbitration, such as the New York Convention and the International Center for Settlement of Investment Disputes Convention, signal a government's commitment to the rule of law and the protection of investor rights.

Source: World Bank, Investment Climate Advisory Services 2010.
Note: a. This is addressed in the section "Intermediate Inputs and Backbone Services" in this module.

MODULE 2

Incentive Framework: Domestic Policies and Institutions (Competition, Business Environment, and Governance)

> **Note to the Practitioner:** Business environment and governance issues have a fundamental impact on competitiveness well beyond export markets. These issues are also covered in quite significant detail in many other analytical products from the World Bank (for example, *Doing Business* reports and Investment Climate Assessments. As such, an in-depth analysis of the business environment and governance should not be required as part of the Trade Competitiveness Diagnostic. Rather, a summary of key issues can be drawn from existing research in most countries. There may be some need to qualify specific impacts in some key sectors and to understand how these factors affect the decisions of exporters, but only limited field research should be required.

Link with Competitiveness Challenges Identified in Trade Outcomes

Main components of domestic policies and institutions	Competitiveness challenge areas			
	General export environment	Cost competitiveness	Product extension and quality	Market penetration
Competition	✓	✓	✓	
Business environment and governance	✓	✓	✓	

Quantitative Analysis: Indicators and Data Sources

		Measures	Sources
Business regulatory environment	Starting a Business	Number of procedures to start a business	*Doing Business* (DB)
		Cost of complying with procedures	DB
		Time (number of days) to complete the procedures	DB
	Closing a Business	Time (number of days) to complete a bankruptcy	DB
		Cost of bankruptcy proceedings as percentage of estate's value	DB
		Recovery rate for claimants through bankruptcy proceedings	DB
	Dealing with Licenses	Number of procedures to build a standardized warehouse	DB
		Median duration (number of days) to complete a procedure	DB
		Cost to complete procedure as a percent of the country's income per capita	DB
	Registering Property	Number of procedures to transfer the property title from a seller to a buyer	DB
		Time (number of days) to complete the procedures	DB
		Cost as a percent of the property value	DB
	Protecting Investors	Transparency of transactions (extent of disclosure index)	DB
		Liability for self-dealing (extent of director liability index)	DB
		Shareholder's ability to sue officers and directors for misconduct (ease of shareholder suits index)	DB
		Degree of protection of property rights and intellectual property	Global Competitiveness Index (GCI)
	Enforcing Contracts	Number of procedures to resolve a commercial dispute	DB
		Time (number of days) to resolve a commercial dispute	DB
		Cost (as percentage of the claim) to resolve a commercial dispute	DB
		Lack of confidence courts to uphold property rights (percent of firms)	World Bank Enterprise Surveys
Taxation	Paying Taxes	Effective corporate tax rate	WDI
		Total tax rate (percent)	WDI
		Administrative burden of paying taxes (number of taxes, agencies involved, methods for payment, frequency)	DB
		Time (in hours per year) to prepare, file, and pay taxes	DB
		Management time dealing with officials (percent of management time)	ICS

Competition	Competition	Intensity of domestic market competition	GCI
		Extent of market dominance (rating)	GCI
		Effectiveness of antimonopoly policy (rating)	GCI
	Services and FDI	Investing across Borders (IAB)	IAB
		Starting a foreign business (time and procedures)	IAB
		Accessing industrial land (time to lease, strength of legal rights, availability of and access to information)	IAB
		Arbitrating commercial disputes (strength of laws, ease of process, extent of judicial assistance)	IAB
Governance	Governance	Number of firms paying bribes	World Bank Enterprise Surveys
		Average bribe as percentage of total sales	ICS
		Irregular payments in exports and imports	GCI
		Losses due to crime and violence	Enterprise Surveys; GCI
		Losses due to security issues	Enterprise Surveys; GCI
		Unpredictable interpretation of regulations	Enterprise Surveys
		Corruption perception Index	Transparency International
		Degree of undue influence in the judicial system and among government officials	GCI
		Government efficiency	GCI

Sources for Cross-Country Indicators of the Business Environment

World Competitiveness Yearbook

- Published by the Institute for Management Development in Lausanne. Until 1996, a joint publication with the World Economic Forum (WEF). Analyzes the international competitiveness of 49 countries, on the basis of hard data from international organizations and perception surveys of enterprise managers.
- Hard data cover economic performance, international trade and investment, public finance and fiscal policy, education, productivity, and infrastructure quality. Survey questions cover institutional framework (government efficiency, justice, and security), business legislation (openness, competition regulations, labor regulations, and capital market regulations) and management practices.
  Source: http://www.imd.ch.

Global Competitiveness Report

- The Global Competitiveness Index, published annually by the World Economic Forum since 1996, is another good example of benchmarking. Analyzes the international competitiveness of more than 100 countries, on the basis of hard data from international organizations and perception surveys of enterprise managers.
- Survey questions cover access to credit, public institutions for contract and law enforcement, corruption, domestic competition, labor regulations, corporate governance, environmental policy, and cluster development. Hard data cover economic performance, international trade and investment, public finance and fiscal policy, education, technological innovation, information and communications technology, and infrastructure quality. Starting in 2003, the analysis includes six *Doing Business* indicators on starting a business and enforcing a contract.
  Source: www.weforum.org.

Global Enabling Trade Report

- Measures and analyzes institutions, policies, and services enabling trade in national economies around the world. Includes the most current data and recent analysis of the factors enabling trade in industrial and emerging economies, as well as the latest thinking and research from trade experts and industry practitioners.
  Source: www.weforum.org.

Index of Economic Freedom

- Published since 1995 by the Heritage Foundation and the *Wall Street Journal*. Analyzes economic freedom in 161 countries and is based on assessments by in-house experts, drawing on many public and private sources.
- The index covers 10 areas: trade policy, fiscal burden, government intervention, monetary policy, foreign investment, banking and finance, wages and prices, property rights, business regulation, and black markets.
  Source: www.heritage.org.

MODULE 2

Economic Freedom of the World

- Published since 1997 by the Fraser Institute. Analyzes economic freedom in 123 countries on the basis of assessments by in-house experts, drawing on many public and private sources. The ratings on the business environment are derived from the Global Competitiveness Report.
- The index covers eight areas: size of government, legal structure, security of property rights, access to sound money, freedom to exchange with foreigners, regulation of credit, regulation of labor, and other business regulation.
  Source: www.freetheworld.com.

World Markets Research Center

- Published since 1996 by the World Markets Research Center in London. Analyzes the investment climate in 186 countries and is based on assessments by 180 in-house experts, drawing on many public and private sources.
  Source: www.worldmarketsanalysis.com.

Country Risk Service

- Published quarterly since 1997 by the Economist Intelligence Unit. Provides international investors with risk ratings for 100 countries on the basis of assessments by in-house experts, drawing on previous ratings.
- The index covers seven areas of country risk: political, economic policy, economic structure, liquidity, currency, sovereign debt, and banking sector.
  Source: www.eiu.com.

Business Environment Risk Intelligence

- Published by Business Environment Risk Intelligence three times a year since 1966, in Geneva, Switzerland.
- Provides international investors with risk ratings for 50 countries on the basis of assessments by in-house experts, drawing on previous ratings and outside experts. Their assessments are evaluated by a panel of about 100 external experts.
- The index covers two areas of country risk: political and operational. Operational risk covers the enforceability of contracts, labor costs, bureaucratic delays, short-term credit, and long-term loans.
  Source: www.beri.com.

FDI Confidence Index

- Published since 1997 by A.T. Kearney. Provides subjective views on the attractiveness of 60 countries for foreign investment. Based on assessments by executive managers of 1,000 global companies. Only the aggregate index is published.
  Source: www.atkearney.com.

Source: World Bank 2008.

Qualitative Analysis: Interview Targets and Issues for Discussion

	Interview targets	Key issues for discussion
Business regulatory environment	• Ministry of Trade • Ministry of Industry • Ministry of Finance • Ministry of Labor • Local government • Company registrar • Other agencies responsible for issuing permits and licenses • Commercial banks • Investment promotion agency • Customs	• Main constraints faced by firms • Constraints to set-up versus day-to-day operations • Which issues affect importing and exporting directly? • Reform policies/programs in place or planned
Taxation	• Ministry of Finance • Local government • Agencies responsible for tax audit and collection	• Structure of tax regime • Any taxes or administrative issues (for example, audits) that keep firms informal or create anti-export bias • Tax incentives/subsidies linked to exporting
Competition	• Ministry of Trade • Ministry of Industry • Competition Authority • Academia	• Current competition law • Nature of existing anticompetitive behavior • Existence of state-owned enterprises or state-trading monopolies • Structure of ownership of major input industries • Cost and service implications • Quality of local suppliers

| Governance | • Ministry of Trade
• Ministry of Industry
• Ministry of Finance
• Local government
• Academia | • Incidence of corruption and nature (for example, large-scale corruption linked to securing government contracts versus petty corruption linked to licensing, customs, and other regulatory processes)
• Other governance issues affecting investment and exporting (linked to judicial system, political processes, and so on) |
| Private sector (relevant for all issues above) | • Domestic investors
• Private investors
• Informal firms
• Law and accounting firms
• Chambers of Commerce | • How do individual firms respond to these issues in terms of investment? in terms of importing and exporting?
• How do responses differ by nature and size of firms? |

Tailoring the Diagnostics to Country and Sector Characteristics
Summary of Specific Considerations by Country Type

Country type	Relative priorities and issues for consideration
Small (population) and remote/ landlocked	• Competition issues may arise due to limited scale of domestic market—greater likelihood of strong links between business and government elite, which contributes to competition and wider governance issues • FDI policy and business regulations likely to be critical—these countries are less able to afford weaknesses in the business and investment climate • May have limited tax base and so there may be pressure on tax instruments • May have more limited institutional capacity
Resource rich	• Historically, many resource-rich economies face particular problems with governance issues—this may manifest itself in business regulatory issues as well as in high- and low-level governance problems (for example, corruption) • Assess how the tax and competition environment affects the resources sector versus the nonresources sector (potential for an environment that creates barriers to competitiveness and adjustment toward nonresources sectors)
Low income, labor abundant	• Important to understand how the tax and regulatory environment affects labor markets • Low-income countries typically face greater problems with regulatory capacity
Middle income	• Competition policy is an important issue to assess, as many middle-income countries have well-established national champions in key industries • Business environment and governance issues likely to vary widely across countries

Summary of Specific Considerations by Sector

Sector	Relative priorities and issues for consideration
Light manufacturing	• Check on competition issues related to key inputs • Many light-manufacturing sectors are targeted with special tax treatment through industrial policies—this may include lower corporate taxes for FDI (through SEZs or otherwise) • Major issues to check on business regulatory environment include procedures for establishing a business, accessing land and property, obtaining permits for construction, and setting up utilities (obtaining electrical and water connections)
Agriculture	• Check on competition issues, including price controls and monopolies in certain parts of the value chains (especially processing and marketing) • Business regulatory issues should focus on land access, zoning, titling, registration, and other processes related to land purchase and lease; issues related to Environmental Impact Assessments (EIA) should be considered
Services	• Competition issues are critical, particularly in key input sectors (energy, transport, telecommunications) • Regulatory restrictions regarding licensing as well as professional and educational credentials can be an important barrier

In spite of the significant impact that business regulation has on overall export competitiveness, the services sector may be one of the most affected by inefficient, unnecessary, and restrictive regulations. Trade in services tends to be more reliant on institutions, with clear and simple rules providing regulation and contract enforcement, than trade in goods for which markets may be more transparent. A sound regulatory framework is the main pillar for business in the services sector, especially when it comes to subsectors in which large initial investments are required,

MODULE 2

such as telecommunications, transportation, and financial services. Managing reforms of services markets requires integrating trade openings with a careful combination of competition and regulation. Governments have an important role to play in generating the preconditions for an efficient set of service industries, giving special importance to the institutional infrastructure. Regulation is generally motivated by a mix of efficiency and equity considerations. The challenge for policy makers is to strengthen such regulation without making it inefficiently strong and, when needed, introducing complementary policies to ensure that the benefits of competition are widely distributed (Hoekman and Mattoo 2008).

Background Reading: Relationship Between Domestic Policies and Institutions and Trade Competitiveness

The business environment plays an important role in firm-level competitiveness in the international context and may act as an enabler or obstacle for their growth. Factors affecting the business environment are diverse and complex. They include a variety of transactions-related costs,[7] the fiscal environment in which firms operate, and institutional quality as well as government effectiveness. An effective business environment should promote firm behavior that is allocatively efficient on a macro basis over the long term (that is, sustainable). This requires (1) a regulatory regime that is adequate to fulfill the task of essential controls of the private sector without creating unnecessary obstacles to running a business, (2) a nondistortionary tax environment, (3) a legal framework that promotes market competition, and (4) sound governance and capable institutions that minimize the wedge between policy (*de jure*) and practice (*de facto*).

The main channels through which the domestic business environment affects export competitiveness are as follows: (1) by introducing distortions to the microeconomic incentives of companies, which ultimately affect their decisions on producing and exporting; and (2) by raising both fixed and variable costs for firms. Although there is no doubt that macro policies are important, consensus is growing that the quality of business regulations and the institutions that enforce it are major determinants of prosperity. Macro-incentives that contribute to the soundness and stability of an economy create opportunities for prosperity, but actual wealth creation occurs through the productivity of firms that combine available resources in the production process. Constraints to entry and exit a business, the regulatory burden, the time and cost of getting licenses and permits, the costs of enforcing contracts, and other factors shape firm-level competitiveness by influencing the microeconomic flexibility of a country (Porter 1998; WEF 2007).

Business regulation may constitute an obstacle to improving firms' competitiveness at the micro level, reducing the options for companies to compete successfully in international markets. Businesses in less developed countries normally face heavier administrative costs, more regulatory procedures, and longer processing times. The regulatory burden is often more costly as the size of the company decreases, constituting a major impediment to start a new business. Although the effect of ineffective business regulation on business is a decreased ability to assert legal or economic rights, the effect on the government side is a structural obstacle for expanding the tax base and generating greater revenue.

A dynamic private sector—with companies engaging in investments, creating jobs, and improving productivity—promotes growth and expands opportunities for international trade. The process by which an productivity grows and economy upgrades works through a series of enablers, which also serve as intermediate indicators of competitiveness. True competitiveness is measured by productivity. Productivity ultimately depends on the microeconomic capability of the economy, rooted in the sophistication of companies (both local and foreign), the quality of the national business environment, and the externalities arising from the presence of related clusters and supporting industries (Porter 1998). In a study conducted to investigate the linkages between business regulation and macro- and microeconomic outcomes, Loayza and Servén (2010) find evidence that some types of regulations have negative effects on labor productivity growth, whereas others have a positive impact. Product market regulations and labor regulations fall under the first group of regulations. The primary connecting link that explains this adverse effect is firm turnover: In countries in which labor and product market regulations are more burdensome, turnover rates are lower on average. The authors found, however, that a third type of regulation—level of taxation—has a positive effect on productivity growth, a result explained as being associated with the higher supply of productive public services permitted by higher taxation. Conversely, an inefficient business environment and burdensome regulations create distortions and discourage firms from competing in the market. Thus, improvements to the existing business regulation can contribute to firms' competitiveness by facilitating procedures and diminishing associated costs (WEF 2007).

Main Components of Business Environment and Governance Analysis

Governance Countries are not endowed with the institutions that make up their economic environments, but rather this is determined endogenously. Policy makers play an important role in shaping future developments on competitiveness. One important component of understanding the microincentives in the business environment that shape firm decision making is the role of the government in protecting against private diversion, including such factors as *the rule of law, bureaucratic quality, corruption, the risk of expropriation by the state*, and the *enforcement of contracts* (Hall and Jones 1999). These meta-institutions are considered fundamental not only for the export sector but also more broadly for a country's overall competitiveness and economic growth. The institutional framework provides the fundamental preconditions for private companies, government, and individuals to interact to produce goods and services in the economy. Owners of land, other physical assets, and intellectual property will invest in the improvement and upkeep of their property only if their rights as owners are not guaranteed. In the same sense, if property cannot be bought and sold with the confidence that the authorities will uphold and enforce the transaction, the market will lack incentives for growth. The result will be an increase in the perceived risk premium of investment, and thus restricted firm entry and reduced investment in innovative activities. This outcome will be particularly evident in smaller markets and in sectors in which the potential rent earnings are limited (for example governance is likely to affect trade and investment more in places like Mongolia and Swaziland than in China and Russia). Analysis of the impact of institutions and governance on export competitiveness may focus on observable channels through which it may affect firm behavior, for example, through a greater understanding of FDI perceptions. At a micro level, governance impacts on trade competitiveness can be analyzed through firm perceptions of corruption and trade-related transactions (for example, licensing, importing, and exporting).

Business Regulations In terms of export competitiveness, extensive compliance requirements associated with government regulatory procedures, such as paying taxes, getting licenses, or dealing with custom procedures for trading across borders, can be detrimental to firms' competitiveness in international markets. In the services sector, more sophisticated regulations on financial and banking services, and specialized delivery services such as telecommunications and transportation, as well as special provisions on FDI and professional licensing and qualification requirements, may constitute significant obstacles for growth and competitiveness.

Excess regulations may add extra costs for regular firms in terms of time and money. Heavier regulation is generally associated with greater inefficiency of public institutions

and more corruption but is not associated with better quality of private or public goods. Frequently, countries that regulate the most have the least enforcement capacity and the fewest checks and balances to ensure that regulatory discretion is not used for private gains. Bad institutions—for example, those involving cumbersome entry procedures, rigid employment laws, weak creditor rights, inefficient courts, and overly complex bankruptcy laws—simply do not get used.

A large part of the business environment is determined by business regulations that affect a company through its different stages of development—that is, from starting the business and hiring and firing workers to paying taxes, dealing with customs, and complying with licenses and permits requirements.

Taxation Although taxation is clearly necessary in all countries, it can have a negative impact on export competitiveness by effectively raising the costs at which firms must sell in export markets. Excessive tax rates (for example, Sweden's notorious former 98 percent marginal tax bracket) create clear disincentives for individuals and firms, but in most cases, the issue is not the rate of the tax per se but rather the way in which it is applied and the distorting effects it may have on firm behavior. For example, excessive tax rates can create a disincentive to invest[8] or an incentive to invest in capital over labor (or vice versa). For large multinationals, the corporate tax rates—which are often the headline figure used in discussions over the competitiveness of tax regimes—matter little, as multinationals make use of transfer pricing, double taxation treaties, and other instruments to reduce their tax burden in any one country. Conversely, Loayza and Servén (2010) find that the level of taxation (what they call fiscal regulation) is positively correlated with GDP growth.

Perhaps more important than the level of taxes is the administrative process involved in enforcing the tax regime. This process may include excessive red tape as well as, more onerous, inspection regimes that can be bureaucratic at best and corrupt at worst. Understanding the basic statutory requirements, procedures, and transparency with which the tax regime is administered is important to analyzing the business environment in which firms operate.

Competition Uncompetitive business practices constrain domestic firms' export competitiveness as well, in particular through practices affecting market access for imports such as domestic import cartels or monopolies, exclusionary abuses of a dominant position, control over importation facilities, vertical market restraints that foreclose markets to foreign competitors, certain private standard-setting activities, and other anticompetitive practices of industry associations. By contrast, robust competition in the home market contributes positively to the international competitiveness of firms by (1) driving prices toward marginal costs, (2) ensuring that firms produce at the lowest attainable costs, and (3) providing incentives for firms to innovate and introduce new products and production methods into the marketplace.

A transparent and effective competition policy can be an important factor both in enhancing the attractiveness of an economy to foreign investment and in maximizing the benefits of such investment. More specifically, competition policy can enhance the attractiveness of an economy for foreign investment by providing a transparent and principles-based mechanism for the resolution of disputes that is consistent with international norms that are widely accepted internationally. This transparency and consistency increases investor confidence and the propensity to invest. Vigorous competition in markets, reinforced by

competition policy, maximizes the benefits of such investment to host countries, by encouraging participating firms to construct state-of-the-art production facilities, to transfer up-to-date technology into host countries, and to undertake appropriate training programs. FDI liberalization can enhance the contestability of markets, which can provide an important stimulus for greater efficiency; it is not a sufficient condition to achieve this result. Rather, effective competition laws, policies, and enforcement machinery are necessary to ensure that preexisting statutory obstacles to contestability are not replaced by anticompetitive practices of firms, thus negating the benefits that could arise from liberalization.

Box 2.10 summarizes some of the key benefits of regulatory reform and the main factors for success. Box 2.11 reviews the benefits and drawbacks of two of the main sources of comparative data on the business environment—the World Bank's *Doing Business* indicators and the World Bank's *Enterprise Surveys*.

Box 2.10. Maximizing the Benefits of Regulatory Reform—Factors for Success

Benefits

International evidence shows that efficient and transparent regulations have a positive impact at macro and micro levels:

- **Economic growth.** Regulatory reform has been estimated to increase the level of real GDP in several OECD countries, ranging from 1 percent in the United States to between 5 and 5.5 percent in France, Germany, and Japan.
- **Export competitiveness.** Supported by efficient trade liberalization reform, export competitiveness transformed Hungary and Mexico from inward-looking to successful export-oriented economies.
- **Investment.** Both domestic and foreign investment responds positively to an effective regulatory framework that provides credibility and certainty to the private sector. The Republic of Korea's FDI inflow increase resulting from regulatory reform was estimated at US$36.5 billion between 1999 and 2003. Trade growth in Hungary was accompanied by a dramatic increase in FDI—during the reform decade, Hungary attracted more than one-third of all FDI in Central and Eastern Europe.
- **Expansion of private-sector activities.** The contribution of the Mexican and Hungarian private sector to the GDP reached nearly 90 percent and 85 percent, respectively, by the end of the 1990s, higher than the ratio for many OECD countries.
- **Increased labor productivity.** A study concludes that economic deregulation in five sectors increased labor productivity in OECD countries, ranging from 0.5 percent in the US to 3.5 percent in Germany.
- **Enhanced competition.** The opening of port operations to multiple parties in Uruguay increased firm productivity by 300 percent. In Chile, deregulation of entry into the long-distance telephone market cut rates by 50 percent.
- **Reduced business costs.** Inefficient regulation in port operations contributed to implicit tariffs of 5 to 15 percent on all Latin America exports. A survey highlights that managers spent between 10 and 30 percent of their time managing process regulation, incurring costs in the range of 5 to 15 percent.
- **Public goals.** Goals such as consumer protection and environmental quality can be reached through efficient reform.

Costs

Regulatory reform can be associated with short-term job losses and reduced government revenues, although evidence shows mixed results:

- **Short-term employment losses.** Can occur in sectors with low levels of productivity and efficiency. However, there is evidence that early job losses can be compensated in the longer run as reforms breed entrepreneurialism and formal employment. In the Republic of Korea, the 1998 deregulation was estimated to create more than 1 million new jobs between 1999 and 2003.
- **Reduced government revenues.** Can occur when reform targets regulations created for revenue purposes (for example, some business licenses). Yet evidence shows that reforms to streamline licenses and eliminate those that are unnecessary or redundant can have a pull effect on potential new users—for example, informal firms—hence increasing the coverage of the revenue base.

(continued on next page)

Box 2.10. *(continued)*

Factors for successful reform

Countries have taken different approaches to regulatory reform based on their intrinsic economic, social, and institutional structures. Underlying factors, however, have contributed to reform success in most countries:

- *A supportive macroeconomic environment.* In an unstable economic environment, it is unlikely that the government will prioritize regulatory reform over macroeconomic stability. Political will has been vital to the success of regulatory reform in Hungary and Mexico.
- *Adapting best practices to local conditions.* In Hungary, international models were adapted using the existing legal and administrative frameworks to implement change.
- *Creating an independent dedicated reform agency.* Ideally composed of influential, skilled technocrats with direct access to the highest levels of policy making, this agency should have the authority to promote regulatory reform, to monitor progress, and to assess the quality and quantity of regulations using cost-benefit and cost-effectiveness principles. In the Republic of Korea, the Regulatory Reform Commission (RRC) was created to maintain a consistent set of principles to control regulatory quality. In Mexico, the government created executive units in key ministries to overcome entrenched resistance to reform.
- *Designing and implementing compensation mechanisms.* Getting the support of interest groups opposed to reform may require a good mix of mechanisms, such as compensatory resources for short-term losses, training for rapid relocation in the marketplace, and prior involvement of labor groups in the design of the reform process. Mexico is a good example of the efficient use of specific adjustment programs during privatization and trade liberalization, although it also highlights that these programs are fiscally expensive.
- *Building effective regulatory structures.* Regulations can be changed in a relatively short period of time, but strengthening the regulatory institutions that implement reform and monitor the quality of regulations needs more time and the government's continuous support.
- *Cost-benefit analysis and monitoring.* As each individual regulation has a cost-benefit balance, a government should be able to know the expected outcomes of its actions on different stakeholders.

Source: World Bank 2009d.

MODULE 2

Box 2.11. Doing Business Data and Enterprise Surveys—Facts and Shortcomings

Doing Business[a]

Benchmarking exercises provide a useful and straightforward way to address competitiveness issues. Examples of these exercises are provided by the World Bank Group's *Doing Business* indicators, which benchmark and rank the cost and quality of business regulations for key cross-cutting investment climate issues. The *Doing Business* indicators use available information on 175 countries and measure the cost of doing business for a hypothetical firm on an annual basis. The two types of indicators in *Doing Business* focus on government regulations and its effect on business—especially on small and medium-size domestic businesses.

The information contains measures of actual regulation, for example, the number of procedures to register a business or an index of employment law rigidity, and measures on regulatory outcomes, for example, time and cost to register a business, enforce a contract, or go through bankruptcy. Frequent observations based on a standard firm description can be extremely useful for monitoring progress in the areas covered under the indicators (that is, costs of starting and closing a business, employing workers, trading across borders, registering property and getting credit, dealing with licenses, and paying taxes; investor protection issues; and contract enforcement) as well as for making cross-country comparisons. The *Doing Business* data do not allow the productivity effects of the cross-firm, within-country variation in investment climate conditions to be studied (Fajnzylber, Guasch, and López 2009).

The main shortcoming with this approach is that it is not enough to know a country's ranking. Rankings are no substitute for a careful evaluation of impact and may be misleading sometimes, as they tend to give equal importance to factors that may influence performance and growth quite differently. For this reason, benchmarking exercises should be seen as complementary to other approaches that try to assess the relative importance of reforms to the selected outcome, be it growth or competitiveness.

Enterprise Surveys

The World Bank Enterprise Surveys (also known as Investment Climate Surveys) collect hard data and perceptions at the firm level. Firm-level data allow for the measurement of some dimensions of the business and investment climate for which limited data sources exist at the aggregate level—notably for indicators of the quality of governance and institutions and, in particular, for measures of the incidence of corruption or regulatory burdens. In addition, microeconomic data allow for the possibility of comparing the different effects and constraints that investment climate conditions have within countries among different type of firms. The idea of directly asking firms about the various aspects of the business environment that affect their performance is the underlying premise of the Enterprise Surveys prepared by the World Bank. The latter cover 105 countries, more than 76,000 firms and dozens of indicators on the quality of the business environment. The surveys capture entrepreneurs' perceptions about the different obstacles affecting firm competitiveness and allow for comparison of these perceptions with hard data on the business environment and firm performance.

(continued on next page)

Box 2.11. (continued)

Business surveys are a direct way of identifying competitiveness constraints. The World Bank Enterprise Surveys include a standard question on the main obstacles for growth of firms. Business professionals are asked to evaluate the severity of some 20 potential obstacles to the growth of their businesses. A five-point scale is used, ranging from extremely severe to not important. These results can be compared across more than 100 countries and can be compared over time as well. This approach provides valuable information on the priorities that entrepreneurs would adopt if faced with the task of designing policies to improve the investment climate. In many countries, business associations also survey firms frequently.

This approach has three main limitations. First, perceptions of the entrepreneurs are volatile and may be biased by recent events reported in the media, and they may also reflect their specific cultural and socioeconomic background. For instance, managers of firms that concentrate on local as opposed to national or international markets may lack the necessary benchmarks to judge the severity of the problems existing in their cities or provinces, and compare them with national or international best practices. Second, the questions tend to focus on obstacles and problems, giving less attention to factors that enable growth, such as technology and innovation. Third, they tend to overestimate the impact of factors whose costs are borne privately and benefits for the economy are more diffused—taxes are perhaps the best example of this.[b]

Sources: Authors.
Note: a. The *Doing Business* methodology, surveys, and data can be found in http://www.doingbusiness.org.
b. Another often-cited shortcoming is the fact that these surveys do not cover firms that have not entered the market. This limits their effectiveness to identify barriers to competition. This can be addressed, in principle, by the survey sample design.

Factor Conditions: Access to Finance

Link with Competitiveness Challenges Identified in Trade Outcomes

Main components of access to finance	Competitiveness challenge areas			
	General export environment	Cost competitiveness	Product extension and quality	Market penetration
Access to investment capital	✓		✓	
Access to working capital	✓			
Trade finance services	✓			✓

Quantitative Analysis: Indicators and Data Sources

	Measures	Sources
General and investment capital	Cost of capital (average of last five years)	IMF International Financial Statistics (IFS) database
	Percent of firms indicating access to finance as a major constraint	World Bank Enterprise Surveys
	Percent of firms obtaining bank credit	World Bank Enterprise Surveys
	Average interest on bank loan and credit line	World Bank Enterprise Surveys
	Average collateral requirement (as percent of loan)	World Bank Enterprise Surveys
Working capital	Average interest on working capital loans	National sources
	Availability of factoring services	National sources
Trade finance	Average cost of confirmed letter of credit (L/C) (percent rate)	National sources
	Average cost of export credit insurance (percent rate)	National sources
	Total export value (US dollars per capita) that can be supported by Export Credit Guarantee Agency (ECGA) fund	National sources
	Share of commercial risk covered by ECGA	National sources

MODULE 2

Qualitative Analysis: Interview Targets and Issues for Discussion

Interview targets	Key issues for discussion
Government • Ministry of Trade and Industry • Ministry of Finance • Development Banks • Export finance institutions (for example, Export Credit Guarantee Agency) • Export promotion agency ***Private sector*** • Individual exporters (small; new and established) across traditional and emerging sectors • Export councils or industry associations • Banks and other financial institutions • Legal/accounting firms (or professional associations)	• Main sources of finance for exporters • Relative availability and terms of investment capital versus working capital? • What restrictions are there on access to capital? What are the main reasons that firms do not take out bank loans? • Cost of loans, terms, and collateral requirements • Are there any restrictions that prevent firms from collateralizing certain assets? • What trade finance support is provided to exporters—L/C? Guarantees? Subsidized insurance? Subsidized loans for export-related projects? Factoring? • Is there any specific support related to smaller/new exporters? • What are the main areas for which additional support would facilitate exports? • Do most exporters make use of bank financing for exporters? • Do exporters make use of the above services? What are the barriers to greater take-up?

Tailoring the Diagnostics to Country and Sector Characteristics

Summary of Specific Considerations by Country Type

Country type	Relative priorities and issues for consideration
Small (population) and remote/landlocked	• No specific issues inherent to being small and remote
Resource rich	• Dutch disease effects may raise the nominal and relative cost of capital for many nonresource export activities
Low income, labor abundant	• Cost of finance often high and collateral requirements excessive • Working capital a major constraint for export entry and survival
Middle income	• Trade finance likely to be a particularly important factor determining export entry and survival • More sophisticated products like factoring and insurance likely to be well established

Summary of Specific Considerations by Sector

Sector	Priorities and issues for consideration
Light manufacturing	• Working capital and trade finance more important for SMEs and firms operating outside global value chains (otherwise should be able to access credit within the supply chain)
Agriculture	• High-volume, low-margin commodity agricultural trade reliant on trade finance • Some countries will have specific programs for agricultural exports
Tourism	• Access to finance, particularly for local and smaller-scale tourist sectors
Business and IT services	• Firms tend to have few tangible assets to use as collateral • Most firms in these sectors are SMEs

Background Reading: Relationship Between Access to Finance and Trade Competitiveness

One of the most important inputs to the production process is capital—that is, access and cost of finance to fund investments and working capital. As is well documented through many ICAs, access to finance is almost always identified as one of the biggest barriers facing firms. Access to finance is a bigger constraint for certain types of firms. Small firms tend to be most constrained in accessing finance, but access to finance is also a particular challenge to firms (of all sizes) that have low levels of asset tangibility (Rajan and Zingales 1998)—that is, firms that have limited physical assets that can be used as a basis of collateral. This is a problem for firms in the services sector as well as for manufacturing exporters in the apparel sector, for instance, who tend to have relatively few assets relative to the size of their working capital requirements. Finally, exporters operating within global value chains tend to have better access to finance than firms that are disconnected from such global networks, as credit is typically extended across the supply chain. The downside for these exporters is that liquidity shocks such as in the recent global financial crisis can transmit quickly across these production networks, drying up exporters' sources of trade credit.

Although many firms face challenges accessing capital, in most cases, it is not access itself that creates these challenges but rather the terms of the loans that are available

(for example, often only short-term credit is made available) and the cost of loans. Two main issues related to cost are most important: (1) the actual interest rate charged and (2) the collateral requirements. On the former, high interest rates mean that only prospective investments with particularly high return expectations and relatively limited riskiness will be considered "feasible." On the latter, high collateral requirements make it virtually impossible for smaller firms to qualify for credit.

The implication of lack of access or high cost of finance on export competitiveness is significant. First, lack of access to finance to fund working capital may be a barrier to participation in export markets, particularly given the greater risks and often longer payment terms involved in exporting. Second, lack of access to affordable finance will mean that producers fail to undertake investments that will improve productivity or that they substitute variable costs (like labor) for capital, resulting in nonoptimal production structures.

Trade finance mechanisms exist to support two fundamental aspects of the trading process: risk mitigation (that is, insuring against the risk of nondelivery or nonpayment by one party) and liquidity (that is, bridging the gap between incurring liabilities for export-oriented production and receiving payment from the customer). Some 80 to 90 percent of all international trade transactions are said to be financed by some form of trade credit (Auboin 2009). The provision of trade finance support lowers risks for exporters and so is particularly important during initial stages of exporting (at the extensive margin, new products and new markets) as well as during periods of macroeconomic uncertainty. Lower risk overcomes barriers to entering and sustaining exports (increasing export survival) as well as lowering trade cost (through financing costs).

The case for government intervention in the provision or support of trade finance stems from unique aspects of trade finance that may imply greater potential risk. The most obvious is its exclusively international context, which tends to increase both macrolevel risks (for example, exchange rate fluctuations, changes to policy, conflict, political upheaval) and counterparty risk, linked to the greater difficulty of enforcement across borders (Menichini 2009). Weak cross-border enforcement raises the risk of strategic default on the part of suppliers, which, combined with information asymmetries, creates a problem of "credible commitment" across borders (Ellingsen and Vlachos 2009). Finally, the cross-border nature of trade financing means that data on which to assess counterparty credit risk are often limited or nonexistent (for example, limited public credit registry coverage or public access to accounts or court proceedings).

The vast majority of trade finance involves credit extended bilaterally between firms in a supply chain or between different units of individual firms.[9] Banks also play a central role in facilitating trade, both through the provision of finance and bonding facilities and through the establishment and management of payment mechanisms such as telegraphic transfers and documentary L/Cs. Among the intermediated trade finance products, the most commonly used for financing transactions are L/Cs, whereby the importer and exporter essentially entrust the exchange process (that is, payment against agreed delivery) to their respective banks to mitigate counterparty risk. Complementing the activities of the banks are export credit agencies (ECAs), which guarantee and insure domestic exporters; private insurers, which provide trade credit insurance, political risk insurance, and bonding facilities; and multilateral development banks (MDBs), which operate formal trade facilitation programs designed to support banks by mitigating risks in new or challenging markets for which trade lines may be constrained.

Assessing the effectiveness of trade finance support in developing countries relies in part on understanding the provision of credit, in general, or key trade finance products, in particular, those offered through commercial banks. A number of surveys have been conducted in recent years (cf. ICC 2009; Malouche 2009) to assess the perceived constraints in the provision of trade credit during and following the global economic crisis of 2009 (see box 2.12)

MODULE 2

Box 2.12. Financing Trade in a Postcrisis World

By providing liquidity and security to facilitate the movement of goods and services, trade finance lies at the heart of the global trading system. Indeed, as Auboin (2009) notes, trade finance has become ever more critical as global supply chains have increasingly integrated in recent years. During the recent global crisis, the availability trade finance was seen to have been substantially reduced, particularly for SMEs and in developing countries. This acted as a further constraint to trade and became yet another source of contagion that reverberated down supply chains to exacerbate the crisis.

Although governments and multilateral institutions responded aggressively to stave off the trade finance "gap"—involving the provision of up to US$250 billion in support—evidence from past crises indicates that trade finance may continue to be a problem long after the crisis ends. For example, in a study of the Asian Financial Crisis, Love, Preve, and Sarria-Allende (2005) find that the total amount of credit provided collapses in the aftermath of a crisis and continues to contract for several years. This is because trade credit is generally a complement rather than an alternative to bank credit. When firms are constrained in their access to bank credit, they tend to reduce the amount of credit they extend in the supply chain; when they are flush with bank credit, they extend more trade.

This highlights the potential vulnerability of trade finance. If banks continue to limit lending (exacerbated by regulatory requirements like Basel II), the integrated nature of global production networks means these credit constraints are likely to amplify across supply chains. Proactive responses by governments to promote not only the provision of trade finance but also wider credit facilities, particularly for SMEs, will be critical to supporting the competitiveness of the export sector.

Source: Farole and Reis 2010.

Factor Conditions: Labor Markets, Skills, and Technical Efficiency

Link with Competitiveness Challenges Identified in Trade Outcomes

Main components of labor markets, skills, and technical efficiency	Competitiveness challenge areas			
	General export environment	Cost competitiveness	Product extension and quality	Market penetration
Labor regulations and skills		✓	✓	
Firm-level technical efficiency		✓	✓	

Quantitative Analysis: Indicators and Data Sources

	Indicators	Sources
Productivity— top line measures	Total factor productivity (TFP)	Derived from Enterprise Surveys; national sources derived from Labor Force Surveys and Enterprise Census
	Labor productivity	Conference Board database, ILO Key Indicators of the Labor Market (KILM) database; national sources (as above)
	Unit labor cost	Derived from Enterprise Surveys; national sources (as above)
Labor markets	Average wages per category of employee	Country-specific data
	Wages and earnings	ILO KILM; CEIC Data[a]
	Firing costs	*Doing Business*, Enterprise Surveys
	Hiring costs	*Doing Business*, Enterprise Surveys
	Payroll taxes	ILO KILM
	Rigidity Index	*Doing Business*
	Percent of workers unionized	ILO KILM, World Bank Enterprise Surveys
	Strikes and work stoppages (annual average)	ILO KILM
	Share of workers in the informal sector	ILO KILM
Labor skills	Percent skilled labor	World Bank Enterprise Surveys
	Educational attainment of workers	ILO KILM
	Percent of firms offering formal training	World Bank Enterprise Surveys
	Average percent of workforce receiving formal training	World Bank Enterprise Surveys
Firm-level technical efficiency	Capacity utilization	World Bank Enterprise Surveys
	Share of firms having introduced new technologies	World Bank Enterprise Surveys
	Share of firms using technology licensed from a foreign company	World Bank Enterprise Surveys
	Share of firms with ISO certification	World Bank Enterprise Surveys
	Share of firms outsourcing a major activity	World Bank Enterprise Surveys
	Share of firms with process or product innovations in past year	World Bank Enterprise Surveys
	Average/median highest level of education of managers	World Bank Enterprise Surveys
	Average/median years of experience managers have in the sector	World Bank Enterprise Surveys
	Percent of skilled technicians in the workforce (industry specific)	World Bank Enterprise Surveys

a. Commercial database provided by CEIC Data: http://www.ceicdata.com/.

Qualitative Analysis: Interview Targets and Issues for Discussion

Interview Targets

	Government agencies and ministries	Private sector and other institutions
Labor markets and skills	• Ministry of Trade and Industry • Ministry of Labor/Employment • Ministry of Education	• Individual exporters • Export councils or industry associations • Universities, other schools, training institutions
Firm-level technical efficiency	• Ministry of Trade and Industry • Ministry of Labor/Employment • Ministry of Education	• Individual exporters • Export councils or industry associations • Universities, other schools, training institutions • Quality certification bodies

MODULE 2

Key Issues for Discussion in Interviews

Labor markets and skills	• Trends in labor productivity and main drivers
	• Trends in labor market: supply- and demand-side issues
	• Trends in wages—skilled versus unskilled labor
	• Labor relations issues
	• Major concerns raised by private sector over labor market issues: wages, hiring/firing costs, regulations, and so on
	• Any recent labor legislation
	• Main skills challenges and how they are being addressed
	• What is government doing to address it
	• What is the private sector doing
	• Situation with vocational training/higher education
Firm-level technical efficiency	• General perceptions on the quality of management/factors behind this
	• Level of education and experience of most managers
	• Role of local versus foreign management
	• Educational and training institutions—availability and quality of management training
	• Any specific programs/efforts to improve managerial technical capacity

Tailoring the Diagnostics to Country and Sector Characteristics

Summary of Specific Considerations by Country Type

Country type	Relative priorities and issues for consideration
Small (population) and remote/landlocked	• May be limited pool of skilled and managerial talent
	• General worker skills and labor productivity likely to be critical, which suggests importance of tight focus on sectors of comparative advantage
Resource rich	• Wages and other input costs may be high resulting from currency impacts of commodity exports (Dutch disease effects)
	• Depending on market size, access to skilled workers and managers may be limited, as the best may be lured toward the dominant resources sector; understanding the dynamics of this will be important
Low income, labor abundant	• Wage rates should be an important source of comparative advantage—if they are not (for example, in many parts of Africa) understanding the reasons behind this (including labor market issues but also wider transactions costs) is critical
	• Local managerial skills may be limited—importance of openness to FDI but also in having policies to ensure spillovers of knowledge
Middle income	• Avoiding the middle-income trap—identifying skills and other inputs that will facilitate upgrading to services and knowledge-intensive sectors

Summary of Specific Considerations by Sector

Sector	Priorities and issues for consideration
Light manufacturing	• Most issues will be critical—labor market regulations, wages, skills, and technical efficiency often are the most important determinants of competitiveness
Agriculture	• Technical efficiency critical—important to understand capacity/quality of extension services
Tourism	• Wages and skills an important issue, particularly given location of tourism facilities in relation to labor markets
	• Important to assess training and skills development programs
Business and IT Services	• Labor force scale can be an issue in some outsourcing sectors
	• Skills are the most important issue—important to understand number and quality of graduates from technical universities and availability and quality of vocational training programs

Background Reading: Relationship Between Labor Markets, Skills, Technical Efficiency, and Trade Competitiveness

Productivity and Competitiveness

At the heart of competitiveness is the productivity of firms in producing goods or services (at the factory, farm, or office gate).[10] Indeed, productivity (specifically, TFP) is often equated to competitiveness—according to Porter (1990), productivity is "the only meaningful concept of competitiveness at the national level." There are compelling theoretical arguments and mounting empirical evidence of the importance of productivity for the prosperity of

MODULE 2

nations. Although macroeconomic factors play an important role in creating opportunities to create wealth, the process of wealth creation in an economy is actually tied to the increase in the productivity with which a nation utilizes its resources to produce goods and services (Porter et al. 2008).

Recent years have seen resurgence in interest in the role of productivity. At the same time, a sharp debate has focused on the links between productivity and trade. Trade can affect a country's productivity by affecting firm-level productivity directly, or by distorting the allocation of resources across the economy (see box 2.13). The causality, however, can run in the other direction, from productivity to exporting. Considerable research, both at the theoretical and empirical level, shows that exporters are more productive than nonexporters and that this productivity difference predates any entry into exporting (Pavcnik 2002). Firm-level productivity can change with trade because of many reasons: (1) import competition, (2) outsourcing, (3) FDI, and (4) integration and access to research and development (R&D) inputs. In this strand of research Roberts and Tybout (1997) develop a model of exporting with sunk costs of entry and test it on a sample of Colombian firms. In the presence of these entry costs, only the relatively productive firms will choose to pay the costs and enter into the foreign market. The implied relationship between exporting and productivity is positive in a cross-section of firms or industries, but the causality runs from productivity to

exporting. Similar results are found by Bernard and Jensen (2004) for the United States, and by Bernard and Wagner (2001) for Germany. In general, there is some reason to believe that in low-income countries, where exporters can benefit from technology absorption and adaptation, exporting can have significant positive spillovers to productivity. In countries in which exporters are already operating at the technology frontier, however, the stronger causality probably runs the other way—from productivity to exporting.

Abundant empirical evidence suggests that productivity is strongly associated with both the propensity to export as well as with volumes of exports (see Escribano, Pena, and Reis 2010). The same can be said about factor costs and availability, although labor skills can be considered a particularly important ingredient for export diversification in products and markets. In particular, endowments of human capital seem to be one of the key determinants of comparative advantage in services, an area of trade presenting continuous expansion in recent years (cf. Mattoo 2009).

Main Components of Analysis of Productivity A firm's productivity depends on a wide range of factors—the two most important proximate determinants are (1) the costs and quality of the inputs employed in the production, especially labor and capital, and delivering processes[11]; and (2) the efficiency with which the firm employs its resources. In addition, structural features such as the potential for

---

Box 2.13. Channels Linking Trade and Productivity

Bloom, Sadun, and Van Reenen (2009) document that Chinese import competition in the European Union led to both within-firm technology upgrading and between-firm reallocation of employment toward more technologically intensive plants. In this strand of research, Cusolito (2009) shows that a reduction in trade barriers shifts firms' incentives away from horizontal innovations and toward the introduction of vertically superior goods. The theory underlying these results is that import competition encourages firms to improve the quality of existing products and to create more efficient production techniques to escape from foreign competition.

Arm's-length trade in intermediate inputs is another source of productivity gains. Offshoring enables a firm to relocate its relatively inefficient production process to external providers with cheaper and more efficient production capabilities. This allows the firm to turn its focus to areas where it has a comparative advantage and to expand output with the existing capacity. Evidence on this effect has been recently provided by Criscuolo and Leaver (2005) who show that there is a positive and robust impact of offshoring on productivity, both in the manufacturing and services sectors. The effect comes mainly from firms that are domestic and nonglobally engaged, that is, do not export and are not parts of a multinational firm.

Another channel between trade and productivity relates to FDI. Plant productivity could rise through the spillovers and linkages between foreign and local firms. The international exchange of goods and services opens channels of communication that facilitate the transmission of technical information. Firms in each country learn not only from the R&D projects undertaken locally but also from the novel experiments that are carried out abroad (Grossman and Helpman 1991). Integration also enlarges the markets in which firms operate, and by itself this effect increases the profit opportunity available from innovating. Finally, trade allows domestic firms to have access to a larger and highly qualified set of inputs needed to conduct R&D.[a]

Source: Authors.
Note: a. The evidence on the impact of trade on productivity is not conclusive. A growing body of work has suggested that exporting confers little or no benefit in the form of faster productivity growth at the plant level (Clerides, Lach, and Tybout 1998; Bernard and Jensen 1999; Delgado, Farinas, and Ruano 2002).

achieving scale economies will also impact productivity. Figure 2.6 illustrates these main factors. This figure is followed by a discussion of labor-related issues and technical efficiency scale; the discussion of intermediate inputs and backbone services is covered in the next section of this module.

Labor Markets and Skills

One of the main determinants of the costs of producing a good is labor, including both costs and skills. Labor costs are a function of the labor legislation and the structure of the market. The theory underlying government interventions in the labor market is based on the fact that free labor markets are imperfect, and as a consequence, there are rents in the employment relationship, which lead to both unfair and inefficient situations. The system of civil rights protections that applies to workers encompasses three bodies of law:

1. *Employment laws* govern the individual employment contract.
2. *Collective or industrial relations laws* regulate the bargaining, adoption, and enforcement of collective agreements, the organization of trade unions, and the industrial action by workers and employers.
3. *Social security laws* govern the social response to needs and conditions that have a significant impact on the quality of life, such as old age, disability, death, sickness, and unemployment.

Labor legislation may work through various channels to affect firm labor productivity and eventual profits. On the demand side, labor legislation may change the cost of employing workers (figure 2.7, arrow 1)—through minimum wages, payroll taxes, worker benefits—thus constraining firm labor force decisions, including hiring and firing, work shifts and the skill level of a firm's workforce (arrow 3). These effects on the size and composition of a firm's labor force will have implications for firm labor productivity directly (arrow 5) and indirectly through reduced level of R&D (arrows 6 and 7). On the supply side, labor legislation may create incentives for workers to maintain or sever employment contracts (arrow 2), which in turn will affect firm labor force investment decisions (arrow 8), with implications for the composition of a firm's labor force (arrow 4) or firm human capital investment and search budgets (arrow 8), again affecting the labor productivity and profits of firms directly (arrow 5) and indirectly (arrows 6 and 7). Notably, arrow 6 points in both directions.

Labor skills have an equally important role in the determination of productivity at both the firm and economy levels.[12] As discussed by Syverson (2010), much of the work in labor economics has focused on wages as the outcome of interest, whereas only a smaller set of work has looked at human capital's impact on productivity at the firm level. Recent work, however, using matched employer-employee data sets offered evidence on the importance of labor quality for a firm's productivity.[13]

Firm-Level Technical Efficiency

Controlling for external factors, the productivity of any firm is ultimately a function of the effectiveness with which its management makes use of the inputs available to it. This is captured in the concept of firm-level technical efficiency. Although TFP is classically obtained under the

Figure 2.6. The Main Determinants of Productivity at the Factory or Farm Gate

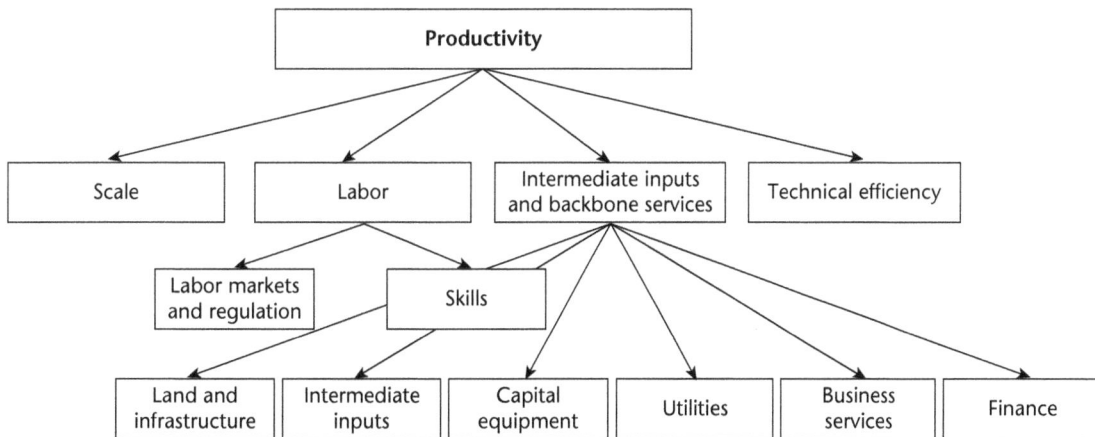

Figure 2.7. The Channels of Impact of Labor Legislation on Firm Productivity and Profits

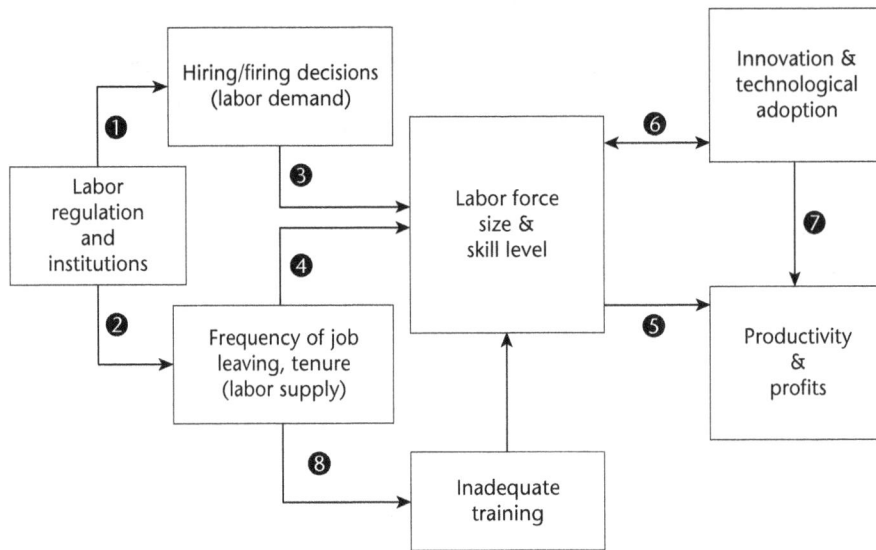

Source: Authors.

assumption that firms optimally allocate their inputs, the reality is that some producers may be systematically more successful in optimizing than others. Technical efficiency takes this fact into account and reflects the ability of a firm to minimize input use in the production of a given output level with no guarantee of achieving optimal allocation.[14] One can thus say that technical efficiency is analogous for firm-level analysis to TFP in macroeconomic and sectoral studies.

Among the most important determinants of technical efficiency is the level of education, training, and experience of its management. Indeed, ICAs have consistently highlighted the importance of management education and experience in firm-level outcomes. More recently, Bloom, Sadun, and Van Reenen (2009) developed a randomized experiment in India designed to measure whether management practices could be improved in badly managed firms and how much difference would result from management improvements. Early results suggested that management practices can be improved and that improvements in management practices may lead to large increases in performance—productivity levels rose by about 15 percent and profits by about 24 percent in the treatment firms compared with control firms.[15] In addition to management skills and experience, many firms (especially SMEs) suffer from lack of access to information on new technologies and methods of organizing production.

The average capacity utilization of a firm, which is the amount of output actually produced relative to the maximum amount that the firm could produce with the existing machinery and equipment, is often indicative of the efficiency with which the firm employs its fixed assets.

Factor Conditions: Intermediate Inputs and Backbone Services

Link with Competitiveness Challenges Identified in Trade Outcomes

Main components in intermediate inputs and backbone services	Competitiveness challenge areas			
	General export environment	Cost competitiveness	Product extension and quality	Market penetration
Scale economies	✓	✓		
Intermediate inputs	✓	✓		✓
Land and infrastructure	✓		✓	
Services inputs		✓	✓	

Quantitative Analysis: Indicators and Data Sources

	Measures	Sources
Scale	Median firm size (output, workers, exports, and so on); overall and exporters	Enterprise Surveys, national sources
	Number of firms in the sector; number exporting	Enterprise Surveys, national sources
	Level of intraindustry trade—domestic and regional	Comtrade (regional); national sources (input-output [I-O] tables)
Intermediates and capital equipment	Comparative regional/global prices of key production inputs	Country-specific analysis
	Tariffs on key inputs and capital equipment	WITS-TRAINS
	Domestic resources costs (DRC) of producing inputs in local market	Requires data on domestic and world prices and value added of inputs[a]
	"Machinery and equipment" price index	International Price Comparisons database
	Share of material inputs and machinery inputs sourced from domestic versus foreign markets	National sources (I-O tables)
Land and infrastructure	"Housing and utilities" price index	International Price Comparisons database
	"Construction" price index	
	Industrial land rent (per square mile) in main commercial city	National sources
	Factory rent (per square mile) in main commercial city	National sources
	Office rent (per square mile) in main commercial city	National sources
Backbone services, utilities	See "housing and utilities" above	International Price Comparisons database
	Electricity cost	National sources
	Electricity quality (value lost due to power outages)	World Bank Enterprise Surveys
	Water cost	National sources
	Water quality (value lost due to water shortages)	World Bank Enterprise Surveys
	ICT price basket	International Telecommunications Union (ITU)
	International internet bandwidth (bits/person)	WDI
	Fixed broadband Internet connection charge and monthly subscription	ITU
	"Communications" price index	International Price Comparisons database
Business services	Local supplier quantity and quality ratings	Global Competitiveness Index (WEF)

a. For a discussion and training presentation on calculating DRC, see http://www.fiscalreform.net/index.php?option=com_content&task=view&id=966&Itemid=1.

MODULE 2

Qualitative Analysis: Interview Targets and Issues for Discussion

Interview Targets

	Government agencies and ministries	Private sector and other institutions
Scale and structural features	• Ministry of Trade and Industry • Competition Agency	• Individual exporters (small/new and established) across traditional and emerging sectors • Export councils or industry associations
Inputs and backbone services	• Ministry of Trade and Industry • Ministry of Finance • Ministry of Energy/Communications • Utilities regulators • Customs Authority • State-operated industrial parks	• Individual exporters • Export councils or industry associations • Private utilities providers: electricity, water, telecommunications, IT • Industrial property developers • Banks and other financial institutions • Legal/accounting firms (or professional association)

Key Issues for Discussion in Interviews

Scale and structural features	• General trends in productivity in the economy/specific sectors • Trends in terms of capacity utilization in the economy/specific sectors • Has there been any significant merger activity/consolidations? Why or why not? • What is the participation of firms from outside the country in the value chain of key sectors? Is there any evidence of mergers or value chain integration on a regional basis? • What are the impediments to integration into global and regional values chains? • To what degree are external economies being exploited in industry agglomerations/clusters? What are the barriers to exploiting these opportunities?
Intermediate inputs and capital equipment	• Any major restrictions to imports of key raw materials? • Do existing programs allow for duty-free access or duty drawback on key raw materials? If so, how effective? What barriers to take-up? • Availability and cost of key inputs in the domestic market. • Any factors constraining availability of quality local inputs: scale, competition, protection, and so on? • What are the implications on competitiveness (cost, time, quality) of using imports versus local supply of key inputs? • Local or regional market access to capital equipment and main intermediates (industry-specific). • Any protection of local suppliers? • Any border restrictions on importing capital equipment or important inputs (tariffs, quotas, technical barriers)? If so, what is behind this? • Any restrictions imposed by exporters of capital equipment (collateral, terms, and so on)? • Availability of capital to finance equipment imports. • Any special programs for duty-free imports of capital equipment and/or intermediates? How effectively does it work?
Land and facilities	• To what degree is access to serviced land (or agricultural land) a problem? Is it an issue of space, titling, or regulation? • Any issues related to zoning, regulations, requirements to pay compensation, and so on? • Any issues around security of property rights? • Where are export-oriented sectors based and what is the land availability for them? • What reforms have taken place/are planned to address any legal and regulatory constraints to land access? • Are any special facilities available for FDI or export-oriented investors, including location, types of facilities, flexibility, and so on?
Backbone services—Utilities	• General situation with cost, access, and reliability of utilities—what are the main factors contributing to poor reliability? • Structure of the utilities sectors—who are the providers and what is the general state of competition? • What is the degree to which foreign investment is restricted in these sectors? • Role and effectiveness of the regulator. • Is there existing or planned PPP for delivery of power generation/distribution, water distribution, ICT, and so on? • Recent or future changes to regulatory structure.
Business services	• Access to quality business services in local market. • Services provided by local versus foreign firms. • Are there areas where no quality local services are provided?

MODULE 2

Tailoring the Diagnostics to Country and Sector Characteristics

Summary of Specific Considerations by Country Type

Country type	Relative priorities and issues for consideration
Small (population) and remote/ landlocked	• Scale issues may limit productivity potential in some sectors • Access to quality business services likely to be limited • Likely to be reliant on imports of many intermediates and capital equipment; therefore, importance on understanding trade policy and other barriers to this
Resource rich	• May have access to certain raw material inputs at advantageous cost—this may offer source of competitive advantage but may also act as a bias toward activities in which the country may not have comparative advantage • Depending on the resources available (coal, oil) energy costs could be a source of competitive advantage—is this in fact the case or are the rents being taken by a monopoly?
Low income, labor abundant	• Industry structure usually characterized by SMEs, so scale economies are a problem • Input costs (intermediates, utilities, capital equipment) often major barriers, but these are often policy induced and are not inherent
Middle income	• Achieving greater scale economies in production often a major opportunity • Focus on input markets (especially utilities) and moving toward greater competition and PPPs; trade barriers may remain for key inputs • Focus on inputs that will facilitate upgrading to services and knowledge-intensive sectors, particularly ICT (regulatory, rather than infrastructure, issues are probably most important)

Summary of Specific Considerations by Sector

Sector	Priorities and issues for consideration
Light manufacturing	• Access to cost-effective, quality raw materials is critical • Access to utilities also is critical in some subsectors • The importance of scale economies will vary significantly by subsector (for example, very important for textiles, but less so for garments)
Agriculture	• Scale issues often critical—both in terms of production (in many low-income countries, average farm sizes decline from generation to generation; many middle-income transition countries have shifted from large collectives to highly fragmented ownership structures) and also postharvest processes • Access to cost-effective inputs critical—important to understand government policies on tariffs and technical barriers to key inputs and capacity/quality of extension services • Land access issues (both for FDI and domestic investors) obviously fundamental as is core inputs infrastructure (for example, irrigation, power)
Tourism	• Land and infrastructure issues obviously important—policies on FDI can be important for land issues and PPP possibilities for infrastructure
Business and IT Services	• ICT infrastructure and pricing critical—regulatory and competition are the most important to understand

MODULE 2

Background Reading: Relationship Between Inputs and Backbone Services and Trade Competitiveness

Scale Economies

The potential to produce at an economically efficient scale can play an important role in determining productivity. While scale almost always plays some role, its influence varies significantly by sector. For example, producing at scale in textiles matters much more for competitiveness than in the manufacture of garments. Generally, the capital intensity of the sector will be closely related with the relative importance of scale. The potential to operate at scale may vary significantly across countries, both for structural and policy reasons. In general, larger countries (for example, China) are often in a better position to have firms operating on a large scale than in smaller countries. Ultimately, factors like market access, openness to FDI, and the degree of openness to cross-border trade mediate the potential for reaping scale economies, as it is frictions in trade and investment that prevent achieving scale through firm mergers and consolidation of value chains across or within countries.

In considering the role of scale economies, it is also important to recognize that scale economies can be realized externally as well as internally. This tends to be particularly important in sectors closer to the technology frontier, where requirements for specialization and other market uncertainties make the consolidation of activities within single firms less economically efficient (although it can also happen in traditional craft-linked sectors like clothing and footwear, for reasons linked to design, skills, and labor market factors). In this case, the emergence of proximate industry clusters (agglomerations) may offer the potential for reaping the benefits of scale externally, through access to deep pools of specialized labor and suppliers and through access to industry-specific public goods (for example, testing facilities, logistics platforms, and so on).

Production Inputs and Backbone Services

In addition to labor, firm productivity is also a function of the physical capital that it employs in the production process. This includes the cost and quality of land and facilities, capital equipment, intermediate inputs, and utilities.[16] It also includes the financing costs involved in employing these resources. Access to high-quality, efficiently priced inputs and backbone services can strengthen the export response to market access opportunities by lowering the costs of production and export. For almost all of these issues, analysis should focus on understanding the regulatory structure of the market and the degree of competition.

Intermediate Inputs and Capital Equipment

Local market availability (or availability of competitive local supply) and the impact of trade policy measures affect the degree to which firms can access materials and especially intermediate inputs cost effectively. In cases in which trade policy places tariffs or restrictions on imports, production costs rise; in cases in which local producers of these inputs are protected from international and domestic competition, quality eventually declines and productivity down the value chain faces knock-on effects.

Because most developing countries lack market scale and in many cases technical capacity, most of the capital equipment for production tends to be imported from abroad. This puts these countries at a competitive disadvantage from the start because of the higher transport costs involved in acquiring the equipment from abroad. In addition, in many developing countries, maintenance costs of equipment also rise significantly because of the need to bring in not only parts but also technicians from abroad (because of the lack of skills or proprietary knowledge of the equipment). The alternative in other firms is to not maintain or operate the equipment properly, shortening its usable life or lowering its day-to-day productivity. These disadvantages are compounded in many countries by factors like currency fluctuations, high costs of capital, and—most problematic—high tariffs and duties on capital equipment (although many

countries have schemes whereby producers can access capital equipment on a duty-free or reduced basis).

Land and Facilities

Access to land, and especially to serviced industrial land, is a major barrier to competitiveness in many countries. The challenge is often particularly acute for FDI, but it can affect local investors equally (or in some cases even more acutely, as foreign investors may have access to certain preferential arrangements for accessing facilities, for example, through SEZs). In addition to the simple availability of land and facilities, key issues that determine the impact on firm-level productivity include the following:

- *Location* where serviced land and facilities are available, in relation to labor markets and major transport infrastructure;
- *Time and cost of acquiring and registering the property*, including obtaining titles, if necessary;
- *Land costs*, including taxation;
- *Zoning*/regulatory issues, including the process of obtaining environmental and other permits;
- *Flexibility* of lease terms—in many sectors, investors seek to limit risk by taking on relatively short-term leases of factory "shells" or other units (for example, on leases as short as five years);
- *Quality* may be an issue in some locations and particularly in some industries—this relates particularly to industrial buildings and facilities for services activities (for example, high-end ICTES); and
- Security of property rights.

Utilities

Having access to relatively cost competitive and (most important) reliable power, water, and ICT services is a critical determinant of firm-level productivity. Indeed, evidence from ICA reports suggests that inadequate supply of electricity is one of the top two or three biggest constraints facing firms in most low-income countries. The key utilities that need to be considered include the following:

- *Power:* This may include gas, but in most cases the biggest issue is electricity. The relative importance of power costs and reliability will vary significantly by sector, with capital-intensive sectors (for example, aluminum) being extremely reliant on power costs as are many light-manufacturing sectors (like textiles and garments). ICT and other professional services sectors are also reliant on adequate power supply. The biggest issue for firms in many low-income countries is the lack of reliability of power supply, which results in many firms having to rely on generators (usually diesel-powered and often doubling or tripling the cost of power) or face long periods of production downtime.

- *Water:* Although not as critical across all sectors, access to quality, efficiently priced water is fundamental in most agricultural sectors as well as some manufacturing sectors (including iron, steel, and other metals as well as some agriprocessing activities like cocoa processing). Again, although cost is important, the issue of reliable access is usually paramount.
- *Telecommunications:* This includes fixed line and (increasingly more important) mobile telephony, and broadband Internet access. This is obviously most critical in the services sectors, particularly ICTES and other business services. Again, reliability issues are critical here, although access (especially to Internet bandwidth) is also an issue in many developing countries. Even more so than with electricity, price is often the biggest determinant of the degree to which telecommunications backbone services facilitate or hinder competitiveness.

In assessing the impact of utilities, the biggest issues tend to relate to infrastructure investments and (related to this)

market structure, including the degree of private sector participation and the level of competition in the market. In addition, the regulatory and tax regime will have an impact on cost structures.

Business Services The available and quality of local supply of business services can have an important impact on firm-level productivity. Specialized business services tend to agglomerate in larger markets and in larger cities (within markets) and so the level of choice and quality of such services may be limited in smaller, developing countries. Among such input services are accounting, legal, marketing, business strategy, printing and publishing, ICT, and industry-specific technical services (for example, research, testing, certification, and so on). In relatively unsophisticated sectors and those in which a country has been operating for some time, access to these business services inputs is likely to have only limited impact on competitiveness. These services, however, play a bigger role in the establishment and development of new firms and particularly in new sectors.

MODULE 2

Factor Conditions: Trade Facilitation and Logistics

> **Note to the Practitioner:** This section addresses issues related to trade facilitation and logistics. Analysts looking to conduct a comprehensive analysis of the transport and trade facilitation environment should consult "Trade and Transport Facilitation Assessment: A Practical Toolkit for Country Implementation" (TTFA; World Bank 2010d). This document (available in hard copy and CD-ROM from the World Bank International Trade Department) provides a detailed, step-by-step program for analyzing the trade facilitation and logistics environment in any country. This section draws heavily from the TTFA, but the information presented here is less detailed. The analyst will be guided to various parts of the TTFA, where appropriate.

Link with Competitiveness Challenges Identified in Trade Outcomes

Main components in trade facilitation and logistics	Competitiveness challenge areas			
	General export environment	Cost competitiveness	Product extension and quality	Market penetration
Distance	✓	✓	✓	✓
Inbound trade facilitation and logistics		✓		✓
Outbound trade facilitation and logistics	✓	✓	✓	✓

Quantitative Analysis: Indicators and Data Sources

	Indicators	Sources
Cost	• Export cost (by land and sea/air) • Import cost (by land and sea/air) • Cost to export and import	Logistics Performance Index (LPI)
	• Cost per kilogram (kg) for a 500 kg shipment by air (benchmark to key markets)	*Doing Business* Freight forwarders
Time and reliability	• Export time (by land and sea/air) • Import time (by land and sea/air) • LPI score (overall)	LPI, *Doing Business*
	• *Doing Business*; Trading Across Borders(overall; time to export and import)	
	• Percent of value lost in transit because of breakage or theft	World Bank Enterprise Surveys
Distance	• Distance to markets by sea and road	LPI, websites of shipping lines, other shipping related websites (for example, portworld.com; e-ships.net; distances.com)
Connectivity	• Liner shipping connectivity index	UNCTAD
	• Air traffic statistics	International Air Transport Association (IATA)
Physical infrastructure	• Infrastructure score	LPI
Customs and trade facilitation	• Customs score	LPI
	• Clearance time: with and without inspection; import and export	LPI; World Bank Enterprise Surveys
	• Physical inspection rate	LPI
Transport and logistics services	• Logistics quality and competence score • Tracking and tracing score • International shipments score	LPI

Note that in large countries, national metrics on costs, time, and reliability performance may have little relevance for some producers, particularly those in more peripheral regions. As such, it may be necessary to collect some data at the subnational level. Although comparative data may be limited, it may be possible in some countries to map out market access to and from nearby ports and airports, to get performance statistics on specific ports, and (making use of World Bank Enterprise Surveys or national manufacturing census) to get an indication on relative shipping costs, customs clearance times, and other performance criteria at a subnational level. *For additional sources of data on a wide range of transport and logistics related factors that may be included in the Diagnostic, please refer to the World Bank's TTFA Toolkit* (World Bank 2010d).

Qualitative Analysis: Interview Targets and Issues for Discussion

Interview Targets

Importers and exporters	Export manufacturers and other producers
	Importers: manufacturers, wholesalers, retailers, traders
Transport service providers	Road transport
	Railways
	Ocean shipping
	Air freight
	Container terminal operator
Logistics service providers	Customs—land border
	Customs—international gateway
	Clearing and forwarding agent
	Integrated third-party logistics (3PLs)
	Consolidator, storage
	Bonded warehouse operator
	Free zone operator
	Banks
Government ministries and agencies	Commerce and trade
	Finance
	Transport
	Agriculture
	Health
	Export promotion agencies
	Preshipment inspection

Issues to be covered during the interviews will necessarily depend somewhat on the supply chains being studied, as well as on country and region-specific factors.

Key Issues for Discussion in Interviews

Exporters and importers	• Type of commodities exported, volumes shipped, and how this has been changing
	• Role of logistics in improving competitiveness of exports
	• Integration of outbound supply chain for principal exports
	• Regulatory procedures significantly increasing documentation, cost, and time for shipments
	• Role of ICT in simplifying transactions, including managing orders, expediting regulatory procedures, and coordinating logistics shipments
	• Problems caused by quality of transport infrastructure and operations, including ports and border crossings
	• Opportunities for mitigating these problems
Road transport	• Principal trades (commodities and routes) handled and volumes shipped
	• Value added services offered
	• Description of typical supply chain for shippers
	• Fleet size and truck types
	• Vehicle annual productivity
	• Typical shipping times and rates
	• Mechanisms for increasing load factors and reducing empty backhauls
	• Use of information and computer technology for contracting trucking services and managing fleets
	• Impact of other government regulation on quality and competitiveness of services
	• Effect of taxes, tolls, and formal and informal road checks on intrastate movements
	• Impact of quality and capacity of the road network on transport time, cost, and reliability
	• Problems with security on primary routes and impact on time and cost
	• Other impediments to improving trucking services
	• Existing programs or proposals to overcome these impediments

MODULE 2

Railways	• Principal foreign trades (commodities and routes) handled and volumes shipped
	• Unit train operations: scheduled and on-demand
	• Value added services offered
	• Description of typical supply chain for shippers using rail service
	• Contractual arrangements and performance standards included in agreements
	• Typical shipping times and rates
	• Procedures for pricing services including backhauls
	• Use of information and computer technology for arranging shipments and scheduling movements
	• Impact of condition and utilization of the rail network on transport time, cost, and reliability
	• Other impediments to improving rail services
	• Existing programs or proposals to overcome these impediments
Ocean shipping	• Principal trades (commodities routes and TEUs[a])
	• Vessel size by route
	• Complementary services offered
	• Description of supply chains for typical consignees and shippers
	• Primary direction for loaded containers and efforts to improve balance
	• Typical shipping times and rates
	• Typical dwell time for containers inbound and outbound
	• Difficulties with clearing containers
	• Electronic transfer of ship manifests, load plans, and other information to expedite movement of cargo and vessels
	• Other government regulatory procedures affecting efficiency of shipping services
	• Impact of quality and capacity of the port facilities and services on transport time, cost, and reliability
	• Other impediments to improving shipping services
	• Existing programs or proposals to overcome these impediments
Air freight (only when the country has a sector that makes significant use of air freight)	• Principal trades (commodities and routes) handled and volumes shipped
	• Value added services offered
	• Aircraft capacity and frequency
	• Primary direction for cargo and efforts to improve balance
	• Description of typical supply chains for shippers and consignees
	• Typical dwell time for inbound cargo
	• Typical shipping times and rates
	• Information and computer technology used for arranging shipments and submitting shipping documents
	• Impact of other government regulation on quality and competitiveness of services
	• Impact of quality and capacity of the airport on efficiency and cost
	• Other impediments to improving airfreight services
	• Existing programs or proposals to overcome these impediments
Container terminal operator	• Principal shipping lines served and trades
	• Traffic volume (vessels and TEU)
	• Vessel size by route
	• Berth and crane productivity
	• Value added services offered
	• Description of typical landside and waterside logistics
	• Terminal handling charge
	• Typical dwell time for containers inbound and outbound
	• Difficulties with clearing containers
	• Congestion in land access to the terminal
	• Impact of other port infrastructure on efficiency
	• Use of information technology for managing storage and berth, scheduling container movements, and notifying shippers and consignees
	• Other impediments to improving shipping services
	• Existing programs or proposals to overcome these impediments
Customs	• Type and volume of activity
	• Principal enforcement responsibility and performance targets
	• Primary source of violations
	• Procedures for clearing inbound and outbound cargo

- Impact of complex regulations on efficiency and effectiveness
- Efforts to modernize processes and increase transparency, including automation and risk management
- Efforts to move clearance activities off the border and to allow movement of goods in transit
- Other problems preventing more efficient and transparent activities
- Opportunities for mitigating these problems.

Clearing and forwarding agents; integrators and 3PLs; consolidator; warehouse operator; free zone operator	- Principal trades (commodities and routes) handled and volumes shipped - Range of logistics services provided including value added - Priorities of clients in term of time, cost and reliability - Ways to establish competitive advantage - Responsibilities for clearing cargo, typical clearance times and problems with clearance procedures - Government regulation that limit type of services and markets served - Use of computerization and modern communications for contracting, scheduling, and coordinating services - Impediments to improving the quality of services - Existing programs or proposals to overcome these impediments
Ministry of Trade and Ministry of Finance	- Role of trade in economy - Reduction of regulation of trade, import, and export - Use of revenue targets for customs - Efforts to simplify customs procedures
Ministry of Transport	- Plans to improve quality of transport infrastructure serving foreign trade, including ports and airports - Procedures and effectiveness of regulations of road safety, security, overloading, and vehicle roadworthiness - Efforts to improve quality and utilization of long distance trucking services - Commercialization and privatization of cargo-handling facilities at ports and airports - Efforts to simplify regulation of truck operators, licensing, rates, and area of operation
Ministry of Agriculture; Ministry of Health	- Principal regulatory responsibilities - Most important commodities that require regulation - Source of greatest threats - Authority responsible for notification of arrival of controlled goods - What are the sources of alerts - Use of risk profiling to determine whether to inspect and test the cargo
Ministry of Agriculture; Ministry of Health	- Proportion of the shipments physically inspected and typical time required - Efforts to develop secure supply chains - Proportion of controlled shipments subjected to laboratory tests and time required - Efforts to simplify regulations - Efforts to improve efficiency and transparency of regulatory procedures - Efforts to improve exchange of information regarding alerts among agencies and with shippers - Other impediments to increasing the efficiency of regulatory function - Existing programs or proposals to overcome these impediments

a. Twenty-foot Equivalent Units—these are intermodal shipping containers.

Analytical Approach

Assessing a country's trade facilitation and logistics environment requires looking at a wide range of issues—including trade-related infrastructure, transport, and logistics services—and at several border and behind-the-border procedures. Table 2.3 summarizes the main components of the trade facilitation and logistics environment that should be covered in a basic assessment. Table 2.3 is based on the *TTFA* framework but is presented here in a reduced form with the aim of conducting a high-level assessment on a countrywide basis. If the analyst requires a more in-depth assessment, for example, wanting to explore in more detail

the institutions and regulations that govern the trade facilitation environment or wanting to understand supply-chain-related issues in a specific sector), the analyst may wish to widen the scope of the analysis. In this case, the analyst is directed to the *TTFA Toolkit* (World Bank 2010d), where additional details on policy issues can be found—specifically, see Table C1 and Box C1 of the *TTFA Toolkit*.

The approach outlined in this section is based on a scaled-down version of the Phase 1 assessment developed in the *TTFA* (World Bank 2010d).

Once the objectives of the assessment are defined, the key starting point is to identify a limited set of commodities

Table 2.3. Summary of Main Components of Trade Facilitation and Logistics Assessment

Components	Policy areas and main issues
Trade logistics performance	**Tools and institutions to measure and assess logistics performance**
a. Trade logistics patterns	a. Statistical instruments for trade in volume
1. Availability of statistics, sources	b. Logistics performance on main routes and at gateway in terms of cost, time, and reliability
2. Volume by routes, modes, and gateway	
3. Main commodities in volume	
b. Logistics performance: cost, time, reliability on the main routes; arbitrage costs reliability by exporter and importers, specific commodities	
c. Other issues: economies of scale, backload	
Availability, quality, and performance of services	**Regulation of transport and logistics services**
a. Logistics competence: practices and skills with consignees	a. Licensing of transport—equipment and operations
b. Trucking market structure	b. Effectiveness of freight regulations (e.g., axle load)
c. Trucking operational performance	c. Domestic and regional regulation of long-distance transport
d. Freight-forwarding and integration	**Quality, reliability of logistics services**
e. Customs brokers	a. Foreign participation in logistics services
f. Railways services	b. Availability of value added logistics services, and conducive regulations
g. Express	c. Access to information on available services
h. Banking and insurance	
i. Warehousing, 3PLs (3rd party logistics)	
j. Others: air cargo, river services	
Trade and customs facilitation	**Customs modernization**
a. Coordination, transparency, security and IT	a. Transparency and consistency of customs clearance procedures
b. Customs clearance	b. Improvement of clearance and border facilities (physical and IT).
c. Customs regimes	c. Introduction of modern practices conducive of professionalism (risk management, authorized operators)
d. Import and export chains, main steps, and structure of delays	d. Coordination among border agencies and procedural consistency with customs
International connectivity and transit systems	**Transit regime**
a. Transit systems	a. Transit systems applicable on international road and rail corridors
b. Port/shipping connectivity	b. Reduction of controls at the border and en route
c. Customs performance	c. Domestic and regional regulation of entry of transit operators
d. Facilitation of multimodal transportation	**Air and sea connectivity and liberalization of services**
	a. Air transport services, passenger, and cargo
	b. Shipping services, impact of feeder services
Trade supporting infrastructure	**Public infrastructure**
a. Roads	a. Adequacy of maintenance funding and policies
b. Ports	b. Port development
c. Railroad	c. Improvement in service delivery (price and quality) and private participation.
d. Airports	d. Development of logistics hubs, such as logistics centers (in or not in free zones), inland clearance facilities, and dry ports/inland container depots
e. Other backbone infrastructure	e. Addressing congestion problems in rural areas
	f. IT infrastructure

Source: World Bank 2010d.

and products and trade relationships on which to focus. This is necessary because the structure of the supply chain, the nature of transport, and the regulations and procedures involved will vary significantly across products—for example, the trade logistics issues facing an exporter of fresh-cut flowers vary dramatically from those facing an exporter of coal or of consumer electronics. It will be critical to address the import side of supply chains, as this is where many of the biggest performance gaps are found. Selection of the supply chains to study should focus on those supply chains that represent particularly important export sectors or potential new opportunities. Decisions on selection should balance the needs of comprehensiveness and strategic importance with potential implications of time, cost, and complexity.

Following this, desk research can be undertaken—in most countries, significant existing research is likely to have been conducted in recent years by the World Bank and other development partners. This can provide valuable background input before undertaking field interviews.

In conducting the analysis, it is valuable to try to understand the degree to which the constraints are related to the transport environment or the border and trade facilitation environment. Experience shows that in many countries in which problems exist in the transport environment, the border environment is also poor. Indeed, in many cases some links will exist between the two. In cases in which it is possible to isolate the main sources of constraint, however, identifying the policy levers to address it will be a much easier task. One way to begin to focus the direction of the analysis is through the first stage of comparing performance through benchmarking key quantitative metrics (see next section). For example, if analyzing Rwanda, a quick look at its relative performance across the LPI measures (see figure 2.8) suggests that customs and infrastructure are major constraints that should be assessed.

Institutions and regulations play a major underlying role in establishing the trade facilitation environment, and so they are likely to be at least part of the problem, wherever constraints exist. For the purposes of the Diagnostic, however, the framework does not focus on understanding institutions and regulations in detail. Rather, the emphasis is in trying to identify broadly the observable areas in the trade facilitation environment in which the binding constraints exist. A second stage of work could then drill down into understanding the institutional and regulatory factors behind this. For analysts who wish to address these issues in more depth, the *TTFA Toolkit* (World Bank 2010d) provides a guide to assessing institutional and regulatory issues.

Finally, the analytical framework described here is designed to analyze a country's overall trade and transport facilitation environment. In many countries, the analyst may wish to assess specific export sectors. Although the above framework may still be adopted for a sector-specific analysis, the analyst may want to consider making use of *value chain analysis*, to study the sector in greater depth, including understanding the impact of the inbound trade logistics environment in shaping access to competitive inputs.

MODULE 2

Figure 2.8. Comparison of Rwanda LPI Performance

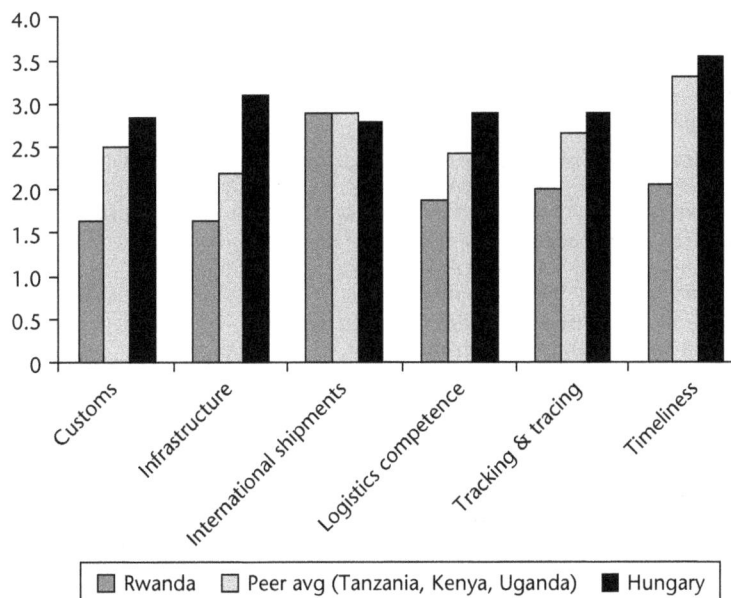

Tailoring the Diagnostics to Country and Sector Characteristics

Summary of Specific Considerations by Country Type

Country type	Relative priorities	Other issues for consideration
Landlocked	• May need to emphasize role of air transport (depending on export sectors) • Greater emphasis on border-related issues (including customs and other border processes) as well as transit regimes and cross-border trade regulation	• Likely to be necessary to extend analysis to cover regulations, processes, and agencies in bordering (especially those where the main regional port is based) • Corridor analysis may be a useful approach • Cost and time comparisons should include benchmarks against other landlocked countries • Landlocked countries may have potential to develop logistics sector as important regional transit hubs
Small (population) and remote	• Greater emphasis on speed and efficiency of logistics environment • Greater emphasis on role of air transport • Exporters tend to be more dependent on imported inputs—so emphasis on efficiency of inbound supply chains	• Small and remote countries often also landlocked • Explore the implications of scale in logistics costs and the potential for improving consolidation in supply chains • Lack of scale increases importance of ensuring local logistics market is open to foreign service providers
Resource rich	• Existing infrastructure and supply chains often designed for resource extraction; focus on understanding effectiveness of supply chains (for example, rail and ports systems as well as customs and trade facilitation) to support export diversification	
Low income, labor abundant	• No specific focus inherent to these countries—often face challenges across the board	
Middle income	• Emphasis on processes, institutions, and supply chain issues	

Summary of Specific Considerations by Sector

Sector	Relative priorities	Other issues for consideration
Light manufacturing	• High reliance on imported inputs in most light-manufacturing sectors requires a focus on inbound logistics processes • Clearance speed and processes often critical (outbound and inbound) • Air transport will also be a important channel for some subsectors	• Many sectors will have special customs regimes for imported inputs designed for export manufacture
Agriculture	• Perishability of many agricultural products means that cold chain networks (including infrastructure and transport/logistics services) should be a priority • For bulk commodities, rail and even river-based transport infrastructure and services tends to be more important than it is in other sectors • Border-related issues are critical, linked to both tariff and nontariff barriers (health and safety)	• Individual agricultural sectors often have quite customized logistics networks that will need to be analyzed closely
Tourism	• Traditional logistics issues are relevant for supply side of the sector, but otherwise focus is on the passenger transport network—especially road and air transport • Primary emphasis on connectivity and cost (internal and to key source markets)—infrastructure and services are critical, as are institutions and regulatory issues (for example, air transport liberalization)	• Quantitative and qualitative analysis should focus on connectivity, which may require assessment not only of focus country but also of its main tourism source markets • Assessment of public transport systems and of safety and security may also need to be included in the analysis
Business and IT services	• As with tourism, the traditional logistics issues are less relevant for this sector—primary focus will be on the passenger transport network and issues of connectivity	• Note that the logistics services sector may itself be a focus of assessment, in which case all aspects of the logistics environment in the country will be important in the assessment.

MODULE 2

Background Reading: Relationship Between Trade Facilitation and Logistics and Trade Competitiveness

For exporters in many developing countries, comparative advantage is eroded step by step across the miles between production and markets. Distance alone will, in many sectors, determine the potential to compete in international markets. But more controllable factors, such as transport and communications infrastructure, border-related processes, and local logistics markets, will play a critical role in shaping exporters' competitiveness through their impact on cost, time, and supply chain reliability.

Indeed, in recent decades, the role of trade facilitation and logistics as a source of trade competitiveness has increased substantially. This is for two main reasons. First, with increased trade liberalization, the transactions costs imposed by trade facilitation environment have become, in most cases, more significant than tariffs. Second, the emergence of highly integrated global production networks and the shortening of product life cycles has raised the importance of timely and cost-effective logistics. Thus, the cost and quality of the logistics environment often play an important role in determining firm-level decisions about where to locate production, where to source supplies, and how to serve consumer markets.

Data from the LPI (World Bank 2010a) show a clear relationship between logistics performance and exports (see figure 2.9). Empirical literature tracing the effect of trade facilitation constraints on trade flows, while limited by the difficulties of properly measuring these barriers, shows unequivocal impacts of time and costs on developing country exports and particularly perishable agricultural products (Djankov, Freund, and Pham 2006) and on the composition of trade (Li and Wilson 2009).

Developing countries tend to suffer from myriad issues—including poor infrastructure, inefficient systems,

corruption, and lack of competitive logistics markets—that contribute to high cost and unpredictable trade logistics environments (see box 2.14)

Trade facilitation and logistics affects export competitiveness through several channels. Although structural factors like distance may act as an absolute barrier to participation in exports markets (in certain sectors), the main channels through which trade facilitation impacts export competitiveness are through transactions costs and risk (which is a function of time and reliability). These are summarized briefly in the remainder of this section.

Direct Costs of Exporting and Importing The direct cost of exporting includes, among other things the cost of transport, insurance, fees to logistics service providers (for example, freight forwarders), and administrative fees for customs and other border procedures. The largest component of these costs is transport and, in this regard, two of the biggest determinants are *distance to market* and *the transport mode* required. Indeed, landlocked countries—which tend to be located far from markets but, most important, are forced to ship much greater distances by ground transport rather than sea transport—tend to face much greater direct costs of exporting. For exporters with products that are particularly time sensitive (for example, because they are physically perishable), reliance on air transport raises costs dramatically—the cost for air freight is typically four to five times that of road transport and 12 to 16 times that of sea transport (World Bank 2009a). Cut flower exports, for example, often incur air transport costs of up to 50 percent of cost, insurance, freight (CIF) value.

Scale economies also affect transport costs. In small economies, the costs of maintaining trade-related infrastructure (both public and private sector) raise the costs

Figure 2.9. Relationship Between Logistics Performance and Exports, 2008

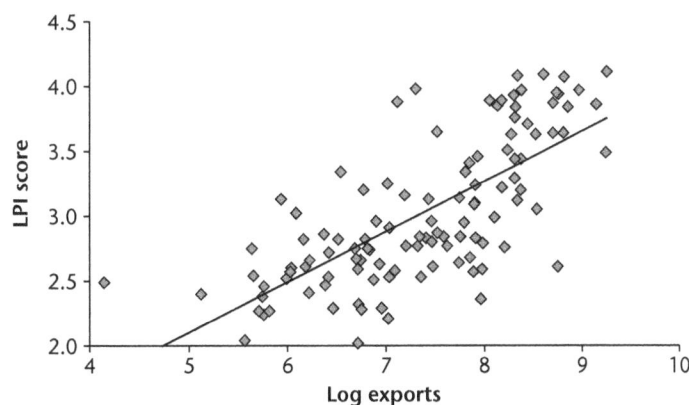

Sources: World Bank 2010a; COMTRADE (US$ exports, 2008).

Box 2.14. The Gap Between Industrial and Developing Countries in Trade Logistics

High logistics costs and low levels of service are a barrier to trade and FDI and thus to economic growth. Countries with higher overall logistics costs are more likely to miss the opportunities of globalization. Take landlocked Chad. Importing a 20-foot container from Shanghai to its capital N'djamena takes about 10 weeks at a cost of $6,500. Importing the same container to a landlocked country in western or central Europe would take about four weeks and cost less than $3,000. The shipping costs and delays from Shanghai to Douala, the gateway for Chad, and to West European ports are essentially the same. And the same international freight forwarding company would handle the container from Douala to N'djamena and within Europe. But what accounts for the large difference in time and cost?

The answer lies in better processes, higher-quality services, and the operating environment. The forwarder in Europe would use a seamless, paperless system to manage the inland shipment from its eight-hectare campus in the gateway port of Le Havre. The transport inside Europe would take less than three days. And to add value for its client and generate more business, the forwarder would provide additional services, such as improving the client's internal distribution practices.

In Chad, the process would be different. Although only five days should be needed to move the container from Douala to N'djamena, the actual time likely would be as long as five weeks. In a difficult governance and security environment, the freight-forwarding company would be trying simply to avoid a breakdown in its client's supply chain. It would maintain company staff along the trade corridor to physically track the goods and trade documents. And it would have to be ready to mediate with the trucking syndicate, the security forces, and myriad government agencies.

Source: World Bank 2010a.

---

for exporters. Moreover, exporters are often unable to take advantage of less-than-truckload or shared container shipments, and the lack of two-way traffic means they must often bear the cost of shipping empty containers or trucks.

Beyond mode, distance, and scale, however, other factors—which are in theory more controllable—shape the transactions costs involved in exporting. One of the most important of these is the *level of competition* in local transport and logistics markets. In many markets, transport and logistics services operate as oligopolies or engage in collusion (for example, *tour de role*) to maintain high prices (and usually poor service). Regulations that often restrict the provision of services from foreign transport providers contribute to uncompetitive local markets in many countries. On top of competition, other factors include *high fees for customs and other documentation, high port and handling charges, the need to hire agents to facilitate clearance, and the need to pay bribes to facilitate the movement of goods.*

Induced Costs: Time, Risk, and Reliability Perhaps even more important than the direct costs are the induced costs that firms must bear related to timeliness, and particularly, reliability of the trade and transport facilitation environment. Time in itself raises costs, in terms of *financing, insurance, and warehousing.* Research by Hummels (2001) finds that each day saved in shipping time is worth 0.8 percent ad valorem for manufactured goods. In West Africa, for example, additional delays from other sources—including goods being held in customs at the port, border crossing delays, and formal and informal road

checkpoint—combine to make round-trip times for a 2,000 km journey as much as 40 days in the region (that is, an average of only 50 km per day). This has significant implications on the capital utilization of the transport fleet in the region and subsequently on the cost of trade. Although the average monthly mileage for trucks in Southern African regional transport is 8,000–9,000 km, in countries like Mali and Niger, it is no more than 2,500 km (Egis BCEOM International 2008).

The most important issue is the predictability and reliability of the supply chain. The absence of predictability and reliability raises risks for firms, forcing them to hedge, for example, *by carrying greater inventory* of supplies and end products, to source from alternative suppliers, or to shift to air transport or other more expensive modes to meet delivery schedules. According to the World Bank's *LPI,* suppliers to the same automobile manufacturer will carry seven days of inventory in Italy, but 35 days in Morocco; and garment exporters in Bangladesh have to export, on average, 10 percent of production by air to be certain to meet the schedules of European buyers.

Finally, most exporters (particularly those operating in these global value chains) also rely on *importing* critical raw materials and intermediate inputs from international suppliers. As such, all the direct and indirect costs discussed in this section also raise production and inventory costs for exporters. The impact of poor reliability in the trade and logistics environment imposes a significant opportunity cost on exporters, restricting their ability to diversify into higher value added production and to integrate into global value chains, both of which rely on predictable, just-in-time production and delivery.

Trade Promotion Infrastructure: Export and Investment Promotion

Link with Competitiveness Challenges Identified in Trade Outcomes

Main components in export and investment promotion	Competitiveness challenge areas			
	General export environment	Cost competitiveness	Product extension and quality	Market penetration
Export promotion	✓	✓	✓	✓
Investment promotion		✓		✓

Note: Trade Finance is covered in the section "Access to Finance."

Quantitative Analysis: Indicators and Data Sources

	Indicators	Sources
Export-promotion agencies (EPA)	Exports per US$ EPA budget	World Bank EPA survey
	EPA budget (percent GDP or per capita)	
	Share of EPA expenditure: market research/information; training/tech support; marketing/other	
	Share of EPA expenditure by main sector	
	Share of EPA expenditure: new versus established exporters	
Investment-promotion agencies (IPA)	FDI flows and stock (share of GDP; per capita)	UNCTAD
	FDI flows and stock per US$ IPA budget	National sources; IMF
	IPA performance score: overall	World Bank Global Investment Promotion Benchmarking (GIPB)
	IPA performance score: website	
	IPA performance score: enquiry handling	

Qualitative Analysis: Interview Targets and Issues for Discussion

	Government agencies and ministries	Private sector and other institutions
EPA	• EPA (national and, if relevant regional) • Ministry of Trade and Industry or other ministry with responsibility for export promotion	• Individual exporters (small/new and established) across traditional and emerging sectors • Training institutions • Export councils or associations • Consultants/service providers
IPA	• IPA (national and, if relevant, regional) • Ministry of Trade and Industry or other ministry with responsibility for investment promotion • Agencies responsible for company registration, land purchase, and registration • Embassies of major investors	• Existing investors—across traditional and emerging markets and sectors • Potential new investors (or investors considering the country) • Chambers of commerce • Industry associations

Key Issues for Discussion in Interviews with Government Agencies and Ministries

EPA	• Structure of the EPA: Single or multiple agencies? Links to government ministries? Structure of executive board and level of private-sector participation on the board? • Management structure: Is it operated by the private sector? • Structure of budget and sources of funding? • Is there a broad sector focus to export promotion support activities? • Is there a focus on nontraditional exports? • Is there a focus on new exporters versus established? Also small versus large firms? • What is the focus on breaking into new markets versus survival of existing exporters? • What efforts are made to track support on an ongoing basis? • What is the focus of information provision? • What is the focus on marketing and trade fairs? • What is the focus of training and capacity building—regulatory compliance, documentation, accessing trade finance, logistics and customs, packaging, pricing, and so on? • What is the focus on regional markets versus major global markets? For the latter, on the European Union versus the United States, Japan, China, and/or other markets?

MODULE 2

IPA
- Structure of the IPA: Links to government ministries? Structure of executive board and level of private sector participation on the board?
- Structure of budget and sources of funding?
- What is the emphasis of efforts between image building, investment attraction, aftercare, and policy advocacy?
- What are the main targets in terms of sectors and markets?
- What explicit links are made between the IPA and the EPA?
- What incentives are offered and how important are these in the overall offering to potential investors?

Key Issues for Discussion in Interviews with the Private Sector and Other Institutions

EPA
- What are the main challenges in terms of entering and staying in export markets?
- Are there specific markets (product or geographic) that are seen as high opportunity or a particular challenge?
- How effective is the EPA and other government support agencies? What are the main strengths and weaknesses?
- To what degree are the main challenges related to marketing? Building contacts/networks in export markets? Meeting technical/regulatory requirements? Other?

IPA
- What are the main requirements for investors in terms of infrastructure, regulatory framework, transport, incentives, and so on?
- To what degree have they invested in Country X to access local markets or to establish a base for exporting?
- How do they view Country X as a location for investment? Across sectors and relative to alternatives in the region?
- What are the main advantages and disadvantages of the country as an export platform?

Tailoring the Diagnostics to Country and Sector Characteristics

Summary of Specific Considerations by Country Type

Country type	Relative priorities and issues for consideration
Small (population) and remote/landlocked	• Strategic prioritization across all aspects of trade promotion will be critical given limited resources • Importance of targeted and efficient EPAs and IPAs
Resource rich	• Emphasis on use of trade-promotion tools to support diversification—EPA and IPA roles likely to be priorities • Does the program of trade promotion effectively leverage the existing natural resources sectors (by facilitating development of supply and services sectors/clusters)?
Low income, labor abundant	• Strategic prioritization across all aspects of trade promotion will be critical given limited resources • Importance of targeted and efficient EPAs and IPAs
Middle income	• Often the main issues will focus on adjustment processes and moving to higher value added activities—how does the incentive system, and the wider programs of trade promotion, support facilitate efficient adjustment (toward sources of comparative advantage) versus support traditional sectors? • Analysis of EPA and trade promotion may focus more on survival and effectiveness in reaching nontraditional markets

Summary of Specific Considerations by Sector

Sector	Relative priorities and issues for consideration
Light manufacturing	• The need to move beyond traditional promotion activities to training, market information, and other enterprise support • For any sector-specific analysis, check on IPAs expertise in the sector and their links with sector bodies • Importance of link between EPA and IPA with regard to attracting investment in export-oriented activities/global production networks
Agriculture	• Many EPAs and IPAs have limited expertise in this area • Role of state trading firms or marketing monopolies in export promotion
Tourism	• Focus analysis beyond EPA/IPA to tourist board or related agency, which may control all investment and export promotion in the sector
Business and IT services	• Assess capacity of EPA for addressing services sector needs

Background Reading: Relationship Between Export and Investment Promotion and Trade Competitiveness

Establishing and maintaining competitiveness in export markets requires not only getting the microeconomic environment right to support exporters and ensuring investment is channeled to the firms and sectors that are most able to exploit sources of comparative advantage, but also addressing market and information failures, providing public goods, and improving coordination and the diffusion of knowledge and best practices. Governments play an

MODULE 2

important role—through EPAs and IPAs—in the provision of a broad range of instruments designed to support exporters and to attract investment in export-oriented activities. Table 2.4 provides a summary for each, including their purpose, the reasons for government intervention, and how these interventions might support competitiveness of firms or the export sector more widely. Trade and investment support focuses largely on the *extensive margin*— on new products and new markets—although many measures listed in in the table will affect the intensive margin, particularly in terms of addressing *export survival* and facilitating *quality upgrading* within existing products.

Although these interventions can all be defended as addressing some form of market, information, or coordination failure, it is by no means certain that they represent efficient or effective mechanisms to promote trade competitiveness. It can be argued that, in many cases, some of these interventions are in fact distortions to competitiveness that not only may harm trading partners by artificially changing the terms of trade but also undermine competitiveness in the long term. Conversely, some interventions by EPAs and IPAs are designed to address problems of information and coordination failure that can be particularly acute in export markets.

Export Promotion (Agencies)

Trade-promotion support is designed to help existing and potential exporters to understand the requirements of export markets (tastes, standards, regulatory requirements) and to identify and exploit markets for their products. In most cases, this support is delivered through an EPA. The case for government intervention to support exporters is usually made on the basis of the (mostly nonrival) entry barriers to exporting (for example, high fixed costs of making contacts, establishing distribution networks, learning about compliance, obtaining licenses), which in particular would deter "pioneer" exporters (Hausmann and Rodrik 2002).

There has been limited empirical analysis of the effectiveness of EPAs, but recent evidence (Lederman,

Olarreaga, and Payton 2009) finds that they have a positive and statistically significant impact on national exports, with important heterogeneity. First, returns to EPAs increase in line with GDP per capita—that is, richer countries have more effective EPAs (or EPAs can be more effective in richer countries). Second, they find decreasing returns to EPA spending, with negative marginal returns after US$1 per capita. Finally, the return on investment in EPAs was highest in Eastern Europe and Asia, with agencies in the Middle East and North Africa lagging furthest behind.

The impact of trade-promotion support on competitiveness comes by supporting "discovery" as well as by improving exporters' technical capabilities to participate in export markets. Essentially, trade promotion reduces start-up costs and lowers risk, and it potentially facilitates *higher-quality* and *lower-cost* exports. In terms of discovery, trade-promotion support can help exporters find and access product-market combinations that they otherwise might not be able to exploit. This means there may be a potential for economy-wide efficiency impacts from export promotion, in terms of helping *deepen specialization* in areas of comparative advantage. Export-promotion support also lowers *market entry costs*, providing a direct cost advantage to exporters. An indirect cost advantage may subsequently follow, if this facilitates greater *scale* of exports—for example, by lowering the cost of transport and compliance. Finally, through the provision of technical support, capacity building, and informational support, EPAs can help ensure compliance to standards, thus lowering *risk* and potentially increasing *quality* of exports.

Investment Promotion (Agencies)

Attracting FDI is an important component of export development strategies in most countries. FDI not only contributes to economic growth through the provision of capital and employment, but most important, in the medium and long term, through its dynamic effects. It is a source of significant positive externalities through

MODULE 2

Table 2.4. Summary of Key Trade and Investment Support Measures

	Purpose	Reason for government provision	Potential impact on competitiveness
EPAs	• Enable existing and new exporters to access information, establish contacts, and initiate trade in export markets	• Information failures (mostly nonrival) • Entry costs as barriers to exporting	• Reduces entry costs • Reduces risk/improves survival
IPAs	• Attract investment (mainly FDI)	• Information failures • Spillover benefits	• Diversifies export base • Improves aggregate productivity • Technology/knowledge spillovers

knowledge spillovers, the introduction of new technologies, and demonstration effects (Carkovic and Levine 2005). It is these externalities, along with the market failure inherent in the provision of information on the potential returns in alternative investment destinations, that is the basis for government provision of investment promotion through the establishment of IPAs.

The literature on FDI defines two broad types of investment (Helpman 1984; Markusen 1984): (1) investment seeking to access a local market (often referred to as "horizontal" or "market-seeking" FDI); and (2) investment designed to take advantage of the cost or quality of certain factors of production (often referred to as "vertical" or "efficiency-seeking" FDI) to establish a platform for regional or global exports. For horizontal FDI, the attractiveness of a local market in some cases might be strong enough to obviate the need for significant promotion efforts. Countries like China, Brazil, and Russia are examples of this. For most vertical FDI,[17] however, investors are somewhat footloose between alternative locations. For small countries, especially, the role of promotion may be critical to getting the attention of potential FDI. Singapore and Ireland are two well-known examples of small countries that have been effective in their efforts to attract export-oriented FDI. Empirical evidence (Harding and Javorcik 2007) confirms the positive role of investment-promotion efforts in increasing FDI flows to developing countries.

Investment promotion supports trade competitiveness primarily by attracting competitive investors. If these are exporters, they may contribute to diversifying a host country's export profile. They are likely to increase the aggregate competitiveness of the country's exporters, as foreign investors—like exporters in general—are on average more productive than domestic producers (Melitz 2003). Finally, FDI may contribute the competitiveness of exporters, whether or not the foreign investors are exporters, through the provision of competitive inputs and through the spillovers of the knowledge and technology they bring into the host market.

Main Components of Trade and Investment Promotion Support Analysis

In analyzing a country's program of trade and investment promotion support, it is necessary to assess the specific components and activities involved in each instrument of support. This assessment allows for an understanding of the scope of the support and the areas in which support may be missing or performance lacking.

Export Promotion (Agencies)

Assessment of an EPA and its contribution to export competitiveness should cover the main activities that are traditionally carried out by an EPA, including the following:

- *Country image building*: advertising, promotion, and advocacy (lobbying)
- *Targeted marketing*: trade fairs and missions, and services provided to cultivate contacts in foreign markets
- *Export support services*: training, technical assistance, capacity building, including regulatory compliance, information on trade finance, logistics, customs, packaging, and pricing
- *Market research and sector analysis*: general, sector, and firm-level information, such as market surveys, online information on export markets, publications encouraging firms to export, and importer and exporter contact databases

Although some recent empirical research suggests that EPAs do have a positive impact on export flows, there are many examples of organizations that have failed to meet their objectives and have done little to support the competitiveness of exporters. Drawing on a note by de Wulf (2001), following are some broad principles that determine the effectiveness of EPAs:

- *Incentives that promote exports/avoid anti-export bias*: EPAs can be effective only if the macro-incentive structure does not create an inbuilt bias against exporting.
- *Autonomous structure*: EPAs need to be a policy advocate and also be able to garner and mobilize resources quickly from both the public and private sector. As such, they tend to operate more effectively when they are established as an autonomous agency with strong private-sector participation on the board as well as top-level political support.
- *Demand-driven services*: This requires strong private sector involvement.
- *Sufficient focus on supply-side/competitiveness*: Too many EPAs focus their resources almost solely on promoting exporters in new markets (for example, trade fairs). However, ensuring the export sector is competitiveness should be a first and fundamental priority.
- *Sustainable budget*: EPAs must have sources of consistent and sustainable funding. This is likely to include some degree of charging for services, but in many cases there are limits to this.

Investment Promotion (Agencies)

Following the conceptual framework outlined by Wells and Wint (2001), IPAs have four basic functions:

1) *National image-building*
2) Specific *investment generation*, including proactive targeting of investors and selling
3) *Servicing investment,* including converting investment commitments to on-the-ground realization and retaining investment through effective aftercare (facilitating licensing, access to infrastructure/facilities, and so on)

4) *Policy advocacy*, in particular working with government to improve the investment climate for FDI

The relative emphasis across these roles will depend somewhat on countries, resources, and government priorities. In most cases, there is a bias toward investment generation. The effectiveness of IPAs is dependent on many of the same issues as for EPAs, most important the broader investment climate, access to a sustainable and sufficient budget, and institutional design that ensures high-level political commitment and strong private-sector representation.

MODULE 2

Trade Promotion Infrastructure: Standards and Certification

Link with Competitiveness Challenges Identified in Trade Outcomes

Main components in standards and certification	Competitiveness challenge areas			
	General export environment	Cost competitiveness	Product extension and quality	Market penetration
Standards	✓	✓	✓	✓

Quantitative Analysis: Indicators and Data Sources

Quantitative measures of standards performance are limited; and what measures are relevant are seldom tracked in most low- and many middle-income countries. As a result, the Diagnostic on standards will focus primarily on qualitative assessment, including both desk- and fieldwork. Following is a summary of a few quantitative metrics that can be included in the analysis.

	Indicators	Sources
Nonagricultural	ISO certification rates	ISO 2008 Survey of Certificates, WDI
	Budget of national quality body and share of budget focused on exporters	Country specific
Agricultural	Measure of border rejections as a share of exports	Product Risk Index[a]
	Share of exporters with HACCP, ISO 22000 or Eurepgap certification	Country specific

a. Cadot, Jaud, and Suwa-Eisenmann 2009.

Qualitative Analysis: Interview Targets and Issues for Discussion

Interview Targets

Government	• *Bureau of Standards*: It understands the public quality infrastructure and works with private industry to address quality issues. Capacity varies greatly. • *Line ministries* (for example, Ministry of Health, Ministry of Industry, Ministry of Agriculture): They have legal responsibility and understand the public system. • *Border authorities*: Customs, Bureau of Standards, and line ministries are represented at the border. Interviews with border post personnel provide insight into the export process.
Private sector	• *Exporters*: Exporters are the prime source of information. Larger exporters are often readily accessible, but representative information requires interviews with smaller exporters as well. • *Exporter/business associations*: Many associations exist, often organized by industry. Be aware that the associations often speak mainly for selected larger members. In some countries, government influence over associations may be considerable. Associations may have been set up by donors for specific purposes. Information must be supplemented by exporter interviews. • *Private quality service providers*: Societe Generale de Surveillance (SGS) and Bureau Veritas are examples of private service providers. They have a local office in many countries. They have good knowledge of the supply and demand situation for the commercial services they supply, such as testing and certification. • *Shipping companies/transporters*: They are always involved in the export process and will help the analyst to understand the process. They are aware of delays and red tape and of project rejections resulting from quality problems. • *International buyers*: Interviews with exporters should be supplemented with interviews with their buyers. Occasionally, buyers will be represented locally, but phone interviews can be used as buyers may be spread out across the globe.
Other stakeholders	• *Local academics and consultants*: In countries with ongoing capacity-building projects, local specialists are knowledgeable about both technical and economic aspects as well as the local political economy. • *Bilateral donors*: Donors support capacity building in quality infrastructure and may have local experts working in capacity building projects. • *International organizations*: UN technical agencies such as the Food and Agricultural Organization and UNIDO often have projects on quality infrastructure and may have experts based locally. The experts tend to be technical specialists rather than economists. • *Civil society*: Local nongovernmental organizations (NGOs) or international NGOs with local presence are often involved in quality issues. The US NGO TechnoServe, for instance, is often involved in trade and commercialization projects.

Key Issues for Discussion

		Sources of information						
Stage	Exporters and exporter/industry associations	Private service providers	Shipping companies and transporters	International buyers	Bureau of standards	Line ministries	Border authorities
1	Create inventory of requirements by export product: Which quality demands do you meet? From where do you learn about standards and technical regulations? How do quality demands vary across your target markets? How important is it to know the exact quality?	Understand requirements of the customers: For which requirements do you provide compliance services? For which markets are these services relevant? Which industries do you serve? Are there industries that you normally serve in other countries but not in this one?	Understand export requirements: Can you make a list of quality related documents that the exporter need?	Create inventory of requirements by export product: Which standards and technical requirements do you follow? What are the consequences of noncompliance? Do you work with your suppliers to ensure compliance?	Understand Bureau role: In which industries is the Bureau active? What is the role of the Bureau in these industries? Are the standards of the Bureau relevant for exporting? Is the Bureau aware of export requirements?	Understand foreign demands for public certification: Is public activity a prerequisite in the export process (for example, phytosanitary licenses)? For which markets and products? Is this due to domestic or foreign demands?	Understand export requirements: Can you make a list of documents needed for export? Which of these relate to quality?
2	Understand the compliance process and the use of quality services: How do you demonstrate compliance? Could you provide a flow chart of activities necessary to ensure compliance? Which services do you use? How do you access services? What is the source of services? Have you shifted suppliers of services in the past?	Understand the portfolio of compliance services offered: Which services do you offer? Do you work on behalf of domestic companies or their international buyers? Why have you chosen the portfolio you have? Will you expand services in the future?	Understand the export process: Can you draw a flow chart showing the range of activities needed for export? Where do quality issues fit in? Can you provide a list of documents needed? What are the consequences of missing documents?	Understand the compliance process and the use of quality services: What is required to demonstrate compliance? Do you specify use of specific service providers Could you provide a flow chart of activities necessary to ensure compliance?	Understand Bureau role in compliance process: Could you draw a flow chart of the compliance process and indicate where the Bureau plays a role? Which services does the Bureau offer exporters?	Understand government role in compliance process: Could you draw a flow chart of the compliance process and indicate where government plays a role?	Understand the export process: Can you draw a flow chart of the export process? Which steps are relevant for quality issues? Can you provide a list of documents needed? What are the consequences of missing documents?

MODULE 2

Key Issues for Discussion

Stage	Exporters and exporter/industry associations	Private service providers	Shipping companies and transporters	International buyers	Bureau of standards	Line ministries	Border authorities
				Sources of information			
3	Understand use of public services: Do you use national standards and public compliance services? Costs of public services? Do you face unnecessary high costs and red tape due to public activity in quality? Is the government helpful?	Understand the competition they face: Do you compete with government or donor subsidized services? What are the regulations that you follow to operate? Does the government fulfill or exceed its role?	Understand interaction with government agencies: Could you specify the role of government agencies in the export process? Do you regard government agencies as helpful or constraining?	Understand use of public services: Do your suppliers use public services? Do you regard government activity as helpful?	Understand Bureau operations: Compare Bureau operations to international best practice! What is the fee structure? How is the Bureau funded? Use of mandatory standards?	Understand government operations: Compare government operations to international best practice! What is the fee structure? How is government activity funded? Role of mandatory standards?	Understand red tape at the border: What is the fee structure? How much time does it take to complete the export process? How much of that is related to quality issues?
4	Views on supply situation: Do you find an adequate supply of services? How do domestic, imported, public and private services compare? What are your prefered suppliers of services? Do you miss export opportunities?	Understand their supply: Why have you chosen the service portfolio you offer? Do you produce all services in country or do you use affiliates abroad? What is the state of the local compliance service industry? Usefulness of public services?	Not relevant	Views on supply situation: What is the supply situation compared with other countries? Would you prefer upgrades to the existing situation? Do you specify use of services from specific sources?	Understand public quality infrastructure: Could you explain the organization of the national infrastructure? How does the Bureau interact with public and private facilities?	Understand public quality infrastructure: Could you explain the organization of the national infrastructure? How does your agency interact with public and private facilities?	Understand border organization: Which agencies are represented at the border? How much of the paperwork needs to be completed at the border and how much must be done elsewhere?
5	Understand alternatives to compliance: What are the costs of noncompliance? What are the costs of services? Can you shift to alternative markets? What will you gain by improved services?	Not relevant	Not relevant	Understand alternatives to compliance: What happens in cases of noncompliance? Are you able to shift non-compliant products to other markets? At what costs?	Not relevant	Not relevant	Not relevant
6	Consultations	Not relevant	Not relevant	Consultations	Consultations	Consultations	Not relevant

Analytical Approach

Product standards have the potential to impact exporters in both existing products and markets (as standards and certification requirements change/become more stringent) as well as in new markets or product ranges, which may require meeting new sets of standards. They affect firms in diverse ways as well, raising transactions costs, and either restricting or facilitating investment in innovation (depending on risk perception and thus the willingness of firms to invest in meeting new standards).

Many international organizations, bilateral donors, and agencies working in the quality field have produced material on how to assess a country's quality system (see box 2.15). Quality is a multidimensional issue, so contributions often specialize in particular aspects. Gap analysis is the most common technique used to assess standards systems. In gap analysis, a desirable configuration of a quality system is defined and the analysis then assesses the current state of a country's system against this ideal. Gap analysis suffers from the drawback that the ideal system is not defined according to observed demand. Most commonly, the ideal system is a description of an industrial country system that is beyond the means of most developing countries, and therefore maybe inappropriate to the needs of the particular country.

The main task of the analyst is to identify the constraints to the exploitation of the full potential of the quality system. In doing so, it is critical to distinguish between private and social constraints. For example, companies may complain about the high costs of certification and argue that high costs hurt their competitiveness. Whether this is true in a social sense depends on the cost structure (see figure 2.10). Imagine that certification costs are high because of a government monopoly. Private companies may be legally bound to use the laboratory of the local bureau of standards. The bureau operates inefficiently and the costs of testing and certification are excessive. A reform of the legal framework for testing and certification will remove the deadweight loss to the economy represented by excessively high testing costs. In this case, high certification costs are a constraint to competitiveness. Imagine a second scenario. The country in question is a small low-income country located far from the target market. The industry that complains about high certification costs is much smaller than similar industries elsewhere. In this case, high certification costs are the result of low economies of scale. The size of the local industry precludes investments in testing facilities, and the local industry will have to use high-cost imported services. The industry calls for subsidized domestic testing facilities to remove the claimed constraint to competitiveness. But subsidizing testing facilities, in this case, are only likely to improve competitiveness and national income in the long run. In the case of an industry that is in the early stages of exploiting comparative advantage this often will not be the case.

It is often difficult to diagnose competitiveness problems without a social cost-benefit perspective in mind. The analysts, however, rarely will have the time and resources to generate the data for a formal analysis of this kind. The methodological problems of quantifying the

MODULE 2

Box 2.15. Examples of Existing Handbooks, Manuals, and Diagnostic Tools for Standards Assessment

Guasch, J. L., J.-L. Racine, I. Sánchez, and M. Diop. (2007). *Quality Systems and Standards for a Competitive Edge*. Washington DC: World Bank.

ISO/UNIDO. (2010). *Building Trust—The Conformity Assessment Toolbox*. Geneva/Vienna: International Organization for Standardization/United Nations Industrial Development Organization.

ISO/UNIDO. (2008). *Fast Forward—National Standards Bodies in Developing Countries*. Geneva/Vienna: International Organization for Standardization/United Nations Industrial Development Organization.

ITC. (2005a). *Innovations in Export Strategy—A Strategic Approach to the Quality Assurance Challenge*. Geneva: International Trade Centre.

ITC. (2005b). *Building Corresponding Technical Infrastructure to Support Sustainable Development and Trade*. Geneva: International Trade Centre.

IPPC. (2010). *Building National Phytosanitary Capacity (Strategic Framework)*. Draft of February 2010. Rome: International Plant Protection Convention.

OIE. (2006). *Performance, Vision and Strategy: A Tool For Governance of Veterinary Services*. Paris: World Organisation for Animal Health.

Sanetra, C., and R. Marbán. (2007). *The Answer to the Global Quality Challenge: A National Quality Infrastructure*. Berlin: *Physikalisch Technische Bundesanstalt*.

UNIDO. (2006). *Product Quality—A Guide for Small and Medium-Sized Enterprises*. Vienna: United Nations Industrial Development Organization.

Source: Authors.

Figure 2.10. Distinguishing between Factors Influencing Competitiveness

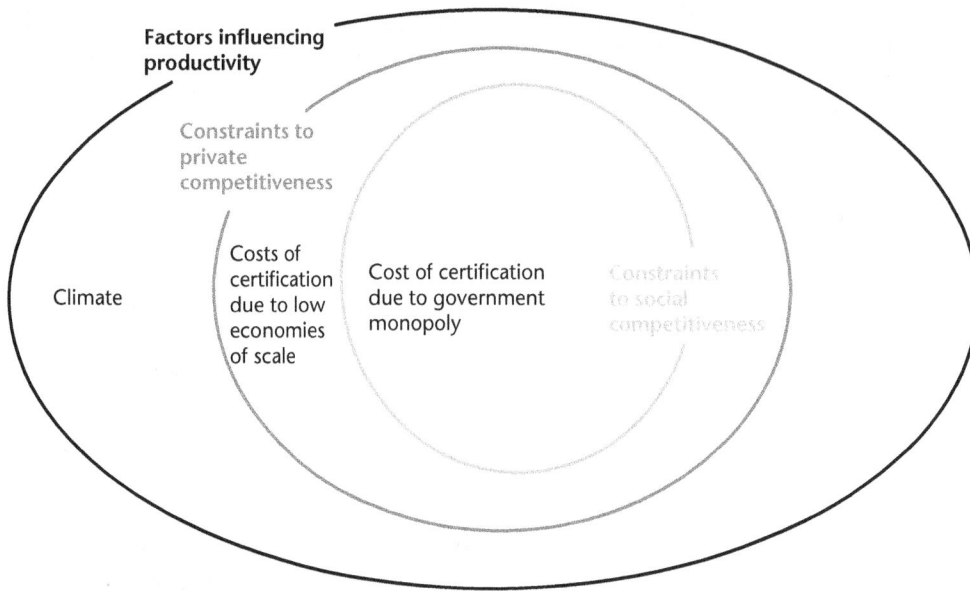

Source: Authors.

costs and benefits of quality are also substantial even with access to ample resources. Yet, it is important to keep the cost-benefit perspective as a guiding principle even for a rapid assessment.

The individual stages of the analysis are presented table 2.5 and are discussed in detail below. The sources of information and the individual stages are linked to the interview discussion guide shown at the start of this section, which identifies some of the key issues to cover and provides examples of typical questions that the analyst will seek to answer. Naturally, as quality issues are highly complex and often country specific, the sources indicated should be understood as typical sources and the questions as prototype questions; it is up to the analyst to adapt the list of sources and questions to the specific areas of investigation.

The stages presented here necessitate deskwork as well as rapid fieldwork, the latter including two to three weeks of on-the-ground fieldwork. The rapid assessment technique is designed to identify specific areas of focus, which would then most likely be analyzed in greater depth as part of a program of reform.

The area of quality is broad and technically complex. Teams assembled to assess a country's quality system will have to reflect the technical complexities. Representative industries often can be selected during deskwork rather than attempting to cover the entire export sector. This sector-level approach will allow for the selection of the right

technical experts. The desk analysis will rely on existing published material possibly supplemented by phone interviews with key stakeholders to verify key assumptions made on the basis of the available material before the fieldwork is begun. The fieldwork will mainly consist of interviews with stakeholders. Often stakeholders will be able to identify written material such as project and company reports that the analyst has overlooked during the deskwork phase.

The following outline of the individual stages discusses the focus of each stage and explains how the standards link with competitiveness:

Stage 1. What Is the Foreign Demand for Quality?

The first task is to identify current and potential future export markets. Only by understanding the quality requirements in these markets may the analyst be able to grasp the demand for quality infrastructure. This stage requires a desk analysis of export trade data as well as a literature study on export performance and strategies in the country in question. Many developing countries have formal trade strategies and donors have assisted in the elaboration of detailed studies of the potential of specific value chains. The Diagnostic Trade Integration Studies elaborated under the Integrated Framework, for instance, have been produced for many low-income countries after a careful process of stakeholder consultation. The identification of export products and target markets will allow the analyst to use industry literature to identify quality issues.

Table 2.5. Assessing the Quality System

Stage 1	**What is the foreign demand for quality?**
	During deskwork, stage 1 analyzes the composition of current exports and the likely quality demands for future exports to get a first impression of the challenges. Does the country export high-value foods or basic commodities? Is the country linked up with global supply chains for manufacturers requiring inputs with exact quality attributes? During fieldwork interviews with private companies and public authorities, the nature of foreign demand should be explored in greater detail.
Stage 2	**What is the derived demand for quality services?**
	Does the demand for quality lead to a derived demand for quality services? During deskwork, the analyst may become familiar with common ways of ensuring compliance for present and future exports. During fieldwork interviews, the analyst may identify which quality services are in demand and how they are supplied by the quality system. Which quality services (including standards and technical regulations) are demanded by business or national regulatory authorities?
Stage 3	**Which constraints emerge from the quality system itself?**
	The quality system provides both opportunities and constraints. Standards and technical regulations often are used as barriers to trade and as vehicles for rent-seeking by public and private actors. Badly designed quality policies may produce constraints rather than facilitate trade. The analyst must use fieldwork interviews to listen to the perceptions of the private sector toward government policy and to assess how well the public parts of the quality system operate as compared with international best practice in standard setting and organization.
Stage 4	**What is the current capacity for quality service delivery?**
	During deskwork, the analyst may become familiar with the basic outline of the quality system. Fieldwork interviews may be used to understand the current system and its limitation in detail. The analysis must include all potential sources, including public, domestic private, and imported services.
Stage 5	**What are the costs and benefits of improved quality services?**
	A formal cost-benefit analysis will not be possible because of resource constraints and methodological problems, yet a cost-benefit perspective must be used to discuss which issues are truly social competitiveness constraints.
Stage 6	**Make a prioritized list of competitiveness constraints.**
	The analyst should create a prioritized list of competitiveness constraints. Priorities may be set with the help of stakeholder consultations.

Source: Authors.

The desk analysis must be supplemented by the field-work. Private-sector interviews and interviews with other knowledgeable stakeholders will reveal the quality requirements with which exports must comply. The analyst must be aware that compliance is often a relative term. Some buyers may require strict compliance, that is, noncompliance will have grave consequences like lost markets, whereas others may work with their suppliers to improve quality if problems arise. Given the often-complex requirements that exporters meet, especially in high-end segments, many exports will only comply with parts of the requirements. Industry interviews will reveal the nature of the compliance process. Both private- and public-sector actors should be consulted during the fieldwork, but the analyst should recognize that the degree to which public representatives are aware of private export markets varies considerably.

Stage 2. What Is the Derived Demand for Quality Services?

The demand for quality services is specific. The services that will prove compliance with the requirements in an emerging electronics industry are totally different from what is needed to comply with seafood quality specifications.

Stage 1 has laid out the export opportunities and the potential constraints with respect to quality. Stage 2 will link these opportunities and constraints with demand for specific services. The experienced analyst will get a good impression of the range of relevant issues during the deskwork. Exports to specific markets are often linked with the use of the same quality services. Considerable variation exists across quality services, however, even for seemingly identical products. Thus, the fieldwork is the primary source of information. Industry interviews with both buyers and sellers will provide specific information. As an illustration of the degree of precision needed, consider the export of fresh produce to the European Union. The exact nature of the end market targeted is important. Fresh produce produced for bulk markets in southern Europe is radically different quality-wise from produce destined for UK supermarkets. Table 2.6 gives an example of specific quality services and how they fulfill demands. The analyst must know which quality services are in demand to understand the constraints to competitiveness.

The analyst involved in stage 2 will face the difficult problem that the product- and market-specific knowledge necessary to understand quality constraints very often

Table 2.6. Examples of Specific Quality Services

Compliance Area	Needs of the exporter	Necessary services
Product standards/technical regulations, including packaging and labeling	Access to standards/technical regulations	Reference center in standards body
Product testing	Conformity assessment recognized by the (international) client	Testing laboratory upgrading toward internationally recognized accreditation
Accuracy of measurement	Internationally recognized equipment calibration, measurement traceability to SI (measurement) standard	Metrology laboratory upgrading toward internationally recognized accreditation, intercalibration schemes
Consistent product characteristics and quality	Enterprise Quality Management System Certification (ISO 9000)	Certification capacity and internationally recognized certifiers
Management of environmental impact	Enterprise Environmental Management System Certification (ISO 14000)	Certification capacity and internationally recognized certifiers
Food safety	Management system to control food contamination (HACCP)	Certification capacity and internationally recognized certifiers; laboratory/testing capability
Social accountability	Insurance of consumer concerns relating to child labor, worker exploitation, and so on (for example, SA 8000, the Base Code)	Certification capacity and internationally recognized certifiers
Examinations of shipment content to order	Product inspection	Development of cross-border inspection services
Traceability of products and inputs from farm to fork	Traceability system	Development of consultancy capacity and internationally recognized certifiers

Source: Henson et al. forthcoming.

requires specific technical expertise. The deskwork accomplished during stage 1 must identify the types of expertise needed early on. It may be necessary to include technical experts in the fieldwork. It also may be necessary to concentrate on only a few representative export products rather than attempting to cover all exports to get the depth of analysis required.

The sources for stage 2 work is value chain and market specific literature as well as interviews with key stakeholders, notably private-sector exporters in the country in question and their buyers in the importing countries. The analyst may find phone discussions with buyers enlightening as part of the preparation for this fieldwork. A large body of business literature on supply chains is available for consultation. The most important source of information remains the private operators in developing countries.

Some quality demands may be highly codified like the private quality assurance schemes of retailers and branded product producers, such as Marks & Spencer, Nestle, Nike, and so on. Often the quality requirements are set out in great detail in readily available codes of practice and quality management manuals. The analyst should be aware that although such material is detailed, an insightful view on how it is interpreted is necessary to identify potential quality constraints.

Stage 3. Which Constraints Emerge from the Quality System?

Standards are a double-edged sword. Benefits like coordination and market access are enjoyed by those who comply, but those who do not comply are excluded or at the least burdened by additional costs. The quality system provides opportunities for improving social efficiency but also induces rent-seeking by both private and public actors. Parts of the quality system are likely to hinder rather than promote trade facilitation. The analyst should seek to identify these parts of the system as competitiveness constraints.

An example is the practices of the Tanzania Bureau of Standards (TBS). TBS is a provider of various testing services and extensive laboratory capacity has been established with the help of foreign donors. TBS has the power to make otherwise voluntary standards mandatory by recommending that the Minister of Industry make them a requirement. The opportunity to force exporters to comply with Tanzanian standards for which they see little use is of great concern to the business community. International best practice in standard setting and conformity service provision recommends that the roles of the standard setter, regulatory authority, and service provider be kept separate. The analyst should assess the degree to which such international best practices are applied in the target country and whether the existing practices open up the possibility for rent-seeking. Practitioners in the quality field are increasingly concerned that the recent surge in donor investment in quality infrastructure under the pretext of trade facilitation may hinder rather than facilitate trade. The establishment of laboratories, for instance, creates a potential for the generation of fees that would sustain the income of agencies. Such investments therefore create a risk that revenue generation takes precedence over service provision. Comparisons with international best practice and industry interviews about the usefulness of government and donor activity will help identify such concerns.

The analyst may look at whether some quality-related tasks are duplicated by various agencies. The export process may require documentation of quality issues that are either unnecessary or demanded by multiple agencies. The standard-setting process and the degree to which private-sector representation takes place are important. The fee structure for quality services may explain agency behavior, as such agencies often are financially strained. Regulations may be assessed for their transparency. The export process at the border requires special attention, as the understanding of the documentation required will inform the efficiency of the process.

Stage 4. What Is the Current Capacity for Quality Service Delivery?

Stage 4 is the point at which many studies begin. The capacity can often be analyzed using tools produced by specialized agencies as presented in box 2.15. Most tools, however, focus on the national public quality infrastructure and ignore domestic private and imported services. The analyst should describe how quality services are produced by both public and private actors. The mode of delivery is important, too. These services can be delivered within value chains, purchased from third parties, produced internally in some cases, and produced domestically or imported. Very often an exporter will use a combination of these channels of delivery.

The use of imported services is often an area of conflict with authorities that prefer to see a national system. Imports are often less costly in nearby countries that have a more developed quality infrastructure. Tanzania, for instance, may access the Kenyan infrastructure, and Mozambique may access the South African infrastructure. In today's highly global economy, quality services are generally a traded service, and even OECD countries frequently use service imports rather than opting for domestic production.

The assessment of the supply of quality services is made difficult by the absence of good indicators that may be accessed during deskwork. There are no reliable quantitative indicators for quality issues. This is an areas in which the trade analysis of quality differs from traditional trade analysis for which trade regulations such as tariffs are available from international databases. The analyst will have to be creative during deskwork and try use the existing but scarce material before beginning fieldwork. Some information may be available depending on the export industries and countries under scrutiny.

For example, ISO publishes a yearly report on the number of certificates issued by members of the International Accreditation Forum (IAF). The standards covered are mainly ISO 9001, 14001, and 22000, which gives the requirements for, respectively, quality management, environmental management, and food safety management systems. The ISO survey for 2010 is the 18th survey. The standards counts may be used as an early indicator of the state of the quality infrastructure in manufacturing, but the data are not flawless. The survey covers the number of certificates not the number of sites certified. Many companies have multiple sites under one certificate. The survey only covers certificates issued by IAF members; however, certificates are also issued by other certification bodies and an organization may choose to implement the standards for their own internal and external benefit without seeking certification.

Information available about other standards may be accessed during deskwork to learn about the state of portions of the quality infrastructure. High numbers of advanced food management certificates, such as Global Partnership for Good Agricultural Practice (GLOBAL-GAP) and Safe Quality Food (SQF), would indicate a relatively advanced agribusiness sector with export interests in high-end markets.

Regulatory authorities may produce useful evidence. The analyst interested in the state of animal products exports to the European Union, for example, should consult publically available reports from the EU's Food and Veterinary Office (FVO). The FVO regularly monitors and publishes reports on developing country regulatory systems as any country exporting animal products to the European Union must have food management systems that are equivalent to EU systems. Many regions and countries, like the European Union and the United States, also register quality problems at the point of import. Such data are often confidential and may be difficult to access, except for in the United States. Media stories on product recalls are another source of information about potential quality problems. Most information tends to be anecdotal, and the

MODULE 2

nature and extent of any problems must be confirmed during fieldwork.

Stage 5. What Are the Costs and Benefits of Improved Quality Services?

The time and resources for desk- and fieldwork are unlikely to allow for any rigorous cost-benefit analysis. The analyst should take care that all costs and benefits have been properly identified and discussed, even though exact quantification may not be feasible. Keeping a cost-benefit perspective is more important that quantification. Without a cost-benefit perspective, many competitiveness analyses degrade into mercantilist statements. The analyst should distinguish clearly between private and social costs and benefits.

During deskwork, the analyst will identify export industries. The analyst may use comparable case studies from similar industries in other countries to identify the range of costs and benefits to be addressed during fieldwork. Technical specialists with insight into specific industries and quality issues often can assist in the identification of costs and benefits at the company level. Social analysis at a higher level often is conducted by an economist.

Stage 6. Make a Prioritized List of Competitiveness Constraints.

The work of the analyst will be most useful if it includes a good discussion of priorities rather than enumerating a "laundry list" of constraints. The analyst should aim for a rough categorization of urgent, important, and minor constraints. Because quantitative methodologies can be applied given the constraints in time and other resources, setting priorities will be a normative exercise.

Stakeholder consultations ensure that the industry and government share the conclusions of the analyst to the extent possible. This consultation also provides an opportunity for error correction as a list of priorities often stimulates discussion and provokes reactions. Stakeholders are unlikely to react to abstract and unbinding discussions. When the analyst presents a draft of priorities, extra resources are often mobilized by stakeholders who fear that their concerns are being ignored. The analyst may organize a stakeholder meeting by the end of the fieldwork period; however, sensitive issue might be better discussed during one-on-one meetings. Box 2.16 summarizes some of the main analytical challenges in assessing the relationship between quality infrastructure and competitiveness.

Box 2.16. Analytical Challenges and Issues for Consideration

The area of quality and competitiveness is prone to misunderstandings about how quality infrastructure may improve competitiveness. It is therefore useful to discuss some common misperceptions, including the following:

- *Contributing to competitiveness through standards is not about lowering the private costs of business by subsidized public quality services.* It follows that competitiveness is not associated with picking specific value chains as "winners" and subsidizing their access to quality services.
- *Competitiveness is not necessarily (but it may be) about raising product quality.* Increased quality is one approach to supporting export industries that may or may not be successful given the social cost-benefit ratio of the necessary interventions. Sometimes it pays to invest in quality, but sometimes it does not pay. There is a risk of overinvesting in quality services if the market is unwilling to pay for extra quality. The use of quality infrastructure is mostly not about raising (or lowering) quality. It is about knowing the quality.
- *Competitiveness is not necessarily achieved by building government quality systems.* The government is a major player in quality services in many countries, but it is far from the only one. The role of the government is determined as much by historical tradition and ideology as by income levels. Low-income countries tend to have little government intervention in quality systems (mainly because of public finance constraints), but major differences exist even among high-income countries. In the United States, for instance, the government only provides knowledge to standard-setting organizations, whereas in the European Union, national governments have a much more hands-on approach. Government activities must be carefully designed to complement private activities. This is particularly important in low-income countries, where the social loss associated with the crowding out of private activity is particularly costly.
- *Competitiveness is not necessarily about building national quality systems.* Many services may be imported either through buyer relationships or as third-party services. Often these imports are costly, but so is the establishment of national systems. Low-income countries are at a disadvantage simply because of the small size of their economies and often because of their isolation.
- *A quality infrastructure is not a necessary condition to achieve competitiveness.* Quality infrastructure often is discussed in absolute terms like "The use of standards is increasingly becoming a prerequisite to worldwide trade." This may be correct, but not all standards are the same. Some are simple and easy to meet, some are complex and require support infrastructure in the form of technological hardware (for example, laboratories) and software (for example, a cost-efficient value chain such as vertically coordinated chains). Only some developing country exports are of the latter variety. The choice of which type of market to aim for is a social cost-benefit consideration. Exports generally follow the principle of comparative advantage. Each country will end up exporting what it does relatively best. Part of the basis for a country's export performance is the nature of its quality system. If the country performs badly in this regard, it will end up exporting goods and services that rely little on quality services.

(continued on next page)

Box 2.16. *(continued)*

- *Competitiveness in quality is not necessarily about harmonizing with international standards.* The WTO SPS and TBT agreements have caused some confusion about the appropriate role of international standards. Compliance with these two trade agreements is made easier if a national standard is based on an international standard. Yet, achieving harmonization does not warrant the blind import of international standards. Countries are free to choose whichever standards they feel fit their situation as long as the standards are supported by a risk assessment. The use of international standards only makes the risk-assessment process a little easier. The choice of appropriate standards is a cost-benefit consideration. If a country deviates significantly from the countries for which an international standard has been developed, the import of the international standard is likely to lead to an economically inefficient situation. Furthermore, international standards abound. Many institutions develop international standards and the choice of one particular international standard therefore does not necessarily guarantee a perfect match with the demand of the customer. Only the customer can formulate the need for a standard, not an international trade agreement. The trade agreement sets some parameters for the use of standards; commercial relationships determine the standard.
- *Standards (and quality infrastructures) are not the same as quality.* The instruments of standards, technical regulation, and the supporting quality infrastructure are often mistaken for quality itself. Quality is a much broader concept. It distinguishes between *producing quality* and *proving quality*. Quality infrastructure is mainly about the latter. Producing quality takes basic capacity building in the value chains through such means as training programs, extension, and advisory services, new technology, and so on. If a first investigation demonstrates a low quality level of the exports of a given country, the reason is often a lack of capacity to produce quality in the supply chain.

Source: Authors.

Tailoring the Diagnostics to Country and Sector Characteristics

Standards tend to be driven by requirements in end markets—as such, the assessment of standards needs to take into account the markets being targeted by exporters. Indeed, any diagnostic assessment of how a country's quality standards system contributes to trade competitiveness must take into account not only the supply side but also the demand side of quality standards. In high-income end markets, pressures from consumers (for high-quality differentiated products), governments (for health and safety protection), and civil society organizations (on ethical and environmental issues) has contributed to a steady increase in the range and stringency of standards to which exporters must comply. When selling into low-income markets, however, the demand for standards tends to be less clear but often less rigorous. Recent research (Kaplinsky and Farooki 2010; Kaplinsky, Terheggen, and Tijaja 2010) suggests that standards play a much less important role in exports bound for low-income markets (see box 2.17).

MODULE 2

Summary of Specific Considerations by Sector

Sector	Priorities and issues for consideration
Light manufacturing	• Focus on product safety and consistency • Standards will be strongly driven by end markets or lead firms in global value chains; however, they can be strongly influenced by in-country quality systems • Standards will be highly sector specific • Both process and product-related standards should be included • Emphasis on testing facilities, role of local bureau of standards, overall certification costs
Agriculture	• Main emphasis on health (food safety) and environmental issues • Focus on SPS standards as well as process-related hygiene standards (for example, HACCP) • For some agricultural products, issues of certification (organics) and traceability (for example, Eurepgap) will require significant technical capacity and considerations of compliance costs • Key government agencies will be linked with Ministries of Health and Agriculture/Environment
Tourism	• Standards and certification usually include both government and private processes • Safety standards are of primary concern (from government regulatory perspective), but quality and consistency of service offerings tend to be the main focus of private initiatives
Business and IT Services	• Importance of ISO (9000) but also many industry-specific standards (ICT; business process outsourcing [BPO] services) • Importance of professional certification schemes—for example, Software Engineering Institute

Box 2.17. Standards in South-South Trade

Thailand's Cassava Exports
Thailand's exporters of cassava pellets to the European Union are required to meet two demanding sets of standards: GMP (Good Manufacturing Practice) covering sanitary and processing procedures, and HACCP as cassava pellets are an input into animal feeds. By contrast, their exports of dried cassava to China are not subject to either GMP or HACCP certification, but only require a minimum level of starch content (Tijaja 2010).

Gabon's Timber Exports
Gabonese timber exporters selling into the European Union and China face different markets in terms of standards (Terheggen 2010). Entry into Europe is covered by much more intense standards, both private standards specified by global buyers and mandatory standards set by governments and international bodies. These differences are illustrated in the figure:

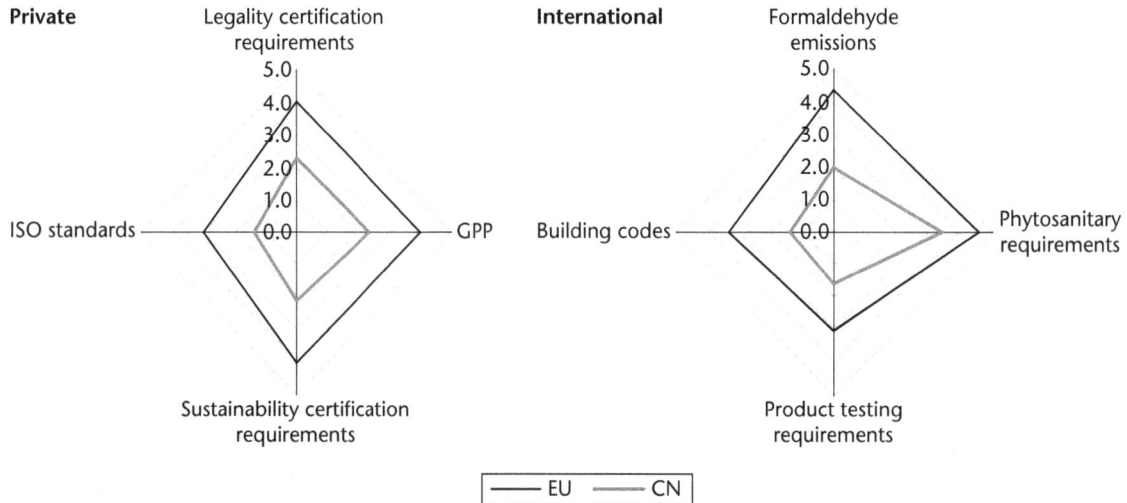

Source: Kaplinsky, Terheggen, and Tijaja 2010.

Background Reading: Relationship Between Standards and Trade Competitiveness

Standards are essentially descriptions of the quality parameters of a product. New public safety threats, such as food safety hazards, and the emergence of ever more complex global supply chains with an associated increased demand for the interoperability of inputs create a strong push for knowing the exact quality of traded products. For instance, the consumer wants to know the content of cancer-causing aflatoxins in peanuts, and the power companies need to know the strength of cables produced abroad. In short, standards are used to transfer product information from seller to buyer. This is not easy. The standard is simply a document outlining the desired characteristics. For the standard to be credible, a compliance infrastructure is needed. For some issues, such as food safety, the public has a key interest and the government is often involved. In that case, standards are often included in legislation, and the resulting document stipulating quality is known as a technical regulation. But for many other issues, standards and the

use of compliance infrastructure are purely private matters and all exchange of information about the nature of the product takes place efficiently on the basis of private transactions. Many activities are part of the quality infrastructure. Standards and their regulatory counterpart (technical regulations) set out the specifications, but a range of quality services are part of the picture too. Box 2.18 provides basic definitions of key terms related to quality standards.

For low-income countries, in particular, the emergence of standards as a form of governance in global trade raises some threats, most important, the risk of being excluded from profitable markets. Three distinct but related characteristics of standards act as a barrier to global trade (versus traditional barriers like tariffs and quotas):

- Unlike tariffs and quotas, standards are not established just by governments but also involve a range of private actors.
- Unlike tariffs and quotas, which are publicly codified, many standards are opaque. The rules and regulations

> **Box 2.18.** Definitions
>
> **Quality**—the value of a set of parameters that describe the nature of a product, service, or management system. An apple, for instance, is a fruit with edible flesh, certain sugar content, a given color, and so on. There are many apple qualities differentiated by, for instance, sweetness or color. Some qualities may be ranked on a low-to-high quality scale; others cannot be ranked but are fit for different purposes. An economic understanding of quality should not talk about low and high quality but rather efficient quality that is the quality that produces the highest benefit-cost ratio.
>
> **Quality services**—all services relevant to establish the values of the parameters that describe the quality of a product, service, or management system. These are the instruments of standards and technical regulations and conformity services.
>
> **Quality infrastructure**—the institutions and technologies used to provide quality services. The term relates to all the fields of metrology, standardization and testing, quality management, and conformity assessment, including certification and accreditation. Often the term MSTQ (Metrology, Standardization, Testing, and Quality) assurance is used interchangeably with quality infrastructure.
>
> **Standard**—a formal description of the desired quality of a product. Standards are voluntary and many standards often compete.
>
> **Technical regulation**—a mandatory formal description of the desired quality of a product. Technical regulations are often created by referring to a standard, thereby making it mandatory.
>
> **Conformity assessment**—activities concerned with determining that requirements laid out in a standard or technical regulation are fulfilled. Conformity assessment includes the areas of testing, surveillance, inspection, auditing, certification, registration, and accreditation.
>
> **Conformity assessment services**—services used to ensure conformity with a standard or technical regulation.
>
> *Source:* Authors.

that producers have to meet are often neither widely publicized nor stable and consistent.

- Unlike tariffs and quotas for which there are established mechanisms to resolve conflicts (for example, the dispute resolution procedures under the WTO), the determination of performance with respect to standards is generally an asymmetric process, determined solely by the buying party or country, with the producer having little capacity to challenge decisions on conformance.

Standards also offer an opportunity for producers to access high-margin markets. Indeed, standards have the potential to shape a number of aspects of export competitiveness. The channels through which standards shape competitiveness are summarized in the remainder of this section.

Product Compatibility

A well-functioning quality system improves market coordination by ensuring product compatibility. This is a key issue behind the rapid growth in global trade. Standardization ensures that inputs produced in distant locations fit together when assembled in the final product. This often is achieved by referring to voluntary standards and using private conformity assessment services, such as testing and certification. Occasionally, the government intervenes to direct the choice of product variety toward a social optimum that market participants are unwilling to reach themselves. In an export context, the drive for product compatibility often translates into complying with standards set up by global buyers.

Market Access

Standards help create market access by ensuring that the product specifications are aligned with foreign demands, which may be public regulatory requirements or private market demands. The EU seafood regulations, for instance, are highly demanding both in terms of product standards and management practices, as are US regulations. Vietnamese seafood exporters frequently export to both markets. The Vietnamese authorities with the assistance of Danida, the Danish development agency, have designed national standards that combine the EU and US demands, ensuring that complying with the Vietnamese standards simultaneously ensures compliance with EU and US demands.

In some cases, standards help shape and develop markets. The competitiveness of a country or industry is then influenced by the ability to participate in the standard-setting process. The rapidly developing biofuel market is an example. Quality issues include chemical composition to ensure compatibility with the existing stock of combustion engines, environmental parameters to ensure a positive effect on climate change, and social parameters to guarantee ethical behavior of biofuel producers. Environmental and social parameters are important to ensure market access into markets like the United States and the European Union. The ability to follow and, if possible, influence the standard-setting process may be a key factor when a country wants to ensure that its emerging industry complies with regulation. Rules on forest clearance, for example, may exclude countries that have recently converted forests into agricultural lands as opposed to most developing countries where this conversion took place centuries ago.

MODULE 2

For exporters, compliance with international product and process standards can open doors to important markets. The flip side, of course, is that firms that fail to comply risk being excluded from global value chains.

Quality Signaling and Value Addition

The market access aspect of standards is linked to the widespread use of standards as the basis for technical regulations. The right product specifications (formulated as either voluntary standards or mandatory technical regulations) safeguard human, animal, and plant life and protect the environment. The gap in regulations is widening between industrial countries and many developing countries, specifically regarding environmental and social issues such as labor practices. Private operators expect production and trading practices to comply with various codes of practice in many markets. The quality system must be able to understand new requirements and prove compliance in a cost-effective way if industries are to remain competitive.

Developing countries are most often standards takers rather than setters. That is, their exports must be compatible with quality demands determined elsewhere. For example, following emerging international standards on the chemical composition of biofuels, ensures Mozambican exporters a market because their product is compatible with car engines in export markets. The biofuel standard creates a *network effect*. The value of Mozambican biofuel increases with the number of people using compatible technologies. Awareness of emerging standards therefore becomes a key factor in a competitive industry, as market participants must lock into the right technologies as soon as possible.

Standards can identify specific product attributes and add value to exports by allowing producers to be rewarded for their efforts when producing them. In this way, standards allow exporters to tap into their willingness to pay for specific product attributes by ensuring them of the nature of the product that is traded. For example, most African agricultural export is de facto organic as chemicals are little used because of their high costs. The average consumer does not know this, however. Organic labeling communicates the information to the consumer.

Cost—Scale Economies and Efficiencies

Standards affect firm cost structures, and therefore product prices, in a variety of ways. Product compatibility makes long-distance trade and the inherent specialization possible, which leads to national and global gains of economies of scale. In an emerging industry, many product configurations may exist, but agreeing on one configuration will allow private operators to mass produce compatible inputs, thereby reaping greater economies of scale. For example,

common regulations on pesticide use will allow extension agencies to advise on the pesticides that are acceptable in export markets. This is less costly than having to fine-tune crop protection management to individual market demands.

Meeting standards is generally a costly process, and this can act as a barrier to entry for small-scale and informal producers (see further discussion in the section "The Costs of Achieving Standards"). On the other hand, in many cases, firms adopting the various sets of standards required to access global markets have experienced considerable improvements in both process and product upgrading. Meeting the needs of demanding corporate value chain leaders to enhance quality, cost, and delivery has invariably meant that firms have had to change their practices on inventories (reducing working capital costs), to restructure their plant layouts, to move from quality at the end of the line to quality at the source, and to introduce new equipment that boosts productivity and enhances product quality (Womack and Jones 1996). Similarly, firms participating in global value chains that require conformance to civil-society driven standards on health, safety, work practices, and the environment generally are able to participate in high-margin niche markets.

There is an important caveat here, however, because, as in the case of ISO standards, the adoption of process standards may provide the capability to enhance productivity and reduce costs, but this capability may or may not be utilized to achieve these ends. Firms may be able to monitor quality performance at each stage of the production cycle through the use of ISO 9000 procedures, but unless these performance indicators are actually used to stretch efficiency—through setting and meeting a series of targets for systematic improvement—the achievement of standards accreditation will have little impact on a firm's capacity to upgrade.

Innovation

The right standards are codified specifications of state-of-the-art technology and best practices in meeting consumer expectations. Standards are platforms on which to add new insights. As the world changes, new standards are introduced to reflect the latest technologies, innovations, and community needs, and redundant standards are discarded. The role in innovation in developing countries is often to diffuse cutting-edge practices as these countries catch up with industrial countries. Often, the knowledge built into standards is transferred through the global supply chains that link distant markets. In Kenya, knowledge about food safety management has been transferred through the country's successful fresh produce exports. New innovations such as prepacked vegetables and ready-to-eat salads have been created using food safety management standards as the underlying basis. These standards ensured that final products were acceptable in end markets and concentrated innovation efforts.

The Costs of Achieving Standards

Although there may be a payback to the firm in effectively implementing standards arising from higher product prices, lower costs, and larger volumes (due to selling to large-scale buyers), the achievement of standards will not be costless. The financial costs of accreditation may be low, but there will be resource costs in acquiring, and then maintaining, accreditation—for example, managerial time, training, new procedures, and new equipment. Moreover, there may also be significant lock-in costs when suppliers invest heavily in meeting the specific standards of a particular firm (as in traceability in horticulture, in which different retail firms have different types of paper trails), and suppliers may find it costly to make the switch to a different lead buyer's standards and procedures.

These costs will necessarily vary across industries. Achieving the standards required to sell into the defense sector will be orders of magnitude more costly than those involved in the certification of organic coffee. See box 2.19 for an example of compliance cost differences across industries.

The key issue in considering the costs of standards accreditation is thus best seen in relation to the size and financial viability of the suppliers involved. Although these levels of expenditure may be affordable to MNCs or large locally owned suppliers, they often exclude small-scale suppliers. One reason for this exclusion is the financial cost. Therefore, in the Thai cassava value chain, a number of smaller plants have had to withdraw from exporting to the European Union as the costs of achieving GMP and HACCP accreditation are too high. These firms reported that it was not just the cost of accreditation but also the fact that HACCP implementation requires trained staff and the maintenance of records (Kaplinsky 2010). Small-scale, and especially informal sector, firms also may be excluded from participating in global value chains because they lack the capacity and culture to systematically record and store the information required to achieve and maintain standards accreditation. Therefore, because of this combination of acquisition costs, costs of maintaining accreditation, and the lack of capabilities to implement and sustain accreditation, the advance of standards in global value chains excludes many small-scale and informal sector producers from global markets.

Main Components of Standards Analysis Two main types of standards can be defined—product and process:

- *Product standards*: Product standards address the characteristics of the output from production. They are relatively unambiguous and are defined by the quality requirements set by particular standards setters. For example, in the case of standards set by lead firms seeking to reduce costs and increase flexibility, this may involve the definition of minimum levels of permitted defects. Thus, in the auto sector, permissible levels of defects that suppliers must achieve have been progressively reduced from 10,000 parts per million to less than 400 parts per million. In the food-retailing sector, the product standards that are tested include pesticide residues. In a relatively new development, Walmart is increasingly focusing on green standards, including on

MODULE 2

Box 2.19. Sectoral Differences in Compliance Costs

Gabonese Timber Industry

In the Gabonese timber industry, one large forest-holding reported the cost of acquiring initial Forestry Stewardship Council (FSC) certification (which requires action through the chain of production) at €4 million, with an annual cost of maintaining accreditation of around €100,000. A second Gabonese firm estimated its environmental compliance cost at €2.10 per hectare, in the context of an estimated minimum economic forest-holding of 50,000 hectares. A third large forest-holding company estimated the cost of achieving the CFAD (Sustainably Managed Forest Concessions) accreditation to be in excess of €1.5 million.

Source: Terheggen 2010.

Malaysian Electronics Industry

By comparison, the cost of compliance to health and safety and the ISO 14001 environmental standard in the Malaysian electronics industry was considerably lower. A large multinational company estimated the annual costs of maintaining its ISO14001 certification and the international occupational health and safety management system standard (Occupational Health and Safety Accreditation Standard [OHSAS] 18001) certification to be around US$4,600. A second multinational reported the cost of OHSAS certification to be $278 per year. Two second-tier suppliers estimated the costs of maintaining ISO14001 accreditation at between $4,600 and $9,275 per year. Most of these cost estimates, however, are based on previous investments by the firms in setting in place the processes and procedures for certification, and these relatively low cost estimates relate only to the annual costs of maintaining registration.

Source: Kaplinsky 2010.

the carbon content of products that it sources from its supply chain. In general, these product standards are unambiguous and require single-point verification at the end of the production process.

- *Process standards*: Process standards are more complex and more varied than product standards:
  - They are more *complex* because they typically involve the documentation of *procedures* involved throughout the production process rather than measuring a single outcome (as in the case of a product). For example, the ISO quality and environment standards (respectively the ISO 9000 and ISO 14000 series) require the documentation of practices and outcomes at various stages of the production process. Unlike product standards, they do not set the levels that must be achieved but require only that these levels be checked and documented.
  - They are more *varied* because, in some cases, they include both the documentation of procedures and the achievement of clearly defined and measured outcomes. This may involve indicators, such as the level of the minimum wage, the age of workers, and the rights of workers to engage in collective bargaining, as well as the introduction of processes to reduce hazardous work practices.
  - They are more *systemic* than product standards because they typically involve the documentation or achievement of standards *throughout the chain*. For example, the FSC certification that addresses sustainability in the timber and wood products value chain involves a chain of custody that follows the timber from its forestry cultivation, through the sawmills, to the manufacture of processed wood, and its transformation into furniture and other final products. A similar process of verification is required throughout the chain if producers are to meet the demanding pesticide-residue requirements of global retailers, who demand that a defaulting shipment can be traced all the way to the individual plot of land in which a particular leaf in a salad was grown.

It is not always possible to separate product from process standards. For example, is organic food a product standard (whose characteristics can be measured) or a process standard (the documentation throughout the chain that inorganic materials are not entering the chain)? In most cases, therefore, particular product standard outcomes require the application of particular process standards. But the obverse is not always the case—that is, given process standards do not necessarily produce the targeted product standards. For example, the ISO quality and environmental standards specify only that pertinent information is systematically collected, which will make it easier to achieve given product standards. But it is entirely possible—and indeed often the case—that producers have achieved the required process certification but that this is not used systematically to improve quality and environmental performance.

Four major sets of actors are involved in setting standards—private sector actors, governments, civil society organizations, and international industry bodies. These actors, and their roles, are outlined in table 2.7.

The other key actors in the standards process are the *providers of quality services*. Conformity assessment and other quality services may be provided from both public and private actors. Many exporters conduct some of their own tests and quality control (first-party assessment), are tested or audited by their buyers (second-party assessment), and buy services from neutral actors (third-party assessment). When quality is regulated by mandatory

Table 2.7. Actors in Standards Setting

Actor	Role
Private sector	Individual lead firms have developed standards to determine the efficiency of their value chain operations. Initially these corporate standards largely defined the nature of the product and were generally unique to the firm. But, in some cases, firms began to cooperate to widen the pool of suppliers on which they could draw. GLOBALGAP is one such example. GLOBALGAP is a private sector body that sets stringent standards for the certification of production processes of agricultural products primarily for food safety purposes. The standards are voluntary in principle, but the fact that some large buyers such as British supermarkets use them have made them de facto mandatory in some markets. Another example is in the automotive industry, where ISO-TS16949 has now been adopted globally, replacing country-specific standards.
	In addition to focusing on flexibility, inventories, quality, and cost and focusing on product standards, lead firms increasingly have needed to respond to civil society pressures on labor standards and the environment. One example is the Marine Stewardship Council (MSC), which sets standards for environmentally sustainable fishing. The electronics industry adopted the Electronic Industry Code of Conduct (EICC), based on the HP Supply Chain Social and Environmental Responsibility Code of Conduct, to replace company-specific codes, following a campaign by civil society organizations that exposed poor working conditions in the industry's global supply chains.

(continued on next page)

Table 2.7. (continued)

Actor	Role
Government	Unlike corporate sector standards for which suppliers can perform at differential levels (and for which they may be rewarded or punished for over- or underperformance) government-legislated standards are mandatory, are transparent, and provide little leeway to producers. Government standards also can vary in their sectoral purview. For example, the United States mandates HACCP certification (which requires processes to reduce the risk of contamination in food production) for imports of juice and meat, but for other foodstuffs, conformance is voluntary. With growing international cooperation, particularly in Europe, many legislated standards are no longer set by individual governments, but rather by groups of governments, as in the case of standards set by the EU Commission. For example, the European Union has adopted a suite of standards governing the farm-to-table chain, targeting a series of linked product and process standards governing food safety, animal health, animal welfare, and plant health. These cover both domestic firms selling into the European Union and exporters to the European Union.
	In addition, governments agree to multilateral standards—for example, WTO SPS agreements. Member states are encouraged to base their technical regulations on international standards, although they may choose to deviate from such standards, if they find that they are inappropriate in the local context. The SPS agreement defines international standards for food safety, animal health, and plant health as the standards set by, respectively, the Codex Alimentarius, the International Office of Epizootics, and the International Plant Protection Convention.
Civil society organizations	Unlike either the standards that pertain in corporate-governed value chains or those standards set by national and international governmental bodies, civil society standards are voluntary. This does not make these standards less important, particularly if producers are seeking to sell into high-margin niche markets. Many of these standards fall under the fair trade umbrella, covering items such as foodstuffs (for example, coffee, where the emphasis is on ensuring minimum incomes for producers), intermediate products (such as organic cotton and FSC timber, covering environmental issues), and final consumer goods (such as apparel, addressing labor standards). Although still a small segment of the global market for these items, the pressures leading to the adoption of fair trade–type certification are forcing many value chains to adopt their own or analogous standards in their value chains. One example of this is Starbucks, which has adopted a non–fair trade scheme to regulate its supply chain (the Rainforest Alliance). Unlike fair trade, which explicitly targets minimum prices paid to farmers and other socioeconomic standards, the Rainforest Scheme focuses on environmental and sustainability issues. Similarly, Walmart, which, under pressure, has tried to resist labor standards, has struck out against criticism by pushing through a series of greening standards to its supply chain, involving second- and third-tier suppliers (with chain-of-custody type accreditation) as well as first-tier suppliers.
	One of the major difficulties associated with the standards driven by civil society organizations is the plethora of confusing and overlapping standards that confront producers. This difficulty arises as a direct consequence of the multiplicity of civil society organizations that are involved. Thus, in the apparel industry, many producers in low-income economies are involved in a costly and often bewildering process of multiple audits of their labor standards as each of the lead buyers bows to pressures from particular civil society organizations in their different final markets. Therefore, in some cases, large global branding firms have approached neutral bodies like the ILO to develop a single globally recognized and transparent labor standard that they can apply to their value chains and meet the demands of civil society organizations across their final markets
International industry bodies	International industry bodies are involved in both general and industry-specific standards setting. For example, the ISO 9000 quality standards grew out of the British Standards BS 5750 certification scheme to address an international audience of participating firms. ISO standards generally cover a range of sectors, as they target internal processes; hence, ISO 9000 certification has been adopted in manufacturing as well as services and marketing companies. In other cases, these international standard-setting bodies are industry specific. For example, the International Maritime Organisation (IMO) has grown into the major body regulating practices and safety in the shipping industry. Its explicit purpose is to safeguard transport and to prevent unfair competition from low-cost and less scrupulous shipping lines. In cooperation with governments and civil society organizations, the IMO has developed in a series of standards, some of which have been enacted into law by most governments, and others that are considered to be beneficial and that are advisory.

Source: Authors.

MODULE 2

technical regulations, government agencies in the importing country and occasionally in the exporting country often get involved. A myriad of private actors offer quality services, ranging from global quality service giants like SGS and Bureau Veritas with offices in many countries, to small companies specialized in particular services. Many national bureaus of standards offer conformity assessment services. The global quality system is marked by competition between service providers who offer standards and the associated conformity services and attempts to harmonize these standards and compliance procedures. The trade-off between competition and the specialization of services and harmonization is difficult to achieve, yet the right balance is often crucial for trade concerns.

Trade Promotion Infrastructure: Special Customs Regimes and Special Economic Zones

Link with Competitiveness Challenges Identified in Trade Outcomes

Main components in special customs regimes and SEZs	Competitiveness challenge areas			
	General export environment	Cost competitiveness	Product extension and quality	Market penetration
Duty drawback and manufacturing-in-bond	✓	✓		
EPZs and SEZs	✓	✓		

Quantitative Analysis: Indicators and Data Sources

	Indicators	Sources
Duty drawback and manufacturing under bond (MUB)	Share of exporters making use of duty relief regimes	National sources
EPZs/SEZs	Share of exports from SEZ	National sources; World Bank International Trade Department (PRMTR) database
	SEZ exports per capita	National sources; PRMTR database
	Number of SEZs	National sources; PRMTR database
	Number of companies operating in SEZs	National sources; PRMTR database
Clusters and collective action	Existence of national cluster programs	National sources
Subsidies and incentives to sectors and exporters	Existence of subsidy programs	National sources
	Share of exporters benefiting from subsidies	National sources
	Cost of subsidies (actual and percent of export value)	National sources
	WTO actions over past X years	WTI

Qualitative Analysis: Interview Targets and Issues for Discussion

Interview Targets

	Government agencies and ministries	Private sector and other institutions
Duty drawback and MUB	• Customs and excise • Other border agencies (police, health, and so on) • Ministry of Trade and Industry or other ministry with responsibility for scheme	• Individual exporters (small/new and established) across traditional and emerging sectors • Export councils or associations • Private sector administrators or service providers to drawback schemes
EPZs/SEZs	• SEZ regulatory authority • Ministry of Trade and Industry or other ministry with responsibility for SEZ program • Customs and other border authorities • Port operators	• Private SEZ operators • Investors operating in SEZs

Key Issues for Discussion in Interviews with Government Agencies and Ministries

Duty drawback and MUB	• What duty relief regimes are offered and why? • Do exporters (of all sizes) make appropriate use of the regimes? • What is their approach on the balance-of-trade facilitation and risk management? • What are the main challenges they face and how are they addressing them?
EPZs/SEZs	• How effective have SEZs been in attracting export-oriented investment? • Structure of the SEZ regulatory authority: links to government ministries? Structure of executive board and level of private-sector participation on the board? • Are the SEZs operated publicly, privately, or both? What is the strategy for this? • What are the challenges in delivering infrastructure, "one-stop" registration, efficient customs, and so on? What are they doing to address these? • Is there any evidence of the SEZs linking effectively with local producers—for example, accessing supplies from local markets, contributing to indirect exports?

MODULE 2

Key Issues for Discussion in Interviews with the Private Sector and Other Institutions

Duty drawback and MUB	• What duty relief regimes do they make use of and why? • How effective are the regimes in terms of registration, paperwork requirements, financial commitments, and repayment times? • What are the main problems that arise with the regime and how could they be improved?
EPZs/SEZs	• How does the investment environment for exporters compare with what would be available outside the zones—in infrastructure, transport access, regulatory burdens, set-up, and so on? • Are incentives offered within the SEZs? How important are they? • What are the main issues that still constrain exporters on a day-to-day basis? • Do investors make significant purchases from local suppliers? What restricts greater links with local suppliers?

Tailoring the Diagnostics to Country and Sector Characteristics

Summary of Specific Considerations by Country Type

Country type	Relative priorities and issues for consideration
Small (population) and remote/landlocked	• SEZs may be difficult to make work due to lack of scale • Logistics or border-oriented zones may be worth consideration
Resource rich	• How can zones support diversification and value addition?
Low income, labor abundant	• Traditional processing zones may be relevant
Middle income	• Greater emphasis on science parks, IT parks, and services-oriented zones

Summary of Specific Considerations by Sector

Sector	Priorities and issues for consideration
Light manufacturing	• Duty drawback particularly relevant for sectors with substantial imported inputs (for example, garments, electronics, automotive) • SEZs may be a critical issue to explore; in many countries and sectors, the majority of exports will be based in zones • Infrastructure, regulatory frameworks, and incentive policies of SEZs must be understood
Agriculture	• SEZs are a possible area of interest for consolidating agricultural value chains, particularly when land is scarce
Tourism	• Increasingly being integrated into SEZ projects but unlikely to be a major area of focus
Business and IT services	• Assess effectiveness of IT and science parks infrastructure and services; location (nearness to skilled labor) is often a critical issue

MODULE 2

Background Reading: Relationship Between Special Customs Regimes and SEZs and Trade Competitiveness

A majority of countries provide support to exporters through duty deferral and drawback or through a spatial program like EPZs or SEZs. Although these interventions can all be defended as addressing some form of market, information, or coordination failure, it is by no means certain they represent efficient or effective mechanisms to promote trade competitiveness. It can be argued that some of these interventions are in fact distortions to competitiveness, which may harm trading partners or create an unlevel playing field within the country. Conversely, they address constraints that hinder investment and trade. Table 2.8 provides a brief summary of the purposes, rationale, and potential impact on competitiveness of these interventions.

Duty Drawback and Manufacturing Under Bond

Most countries have established duty relief or exemption schemes designed to promote competitive exports by reducing or removing taxes on imported inputs for use in further export-oriented manufacturing, through either duty drawback or MUB regimes. The rationale for specific exemption or duty relief for exporters is that the imposition of a tariff on imported inputs acts as a tax on exporters, which may reduce the competitiveness of exporters in world markets.

Fundamentally, duty drawback and MUB regimes provide the potential for exporters to improve competitiveness through both cost (access to lower-cost inputs) and quality. To the degree that they facilitate imports of higher technology inputs than might be available in the domestic market, they offer the potential to improve aggregate productivity through knowledge and technology spillovers.

Table 2.8. Summary of Special Customs Regimes and Economic Zones

	Purpose	Reason for government provision	Potential impact on competitiveness
Duty drawback and MUB	• Allows exporters to access imported inputs for exports on duty-free basis	• Reduce anti-export bias of tariff regime	• Lowers production costs for exporters • Allows for access to high-quality inputs
EPZs/SEZs	• Provides exporters with an environment of high-quality infrastructure, more liberal environment, improved administration, and possibly fiscal incentives	• As above and overcomes poor investment climate more generally	• As above • Improves quality and flexibility (speed) of production and distribution

Source: Authors.

The administration of such schemes is sometimes problematic, however, and so their existence alone does not necessarily contribute to competitiveness. Indeed, it is recommended that duty and tax exemptions for exporters be kept to a minimum to reduce the burden on customs administrations.

Export Processing Zones and Special Economic Zones

SEZs[18] are demarcated geographic areas within a country's national boundaries inside which the rules of business are different—generally more liberal—from those that prevail in the national territory. SEZs act as a tool of trade and investment policy, aiming to overcome barriers that hinder investment in the wider economy, including restrictive policies, poor governance, inadequate infrastructure, and problematic access to land.

Specifically, SEZs tend to offer export-oriented investors three main advantages relative to the domestic investment environment. First, they generally offer a *special customs environment*, including efficient customs administration and (usually) access to imported inputs free of tariffs and duties. Second, historically at least, zones have offered a range of *fiscal incentives*, including tax holidays, exemptions, and reductions, as well as unrestricted movements of capital and repatriation of profits. Finally, SEZs offer a high-quality *investment climate* that is a marked improvement over what is available in the country overall. By concentrating on a relatively narrowly defined area, SEZs make it more feasible to deliver a high-quality investment environment—from the perspective of financial investment, governance, and delivery capacity—than otherwise may be possible across the economy as whole.

Main Components of Interventions

In analyzing a country's program of sectorally and spatially targeted support to the export sector, it is necessary to assess the specific components and activities involved in each instrument of support—a summary of these components follows.

Duty Drawback and Manufacturing Under Bond[19]

Exporters have a wide range of possible approaches to duty and tax relief on imported inputs; however, two main mechanisms are of most interest:

• *Duty drawback*: Under a duty-drawback regime, the exporter pays full duty upon importing the relevant good but then can claim a refund on the basis of specific information on the content of its exports.
• *MUB*: This mechanism is particularly relevant for exporters who make substantial use of imported inputs. MUB is similar to a duty drawback, but in this case, the imported input remains under bond until it is processed and reexported. Thus, the exporter is not required to pay the duty for each individual importation, although exporters are usually required to maintain a credit with customs as financial security against the value against the tax liabilities that otherwise would be payable for the imported raw materials. An MUB scheme requires that the raw materials be kept within a specific bonded warehouse or factory that has been licensed by customs. Box 2.20 provides an example of an MUB program.

Assessment of a duty and tax relief regime should consider the nature of the program and how it is administered. Specifically, it comes down to a balance between meeting the needs of exporters for limited bureaucracy and cash-flow commitments and the needs of government to minimize the risk of diversion. Exporters prefer mechanisms whereby duties are exempted, whereas governments prefer some financial guarantees, either through exporters putting up a bond or paying and reclaiming duties. For exporters, particularly small exporters, the burden of drawback mechanisms in some countries often undermines its potential value as a source of competitiveness. This is because extremely detailed paperwork requirements may make it costly or difficult for the exporter to prove its right to the refund, and because in many

---

Box 2.20. Kenya's MUB Program

Kenya maintains an MUB program that is designed to encourage manufacturing for export by exempting approved applicants from import duties and VAT on the raw materials and other inputs that they import and also providing a 100 percent investment allowance on plant, machinery, equipment, and buildings.

If the goods that are produced from the raw materials and other inputs are not exported, the scheme's participant is subject to a surcharge of 2.5 percent and the imported inputs used in their production are subject to all other duties. Under this scheme "manufacture" includes any process by which a commodity is finally produced. This includes assembling, packing, bottling, repacking, mixing, blending, grinding, cutting, bending, twisting, and joining or any other similar activity. The remission, however, is not available for the importation of plant, machinery, equipment, fuel, and lubricants, or for suspended duty or dumping duty.

The scheme can be used by both direct exporters (that is, manufacturers who import raw materials, manufacture, and then export the finished product) and indirect exporters (that is, a manufacturer/producer who imports goods for use in the production of goods for supply to another manufacturer for use in the production of goods for export).

Application for participation in the scheme must be supported by a bona fide export order or contract for specified export goods or a letter of credit; a detailed production plan; a list of imported goods, including their description; and the tariff classification, quantity, value, and amount of duty/VAT to be waived. Furthermore, the value of the imported goods must exceed K Sh 1 million (approximately US$10,000).

Source: World Bank 2009a.

---

countries, exporters face extraordinarily long delays in receiving their refunds. It is, therefore, critical to have the right legal and regulatory environment to manage the schemes effectively and efficiently. Customs needs to have processes in place to ensure that claims for duty relief are legitimate and can be audited, but it needs to be able to do this in an efficient way.

Export Processing Zones and Special Economic Zones

Several specific aspects of the investment climate are usually targeted for improvement inside SEZs.

- First, SEZs are designed to overcome *land and infrastructure* constraints that may hinder investment in the national economy by providing investors access to long-term leases, prebuilt factory shells, and reliable utilities (electricity, water, telecommunications).
- Second, SEZs normally improve the overall *administrative environment*, particularly with regard to the procedures required to register a business, acquire the licenses required to operate, obtain visas and work permits, and access key services like utilities and construction. This is often facilitated through the establishment of "single-window" or "one-stop shop" services, whereby the SEZ authority will be a single point of contact to arrange the delivery of these administrative services through coordination with the relevant government agencies.

- Third, another important component of the administrative services offered in zones is a privileged and expedited *customs administration*. Such services often involve the stationing of customs officers inside or at the gate of the free zone to offer on-site clearance to speed up import and export procedures. It is usually also combined with a range of other advantages, including the ability to move and hold goods in bond as well as the removal of financial requirements for bonded and duty-free inputs.

Recent research (Farole 2011) suggests that the following factors are important determinants of the potential success of SEZs as a tool to promote exports:

- *Infrastructure quality:* The quality and cost of electricity is the most important determinant of competitiveness for manufacturing-related exporters (for services exporters, telecommunications infrastructure tends to be equally important). In too many SEZs, infrastructure provision remains of relatively poor quality.
- *Trade and transport facilitation:* Efficient on-site customs clearance, effective transport links to key trade gateways, and (perhaps most important) efficient port operations are critical determinants of SEZ success.
- *Investor servicing (one-stop shops):* Although less critical in the long run, access to an effective one-stop service is often important for attracting and converting initial investors.

MODULE 2

Trade Promotion Infrastructure: Industry Coordination and Sector Support

Link with Competitiveness Challenges Identified in Trade Outcomes

Main components in industry coordination and sector support	Competitiveness challenge areas			
	General export environment	Cost Competitiveness	Product extension and quality	Market penetration
Industry associations and bodies	✓			
Clusters	✓	✓	✓	✓
Subsidies and incentives to sectors and exporters	✓	✓		

Quantitative Analysis: Indicators and Data Sources

	Indicators	Sources
Industry associations	Share of firms/exporters that are members of industry bodies (taking into account only those that are dues-paying members)	National sources
Clusters	Existence of national cluster programs	National sources
Subsidies and incentives to sectors and exporters	Existence of subsidy programs	National sources
	Share of exporters benefiting from subsidies	National sources
	Cost of subsidies (actual and percent of export value)	National sources
	WTO actions over past X years	WTI

Qualitative Analysis: Interview Targets and Issues for Discussion

Interview Targets

	Government agencies and ministries	Private sector and other institutions
Clusters and industry bodies	• Ministry of Trade and Industry or other ministry with responsibility for clusters, sectors, and industrial policy • Any relevant local or regional government • National Competitiveness Council (if established)	• Individual exporters (small/new and established) across traditional and emerging sectors • Established cluster and industry representative bodies • Universities and training institutions • Relevant research institutions
Subsidies and incentives to sectors and exporters	• Ministry of Trade and Industry or other ministry with responsibility for administering incentive regimes • Export promotion agency	• Individual exporters (small/new and established) across traditional and emerging sectors • Established cluster and industry representative bodies

Key Issues for Discussion in Interviews with Government Agencies and Ministries

Industry bodies	• What is the nature of interaction between industry bodies and government? • Does the government provide financial or other support to facilitate the creation and sustainability of industry associations? What are constraints to more collective action on part of industry/exporters? • What role do they see for industry bodies going forward?
Clusters	• Do they take a sectoral or cluster approach? • What sectors/clusters are officially being supported with policy? How are these chosen? • How are they organized to deliver support? • What public goods are they focused on delivering?
Subsidies and incentives to sectors and exporters	• What subsidy and incentive programs do they offer to exporters? • What is the take-up rate on these? What constraints are there to higher take-up (awareness, administrative burdens, and so on)? • Are they monitoring the cost and impact of these programs? What are the results?

MODULE 2

Key Issues for Discussion in Interviews with the Private Sector and Other Institutions

Industry bodies	• What is the level and nature of membership? • What share of members are exporters? • What are the main services they offer? • What specific services for exporters? • What is the nature of interaction between industry bodies and government? • What are constraints to more collective action on part of industry/exporters?
Clusters	• How are the clusters organized? What is the role of private and public sector and other institutions? • How are they funded? Is it sustainable? • How effective is public-private dialogue? • What public goods are being delivered through the cluster or provided by government? • To what degree does the cluster actually contribute to greater competitiveness for individual exporters?
Subsidies and incentives to sectors and exporters	• What subsidy and incentive programs are available? • Do exporters take advantage of these? What constraints are there to higher take-up (awareness, administrative burdens, and so on)?

Tailoring the Diagnostics to Country and Sector Characteristics

Summary of Specific Considerations by Country Type

Country type	Relative priorities and issues for consideration
Small (population) and remote/landlocked	• May have limited scale through which to support clusters in many industries; it is critical that sectoral support be tightly matched with comparative advantage • Industry bodies likely to be dominated by a small group (elite)
Resource rich	• May be strong industry bodies from natural resources sectors (potentially dominated by FDI) with effective lobbying • Role of subsidies and incentives may be important to probe; how effective is the incentive structure in facilitating investment in sectors in which the country has comparative advantage?
Low income, labor abundant	• Building capacity of industry bodies and clusters should be a priority
Middle income	• May have well-established, strong industry bodies • Emphasis on cluster support to facilitate innovation and upgrading

MODULE 2

Industry representation, cluster, and sector support will vary tremendously across sector and country. In this respect, there are no specific considerations inherent to the sector.

Background Reading: Relationship Between Industry Coordination and Sector Support and Trade Competitiveness

Governments provide a range of support targeted to individual sectors, which may be specifically targeted to promote export competitiveness or may do so implicitly. In the past, such support normally came under the banner of "industrial policy" and targeted specific sectors according to their traditional importance to the economy or their potential to act as a catalyst for diversification and upgrading. Although such targeted sector policy remains popular in many countries, more recently, government intervention has focused on a comprehensive cluster approach. A cluster is an agglomeration of companies, suppliers, service providers,

and associated institutions operating in the same broad field, and usually is located within a relatively narrow geographic area (World Bank 2009b). Cluster support differs fundamentally from traditional industrial-policy-inspired sectoral approaches principally in their focus on related and supporting institutions, their preoccupation with competitiveness, and their openness to imports and foreign investment.

Clusters contribute to competitiveness by offering a rich environment for realizing externalities, including access to specialized labor, specialized suppliers, and knowledge spillovers. This allows individual firms to realize the benefits of scale economies, contributing to greater productivity and innovation (for example, the ICT clusters in Silicon Valley in the United States and Bangalore in India). As clusters rely on external scale economies, however, they face a challenge of collective action. Thus, the government often has an important role to play in facilitating clusters, particularly in cases in which the cluster remains latent and in countries and regions in which cooperation is lacking. Governments support clusters in various ways, including facilitation of dialogue to overcome coordination challenges, and support for the provision of public goods to enable clusters to realize opportunities for scale or quality upgrading (see box 2.21). Because many clusters in their initial stages are composed of companies that may compete aggressively in domestic markets, facilitating clusters to address export market opportunities can be a valuable first step to cluster development.

Many governments around the world offer a range of subsidies and incentives to promote exports—in many cases, linked with some of the instruments discussed thus far. Such incentives may include direct subsidies, low-cost loans, or tax relief. Export subsidies are most commonly applied in the agricultural sector, in which the establishment of price floors (as part of income support programs for farmers) encourages overproduction.[20] It is also common in other sectors in which governments want to encourage production for export rather than domestic markets, or in which export sectors are seen as particularly important to protect (for example, the automotive industry in South Africa and elsewhere, the textile and garments sector in India, and so on).

Several arguments have been raised to support government intervention to subsidize exports, most notably, the case of "infant industries"—that learning by doing and external scale, in combination with imperfect capital markets (information asymmetries), justify temporary industry protection through such schemes as export incentives and subsidies. Many such schemes create significant market distortions and may not be compatible with WTO agreements. Although subsidies may not affect underlying firm competitiveness (and may be harmful to competitiveness in the long run), they do alter the terms of trade and, as such, are important to consider when evaluating a country's performance in global trade, particularly within specific sectors.

It is beyond the scope of this Diagnostic to assess the performance of individual clusters and of sectors more broadly. The more relevant issue is to understand the nature of government policy support to clusters and the degree to which it is playing a positive role in supporting competitiveness. Components of support that can be assessed include the following:

- *The degree to which cluster support is targeted to industries with comparative advantage:* Too often, cluster strategies target areas beyond what is reasonable for a country to become competitive in, even in the medium term (for example, biotech and nanotech). Good practice cluster approaches focus on sectors in which the country or region has already shown some success or in which it has a clear source of comparative advantage.
- *The institutional structure for delivery of sector and cluster support:* Good practice would call for participation of both national and local or regional government as well the private sector and other institutions such as universities, training centers, and so on. Within government, interministerial coordination is critical to success.
- *The role of the private sector in driving the initiatives:* Although the government has a clear role, the most successful cluster initiatives are, at least in time, strongly private sector driven with active commitment from the leading companies, both domestic and foreign-owned.

A wide range of incentives and subsidy regimes have been developed to support exporters. Among the most common are the following:

Box 2.21. Upgrading Quality for Competitiveness in Pakistan's Sialkot Surgical Instruments Cluster

Of Pakistan's clusters, the one with most success in exporting has been Sialkot's surgical instrument cluster. The city hosts around 300 producer firms, supported by more than 2,000 subcontracted supplier firms. Together, the firms produce more than 2,000 different types of surgical instruments, most of which are exported to the United States (59 percent) and Europe (27 percent), making Pakistan the world's second-largest exporter of surgical instruments (Nadvi 1997). The vast majority of firms in Sialkot's surgical instrument cluster are composed of SMEs with less than 20 employees, mostly family run. These firms share a defining characteristic—that is, a vast social network between firms at all levels. The industry faced a serious crisis in the mid-1990s when the US Food and Drug Administration revealed that Sialkot surgical instruments failed to meet quality standards (under the Good Manufacturing Practice System) and thus prohibited import of its products. The industry had no choice but to adapt.

Under the effective guidance of two existing local institutions, the Surgical Instrument Manufacturers Association and Sialkot's chamber of commerce, the cluster achieved rapid quality upgrades, resulting in the US embargo being dropped. By 1996, the industry more than recovered its market, exporting 10 percent more than in previous years. The cluster has been able to respond successfully to subsequent quality challenges, and a number of firms in the cluster have adopted the ISO 9000 quality standard. The surgical instruments sector is now Pakistan's second in numbers of quality-certified firms, with the textile sector in first place.

Source: UNIDO 2006.

Box 2.22. WTO Prohibitions against Export Subsidies—the SCM Agreement

Article 3 of the Agreement on Subsidies and Countervailing Measures (SCM) identifies export subsidies as prohibited and provides clear examples of interventions that constitute export subsidies. The SCM Agreement defines export subsidies as subsidies that are contingent in law or in fact upon export performance. Examples of prohibited export subsidies include (but are not limited to) the following:

- A direct subsidy contingent on export performance
- Currency-retention schemes involving a bonus on exports
- Preferential transport and freight charges for export shipments
- Provision of domestic products and services for exports at terms more favorable than those for domestic goods
- Exemption, remission, or deferral of direct taxes or social welfare charges if contingent on exports
- Allowance of special direct tax deductions for exports above those granted on goods for domestic consumption
- Exemption or remission of indirect taxes on exports in excess of those on goods sold for domestic consumption
- Exemption, remission, or deferral of prior-stage cumulative taxes on goods or services used in the production of exported products in excess of products sold for domestic consumption (except for the exemption, remission, or deferral of such taxes on "inputs consumed" in the production process)
- Provision of export credit guarantees or insurance programs at premium rates inadequate to cover long-term costs
- Grants of export credits at rates below those that they pay for the funds, or at below market rates, or payment of all or part of the costs of obtaining credit.

Source: Creskoff and Walkenhorst 2009.

- *Direct subsidization of exports*: This may be on a nominal or an ad valorem basis.
- *Transport subsidies:* This involves cost reduction or refund on transport or customs-related costs for exporters; it is most commonly used when transport costs rise substantially (for example, to mitigate the impact of petroleum price increases on exporters reliant on air cargo).

- *R&D or training subsidies:* These tend to be less directly linked with exports.
- *Tax incentives:* These include tax holidays or reductions linked to export participation or export volumes.

Many of these incentives, however, are not compliant with WTO agreements, as outlined in box 2.22.

MODULE 2

Trade Promotion Infrastructure: Innovation

Link with Competitiveness Challenges Identified in Trade Outcomes

	Competitiveness challenge areas			
Main components in innovation	General export environment	Cost-Competitiveness	Product extension and quality	Market penetration
Product Innovation			✓	
Process Innovation		✓	✓	

Quantitative Analysis: Indicators and Data Sources

Indicator	Sector relevance	Stage of development relevance	Measure/Description	Source
A. Absorption and Innovation Local Capacity				
A1. Scientific/Design Capabilities				
Patent applications, nonresidents	all most science based and scale intensive	all but mostly middle income	Worldwide patent applications filed through the Patent Cooperation Treaty procedure or with a national patent office for exclusive rights for an invention—provides protection for the invention to the owner of the patent for a limited period, generally 20 years.	World Intellectual Property Organization (WIPO), WIPO Patent Report: Statistics on Worldwide Patent Activity
Patent applications, residents				
Patents in the United States			Number of patents filed in the United States by residents of a country.	US Patent and Trademark Office
Patents in Europe			Number of patents filed in the European Union by residents of a country.	European Patent Office
Trademark applications, direct nonresident	all but mostly supplier dominated and specialized suppliers	all	Trademark applications filed are applications to register a trademark with a national or regional Intellectual Property (IP) office. A trademark is a distinctive sign that identifies certain goods or services as those produced or provided by a specific person or enterprise. A trademark provides protection to the owner by ensuring the exclusive right to use it to identify goods or services or to authorize another to use it in return for payment.	WIPO, WIPO Patent Report: Statistics on Worldwide Patent Activity
Trademark applications, direct resident				
Royalty and license fees, receipts (balance of payments [BoP], current US$)	all but mostly science based also nature based	all but mostly middle income	Royalty and license fees are payments and receipts between residents and nonresidents for the authorized use of intangible, nonproduced, nonfinancial assets and proprietary rights (such as patents, copyrights, trademarks, industrial processes, and franchises) and for the use, through licensing agreements, of produced originals of prototypes (such as films and manuscripts). Data are in current US dollars.	International Monetary Fund, BoP Statistics Yearbook and data files
Licenses			Percent of establishments in the country/sector that have purchased either a foreign or local license.	World Bank Enterprise Surveys

Indicator			Description	Source
Researchers in R&D (per million people)	all but mostly science based		Researchers in R&D are professionals engaged in the conception or creation of new knowledge, products, processes, methods, or systems and in the management of the projects concerned. Postgraduate doctoral students engaged in R&D are included.	WDI
Research and development expenditure (percent of GDP)			Expenditures for research and development are current and capital expenditures (both public and private) on creative work undertaken systematically to increase knowledge, including knowledge of humanity, culture, and society, and the use of knowledge for new applications. R&D covers basic research, applied research, and experimental development.	
Scientific and technical journal articles			Scientific and technical journal articles refer to the number of scientific and engineering articles published in the following fields: physics, biology, chemistry, mathematics, clinical medicine, biomedical research, engineering and technology, and earth and space sciences	National Science Foundation, Science and Engineering Indicators
Quality of scientific research institutions	all	all but mostly middle income	"To what extent do you agree that your country has adequate scientific research institutions available? 1 = Disagree strongly, 5 = Agree strongly.	World Economic Forum Global Competitiveness Index (GCI)

A2. IPR/Certification

Intellectual property protection	all	all	"How would you rate intellectual property protection, including anticounterfeiting measures, in your country?" 1 = Very weak, 7 = Very strong,	GCI
International Certifications (ISO)	all but mostly exporters		Percent of establishments in the country/sector that have an ISO certification,	Enterprise Surveys

A3. Human Capital

Technicians in R&D (per million people)	all	all but mostly middle income	Technicians in R&D and equivalent staff are people whose main tasks require technical knowledge and experience in engineering, physical and life sciences (technicians), or social sciences and humanities (equivalent staff). They participate in R&D by performing scientific and technical tasks involving the application of concepts and operational methods, normally under the supervision of researchers.	WDI
Availability of scientists and engineers	all mostly science based		"To what extent do you agree that scientists and engineers in your country are widely available?" 1 = Disagree strongly, 5 = Agree strongly.	GCI
Enrollment in Science, Technology, Engineering, Mathematics (STEM) disciplines		all	Registered students in STEM.	Country statistics
School enrollment, tertiary (percent gross)			Gross enrollment ratio is the ratio of total enrollment, regardless of age, to the population of the age-group that officially corresponds to the level of education shown. Tertiary education, whether or not to an advanced research qualification, normally requires, as a minimum condition of admission, the successful completion of education at the secondary level.	United Nations Educational, Scientific, and Cultural Organization (UNESCO) Institute for Statistics

MODULE 2

Share of population speaking English	all but less supplier dominated			Economic Growth Center at Yale University
Percent of tertiary-educated individuals in OECD countries				Docquier and Marfouk (2004)

A4. Production Capabilities

State of cluster development	all, mostly supplier dominated and specialized suppliers	all, mostly low income	"In your country, how extensive is collaboration among firms, suppliers, partners, and associated institutions within clusters?" 1 = Collaboration is nonexistent, 7 = Collaboration is extensive.	GCI
Local availability of specialized research and training services	all	all	"In your country, to what extent are high-quality specialized training services available?" 1= not available, 7= widely available.	
University-industry collaboration			"To what extent do business and universities collaborate on research and development (R&D) in your country?" 1 = Do not collaborate at all, 7 = Collaborate extensively.	
Production process sophistication			"In your country, how sophisticated are production processes?" 1 = Not at all—labor-intensive methods or previous generations of process technology prevail, 7 = Highly—the world's best and most efficient process technology prevails.	

A5. Finance

Domestic credit provided by banking sector (percent of GDP)	all	all	Domestic credit provided by the banking sector includes all credit to various sectors on a gross basis, with the exception of credit to the central government, which is net.	WDI
Access to finance	all	all	"Is there sufficient access to financing, which includes availability and cost [interest rates, fees, and collateral requirements]?" Measures share of firms that identify it as a major obstacle to doing business.	Enterprise Surveys

B. Exposure to External Technology

FDI net inflows	all	all	percent of GDP	WDI
FDI in manufacturing	all	all	percent of total FDI	Country investment statistics
Inward FDI potential index	all	all	0–1	UNCTAD
FDI and technology transfer	all	all	"To what extent does FDI bring new technology into your country?" 1 = Not at all, 7 = FDI is a key source of new technology.	GCI
Royalty and license fees, payments	all	all but mostly middle income	BoP, current US dollars	IMF, BoP Statistics Yearbook and data files.
Imports of high-tech goods	all	all	percent of GDP	CEPII BACI (*Base pour l'Analyse du Commerce*) database
Imports of high-tech capital goods	all	all	percent of GDP	
Imports of intermediary goods	all	all	percent of GDP	
Foreign intermediate inputs	all	all	percent of all inputs that are foreign by country/sector	World Bank ES

C. Penetration of Older Technologies

Electrical power consumption	all	all	kilowatt-hours/capita	WDI
International outgoing telephone traffic	all	all	minutes	
Air transport, registered carrier departures worldwide	all	all		
Agricultural machinery: tractors	all	all	per 100 hectares of arable land	
Main lines	all	all	per 100 inhabitants	
D. Penetration of Recent Technologies				
Internet users	all	all	per 1,000 inhabitants	WDI
Personal computers	all	all	per 1,000 inhabitants	
Cellular subscribers	all	all	per 100 inhabitants	
Percentage of digital mainlines	all	all	per 100 inhabitants	

Qualitative Analysis: Interview Targets and Issues for Discussion

Interview Targets for Field Research on Innovation

Innovation issue	Government agencies and ministries	Private sector and other institutions
A.1/A3. Skills (scientific, design capabilities/human capital)	• Education Ministry • Science and Technology Ministry	• Universities • Training Institutions • NGOs
A.2. IPR/Certification	• Standards and Norms Agency • Patent and Trademark Agency	• NGOs or donor-funded agencies that promote certification and standards adoption
A4. Production Capabilities	• Ministry of Industry	• Chambers of commerce • Business/cluster associations • Incubator associations
A5. Finance	• Science and Technology Ministry • Ministry of Finance/Economy	• Banks • Microfinance institutions • Venture capital associations
B. Exposure to External Technology	• Ministry of Industry • Investment promotion agencies	• Universities' tech transfer offices

Key Issues for Discussion in Interviews with Government Agencies and Ministries

Education Ministry	• Promotion of STEM careers? • Funding of doctoral studies in local and foreign universities • Percentage of return of foreign-trained doctors
Science and Technology Ministry	• What is the amount of government funds to R&D? • Which type of R&D (basic applied) is funded? • What are the mechanisms to fund R&D: through public R&D labs, higher education institutions, or the private sector? • Who keeps the IP of inventions discovered with government-funded R&D?
Standards and Norms Agency	• Type of certification more demanded by firms? • Sectors with highest demand • Are standards usually adopted by large firms? By SMEs?

MODULE 2

Patent and Trademark Agency	• Extent of use of IPR in its different modalities: local patents, utility models and industrial designs • Does the local IPR agency also provide guidance in international patenting (for example, the United States and Europe)?
Ministry of Industry	• Is there a strategy/policy for innovation? What are the main components? • Is there a special tax treatment for R&D investments? • What are the policies related to cluster development?
Ministry of Finance/Economy	• Is there a special tax treatment for R&D investments? • What is the amount devoted for government-funded R&D?
Investment Promotion Agencies	• FDI legal regime: do foreign investors have the same legal rights as local investors? • What are the incentives that MNCs receive for installing plants in the host country? For technology licensing? • Do the incentives differ by sector?

Key Issues for Discussion in Interviews with Private Sector and other Institutions

Universities	• Are there tech transfer offices in the university? • What about spin-off companies initiated by professors? • Structure of the R&D funding: own funds, government-funded R&D, private sector–funded R&D • Joint applications with firms to government-funded R&D
Training institutions	• Are there tech transfer offices in the institution? • What about spin-off companies initiated by professors? • Structure of the R&D funding: own funds, government-funded R&D, private sector–funded R&D • Joint applications with firms to government-funded R&D
NGOs and donor-funded agencies	• What programs exist to promote standards adoption? • What are the main shortcomings in the current standards and certification regime?
Chambers of commerce	• What is the role of public and private sectors on the organization and structure of production clusters? • Issues with access to government funding and programs • Linkages between local firms and FDI • Schemes to link firms with universities
Business associations	• Use of government-funded R&D • Use of financial institutions funding for R&D • Schemes to link producers with input suppliers
Banks	• Funds for R&D—basic • Funds for R&D—applied • Funding for early stage research • Is any sector(s) prioritized?
Microfinance institutions	• Funds for R&D—basic • Funds for R&D—applied • Funding for early stage research • Is any sector(s) prioritized?
Venture capital associations	• Funds for R&D—basic • Funds for R&D—applied • Funding for early stage research • Is any sector(s) prioritized?

Analytical Approach

The analytical framework distinguishes between the factors that dictate the efficiency with which an economy absorbs and creates technology, on the one hand, and the extent to which it is exposed to external technologies, on the other hand. First, the speed with which a country absorbs and adopts technology depends on many factors, including the extent to which a country has a technologically literate workforce and a highly skilled elite; promotes production capabilities that encourage investment and the creation and expansion of firms using high-technology processes; permits access to capital; and has adequate public sector institutions to promote the diffusion of critical technologies for which private demand or market forces are inadequate. Second, among the most important channels through which low- and middle-income countries are exposed to foreign technologies are trade, FDI, and contacts with highly skilled diaspora members (nationals working abroad) and with other information networks, including those of academia and the media.

The framework considers four key dimensions: *A. Absorption and Innovation Local Capacity, B. Exposure to External Technology, C. Penetration of Older Technologies, and D. Penetration of Recent Technologies.* The assessment will collect its data from two components: (1) a quantitative part that uses secondary sources to capture innovation metrics; and (2) a qualitative section to be formulated to key actors in the innovation ecosystem, both in the public and private spheres as well as the nonprofit.

Previous sections have stressed the particularities of different innovation patterns. Table 2.9 provides a summary of the degree of influence of each innovation dimension on

trade competitiveness, taking into account the importance of innovation dimensions for each innovation pattern, in terms of (1) whether these measures are likely to have an impact on export diversity or export sophistication—specifically, in terms of new products for the former and quality upgrading for the latter; (2) how these measures affect the cost-competitiveness of exporters. For example, if traditional manufacturing is important in an economy and therefore supplier dominated is the prevalent innovation pattern, design capabilities and certification compliance are likely to be vital for both introducing new products and upgrading existing products. As explained, the nature of innovation in supplier-dominated sectors is not based on developing new technologies but rather on improving designs and branding. This innovation pattern relies on technology embodied in foreign capital goods; therefore, exposure to external technology is paramount. A big opportunity to innovate resides in improving production processes using embodied new technology and human capital held by technicians and engineers. The funding needed in traditional industries to enter the market is usually low compared with higher entry barriers in all other sectors.

Table 2.9. Framework for Analysis of Innovation Characteristics and Trade Competitiveness

	Diversification: New products	Sophistication: Product upgrading	Cost saving: New processes
A. Absorption and Innovation Local Capacity			
A1. Scientific/Design Capabilities	SD *** design SI *** both SS *** both SB ***scientific	SD *** design SI *** both SS *** both SB ***scientific	Not determinant
A2. IPR/Certification	SD ** certification SI * **IPR SS *** IPR SB ***IPR	SD * certification SI *IP SS * IPR SB *IPR	Not relevant might even increase costs
A3. Human Capital	SD * SI ** SS ** SB ***	SD * SI ** SS ** SB ***	SD ** SI ** SS ** SB **
A4. Production Capabilities	All***	All***	All***
A5. Finance	SD * SI ** SS *** SB **	SD * SI ** SS *** SB **	SD * SI * SS * SB *
B. Exposure to External Technology	All ***	All ***	All ***
C. Penetration of Older Technologies	All ***	All ***	All ***
D. Penetration of Recent Technologies	SD ** SI *** SS *** SB ***	SD ** SI *** SS *** SB ***	SD * SI ** SS ** SB **

Source: Authors.
Note: SD = supplier dominated; SI = scale Intensive; SS = specialized suppliers; SB = science based.
*important, **more important, ***very important.

Tailoring the Diagnostics to Country and Sector Characteristics

Summary of Specific Considerations by Country Type

Country type	Relative priorities and issues for consideration
Small (population) and remote/landlocked	• May have limited scale and market access to support leading-edge innovation • However, obtaining knowledge through suppliers may be restricted because of difficulties in access • Certification and standards-related issues may be important barriers
Resource rich	• May have strong technical skills linked to the resource sector that could be applied to support upgrading and diversification • Important to understand whether linkages with local firms (or lack of them) are supporting (restricting) knowledge spillovers
Low income, labor abundant	• Focus on technology absorption and generating spillovers from FDI • Certification and standards-related issues may be important barriers • Technology transfer policies and institutions may be critical to assess
Middle income	• Main challenges will be in developing scientific and design capabilities • Access to recent technologies likely to be a critical issue • IPR and patenting issues likely to be important to attracting science-based activity • Skills development, particularly tertiary education critical • Assess role of industry-university linkages and government research institutions

To better understand a country's innovative capabilities, it is necessary to map the country's economic and export structures to understand specific sectoral patterns. Using table 2.10, we can classify specific industries according to the innovation patterns and export propensity. Table 2.10 provides a guideline to match innovation patterns with International Standard Industrial Classification (ISIC) and the OECD classification of industries using sectoral technological content.

The reclassification exercise provides a tool for identifying main innovation patterns in a country's economy. Nevertheless, not all manufacturing or services sectors show the same degree of tradability in external markets nor the same potential for product differentiation (a proxy of production and export diversification). We can link then the economic sector structure with its tradability and its potential diversification using table 2.11. Manufacturing products are the most tradable, especially in R&D-intensive manufacturing and manufacturing (see table note to table 2.11 for detailed industry list). Services are not highly tradable. Product differentiation varies within services subsectors as well as in manufacturing subsectors.

Background Reading: Relationship Between Innovation and Trade Competitiveness

Diversification and sophistication are important dimensions of trade performance. Recent research suggests that the developing countries that have been more successful in terms of growth of both exports and output have tended to increase the diversity and sophistication of the products they produce and export (UNIDO 2009). Diversification tends to be more important for countries climbing the stages of development. Imbs and Wacziarg (2003) find an inverse U-shaped relationship between specialization in production and exports and per capita income. As incomes rise, countries diversify their production and export structures. New product lines are introduced and new activities are taken up within existing sectors until countries reach high levels of income. They also find that poor countries and—to a lesser degree—rich countries tend to specialize in the production of a fairly narrow range of activities. Across a wide range of incomes, however, the diversity of what a country produces increases with the level of per capita income.

In most cases, when diversification and sophistication are coupled, they are an outcome of "moving up the production ladder" from relatively simple mass-manufacturing activities, such as textiles or footwear, to increasingly more complex production processes, such as metal-mechanical, chemical, or electronics industries. Indeed, although successful low-income countries tend to expand their export market share of unskilled labor-intensive products, success for middle-income countries typically involves moving vigorously up the ladder of product sophistication. Diversification is fostered through a strong network of linkages generated across economic sectors. Linkages to other sectors of the economy are related with trade because industrial diversification appears to lead to export diversification. More diverse economies may

Table 2.10. Comparative Industrial Classification

	ISIC Rev. 31	Innovation Patterns	OECD Technology Intensity Index Index R&D/Production	
			Aggregate intensity 2	Median Intensity
High-technology industries				
Aircraft and spacecraft	353	Science based/scale intensive	10.3	10.4
Pharmaceuticals	2423	Science based	10.5	10.1
Office, accounting, and computing machinery	30	Science based/scale intensive	7.2	4.6
Radio, television, and communications equipment	32	Science based/scale intensive	7.4	7.6
Medical, precision, and optical instruments	33	Specialized suppliers	9.7	5.6
Medium-high-technology industries				
Electrical machinery and apparatus, n.e.s.	31	Scale intensive	3.6	2.3
Motor vehicles, trailers, and semitrailers	34	Scale intensive	3.5	2.8
Chemicals excluding pharmaceuticals	24 excl. 2423	Science based	2.9	2.2
Railroad equipment and transport equipment, n.e.s.	352 + 359	Scale intensive	3.1	2.8
Machinery and equipment, n.e.s.	29	Specialized suppliers	2.2	2.1
Medium-low-technology industries				
Building and repairing of ships and boats	351	Specialized suppliers	1	1
Rubber and plastics products	25	Scale intensive	1	1.1
Coke, refined petroleum products, and nuclear fuel	23	Scale intensive	0.4	0.3
Other nonmetallic mineral products	26	Scale intensive	0.8	0.6
Basic metals and fabricated metal products	27–28	Scale intensive	0.6	0.5
Low-technology industries				
Manufacturing, n.e.s.; recycling	36–37	N/A	0.5	0.5
Wood, pulp, paper, paper products, printing, and publishing	20–22	Supplier dominated	0.4	0.1
Food products, beverages, and tobacco	15–16	Scale intensive	0.3	0.3
Textiles, textile products, leather, and footwear	17–19	Supplier dominated	0.3	0.4
Total manufacturing	15–37		2.6	2.2

Sources: Author's elaboration using OECD (2003), Pavitt (1984), and UN ISIC.
Note: n.e.s. = not otherwise specified; N/A = not applicable; Technology Intensity Index calculated as R&D expenditure as a share of production value.

MODULE 2

Table 2.11. Sectoral Groups According to Degrees of Tradability and Differentiation

Sectors	Tradability[a]	Product differentiation
1. Infrastructure services	Low	Low
2. Local services	Low	Medium
3. Business services	Low/medium	High
4. R&D-intensive manufacturing	High	High
5. Manufacturing	High	Low
6. Resource-intensive industries	Medium	Medium

Source: Author's adaptation from McKinsey Global Institute (2010a).
Note: SD = supplier dominated; SI = scale Intensive; SS = specialized suppliers; SB = science based. **1 = Infrastructure services:** electricity, construction, hotels and restaurants, land transport; **2 = Local services:** real state, post, telecommunications, wholesale and retail, finance and insurance; **3 = Business services:** R&D, computers and related activities; **4 = R&D-intensive manufacturing:** pharmaceuticals, radio, television, communication equipment, chemicals, aircraft and spacecraft, medical instruments. (Comment: Mostly SB, SI, SS); **5 = Manufacturing:** motor vehicles, machinery, and equipment. (Comment: Mostly SI, SS); **6 = Resource-intensive manufacturing:** pulp, paper, printing, publishing, wood products, rubber and plastics, basic metals, fabricated metals, agriculture, forestry and fishing. (Comment: Mostly SI, SD).
a. Tradability is calculated by (M + X)/sector GDP.

be better able to take advantage of export opportunities in global markets. Finland's wood industry and its movement up the production ladder provides an example of industrial and export diversification and sophistication through linkages with other sectors (see box 2.23).

As a major driver of economic growth and productivity, innovation[21] has an obvious impact on exports and trade competitiveness. First, innovation in the form of new products increases diversification, whereas sophistication is fostered by quality upgrading. Recent research in the

MODULE 2

Box 2.23. Moving up the Production Ladder in Finland—Sector Linkages, Diversification, Sophistication, and Exports

Finland's exports 1900–1996

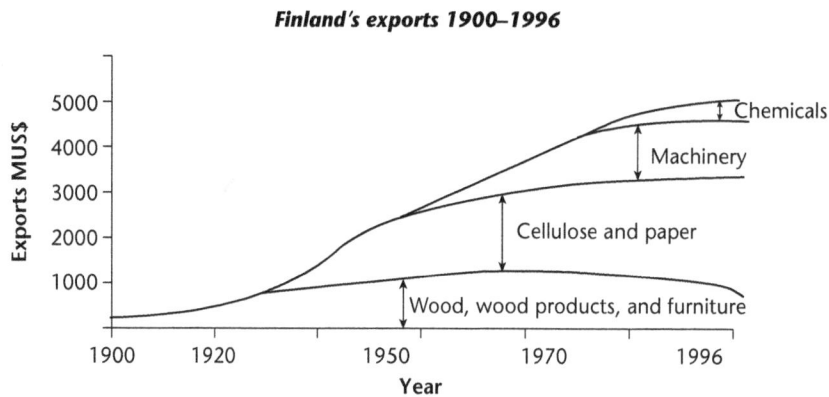

Source: Hernesniemi, Lammi, and Ylä-Anttila 1996.

Finland is an example where linkages to domestic suppliers sprout diversification and sophistication from the wood and paper industry. During the first development phase (approximately from the early 1900s to the mid-1950s), native wood was only minimally processed before being exported, and the majority of required capital goods and production inputs were imported. During a second phase, which lasted until 1970, industries that processed wood into cellulose, paper, and cardboard were established. All the engineering services required in the value chains were provided by local companies and the first local technology-intensive suppliers came into being and developed rapidly. The development after 1970 is characterized by increasing exports of high-valued wood, paper, and chemical products as well as machinery and equipment (Hernesniemi et al. 1996). In 2005, instruments, electro machinery, processing machinery, and transport equipment were already important export products of the Finnish economy representing 21 percent of all exports.

Source: Torres-Fuchslocher 2010.

---

manufacturing sector has found an influence from product innovation to productivity and then to exporting, which may explain how a firm's decision to invest in R&D and make product innovations drives its productivity and triggers the decision to start exporting (Cassiman and Martìnez-Ros 2007). Additionally, participation in global production through exports provides firms with access to knowledge to meet requirements of product quality; delivery time; process efficiency; and environmental, labor, and social standards. Mastering the requirements of global production ("learning by exporting") builds a platform for local innovations in more sophisticated products (Gereffi, Humphrey, and Sturgeon 2005).

Second, exporting may imply the reduction of inefficiencies through the renewal of production processes with resulting cost savings. Process innovations may have labor, capital, and inputs saving effects and therefore are expected to result in significant productivity growth (Hall, Lotti, and Mairesse 2007; Harrison et al. 2005). Through persistently performing an activity over time, a firm may accumulate skills and knowledge as well as learn how to organize and manage the activity in an effective manner (Andersson and Lööf 2009). For example, Damijan, Kostevc, and Polanec

(2008) support this idea by showing the link between exporting to process innovation and subsequently from process innovation to productivity growth using panel data from Slovenian firms between 1996 and 2002.

Main Components of Innovation Analysis—Understanding Patterns of Innovation

There are a number of sources by which firms acquire knowledge and innovate. Certain innovation patterns are more relevant for certain economic structures, and their importance varies by country. Within each pattern, firms tend to have a predominant learning and innovation behavior regarding main sources of technical change, dependence on basic or applied research, modes of R&D (in-house or extramural R&D), use of tacitness or codified nature of knowledge, scale and relevance of R&D activity, and degree of appropriability of the innovations.

Table 2.12 provides the taxonomy of the different innovation patterns, the economic sectors that make up each pattern, their main components of innovation, and typical firm size. It is influenced heavily by Pavitt's (1994) work on sectoral innovation patterns in manufacturing as well

Table 2.12. Sector Innovation Patterns and the Main Components of Learning and Innovation

Broad sector	Industries	Typical firm size	Learning	Innovation components and characteristics
Traditional manufacturing	Textiles and apparel, footwear, furniture, tiles	SME	Mainly supplier driven	Most new techniques originate from machinery and chemical industries
				Opportunity for technological accumulation is focused on improvements and modifications in production methods and associated inputs, and on product design
				Most technology is transferred internationally, embodied in capital goods
				Low appropriability, low entry barriers
				Innovation takes the form of new designs and branding; trademarks would be the ideal way to appropriate innovation efforts
Natural resource based	Sugar, tobacco, wine, fruit, milk, mining industry	Large	Supplier driven, science based	Importance of basic and applied research led by public research institutes due to low appropriability of knowledge
				Innovation is also spurred by suppliers (machinery, seeds, chemicals, and so on)
				Increasing importance of international sanitary and quality standards, and of patents
				Low appropriability of knowledge, but high for input suppliers
Complex products	Automobile and auto components, aircraft, consumer electronics, pharmaceuticals	Large	Scale intensive and also science-based firms	Technological accumulation is generated by the design, building, and operation of complex production systems or products
				In-house R&D is critical for innovation
				Process and product technologies develop incrementally
				In consumer electronics, technological accumulation emerges mainly from corporate R&D laboratories and universities; there is a skill entry barrier
				Appropriability is medium, high
Specialized suppliers	Software, precision equipment	SME	Specialized suppliers	Important user-producer interactions; learning from advanced users
				Low barriers to entry and low appropriability
				High in-house R&D for development of cutting-edge technologies

Sources: Author's elaboration based on Pavitt (1984) and Giuliani, Pietrobelli, and Rabellotti (2005).

as by recent developments (Giuliani, Pietrobelli, and Rabellotti 2005) and the inclusion of the services sectors (Castellacci 2008).

Traditional manufacturing includes labor-intensive and mature technology industries, such as textiles, footwear, tiles, and furniture. This group of industries tends to have stable, well-diffused technologies. SMEs dominate the traditional manufacturing sectors. These sectors are defined as supplier dominated because producers of inputs (machinery, materials, and the like) introduce major process innovations (Pavitt 1984). The technologies are primarily embodied in the capital equipment; the low end of the range has relatively simple skill requirements. Many traded products are undifferentiated and compete on price: Thus, labor costs tend to be a major element of cost

in competitiveness. Scale economies and barriers to entry are generally low. The final market grows slowly, with income elasticities below unity. There are exceptions to these features, however,. There are particular low-technology products in high-quality segments for which brand names, skills, design, and technological sophistication carry large value added, even if technology intensity does not reach the levels of other innovation patterns (Lall 2000).

Firms in traditional manufacturing can upgrade their products (and processes) by developing or imitating new products' designs, and by interacting with large buyers who are increasingly playing a role in shaping the design of final products and the production process (time, quality standards, and costs). The production of traditional manufactures has undergone massive relocation from rich to poor countries, with assembly operations shifting to low-wage sites and complex design and manufacturing functions retained in industrial countries. This relocation has been the engine of export growth in this industry, though the precise location of export sites in textiles, and clothing has been influenced strongly by trade quotas and trade agreements (Gereffi, Humphrey, and Sturgeon 2005). Other exports that have benefited from active relocation in this group are toys, sports and travel goods, and footwear (Lall 2000).

The natural resource-based sector activities imply the direct exploitation of natural resources, for example, copper, marble, or fresh fruit. The output of extractive industries is the internationally standardized product. For example, copper produced by a mine in Latin America is likely to be identical to copper produced in Zambia. An implication is that downstream integration from commodity extraction often fails because buyers can choose any producer of such standardized goods. To date, however, such downstream activities have often been the main focus of government attempts to broaden the economy from its extractive industries base (UNIDO 2009). Traditional manufacturing and natural resource-based sectors are, by far, the most common in developing countries.

The complex products group includes automobiles, auto components, aircraft, ICT, and consumer electronics, among others. These industries are dominated by large firms that take advantage of the economies of scale intrinsic to the sector's technologies. Complex product industries can be separated further using Pavitt's (1984) categories of science-based industries and scale-intensive sectors.

First, science-based industries have an innovation pattern that is closest to the traditional linear model of innovation, for which in-house R&D is critical for innovation (see box 2.24). Science-based innovation has five stages: fundamental research, applied research, engineering development, production engineering, and service engineering (Balconi, Brusoni, and Orsenigo 2008). Innovations are appropriated by the inventor and take the form of a large number of patents. Their products have advanced and fast-changing technologies. The most advanced technologies require sophisticated technology infrastructures, high levels of specialized technical skills, and close interactions among firms and between firms and universities or research institutions. Some products like electronics have labor-intensive final assembly, and their high value-to-weight ratios make it economical to place this stage in low-wage areas. These tend to be lead products in international integrated production systems for which different processes are separated and located by MNCs according to fine differences in production costs.

Second, scale-intensive industries are the heartland of industrial activity in mature economies. They tend to have complex technologies, with moderately high levels of R&D, advanced skill needs, and lengthy learning periods. Those in

---

Box 2.24. Linear Model of Innovation

The linear model of innovation is associated with V. Bush, who claimed that scientific progress is essential to technological innovation and economic development. This thesis was laid out in a policy paper meant to raise support for public funding of basic research (Bush 1945). Basic research is performed without thought of practical ends. It results in general knowledge and an understanding of nature and its laws. The scientist doing basic research may not be interested in the practical applications of his work, yet the further progress of industrial development eventually would stagnate if basic scientific research were long neglected. In general, science does remain an important condition and component of technological progress, and one that is fundamental in science-based industries (for example, consumer electronics, pharmaceuticals, aircraft and spacecraft, and so on). See tables 2.10 and 2.11 for a list of science-based sectors.

The linear model of innovation conceptualized the steps involved in transforming a new concept to a practical reality in the form of a new product. The sequence is as follows:

Basic Research → Applied Research → Development → Production

Applied research is nurtured by the results of fundamental (basic) research, and it emphasizes new products and processes. Development includes the improvement, testing, and evaluation of a process, material, or device resulting from applied research. In the linear model of innovation, to sustain basic scientific research, it is necessary to train a large pool of scientists and to strengthen the centers of basic research, which are colleges, universities, and research institutes.

Nevertheless, there is a clear division of labor along the sequence among different types of agents who specialize in the various relevant stages. Typically, basic research is conducted in universities and public laboratories, whereas applied research and technological development are carried out by firms, especially large ones, that can afford expensive R&D investments.

Source: Balconi, Brusoni, and Orsenigo 2008.

the engineering and automotive subgroups are linkage intensive and need considerable interaction between firms to reach best practice technical efficiency. Automotive products have been of particular export interest to newly industrializing countries, particularly in East Asia (for example, China and the Republic of Korea) and Latin America (for example, Argentina, Brazil, and Mexico) (Lall 2000).

The specialized suppliers group is composed of makers of machinery, equipment, and precision instruments. In this group, innovation benefits greatly from user-producer interactions. A machinery precision instruments industry that serves traditional manufacturing was crucial for the development of the economies of Finland, Germany, and Sweden. Empirical studies show that the strength of local technology-intensive suppliers and the specialized knowledge-intensive services represents a common characteristic of the development path of these countries (Torres-Fuchslocher 2010).

Specialized suppliers have an important role to play in the enhancement of national technological capabilities. Some types of knowledge creation depend on a close relationship between suppliers and customers and the implicit exchange of information. Internationally successful export industries, including natural resources–based sectors, can help local suppliers to internationalize. Clustered industries attract the attention of foreign demand more effectively than an isolated firm. Consequently, specialized suppliers have more chances to follow the industry in the process of internationalization. In Denmark, for example, the export-oriented dairy and fishing sectors have stimulated dozens of supporting industries in such areas as food-processing machinery, fishing boats, varnish for boats, and telecommunications equipment. A number of these industries are internationally competitive.

Location is important in cases such as small-scale specialized supplier firms. Proximity confers an advantage in communicating with each other and their customers, and hence the opportunity to respond quickly to the requirements of the industry. In other cases, such as the case of standardized traditional manufactured products, the distance to other potential markets and the availability of raw materials and inputs may have a larger weight in the location decision.

Notes

1. See Bown (2010). Petitions to apply trade remedy laws increase during recessions. According to the World Bank's Global Antidumping Database, the number of trade remedy investigations increased after mid-2008, only declining in the final quarter of 2009. Yet because several prior investigations were concluded then, the actual barriers imposed increased.

2. An exception to this is fisheries. At the WTO, tariffs on fish products fall under the Non-Agricultural Market Access (NAMA) negotiations.

3. See the World Bank Group's *Investing Across Borders 2010* (World Bank, Investment Climate Advisory Services 2010) report on FDI regulation in 87 economies.

4. A lower tariff is charged until a certain quantitative threshold, after which a higher rate kicks in.

5. See http://go.worldbank.org/C8SJJ4GW50.

6. SPS Agreement Annex A.

7. This includes costs related to setting up a business and remaining in compliance with legal and regulatory frameworks (discussed in this section) but also infrastructure, transport, and trade facilitation costs (covered separately in the section "Factor Conditions: Trade Facilitation and Logistics").

8. For example, if reinvested profits are taxed in the same way as profits distributed as dividends.

9. According to messaging data from SWIFT, approximately 90 percent of trade finance occurs through interfirm, open-account exchange. Estimates from BAFT (2009) suggest that 10-20 percent of trade finance is composed of cash-in-advance payments (these mainly involve SME buyers, and inordinately in developing countries); 45-80 percent is on open account (of which 30-40 percent is intrafirm), and 10-35 percent is bank intermediated.

10. Roughly half of cross-country differences in per capita income and growth are driven by differences in TFP, generally attributed to technological development and innovative capacity (Dollar and Wolff 1988; Hall and Jones 1999).

11. Actually, the productive effects of inputs like labor and capital can affect productivity, if there are input quality differences that standard input measures do not capture (see Syverson 2010).

12. Human capital is a broad topic (Schultz 1961) that encompasses "investments" in health, knowledge, and education at different ages.

13. See, in addition to Syverson (2010), Abowd et al. (2005), Fox and Smeets (2009), and Galindo-Rueda and Haskel (2005).

14. Technically, technical efficiency (TE) is a (one-sided) deviation from a production frontier described by some common production function and is estimated simultaneously with the latter. In a stochastic production frontier model, TE may, roughly, be viewed as a "systematic" component of TFP, as TFP includes random shocks that are beyond managerial control.

15. Bloom and Van Reenen (2007) offer a comprehensive study relating management practices to productivity.

16. Another critical backbone service is, of course, transport and logistics. This is addressed as a separate issue in the section "Factor Conditions: Trade Facilitation and Logistics" of this module.

17. One exception may be where FDI is targeted at a natural resource or other endowment that is not widely available or earns particularly high rents.

18. SEZ is being used here in a generic sense to cover any one of a variety of similar regimes, including industrial-free zones, EPZs, *maquiladoras*, investment promotion zones, foreign trade zones, free zones, and wide-area SEZs.

19. The discussion here is drawn from World Bank (2009a).

20. Export subsidies are a lower-cost alternative to governments having to buy up the excess production.

21. Innovation is defined as new ways to solve problems by combining technology (an improvement in product, process, marketing, or organization) with transformational entrepreneurship (typically involving commercialization of technologies via formal firms but also including value generation by informal, nonprofit, and governmental entities). Innovation ranges from incremental new-to-the-firm adoption and adaptation of existing technologies to radical new-to-the-world creation and commercialization of disruptive products and processes.

MODULE 2

References

Abowd, J., J. Haltiwanger, R. Jarmin, J. Lane, P. Lengermann, K. McCue, K. McKinney, and K. Sandusky. 2005. "The Relationship Between Human Capital, Productivity and Market Value: Building Up From Microeconomic Evidence." In *Measuring Capital in the New Economy,* eds. C. Corrado, J. Haltiwanger and D. Sichel, 153–203. Chicago: University of Chicago Press.

Anderson, J., and P. Neary. 1994. "Measuring the Restrictiveness of Trade Policy." *World Bank Economic Review* 8: 151–169.

Andersson, M., and H. Lööf. 2009. "Agglomeration and Productivity: Evidence from Firm-Level Data." Working Paper Series in Economics and Institutions of Innovation 170, Royal Institute of Technology, CESIS, Centre of Excellence for Science and Innovation Studies.

Auboin, M. 2009. "Boosting the Availability of Trade Finance in the Current Crisis: Background Analysis for a Substantial G20 Package." CEPR Policy Insight No. 35, June 2009, Centre for Economic Policy Research, London.

BAFT. 2009. *IMF-BAFT Trade Finance Survey.* Bankers' Association for Finance and Trade, September 2009, Washington, DC.

Balconi, M., S. Brusoni, and L. Orsenigo. 2008. "In Defence of the Linear Model: An Essay." KITeS Working Papers 216, KITeS, Centre for Knowledge, Internationalization and Technology Studies, Università' Bocconi, Milan, Italy.

Bernard, A. B., and J. B. Jensen. 2004. "Why Some Firms Export." *The Review of Economics and Statistics* 86 (2): 561–569.

Bernard, A. B., and J. B. Jensen. 1999. "Exporting and Productivity." NBER Working Paper No. 7135, National Bureau of Economic Research, Cambridge, MA.

Bernard, A. B., and J. Wagner. 2001. "Export Entry and Exit by German Firms." *Weltwirtschaftliches Archiv* 137 (1): 105–123.

Bloom, N., R. Sadun, and J. Van Reenen. 2009. "The Organization of Firms Across Countries." *CEP Discussion Papers dp0937*, Centre for Economic Performance, London.

Bloom, N., and J. Van Reenen. 2007. "Measuring and Explaining Management Practices Across Firms and Countries." *The Quarterly Journal of Economics* 122 (4): 1351–1408.

Bown, C. P. 2010. "First Quarter 2010 Protectionism Data: A Monitoring Update to the Temporary Trade Barrier Database." World Bank. http://go.worldbank.org/W5AGKE6DH0.

Bush, V. 1945. *Science: The Endless Frontier.* Washington, DC: U.S. Government Printing Office.

Cadot, O., C. Carrère, and V. Strauss-Kahn. 2011. "Trade Diversification: Drivers and Impacts." In *Trade and Employment: From Myths to Facts,* eds. M. Jansen, R. Peters, and J. M. Salazar-Xirinachs, 253–283. Geneva: ILO.

Cadot, O., M. Jaud, and A. Suwa-Eisenmann. 2009. "Do Food Scares Explain Supplier Concentration? An Analysis of EU Agri-food Imports." Working Paper No. 2009-29, Paris School of Economics.

Carkovic, M. V., and R. Levine. 2005. "Does Foreign Direct Investment Accelerate Economic Growth?" In *Does Foreign Direct Investment Promote Development?* ed. Theodore H. Moran, Edward M. Graham, and Magnus Blomström, 195–220. Washington, DC: Institute for International Economics.

Cassiman, B., and E. Martìnez-Ros. 2007. "Product Innovation and Exports: Evidence from Spanish Manufacturing." Mimeo.

Castellacci, F. 2008. "Technological Paradigms, Regimes and Trajectories: Manufacturing and Service Industries in a New Taxonomy of Sectoral Patterns of Innovation." *Research Policy* 37 (6–7): 978–994.

Cattaneo, O. 2010. "Health Without Borders." In *International Trade in Services: New Trends and Opportunities for Developing Countries,* eds. O. Cattaneo, M. Engman, S. Saez, and R. M. Stern 99–140. Washington, DC: World Bank.

Chanda, R. 2006. "Effective Market Access in Modes 4 and 1." Indian Institute of Management, Bangalore.

Clerides, Safronis, Saul Lach, and James Tybout. 1998. "Is learning by Exporting Important? Micro-dynamic Evidence from Colombia, Mexico, and Morocco." *Quarterly Journal of Economics* 113 (3): 903–947.

Creskoff, S., and P. Walkenhorst. 2009. "Implications of WTO Disciplines for Special Economic Zones in Developing Countries." Policy Research Working Paper 4892, World Bank, Washington, DC.

Criscuolo, C., and M. Leaver. 2005. "Offshore Outsourcing and Productivity." Paper presented at the OECD Workshop on the Globalisation of Production: Impacts on Employment, Productivity and Economic Growth, Paris, November 15–16.

Cusolito, A. 2009. "Competition, Imitation, and Technical Change: Quality vs. Variety." Policy Research Working Paper Series 4997, World Bank, Washington, DC.

Damijan, J., Č. Kostevc, and S. Polanec. 2008. "From Innovation to Exporting or Vice Versa?" Working Paper No. 43., I. f. E. Research, Ljubljana.

Deardorff, A. and R. Stern. 1997. "Measurement of Non-Tariff Barriers," Economics Department, Working Paper No. 179, OECD, Paris.

Delgado, M., J. Farinas, and S. Ruano. 2002. "Firm Productivity and Export Markets: A Non-parametric Approach." *Journal of International Economics* 57 (2): 397–422.

de Wulf, Luc. 2001. "Why Have Trade Promotion Organizations Failed, and How They Can Be Revitalized?" PREM Notes #56, World Bank, Washington, DC.

Djankov, S., C. Freund, and C. Pham. 2006. "Trading on Time." Policy Research Working Paper No. 3909, World Bank, Washington, DC.

Dollar, David, and Edward N. Wolff. 1988. "Convergence of Industry Labor Productivity among Advanced Economies: 1963–1982." Working Papers 88-19, C.V. Starr Center for Applied Economics, New York University.

Eaton, J., and S. Kortum. 2001. "Trade in Capital Goods." *European Economic Review* 45 (7): 1195–1235.

Eichengreen, B. 2008. "The Real Exchange Rate and Economic Growth." Working Paper No. 4, Commission on Growth and Development, World Bank, Washington, DC.

Egis BCEOM International. 2008. "West African Road Transport and Transit Facilitation Strategy." ECOWAS Technical Assistance Project.

Ellingsen, T., and J. Vlachos. 2009. "Trade Finance during Liquidity Crisis." International Trade Department, World Bank, Washington, DC.

Engman, M. 2010. "Exporting Information Technology Services: In the Footsteps of India." In *International Trade in Services: New Trends and Opportunities for Developing Countries,* eds. O. Cattaneo, M. Engman, S. Saez, and R. M. Stern, 219–262. Washington, DC: World Bank.

Escribano, A., J. Pena, and J. G. Reis. 2010. "Trade Competitiveness and the Investment Climate: An International Comparison," Mimeo, World Bank, Washington, DC.

Fajnzylber, P., J. L. Guasch, and J. H. López, eds. 2009. *Does the Investment Climate Matter? Microeconomic Foundations of Growth in Latin America.* Washington, DC: World Bank.

Farole, T. 2011. *Special Economic Zones in Africa: Comparing Performance and Learning from Global Experiences.* Washington, DC: World Bank.

Farole, T., and J. Reis. 2010. "Trade and the Competitiveness Agenda." Economic Premise 18, World Bank, Washington, DC.

Fox, J. T., and V. Smeets. 2009. "Does Input Quality Drive Measured Differences in Firm Productivity?" University of Chicago Working Paper, Illinois.

Freund, Caroline, and Martha Denisse Pierola. 2008. "Export Surges: The Power of a Competitive Currency." Policy Research Working Paper Series 4750, World Bank, Washington, DC.

Galindo-Rueda, F., and J. Haskel. 2005. "Skills, Workforce Characteristics and Firm-Level Productivity: Evidence from the Matched ABI/Employer Skills Survey." IZA Discussion Paper No. 1542, Forschungsinstitut zur Zukunft der Arbeit Bonn.

Gereffi, G., J. Humphrey, and T. Sturgeon. 2005. "The Governance of Global Value Chains." *Review of International Political Economy* 12 (1): 1–27.

Giuliani, E., C. Pietrobelli, and R. Rabellotti. 2005. "Upgrading in Global Value Chains: Lessons from Latin American Clusters." *World Development* 33 (4): 549–573.

Grossman, Gene M., and Elhanan Helpman. 1991. "Trade, Knowledge Spillovers, and Growth." NBER Working Papers 3485, National Bureau of Economic Research, Cambridge, MA.

Hall, Bronwyn, Francesca Lotti, and Jacques Mairesse. 2007. "Employment, Innovation, and Productivity: Evidence from Italian Microdata." NBER Working Paper 13296, National Bureau of Economic Research, Cambridge, MA.

Hall, R. E, and Jones, C. 1999. "Why Do Some Countries Produce So Much More Output than Others?" *Quarterly Journal of Economics* 114: 83–116.

Harding, T., and B. S. Javorcik. 2007. "Developing Economies and International Investors: Do Investment Promotion Agencies Bring Them Together?" Policy Research Working Paper Series 4339, World Bank, Washington, DC.

Harrison, Rupert, Jordi Jaumandreu, Jacques Mairesse, and Bettina Peters. 2005. "Does Innovation Stimulate Employment? A Firm-Level analysis Using Comparable Micro Data from four European Countries." Department of Economics, University Carlos III, Madrid.

Henson, M., F. Jensen, S. Jaffee, and L. Diaz Rios. Forthcoming. "Assessing the Demand for Trade-Related Food safety and Quality Interventions in Agri-Food Chains: A Guidance Note." World Bank, Washington, DC.

Hausmann, R., J. Hwang, and D. Rodrik. 2006. "What You Export Matters." CEPR Discussion Papers 5444, Centre for Economic Policy and Research, London.

Helpman, E. 1984. "A Simple Theory of International Trade with Multinational Corporations." *Journal of Political Economy* 94 (3): 451–471.

Hernesniemi, H., M. Lammi, and P. Yl‰-Anttila. 1996. "Advantage Finland—The Future of Finnish Industries." Etla Series B 113, Research Institute of the Finnish Economy (ETLA), Helsinki.

Hoekman, B., and A. Mattoo. 2008. "Services Trade and Growth." Policy Research Working Paper No. 4461, World Bank, Washington, DC.

Hoekman, B., and A. Nicita. 2008. "Trade Policy, Trade Costs, and Developing Country Trade." World Bank Policy Research Working Paper 4797, World Bank, Washington, DC.

Hummels, D. 2001. "Time as a Trade Barrier." Purdue University, Indianapolis, IN.

ICC (International Chamber of Commerce). 2009. "Rethinking Trade Finance 2009: An ICC Global Survey." ICC Banking Commission Market, Paris.

Imbs, J., and R. Wacziarg. 2003. "Stages of Diversification." *American Economic Review*. 93 (1): 63–86.

Jeonghoi, Kim. 2010. "Recent Trends in Export Restrictions." OECD Trade Policy Working Paper No. 101, Organisation for Economic Co-operation and Development, Paris.

Kaplinsky, R. 2010. "The Role of Standards in Global Value Chains." Policy Research Working Paper No. 5396, World Bank, Washington, DC.

Kaplinsky, R., and M. Z. Farooki. 2010. "What Are the Implications for Global Value Chains When the Market Shifts from the North to the South?" World Bank Policy Research Working Paper No. 5205, World Bank, Washington, DC.

Kaplinsky, R., A. Terheggen, and J. P. Tijaja. 2010. "What Happens When the Market Shifts to China? The Gabon Timber and the Thai Cassava Value Chains." World Bank Policy Research Working Paper No. 5206, World Bank, Washington, DC.

Kee, H. L., A. Nicita, and M. Olarreaga. 2008. "Estimating Trade Restrictiveness Indices." *Economic Journal* 119: 172–199.

Lall, S. 2000. "The Technological Structure and Performance of Developing Country Manufactured Exports, 1985-1998." Working Paper, Q. E. House, University of Oxford.

Lederman, D., M. Olarreaga, and L. Payton. 2009. "Export Promotion Agencies Revisited." Policy Research Working Paper No. 5125. Washington, DC: World Bank.

Lee, J. W. 1995. "Capital Goods Imports and Long-Run Growth." *Journal of Development Economics* 48: 91–110.

Li, Y., and J. Wilson, J. 2009. "Trade Facilitation and Expanding the Benefits of Trade: Evidence from Firm Level Data." Asia-Pacific Research

and Training Network on Trade (ARTNeT), an initiative of the United Nations Economic and Social Commission for Asia and the Pacific (UNESCAP) and the Intenational Development Research Center (IDRC), Canada.

Loayza, N. V., and L. Servén. 2010. *Business Regulation and Economic Performance*. World Bank, Washington, DC.

Love, I., L. A. Preve, and V. Sarria-Allende. 2005. "Trade Credit and Bank Credit: Evidence from Recent Financial Crises." Policy Research Working Paper Series 3716, World Bank, Washington, DC.

Malouche, M. 2009. "Trade and Trade Finance Developments in 14 Developing Countries Post-September 2008." World Bank, Washington, DC.

Markusen, J. 1984. "Multinationals, Multi-plant Economies, and the Gains from Trade." *Journal of International Economics* 16 (3/4): 205–226.

Mathew, S. 2003. "Trade in Fisheries and Human Development: Country Case Study of India." Asia Pacific Regional Initiative on Trade, Economic Governance, and Human Development. UNDP. Asia, Hanoi.

Mattoo, A. 2009. "Exporting Services." In *Breaking into New Markets*, eds. R. Newfarmer, W. Shaw, and P. Walkenhorst. Washington DC: World Bank.

McKinsey Global Institute. 2010a. "How to Compete and Grow: A Sector Guide to Policy." McKinsey Global Institute, Washington, DC.

Melitz, M. J. 2003. "The Impact of Trade on Intra-Industry Reallocations and Aggregate Industry Productivity." *Econometrica* 71 (6): 1695–1725.

Menichini, A. 2009. "Study on Inter-Firm Trade Finance in Times of Crisis." International Trade Department, World Bank.

Miao, Y., and A. Berg. 2010. "The Real Exchange Rate and Growth Revisited: The Washington Consensus Strikes Back?" IMF Working Papers 10/58, International Monetary Fund.

Miroudot, Sébastien, Rainer Lanz, and Alexandros Ragoussis. 2009. "Trade in Intermediate Goods and Services." OECD Trade Policy Working Paper No. 93, Organisation for Economic Co-operation and Development, Paris.

Nadvi. 1997. "Cutting Edge: Collective Efficiency and International Competitiveness in Pakistan." IDS Discussion Paper 360, Institute of Development Studies, Brighton.

Nair-Reichert, Usha, and Diana Weinhold. 2001. "Causality Tests for Cross-Country Panels: A New Look at FDI and Economic Growth in Developing Countries." *Oxford Bulletin of Economics and Statistics* 63, no. 2 (May): 153–171.

Nogués, Julio. 2008. "The Domestic Impact of Export Restrictions: The Case of Argentina." IPC Position Paper–Agricultural and Rural Development Policy Series July, International Food & Agricultural Trade Policy Council, Washington, DC.

OECD (Organisation for Economic Co-operation and Development). 2003. *Science, Technology and Industry Scoreboard*. OECD: Paris.

Oxfam. 2004. "Stitched Up: How Rich Country Protectionism in Textiles and Clothing Prevents Poverty Alleviation." Briefing Paper No. 60. Oxfam International, Oxford.

Park, Albert, Dean Yang, Xinzheng Shi, and Yuan Jiang. 2009. "Exporting and Firm Performance: Chinese Exporters and the Asian Financial Crisis." *Review of Economics and Statistics* 92(4): 822–842.

Pavcnik, N. 2002. "Trade Liberalization, Exit, and Productivity Improvements: Evidence from Chilean Plants." *Review of Economic Studies* 69: 245–276.

Pavitt, K. 1984. "Sectoral Patterns of Technical Change: Towards a Taxonomy and a Theory." *Research Policy* 13 (6): 343–373.

Porter, M. E. 1998. "Measuring The Microeconomic Foundations of Economic Development." In *The Global Competitiveness Report*. Geneva, Switzerland: World Economic Forum.

Porter, M. E. 1990. *The Competitive Advantage of Nations*. New York: Free Press.

Porter, M. E., Mercedes Delgado-Garcia, Christian H. M. Ketels, and Scott Stern. 2008. "Moving to a New Global Competitiveness Index." Chapter 1.2 of Global Competitiveness Report 2008/2009, 43–63. Geneva: World Economic Forum.

MODULE 2

MODULE 2

Porter, M. E., Christian H. M. Ketels, and Mercedes Delgado-Garcia. 2006. "The Microeconomic Foundations of Prosperity: Findings from the Business Competitiveness Index." In *Global Competitiveness Report 2006-2007*, ed. Augusto Lopez-Claros, Michael E. Porter, Xavier Sala-i-Martin and Klaus Schwab. Palgrave Macmillan.

Rajan, R., and L. Zingales. 1998. "Financial Dependence and Growth." *American Economic Review* 88: 559–586.

Roberts, Mark, and J. Tybout. 1997. "The Decision to Export in Colombia: An Empirical Model of Entry with Sunk Costs." *American Economic Review* 87 (4): 545–564.

Rodrik, D. 2008. "Industrial Development: Some Stylized Facts and Policy Directions." In *Industrial Development for the 21st Century*, eds. D. O'Connor and M. Kjöllerström, 7–8. New York: United Nations.

Schultz, T. W. 1961. "Investment in Human Capital." *American Economic Review* 51: 1035–1039.

Staiger, R. W., and A. O. Sykes. 2009. "International Trade and Domestic Regulation." Stanford Law and Economics Olin Working Paper No. 387Staritz, C. 2011. "Making the Cut: Is the Clothing Industry Still a Development Path for Low Income Countries?" World Bank, Washington, DC.

Syverson, C. 2010. "What Determines Productivity?" NBER Working Papers 15712, National Bureau of Economic Research, Cambridge, MA.

Terheggen, A. 2010. "The New Kid in the Forest: The Impact of China's Resource Demand on Gabon's Tropical Timber Value Chain." PhD Dissertation, The Open University, Milton Keynes.

Tijaja, J. P. 2010. "The Role of Exogenous Factors and Domestic Agency in Changing Market Conditions: Lessons from the Thai Cassava Value Chains." PhD Dissertation, Development Policy and Practice, The Open University, Milton Keynes.

Tokarick, S. 2006. "Does Import Protection Discourage Exports?" IMF Working Paper, wp/06/20, International Monetary Fund, Washington, DC.

Torres-Fuchslocher, C. 2010. "Understanding the Development of Technology-Intensive Suppliers in Resource-Based Developing Economies." *Research Policy* 39 (2): 268–277.

UNCTAD (United Nations Conference on Trade and Development). 2009. "Training Package on Trade Policy Analysis: Module 1 Descriptive Statistics." UNCTAD Virtual Institute, Geneva.

UNIDO (United Nations Industrial Development Organization). 2009. "Industrial Development Report 2009: Breaking In and Moving Up: New Industrial Challenges for the Bottom Billion and the Middle-Income Countries." United Nations Industrial Development Organization, Vienna.

UNIDO (United Nations Industrial Development Organization). 2006. *Product Quality—A Guide for Small and Medium-Sized Enterprises.* Vienna: United Nations Industrial Development Organization.

Vandenbussche, H., and M. Zanardi. 2010. "The Chilling Effects of Antidumping Proliferation." *European Economic Review.* 54 (6): 760–777.

Waglé, S. 2005a. "International Trade in Textiles and Clothing and Development Policy Options After the Full Implementation of the WTO Agreement on Textiles and Clothing (ATC)." UNDP Policy Paper, Regional Center, Colombo.

Waglé, S. 2003. "Protection in Global Trade: Catfish Dispute Between the United States and Vietnam." UNDP Policy Paper, Regional Center, Colombo.

Wagner, J. 2005. "Exports and Productivity: A Survey of the Evidence from Firm Level Data." University of L¸neburg Working Paper Series in Economics, No. 4, L¸neburg.

WEF (World Economic Forum). 2007. *The Global Competitiveness Report 2007–2008.* www.weforum.org.

Wells, L., and A. Wint. 2001. "Marketing a Country: Revisited." FIAS Occasional Paper 13, Foreign Investment Advisory Service, Washington, DC.

World Bank, Investment Climate Advisory Services. 2010. *Investing across Borders 2010–Indicators of Foreign Direct Investment Regulation in 87 Economies.* Washington, DC: World Bank.

World Bank. 2010a. "Connecting to Compete: Logistics Performance Index 2010." World Bank, Washington, DC.

World Bank. 2008. *Doing Business.* www.doingbusiness.org.

World Bank. 2009a. "Air Freight: A Market Study with Implications for Landlocked Countries." Transport Papers No. 26, August. World Bank, Washington, DC.

World Bank. 2009b. *Clusters for Competitiveness: A Practical Guide and Policy Implications for Developing Cluster Initiatives.* Washington, DC: International Trade Department, World Bank.

World Bank. 2009d. "Lessons for Reformers: How to Launch, Implement, and Sustain Regulatory Reform." World Bank, Washington, DC.

World Bank. 2004. *Global Economic Prospects 2005: Trade, Regionalism, and Development.* Washington, DC: World Bank.

World Bank. 2003. "From Goats to Coats: Institutional Reform in Mongolia's Cashmere Sector." World Bank, Washington, DC.

MODULE 3

POLICY OPTIONS FOR COMPETITIVENESS AND CASE STUDIES

This module of the *Toolkit* provides a discussion of broad policy areas and options for consideration in addressing the specific constraints identified through the Diagnostic exercise. It also includes case studies of good practice showing policies that were effective in addressing specific trade competitiveness constraints across a wide range of countries. However, given the highly context-specific and endogenous nature of policy development (particularly in the area of competitiveness), and the critical need to take into account political economy considerations when crafting policy, it does not provide prescriptive advice on specific policies that should be adopted.

Market Access

Market access issues often appear to be beyond a country's policy purview and control. This need not be so. After the Diagnostics is conducted, and if market access comes across as one of the serious hurdles to export competitiveness, it will be clear whether the problem pertains to the trade policy of other countries or to domestic capacity constraints. Policies can address both sets of issues at least over the medium term.

Develop and Implement a Trade Negotiations Strategy

Countries need to pursue tariff reductions at the WTO in both agricultural and nonagricultural (that is, NAMA) negotiations. The reduction in MFN tariffs is particularly important for exporters that are hurt by preferential tariffs enjoyed by competitors that export similar products. Conversely, LDCs that stand to lose their margins of tariff preference because of fall in MFN tariffs will need to negotiate to benefit from aid-for-trade measures and interim trade-related assistance for export diversification. Until the time tariffs are eliminated, they should also pursue duty-free-quota-free access for *all* their exports. In cases in which existing GSP schemes exclude exports of interest to them, such as textiles and clothing, countries should lobby for their inclusion in the major markets. Because progress on multilateral

trade negotiations is slow, countries could pursue bilateral and regional trade strategies for preferential access in major markets. Scope also exists to reduce tariffs among developing countries, such as the G-77 and China, under the auspices of Global System of Trade Preferences (GSTP).

Monitor and Seek Disciplines against Trade Remedy Measures, and Simplify Rules of Origin

With the reduction in tariffs and elimination of quotas, countries often take recourse to trade remedy measures such as antidumping and antisubsidy petitions to stem the flow of imports. Such trends should be monitored and fought vigorously if they affect market access or may do so in the future. These measures could be taken up in negotiations on WTO rules to reduce the impact of trade remedy measures with protectionist intent. LDCs could push for a moratorium of such actions against their exports. Emphasis must be put to issues like harmonizing the rules of origin so that beneficiaries are not burdened with different criteria in different preferential schemes. Poor countries make greater utilization of preferences when rules on *cumulation* and value added requirements are relaxed. In BTAs/RTAs, lax regional *cumulation* requirements could encourage countries to form more integrated supply chains within their regions.

Enhance Domestic Capacity to Monitor and Upgrade Quality and Standards of Exports

The underutilization of trade preferences and existing market access opportunities indicates that much of export competitiveness is blunted by poor domestic capacity. Foreign markets have legitimate concerns about the safety and the SPS status of goods entering their borders. To avoid rejections, exporting countries need to meet the required minimum of such standards in a cost-effective manner. Countries need effective legal and regulatory frameworks to comply with SPS standards set by international agencies like the Food and Agricultural Organization and the World Health Organization. Although the WTO permits countries to set their own SPS standards, they must instill confidence in importing countries by focusing, among others, on biosecurity, storage, and disinfection of pests and diseases. Especially for agricultural exports, this requires public-private partnerships to establish mechanisms for information sharing and support to organized exporting groups, including the establishment of laboratories and microbiology testing facilities for residues of drugs and pesticides.

Box 3.1 gives an example of the role of bilateral trade agreements in facilitating market access for exporters.

Trade and Investment Policy

In an increasingly integrated world, an open trade policy can improve countries' export competitiveness mainly by reducing the cost of imports and increasing the variety of imports. Policies that restrict access to foreign sources of intermediate goods and services can deny firms access to the goods and services they need to compete internationally, and these policies are more likely to produce firm closures and job losses. Experience has shown that policies that protect domestic production from foreign competition with the goal of protecting jobs and avoiding trade-related structural adjustment are often counterproductive, temporarily saving jobs in vulnerable sectors often at the expense of higher paying jobs in competitive sectors of the economy. Delaying inevitable adjustment almost invariably translates into greater long-term hardship than would be the case if policies of market openness were pursued.

Although an open trade policy is an essential component of sustainable economic growth, complementary policies also are needed to realize full benefits. Other policy choices that matter include adequate institutions and rule of law, which are crucial for property rights and for lowering transaction costs; sound regulatory framework and appropriate labor market, macroeconomic and investment

---

Box 3.1. Case Example of Good Policy Practice—Securing Market Access through a South-South Bilateral Trade Agreement

Frustrated with the slow progress in securing market access through the regional South Asian Free Trade Agreement (SAFTA), Sri Lanka and India signed a BTA, which became operational in March 2000. India committed to give duty-free access, within three years, to all Sri Lankan exports, except tea, textiles, and other items listed in the negative list. Given India's much larger size, it agreed to include in its negative list only 419 tariff lines at the HS six-digit level. Sri Lanka maintained a larger negative list of 1,180 tariff lines primarily to shield its agricultural sector from Indian competition. The BTA spurred trade flows between the countries in the early years. Indian exports to Sri Lanka increased from US$539 million in 1998 to more than US$1 billion in 2003. The share of Sri Lankan imports from India reached 25 percent in 2008 from about 8 percent in 2000. The share of Sri Lankan exports to India also picked up from about 1 percent in 2000 to 9 percent in 2005. It has since declined to less than 5 percent in 2009. Although India's exports were diversified, Sri Lanka's were concentrated in a few commodities such as copper and vegetable oil, which also attracted Indian investors to route developing country imports via Sri Lanka to take advantage of the tariff preference.

Generally considered a successful BTA, experiences with implementing the India–Sri Lanka Bilateral Trade Agreement highlight specific issues that are relevant to other pairs of developing countries seeking similar trade agreements. *First*, the rules of origin need to be negotiated carefully and then implemented well. Because the main export surge from Sri Lanka to India was in products for which the rules of origin were not enforced, the resulting trade disputes led to the introduction of TRQs, with India limiting preferences to imports up to a certain quantity only. This led to a decline in Sri Lankan exports during 2006–09. *Second*, mutual recognition of standards is crucial to reduce NTBs. Exporters suffer when SPS standards are not mutually recognized and shipments are subject to random harassment and lengthy approvals from the partner country. One of Sri Lanka's major export interests, tea, not only was subject to a TRQ but also could enter India only through two designated ports, leading to low utilization of preferences. *Third*, the trade agreement should be comprehensive and set milestones. Both India and Sri Lanka saw their FDI inflows increase into each other's territories. This increase was not only to take advantage of tariff preferences but also a response to signals issued by the signing of a legal agreement that increased business confidence. This success has led the two countries to negotiate an expansion of the current goods-only agreement to cover trade in services and cross-border investment under a Comprehensive Economic Partnership Agreement. This agreement will require the management of domestic opposition and the political economy, as well as a higher threshold of regulatory preparation and changes.

Sources: Jayasekera 2004; Weerakoon 2010.

MODULE 3

policies that facilitate the allocation of resources to increasingly productive employment; and adequate social safety nets and adjustment assistance.

The table below provides some broad guidelines as to the types of trade and investment policy levers that may be appropriate, depending on the constraints identified.

Box 3.2 provides some case study examples of good policy practice in addressing anti-export biases in the trade policy environment.

Policy areas and main issues	Remedies/Project components
Import barriers	• Cut import tariffs to reduce tariff dispersion, escalation, and effective rate of protection • Reduce gap between MFN and preferential tariffs • Analyze revenue impact of tariff reductions • Make tariffs publicly available
Export duties	• Eliminate export duties and quantitative restrictions • If duties used for tax revenues, consider alternative fiscal revenues
Nontariff measures	• Identify NTMs implemented by all government agencies • Encourage dialogue among agencies to avoid duplicate and redundant regulations • Streamline related procedures in terms of time and cost • Improve information on NTMs for private sector • Firm survey on NTMs faced by importers and exporters • Set up a public-private NTM review committee • Discuss less trade distorting alternatives • Use a Regulatory Impact Assessment • Facilitate customs procedures by connecting all government agencies to Single Window • Make NTMs publicly available • Study impact of state-trading enterprises, if any
Exchange rate and FDI policy	• Study the appropriateness of the current exchange rate regime • Liberalize access to key input sectors and/or promote foreign participation in joint ventures • Identify restrictions like licensing requirements and other regulatory requirements that create an unlevel playing field between domestic and foreign investors

Source: Authors.
Note: FDI = foreign direct investment; MFN = Most Favored Nation; NTM = nontariff measure.

Box 3.2. Case Examples of Good Policy Practice—Trade and Investment Policy

Chile: Unilateral Liberalization, FTAs, and an Agribusiness Export Boom
In the past two decades, Chile has become a major export success, particularly beyond its traditional minerals sectors, encompassing the agricultural and agriprocessing sector, including salmon, wine, and horticulture and, more recently, pork, poultry, and dairy. In addition to supply-side initiatives, Chile's trade policy played a key role in stimulating the growth of agricultural exports, through a combination of low tariffs, the removal of NTBs, and the strategic use of FTAs.

Unilateral liberalization of tariffs has played an important role in Chile's agricultural export success. Average tariff rates stood around 20 percent at the end of the 1980s, but they were cut virtually in half within five years, and in half again within another five years. Uniform MFN tariffs now stand at 6 percent, with the effective tariff rate around 2 percent because of the many preferential trade agreements into which Chile has entered. Preferential trade agreements have significantly expanded producers' market access to new markets for agricultural products, for example, pork in the Republic of Korea and Japan. These agreements have been critical in removing regulatory NTBs in Chile's agricultural sector (and in parallel improving export market access), as most of the trade agreements have included strict implementation and monitoring procedures, for example, related to SPS arrangements.

In addition to improving market access potential, the reforms had two important impacts on agribusiness producers and exporters in Chile. First, they improved their access to competitively priced inputs, most important, capital equipment, but also other key agricultural and nonagricultural inputs. This particularly catalyzed investment and growth in the processing sector. Second, they triggered supply chain consolidation and vertical integration in the agribusiness sector, linked in part to a significant increase in FDI, resulting in larger and more competitive exporters.

(continued on next page)

MODULE 3

Box 3.2. *(continued)*

Between 1990 and 2006, annual agricultural exports grew from US$2 billion to US$9 billion, an average growth rate of almost 10 percent per year. In addition, Chile has successfully diversified its destination markets for agricultural exports—in the four years to 2005, for example, 30 percent of agricultural exports went to North America, 25 percent to Europe, 26 percent to Asia, and 18 percent to Latin America. Perhaps more important has been Chile's success in adding value to primary agricultural production—processed food products have risen to be the most important subsector in manufacturing, accounting for 30 percent of all manufacturing output (ahead of even nonferrous metals and chemicals, traditionally important sectors in the country).

Sources: OECD 2008; Ffrench-Davis 2010.

Mexico: Streamlining NTMs
The Mexican government embarked on an ambitious reform agenda to streamline its NTMs as part of a broader competitiveness agenda in the aftermath of the financial crises that hit Mexico in the 1980s and 1990s. Then NAFTA provided a strong political anchor to a reform process by making reversion to protectionism politically impossible. The process was institutionalized through the creation of a regulatory-improvement agency. The Economic Deregulation Unit (UDE), created as early as 1989, was placed under the Secretariat of Trade's authority, but given, by presidential decree, a broader authority than the Secretariat. It was then transformed into a formal federal agency, COFEMER, in 2000. The regulatory reform process was top-down and driven by a small group of 15 to 20 technocrats. These were a mixture of economists and lawyers, many of them trained abroad. The number of licenses, permits, and other information requirements in the commerce and transport sector, for instance, was cut from about a thousand in 1995 to fewer than 400 in 2000, and UDE reviewed more than 500 regulatory proposals between 1995 and 2000. In total, about 90 percent of Mexico's regulatory framework was affected by the process.

Sources: Salas 2005; IFC 2008b.

Domestic Policies and Institutions: Business Environment and Governance

Once areas for improvements are identified and priorities are clearly defined, government authorities need to undertake a series of reforms to tackle the aspects of the business environment and governance that most constrain competitiveness of exporters. Successful countries often combine high levels of human capital in the public administration, and the use of modern technology to minimize the regulatory burden on businesses and ensure greater transparency. Furthermore, in cases in which private markets are functioning, competition serves as a substitute for regulation. By combining simple regulation with good definition and protection of property rights, they achieve what many others strive to do—that is, having government regulators serve as enablers of competitiveness and economic growth. Aside from how much and what they regulate, good practice countries share common elements in how they regulate. For example, countries with the least time to register a business, such as Canada, have single registration forms accessible over the Internet. Countries that take the least time to enforce a collateral agreement, Germany, Thailand, and the United States, for example, allow out-of-court enforcement (IFC 2006).

The design of regulation determines the efficiency of economic and social outcomes. Good practice is not limited to rich countries or countries in which comprehensive regulatory reform has taken place. Previous country experiences have shown that not all reforms need to be done at the same time and that setting priorities is the initial step for successful reforms. Partial reforms may lead to a virtuous circle in which the success of one reform emboldens policy makers to pursue further reforms. Simplification is the most common objective in regulatory reforms. Simplification involves not only a business process change but also cultural change in how regulators view those they regulate, and how those who are regulated perceive the value and effectiveness of the regulatory processes. Simplification does not mean compromising core standards with respect to health, safety, the environment, or labor. Simplification means reducing or eliminating elements of a process to reduce complexity and inefficiency. It also involves limiting the potential of any reintroduction of cumbersome or unnecessary requirements or steps. Simplification does not absolutely require that regulators make radical changes to its processes; rather, it can be achieved through a more gradual and incremental approach.

Box 3.3 provides some case study examples of good policy practice in addressing business environment reforms.

Box 3.3. Case Examples of Good Policy Practice—Domestic Policies and Institutions

Serbia: Business Registration Reform

For decades, starting a business in Serbia was time-consuming and burdened with unnecessary bureaucratic hurdles—the rules inherited from its Communist past were not business friendly. Some of the biggest problems included the following: the $5,000 minimum capital requirement for starting a limited liability company, the necessary inspections before a company could start operating, and the commercial courts checking every document. Sixteen commercial courts were in charge of registering enterprises, and 131 municipalities dealt with registering entrepreneurs. The practice was so inconsistent that even judges in the same court required different documents. Countless reports identified the need to reform the system. By 2001–02 a decision was taken to undertake reform.

The reform had two elements. The first was a radical change of the laws, and the second was making the new system work in practice by establishing a new registry. Using the Irish system as a model, the system was centralized and accessible via the Internet, leading to far greater legal certainty. Another very important change was the five-day deadline to register a company. If no decision is made in five days, the applicant is free to begin operations (that is, silence is consent). For the company law, too, rather than amend the old law, a new one more suitable for a market economy was created. The new company law reduced the minimum capital requirement for limited liability companies (90 percent of all companies in Serbia) from $5,000 (equivalent to around €4,500 at the time) to €500 and eased requirements for establishing companies by making the rules more flexible.

The effects of the reform were felt almost immediately. The time necessary for starting a business was reduced from 51 days in 2004 to 18 in 2005. The new system was a radical change, with a focus on customer service and user friendliness. And the forms for registration are being continually improved to reduce the time to complete them. After the decentralized and inconsistent practices of the commercial courts, the new system is centralized, with Internet access to all registration data. To unify practices, only one person—the registrar—has final authority and the power to interpret the relevant laws. This increases legal certainty and uniformity across the board. During its first year, the Serbian Business Registry Agency registered almost 11,000 new companies, 70 percent more than in 2004, shrinking the informal sector. In two years, the number of registered businesses more than doubled.

Source: World Bank 2008 (http://www.doingbusiness.org/reforms/case-studies/2007/starting-a-business-in-serbia).

(continued on next page)

MODULE 3

Box 3.3. *(continued)*

Arab Republic of Egypt: Tax Reform

With 37 percent of Egypt's workforce in the informal sector, the government realized reform was the way to broaden its tax base and increase revenues. Tax rates were high, the process of making payments was cumbersome, and tax evasion was the norm. In July 2004, a new cabinet took office with a mandate to reform. One of its goals was to increase employment through investment. To do so, a high priority was placed on amending the tax law, customs law, and customs tariffs and on enacting competition and antitrust laws. Making Egyptian tax law closer to international practice would increase Egypt's competitiveness and its attractiveness as a destination for foreign investment.

The boldest reform was to simplify tax law so that every business faces the same tax burden—with no exemptions, tax holidays, or special treatments for large or foreign businesses. Taxation administration also improved. Self-assessment replaced administrative assessment, which was essential for the tax reform. There is also less room for interpretation, reducing the possibility of negotiating taxes.

The results were an immediate increase in taxpayer submissions by almost 50 percent, an increase in corporate tax revenues from £E22 billion in fiscal year 2004 to £E39 billion in fiscal year 2005, despite the fall in corporate tax rates (from a variable rate between 32 percent and 40 percent to a flat rate of 20 percent), and an overall increase in tax revenue from 7 percent to 9 percent of GDP.

Source: World Bank 2008 (http://www.doingbusiness.org/reforms/case-studies/2007/adding-a-million-taxpayers-in-egypt).

Australia: Competition Policy

Australia's competition-oriented reforms happened in three waves, first through increased exposure to international markets in the early 1990s; followed by the development and implementation of the *National Competition Policy* (NCP) in the mid-1990s, and with regular updates in the late 1990s and onward. Comprehensive reforms coordinated across all levels of government aimed to (1) reform all legislation that restricted competition; (2) implement a culture of "continuous improvement" in regulatory quality; (3) implement competitive neutrality for all public businesses; and (4) provide third-party access to significant infrastructure facilities.

The NCP was implemented through an incentive scheme in which the national government financially rewarded (or penalized) achievements of negotiated milestones. A system of "competition payments," defined as the state's share of additional revenue arising from the NCP, was introduced. Federal to state governments made payments that implemented specific reforms, while pecuniary penalties were imposed on slow reformers, in the form of reduced or delayed budget transfers from the central government. Although a majority of reform goals in competition policy were met on time in the 10-year period, in some cases, pecuniary penalties for slow reformers exist. For instance, Western Australia's uncompleted plans for water systems led to a 5 percent suspension penalty of its 2005–06 competition payments. When reform goals were finally met in 2007, suspended payments were then disbursed. Similarly, Queensland's failure to address anticompetitive restrictions in liquor licensing resulted in a 5 percent permanent deduction penalty of the state's 2003–04 competition payments.

The Australian experience is considered to be one of the most successful examples in recent years. The NCP helped make Australia one of the top-performing OECD economies and has enhanced economic flexibility and adaptability to change, showing the quickest recovery from the global crisis among OECD countries. The reforms have reduced barriers to entry and exit and improved competition, estimated to have increased GDP by 2.5 percent (not including dynamic effects).

Source: World Bank 2011b.

Access to Finance

Policy areas and main issues	Remedies/Project components
General access to finance issues	• Improving the regulatory framework and competition in the banking system • Facilitating the development of early stage financing, including "business angel" networks • Improving credit information systems (e.g., credit bureaus) • Establishing or improving the operation of a credit guarantee program • Capacity building to improve bank knowledge and capability in dealing with SMEs or the export sector
Trade finance	• Establishing a focused trade finance institution • Strengthening the capacity of existing institutions (e.g., export credit guarantee agency) • Expanding access to existing services offered through government-owned development banks by enabling them to be distributed through existing commercial banks • Providing backing for an export credit insurance product • Developing markets for factoring and forfeiting products

Source: Authors.
Note: SME = small and medium enterprises.

Box 3.4 provides some case study examples of good policy practice to facilitate access to finance for exporters.

Box 3.4. Case Examples of Good Policy Practice—Access to Finance

Singapore: Financing SME Growth and Internationalization
With a small population and an extremely limited geographic base, growth for Singaporean firms depends on competitiveness in export markets. In line with Singapore's development strategy of broad global engagement, the government has made strong efforts to facilitate the expansion of domestic SMEs into international markets, including through overseas investment. These efforts include, among others, financing, tax incentives, and grants. Among the key programs are the Growth Financing Programme and the Internationalization Finance Scheme.

The Growth Financing Programme, run by the Singapore Economic Development Board (EDB) makes long-term equity investments in early stage SMEs that are seen to have the potential to become globally competitive. Companies that have successfully completed product development and can show some initial "customer traction" can apply for equity financing for overseas market expansion through the program, with the potential that every S$2 raised by the growth company from third-party investors will be matched by S$1 from EDB, subject to a maximum of S$1,000,000 (and with a minimum third-party investment of S$500,000).

The Internationalization Finance Scheme, run by International Enterprise (IE) Singapore, facilitates financing for fixed investments abroad or confirmed overseas projects, including loans, guarantees, and asset-based financing (e.g., leasing). The amount of financing available under the scheme recently was raised from S$15 million to S$50 million. To attract private financing, the government of Singapore assumes 80 percent of the risk of financing. The program is open to Singapore-based firms with less than S$300 million in turnover.

The program has been effective in facilitating outward expansion by Singaporean SMEs. According to a government survey of SMEs in 2009, 69 percent had established overseas ventures. Data from the 2010 Start-up Enterprise Survey shows that 25 percent of Singaporean start-ups now have overseas revenue.

Sources: http://www.iesingapore.com (accessed November 9, 2011); www.edb.gov.sg (accessed November 9, 2011).
Note: S$1 = US$0.784 as of September 21, 2011.

Vietnam: Securing Lending
In Vietnam, accessing credit continues to be a binding constraint for entrepreneurs and the burgeoning sector of smaller businesses in Vietnam. Donor reports estimate 20 to 40 percent of households and small firms do not have access to formal financing channels. IFC responded to a request from the government of Vietnam to streamline the country's secured transactions laws and registry. This effort resulted in a three-point improvement on the relevant *Doing Business* indicator, putting the Vietnamese legal framework on par with the OECD average. Vietnam's "getting credit" ranking in the *Doing Business* 2008 report improved from 80 to 48 among 145 countries. As a result of the law, any asset could legally be used as collateral, creditors would be better able to assess the risk profile of their lending portfolios, and all conflicting legislation was repealed.

Source: IFC 2008a.

(continued on next page)

MODULE 3

Box 3.4. *(continued)*

Mexico: NAFIN Productive-Chain Reverse-Factoring Services for SMEs

Following Mexico's major internationalization in the 1990s, mainly induced through NAFTA, many large companies became highly successful exporters. Yet the large SME sector still struggled with traditional barriers to growth and export participation, most important, access to finance, linked to their lack (or perceived lack) of creditworthiness. In response to this, and partly as a strategic commercial move in its own right, *Nacional Financiera* (NAFIN), a state-owned development bank with 32 branch offices nationwide, developed a so-called productive chains program in 2001 to link large creditworthy buyer firms with small risky firms unable to access formal finance.

The NAFIN factoring program operates an electronic platform that provides factoring services online. The website has a dedicated page for each big buyer, and small suppliers are grouped into chains with those big buyers with whom they have business relationships. The suppliers and NAFIN sign an agreement allowing the electronic sale and transfer of receivables. Once a supplier delivers goods and its invoice to the buyer, the buyer posts a negotiable document equal to the amount that will be factored on its NAFIN webpage. In general, this is equal to 100 percent of the value of the receivable. The supplier will then be able to access its buyer's NAFIN webpage and see all factors that are willing to finance this particular receivable along with their quotes for interest rates. Picking the one it deems has the most favorable terms, the supplier clicks on the name of the factor, and the amount of the negotiable document less interest is transferred to the supplier's bank account. When the invoice is due, the buyer pays the factor directly. The efficiency of the electronic platform means that small suppliers typically have money within one business day.

A few features make the NAFIN factoring program unique, namely, the following:

- The use of the electronic platform and the Internet reduces costs and improves efficiency for all parties involved: sellers, buyers, and factors. More than 98 percent of all services related to the factoring are provided electronically, all transactions can be completed within three hours, and money is credited to the supplier's account by the close of business the same day. This provides immediate liquidity to suppliers.
- The use of reverse factoring transfers the credit risk of the small suppliers to highly creditworthy buyers and enables NAFIN to offer factoring without requiring collateral to SMEs, which often lack a credit history or access to other forms of formal financing. In addition, there is no service fee, and the maximum interest rate charged is about 8 percentage points below commercial banks' lending rates.
- The competitive, instant, online, multifactor structure nurtures competition among factors and allows small suppliers to pick the factor with the most favorable terms. Most factors refinance their factoring activities with NAFIN, earning the difference between the rate they charge the suppliers and the rate NAFIN pays.

Two important steps taken by the Mexican government enabled NAFIN to undertake its successful factoring program. First, in May 2000, the government implemented reforms to legislation pertaining to e-commerce that gave electronic messages the same legal validity as written documents. Passage of the Law of Conservation of Electronic Documents established requirements for conservation of the content of electronic messages regarding contracts, agreements, and accords. The Electronic Signature Law permits substituting electronic signatures for written signatures and allows the receiver of a digital document to verify the identity of the sender. Modifications to the Federation Fiscal Code included amendments necessary to complete electronic transactions, including factoring. Second, favorable taxation treatment helps keep factoring costs low for SMEs and gives them incentives to participate in the factoring program. All interest charges that small suppliers pay to their factors are tax deductible.

The factoring program managed to secure the participation of 190 big buyers (accounting for 45 percent of the output in the private sector) and more than 70,000 SME suppliers. Twenty domestic banks and finance companies act as the factors. Since the program's inception in September 2001, NAFIN extended more than US$9 billion in financing to SMEs in its first few years of operation. The program also contributed to a dramatic turnaround in NAFIN's own finances from a deficit of US$429 million in 2000 to a surplus of US$13 million in December 2003. With the efficiency of its Internet platform, NAFIN's market share of factoring grew from 2 percent in 2001 to 60 percent in 2004. It is able to provide the cheapest form of financing available for small suppliers in Mexico. An example for other countries as well, NAFIN has entered into an agreement with a development bank in Republica Bolivariana de Venezuela to develop a similar product. NAFIN's model is also being considered for replication in other Latin American countries such as Argentina, Chile, Costa Rica, El Salvador, and Nicaragua.

Source: World Bank 2006.

Ghana: Farmers Use of Warehouse Receipts to Finance Exports

Since 1989, the NGO TechnoServe has worked closely with the Department of Co-operatives and the Agricultural Development Bank in Ghana in encouraging small-scale farmers to form cooperatives and use warehouse receipts to store their crops for sale in the lean season. The bank provides loans against the members' grain, at 75 to 80 percent of current market price, and the grain is stored in cooperatively owned warehouses. The scheme is concentrated in the Brong-Ahafo "maize triangle" of Ghana—the major area of agricultural surplus, where annual price fluctuations are high.

From 1992 to 1996, farmers participating in the scheme in this region were able to increase their profits on grain sales by an average of 94 percent per year.

Source: UNESCAP 2003.

(continued on next page)

Box 3.4. *(continued)*

Philippines: Credit Guarantee for Indirect Exporters—the Asparagus Case

An association of small farmers in South Cotabato, Philippines, with landholdings ranging from three to five hectares wanted to enter into a contract to grow asparagus for Dole Philippines Inc. The farmers were beneficiaries of the government's Agrarian Reform Program that distributed rice and corn farm lands. Dole identified the area as suitable for planting asparagus and offered the farmers a contract growing scheme whereby Dole would provide the farming technology and inputs such as asparagus seedlings. Dole planned to export fresh asparagus to Japan. Under the growing agreement, pricing was subject to a floor price with an escalation should the export market price increase.

This was a start-up project and the first commercial-scale production of asparagus in the country. No commercial banks would lend to the farmers association. The farmers' only assets were their small agricultural lands titles that were not yet perfected. A government bank, the Development Bank of the Philippines (DBP), was willing to finance the project under its Window 3 Program, which charged less-than-commercial rates for developmental projects. The bank determined that the asparagus production was developmental as it involved a new agricultural industry, agrarian reform beneficiaries, and foreign exchange earnings. DBP, however, needed a guarantee for the loan. The guarantee was provided by the Guarantee Fund for Small and Medium-Scale Enterprises (GFSME), a quasi-government agency (now the Small Business Corporation, a government-owned financial institution). The GFSME provided an 80 percent guarantee, and Dole Philippines issued a commercial guarantee for 10 percent, for a total of a 90 percent guarantee on the PHP 30 million loan to the farmers from DBP.

Beginning with 90 hectares first planted with asparagus on a commercial scale, more than 3,000 hectares of asparagus have since been planted in South Cotabato and other provinces. Foreign exchange earnings from the export of asparagus mainly to Japan and Europe have made asparagus a major cash crop in the country. Income and employment effects on the local economies have been substantial.

Source: ITC 2009.

Indonesia: Export Credit Guarantees in Times of Crisis

When financial institutions do not have confidence in the stability of the importer's country or in the standing of the financial institution issuing the L/C, confirmed letters of credit become difficult and expensive—sometimes impossible—to obtain. During the Asian crisis (1998), Indonesian banks had difficulty getting foreign counterparties to confirm the L/Cs they issued on behalf of Indonesian importers because of doubt over the stability of the entire Indonesian financial system. Without confirmed L/Cs, Indonesian importers could not import raw materials needed for their own export production.

Both national and bilateral support in terms of export credit guarantees played an important role in freeing up the market. Indonesia's Central Bank deposited US$1 billion in 12 foreign banks to guarantee export L/Cs issued from Indonesian banks. They also provided a short-term hedging facility for exporters to provide additional liquidity. Some relatively stable Indonesian banks also made deposits in foreign banks and used those deposits as cash collateral for their L/Cs. Finally, Japan Export Import Bank (JBIC) provided financing via the Bank of Indonesia to guarantee L/Cs issued by domestic Indonesian banks. Strict qualification requirements restricted its take-up in the market initially, but this improved later.

Sources: ITC 2009; Chauffour and Farole 2010.

MODULE 3

Labor Markets, Skills, and Firm-Level Technical Efficiency

Policy areas and main issues	Remedies/Project components
Labor markets and skills	• Improvements in labor market regulation—for example, hiring and firing practices, shift protection from employment to social policy (e.g., unemployment insurance)
	• Linking regular minimum wage increases with productivity
	• Training and skills development initiatives, including the following: addressing skills mismatches; pre-employment skills training initiatives; and active labor market training programs to reintegrate the unemployed and disadvantaged back into the workforce
	• Ensuring greater portability of education and training credentials
	• Focusing vocational training programs to meet the needs of the private sector
	• Decentralizing provision of vocational training and facilitating greater private provision
	• Improving enforcement of labor standards
Firm-level technical efficiency	• Programs to support public-private initiatives for training and vocational education
	• Encourage high-quality business education
	• Establish a regulatory environment which makes entry easy and which allows quality to determine success
	• Entrepreneurship development training

Box 3.5 includes brief case studies highlighting good practice policies and initiatives designed to improve competitiveness through improving labor skills, productivity, and technical efficiency.

Box 3.5. Case Examples of Good Policy Practice—Training, Skills Development, and Technical Efficiency

Malaysia: The Penang Skills Development Centre (PSDC)
The PSDC is the first skills industry-led training center to be set up in Malaysia. It was conceptualized in 1989 out of urgency that, for Penang to continue to attract FDIs, its human capital must be trained to keep pace with changes in technology. Although the initiative, land, and some financial support came from the state and federal governments, with initial support from some of the US electronics MNCs in the state, the leading role in the center was the private industry. Not only did they provide the initial trainers and equipment, but also were responsible for designing the training programs to meet their needs.

PSDC now has 140 members and operates as a nonprofit society. Its mission is to pool resources among the Free Industrial Zones and Industrial Estates in Penang to provide up-to-date training and education programs in support of operational requirements, as well as to keep abreast of technological progress. The center operates on a full cost basis, and companies that send employees to the center pay for the training. To ensure that the training provided meets the needs of industry, the programs were continually upgraded and adapted to evolving skill needs.

The PSDC now caters to the firms in the free industrial zones and industrial parks in Penang, which as of late 2007, had a total of 1,277 factories employing approximately 220,000 workers. The center has trained more than 150,000 participants through more than 7,000 courses, pioneered local industry development initiatives, assisted in the input and formulation of national policies pertaining to human capital development, and contributed directly to the Malaysian workforce transformation initiatives. More recently, the PSDC has set up a new Shared Services Center to house Malaysia's largest Electromagnetic Compatibility Lab, which will provide training programs to fast-track the work readiness of university graduates. The program will be conducted in partnership with member companies to bridge the competency gap of Malaysian graduates and needs of the industry.

Initially, the PSDC was unique, but its model has since been adopted throughout the country; currently, 11 of 13 states in Malaysia now have skills development centers.

Sources: Penang Skills Development Centre 2010; InvestPenang 2010.

Honduras: *Instituto Politécnico Centroamericano (IPC)*
IPC is a nongovernmental, nonprofit, vocational training institute that was founded in 2005. An assessment of Honduras vocational training system had concluded that the system was broken: instructors were incapable of teaching and 95 percent of equipment was stolen, broken, or irrelevant. Based on these findings, IPC was established to design courses for current and future workers in all sectors of the economy, including in manufacturing and textiles and clothing. The institute's objective is to provide workers with relevant skills demanded by industry. Its curricula are hence strongly influenced by input from employers. IPC strives to offer the best technical equipment, curricula, and test instructors in the region. For example, a majority of the 12 instructors are brought from North America, Europe, and Latin America. In the spring of 2009, IPC had 270 full-time students, and some 1,400 workers were upgrading their skills in courses lasting between 2 and 18 weeks. A majority of the graduates join the *maquila* companies: for example, Gildan, a large Canadian apparel company, hires 60 students from IPC every year.

(continued on next page)

Box 3.5. *(continued)*

Ninety percent of students come from families earning less than US$300/month and the fee for a year of full-time training is US$1,500. The expenses are partly covered by companies, charitable organizations, and governments: a US NGO covers transportation and a daily meal; a Swiss company that supplies chemicals to the textiles industry donated a chemistry lab; a French company provided design equipment; and an Italian company donated sewing equipment. Roughly 95 percent of the students receive a corporate scholarship that covers 75 percent of the fee. In return, they commit to work for the sponsor for two to four years. Foreign multinationals are carrying most of the expenses, whereas Honduran companies have been less willing to invest in training and retraining—a pattern that is common in many developing countries.

Source: IPC 2009.

Mexico: Comprehensive Training to Support Skills Development and Modernization for SMEs

Despite its successful internationalization, Mexico's large SME sector still struggles with traditional barriers to growth and export participation. One such barrier is skills development, including at the managerial level. One program that has proven effective to address this challenge was the Integral Quality and Modernization Program (*Programa de Calidad Integral y Modernización*, known by its acronym CIMO), established in 1988 by the Mexican Secretariat of Labor.

Set up initially to provide subsidized training, CIMO evolved when it became apparent that lack of training was only one of many factors contributing to low productivity among smaller enterprises. All states and the federal district of Mexico have at least one CIMO unit, each staffed by three or four promoters and housed in business associations that contribute office and support infrastructure. Promoters organize workshops on training and technical assistance services, identify potential local and regional training suppliers and consulting agents, both public and private, and actively seek out SMEs to deliver assistance on a cost-sharing, time-limited basis. They work with interested companies to conduct an initial diagnostic evaluation as the basis for organizing training programs and other consulting and technical assistance. The government does not deliver the training; instead, its role is to identify the most qualified local public and private training providers. To reduce unit training costs, providers usually deliver the training on a group or association basis. This strategy is deliberate: One of the program's objectives is to promote the development of regional training markets able to serve the needs of local enterprises. The CIMO program also targets industrial clusters and works with large firms and their SME suppliers to organize and deliver cluster-specific training programs.

By 2000, CIMO was providing an integrated package of training and industrial extension services to more than 80,000 SMEs each year and training upto 200,000 employees. Private sector interest has grown, and in 2004, more than 300 business associations participated in CIMO, up from 72 in 1988. Several rigorous evaluations have found CIMO to be a cost-effective way of assisting SMEs. Although CIMO firms tended to have lower preprogram performance than a comparison group with similar attributes, their postprogram outcome indicators tended to show improvements in key areas, such as labor productivity, capacity utilization, product quality, wages, and employment.

Source: World Bank 2010b.

India: Improving Quality and Technical Efficiency in Software Firms by Adopting Standards

The leading Indian firms have moved up the value chain in software services, developing organizational and managerial capabilities that enable them to offer more comprehensive services than merely low-cost programming. One sign of maturity is that the industry increasingly procures fixed-price contracts, rather than the time-and-materials contracts of earlier years. With the greater risk of fixed-price contracts comes flexibility in organizing work, greater management control, and an opportunity to earn higher returns as efficiency improves. Revenue per worker is increased, indicating a move up the value chain—from an average of $9,000 in fiscal 1995–96 to $20,500 in 2000/01—but revenues are still lower than what they are in product-based companies.

To build client value, companies have expanded their capacity to service a wider range of software-development tasks, as well as to move into new services, such as product design and information services outsourcing. Software development includes analysis and specification of requirements, software design, writing and testing of software, and delivery and installation. Indian companies are trying to move beyond only writing and testing, which require the least skill and account for only a small portion of the overall project costs, to higher skill levels that require deeper business knowledge of the industry for which software solutions are being developed.

In their quest to climb the value chain, India's software firms ensured product quality and reliability by adopting internationally recognized standardized work processes. Because most Indian software firms are export-oriented and serve clients around the world, meeting globally acceptable frameworks and standards has been critical to validating their credentials to new clients, who often demand that vendors adopt ISO and Capability Maturity Matrix (CMM) standards. An increasing number of firms have met international certification requirements for key quality standards. For many, this was an exercise in brand building, but the processes and procedures put in place left their hallmark on the quality of software products and services. Firms seek certification from various sources, beginning with quality management practices that meet ISO 9000 standards to ensure consistent and orderly execution of orders. The next stage focuses on software engineering and certification under the People CMM framework of the Software Engineering Institute (SEI) at increasing levels of process maturity. Another stage focuses on aligning internal practices with the CMM, which is a framework to guide attracting, motivating, and retaining a talented technical staff. The Six Sigma methodology ensures end-to-end quality across all company operations and focuses on improved customer satisfaction by reducing defects, with a target of virtually defect-free processes and products. As of December 2003, India had 65 companies at SEI CMM Maturity Level 5. In October 2002, the SEI of Carnegie Mellon University published a list of high-maturity organizations as part of its Survey of High-Maturity Organizations and High Maturity Workshop research. The full set of 146 high-maturity organizations includes 72 Level 4 organizations and 74 Level 5 organizations. Of the 87 high-maturity organizations assessed outside the United States, 77 are in India.

Source: Guasch et al. 2007.

Intermediate Inputs and Backbone Services

Policy areas and main issues	Remedies/Project components
Inputs and backbone services	• Institutional reform and capacity building in utilities regulators • Liberalization of utilities markets • Land market reforms—development of a land registry, extension of land use rights periods for FDI, surety of title • Establishment of industrial parks/SEZs • Introduction of PPP legislation/frameworks • Trade policy reform (reducing tariffs/NTBs) • Establishing trade credit lines/other access to finance initiatives • Establishing/reforming duty-drawback regimes; establishing manufacturing under bond programs

Source: Authors.
Note: FDI = foreign direct investment; NTBs = nontariff barriers; PPP = purchasing power parity; SEZ = special economic zone.

Box 3.6 provides some case study examples of good policy practice in improving access to competitive inputs.

Box 3.6. Case Examples of Good Policy Practice—Intermediate Inputs and Backbone Services

Kenya: Air Services Liberalization Promotes Goods and Services Exports
Like most countries, Kenya air transport market was highly regulated during the 1970s and 1980s. In East Africa, the breakup of the former regional airline, the East African Airways Corporation, in 1977, led to the emergence of national carriers, which were subsequently highly protected, with implications on the availability, quality, and price of air transport services. Liberalization of Kenya's air transport sector began in the late 1990s with regional agreements through the Common Market for Eastern and Southern Africa (COMESA) and the East African Community, followed by the establishment of the Kenya Civil Aviation Authority as an autonomous regulator in 2004. But what really catalyzed the development of the sector in Kenya actually preceded these regulatory reforms—the privatization of the national carrier, Kenya Airways, in 2006. This led to KLM taking the largest stake in the carrier and bringing in international management expertise.

The result was that Kenya Airways has become one of the leading airlines in Africa. Critically, this has facilitated the development of two major sectors of the Kenyan economy. First, the tourism sector benefited significantly from access to a wider range of domestic and international air services, and the sector has become one of the most important employment and foreign exchange earning sectors in the country. Second, the rapid expansion of air freight capacity in Kenya—both through Kenya Airways and the opening up of the market to other airlines, especially dedicated cargo freighters—has facilitated the massive growth in horticultural exports (particularly cut flowers and vegetables) that is a well-documented Kenyan success story.

Fiji: Duty Suspension Scheme
Fiji's duty suspension scheme is managed by a private sector organization—The Exporters Club—on behalf of Fiji Islands Revenue and Customs Authority. Members must be in the business of importing materials for transformation into products for export. The Exporters Club assesses the qualifications of applicants, recommends a list of materials to be imported and subsequently used in the production of exports, calculates advance credits and entitlement proportion (EP) ratios, and advises Customs when all requirements are met.

The exporter receives credits for every dollar of exports achieved under the system. It can use these credits to import approved materials duty free. The credit is based on the EP, that is, the proportion of imported goods required to produce one unit of the export product. As long as the company operates within its EP ratio, it can continue to import approved goods duty free. The EP is calculated when companies enter the scheme, using the company's import and export history and an audited set of accounts. For the first export operation, companies can be provided with advance credits that would enable them to import for two months using the credits.

Specially developed software has been created for Customs as an attachment to the Automated System for Customs Data (ASYCUDA) system. The software enables the Exporters Club to manage the day-to-day operations of the program and Customs to audit arrangements with individual members. Members have access to their own data but cannot access the details of other members.

The Exporters Club is a nonprofit organization owned by eight peak industry groups involved in promoting exports. A board manages the club, representing owners and the Customs Authority. The club monitors the performance of each club member through a computerized system that calculates the amount of credits earned and automatically reduces these credits when products are imported. To cover the costs of operation, the club charges an application and assessment fee, an annual subscription fee, and an activity fee.

Source: World Bank 2009c.

Trade Facilitation and Logistics

Policy areas and main issues	Remedies/Project components
Regulations of transport and logistics services/quality and reliability of transport and logistics services/ business practices	• Introduce professional standards and certification for logistics services providers • Introduce standard performance contracts for transport and logistics services • Encourage development of large, long-haul trucking fleets • Create incentives to upgrade transport fleet • Allow increased scale of logistics service providers (mergers and acquisitions) • Encourage integration of logistics services for trade and distribution • Allow introduction of new technologies for tracking and security • Introduce modern supply chain management techniques • Support for national logistics council and other mechanisms for self-regulation
Customs modernization	• Reform and automate customs procedures • Improve border facilities • Introduce risk management programs to expedite clearance, including reduced inspections and authorized economic operators • Improve trade security (e.g., scanners, secure supply chains) • Integrate activities of border management agencies • Introduce a single point of entry for information used in clearing cargo • Accept scanned copies for supporting document and e-signatures • Automate and simplify procedures for SPS and for standards certification
Related procedures and trade facilitation initiatives	• Develop public information platforms for sharing trade and logistics data • Introduce e-government services and e-signatures to facilitate government approvals • Strengthen capacity of authorities regulating trade and logistics • Improve collection of key statistical information and performance indicators • Develop capacity to analyze indicators and monitor results of policies and investments
Transit regime/air and sea connectivity and liberalization of services	• Plan and manage multimodal freight corridors • Develop urban and line-haul transport interface (e.g., urban truck terminals) • Liberalization/deregulation of air services policies (e.g., introducing fifth freedom or other bilateral freedoms)
Public infrastructure	• Increase private sector participation to provide and maintain public infrastructure • Introduce commercial management in port and airport operations • Construct new transport links • Upgrade existing transport links • Plan and manage multicountry freight corridors • Establish dryports and inland clearance facilities • Develop logistics hubs (e.g., free zones, distribution centers) • Improve telecommunications services to support logistics

Source: World Bank 2010d.

Box 3.7 provides some case study examples of good policy practice in trade facilitation and logistics.

Box 3.7. Case Examples of Good Policy Practice—Trade Facilitation and Logistics

Cambodia: Risk Management

Cambodian importers of raw materials for garment manufacture and subsequent export "are subjected to as many as 64 documentary inspections, physical goods inspections . . . [and] a requirement for over 70 signatures and 12 separate payments . . . . [and] exporters who are exporting ready-made garments . . . have to fulfil as many as 90 documentary inspections, possibly 100 signatures and 17 different formal payments, in addition to informal payments they have to make in order to get the thing done." (Sovicheat 2006, 1).

The Royal Government of Cambodia has since introduced a comprehensive risk management approach to border management. The approach has consolidated and rationalized the requirements of government agencies involved in the inspection and clearance of goods at the border through the following:

• Raising the level of understanding of all stakeholders—particularly the implementing agencies involved in inspection and audit— of the principles of risk management, compliance management, and information management, and assisting them in the achievement of a strategic approach to risk management and compliance management.
• Providing a framework for risk management whereby the inspection of import and export consignments is focused on high-risk shipments and maintains a balance between facilitation and control.
• Developing an understanding of specific risks

Source: World Bank 2011a.

(continued on next page)

MODULE 3

Box 3.7. *(continued)*

Cameroon: Customs Integrity Initiative

Within the Cameroonian context, customs is perceived as one of the institutions with the most important problems of transparency. A new program financed by the World Bank and introduced in 2006 was designed to strengthen the chain of command by holding each link accountable—with the assistance of activity, performance, control, and risk indicators—to improve understanding of activities on the ground, to provide an effective decision-making tool, and to reduce corruption in customs.

Cameroon Customs had already carried out steps to strengthen accountability. They included the regular publication of revenue collection data, increased contacts with the business community, automation through the use of ASYCUDA software, and reduced information asymmetry through the use of individual performance indicators. The head of Customs still wanted to initiate a second wave of reforms to change the behaviors of frontline officials and to reduce corruption and increase performance. Accordingly, she commissioned the development of an integrity action plan with a specific focus on human resources policies through a monitoring and incentive framework. A pilot was set up and performance contracts for the two largest customs stations were designed. In early February 2010—following a dialogue among frontline officers and senior management—individual and team performance contracts with measurable indicators were signed. Each inspector's performance was to be assessed through eight indicators: four related to trade facilitation and four related to the customs clearance process and fines. For each indicator, a maximum or minimum value was set based on median monthly values in the three preceding years. An inspector achieved his or her contract if he or she improved performance by 15 percent on all indicators after the six-month pilot period. For inspectors below 100 percent contract performance, a system was established that began with warnings and interviews and failure to meet performance goals can lead to the inspector's transfer to another customs station. For the best performing inspectors, a limited financial bonus was granted, along with nonfinancial recognition.

Frontline officers, as well as middle management, supported the initiative because they wanted their performance to be assessed on the basis of objective criteria. Early results show that performance contracts have led to decreased clearance times and reduced poor practices, with revenues maintained at the same level as before. Moreover, the contracts have contributed to increased information flow from inspectors to the Head of Customs.

Source: World Bank 2011a.

Trans-Kalahari Corridor: Document Standardization and Simplification

The Trans-Kalahari Corridor (TKC), the road route between Gauteng province (South Africa) and Walvis Bay (Namibia) via Botswana was opened in 1998, replacing the traditional longer route through western South Africa. Despite major road rehabilitation in 1999, traffic reached only 15 percent of the expected capacity. The major obstacles occurred at the border crossings. This led the TKC Corridor Management Group to seek a partnership with the customs administrations of Botswana, Namibia, and South Africa. This partnership resulted in agreements (October 2000) to extend the operating hours of customs at the Namibia–Botswana border from 22 to 24 hours to enable loading and unloading in Windhoek and crossing the border in the same day.

In August 2003, the TKC started a pilot phase to replace all existing transport documents with a single administrative document (SAD). To complement this effort, South African Customs developed a website with details on the SAD process. Border processing times were cut by more than half, from an average time of 45 minutes to 10–20 minutes. According to the US Agency for International Development (USAID) estimates, reduced border delays created savings of $2.6 million per year along the corridor. As a result, the route became economical, and traffic flows increased. Operators were moving about 620,000 tons annually along the TKC, about 65 percent of expected capacity, until the Botswanan government increased road user charges in February 2004. In some cases, road charges were multiplied by a factor of 10. The customs problem had been settled; but following this unilateral decision affecting the transport sector, traffic decreased significantly.

Source: World Bank 2004.

Northern Corridor Stakeholders Consultation Forum: Trade Facilitation Committees

Since 1999, officials dealing with transport, transit, and private operators along the Northern Corridor (including Ministry of Transport, Ministry of Trade, customs agencies, exporters, and importers associations, and so on) have been regularly meeting twice a year to discuss transit issues. This private-public sector alliance has produced the following positive developments:

- Elimination of charges on imports routed through the port of Mombasa (by Kenya Bureau of Standards and the Kenya Plant Health Inspectorate Service)
- Development of a one-stop processing center
- Reduction of the number of required stamps to go through Mombasa port (from 21 to 11)

As a result of this forum, national transit and trade facilitation committees are being established in the region. Private sector participation has been extended to include insurance clearing agents, bank associations, the shippers' council, and the like. Public-private partnerships to tackle trade and transport facilitation are also being established in West Africa.

Source: World Bank 2004.

Trade and Investment Promotion

Policy areas and main issues	Remedies/Project components
Export promotion agencies	• Consolidating agencies dealing with export promotion • Institutional reform and capacity building of an export promotion agency • Increasing private sector participation • Developing targeted export promotion strategy • Realigning focus—for example, support versus promotion; new versus existing exporters • Improving service delivery through outsourcing—for example, market research and training
Investment promotion agencies	• Institutional reform and capacity building • Increasing private sector participation • Developing targeted investment promotion strategy • Development/implementation of anchor investor strategy • Improving aftercare services • Developing/improving online presence • Development of a land bank portal

Source: Authors.

Box 3.8 provides some case study examples of good policy practice for export and investment promotion.

Box 3.8. Case Examples of Good Policy Practice—Export and Investment Promotion

Tunisia: Targeted Export Support Through a Matching Grant Program

Tunisia's export sector is highly focused on natural resources–based industries and strongly oriented toward Europe. Although the bulk of its exports are dominated by large (state-owned or formerly state-owned) concerns, diversification of the export base relies largely on SMEs, with relatively limited experience and knowledge of foreign markets. As one program to promote the internationalization of Tunisian SMEs, the Tunisian Export Market Access Fund (FAMEX) was established in April 2000; following its success, FAMEX II was launched in 2005.

The creation of FAMEX marked an important shift of focus for export promotion in Tunisia, away from a trade-promotion organization model led by the government to a public-private sector participatory approach. Acknowledging that firms, not countries, compete, the Tunisian government emphasized individual exporters and their associations. FAMEX helped individual firms implement a systematic strategy to enter, sustain, and expand export markets. The $10 million fund was set up by *Centre de Promotion des Exportations de la Tunisie* (CEPEX; Tunisia's export promotion agency) with World Bank assistance. It was privately managed by international and local experts. FAMEX encouraged firms, especially SMEs, to enter export markets by temporarily covering up to 50 percent of the cost of consultant services (up to US$100,000 per firm) and providing technical assistance. Services were offered by local consultants and international experts in response to demand from private firms.

A key factor in the delivery of the program was the process by which exporters were selected to participate. Although the program was designed for SMEs, a minimum size threshold was established (around US$140,000 turnover for manufacturing firms and US$70,000 for services firms). To qualify for the grant, firms were required to prepare an export development plan, within which they would identify specific projects for which they requested grant support. Applicants had to define whether the projects were being linked to new export entry or to new product or market entry (for existing exporters). They were required to show that serious consideration was given to the feasibility of the proposed projects. Plans were reviewed by a panel including senior experts from FAMEX management, and the process included detailed interviews; successful applicants had to sign a letter of intent to bind them to activities in the plan.

In the five years that it existed, FAMEX I helped 700 firms become exporters, export new products and services, or enter new markets. Estimates indicate that each $1 of FAMEX assistance generated more than $20 of additional exports. A recent survey indicates that 60 percent of the firms that benefited from FAMEX assistance are now willing to pay, or are already paying, full market price for export services (FAMEX 2008). A small export consulting industry has also been created as a result of the program. FAMEX thus served as a catalyst to develop business-to-business markets. A more recent detailed evaluation of the FAMEX II program found clearly that participants in the FAMEX program achieved substantially higher export growth than nonparticipants.

Sources: Nassif 2010; Gourdan 2011.

Costa Rica: Coordinating Investment Promotion to Attract Intel

Costa Rica took advantage of a close-knit government and business community to organize a flexible, unified effort to attract Intel to establish a US$300 million semiconductor plant under the country's free zone program in 1996. A team was assembled

(continued on next page)

MODULE 3

Box 3.8. *(continued)*

that included high-level representatives of all relevant government ministries and private sector stakeholders, with close involvement of the president. Key to this was the role of the Costa Rica Investment Promotion Agency (CINDE). As a nonprofit, autonomous organization, CINDE maintained close ties with the government and the private sector and was able to act not only as an effective coordinator of the approach to Intel but also as a credible mediator between Intel and the government. Box figure 3.8.1 gives a perspective of the cross-agency coordination involved in the Intel investment promotion effort in Costa Rica.

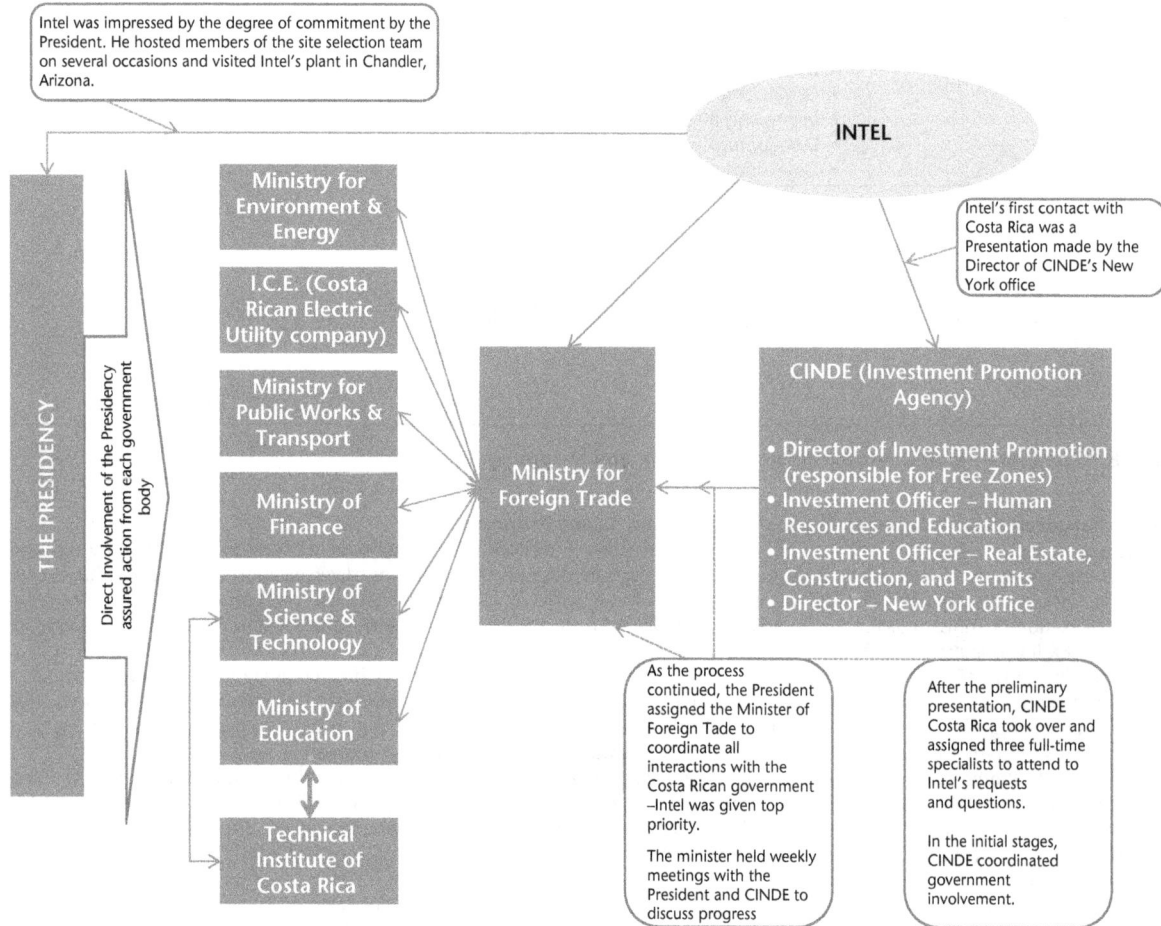

Intel was impressed by the degree of commitment by the President. He hosted members of the site selection team on several occasions and visited Intel's plant in Chandler, Arizona.

INTEL

Intel's first contact with Costa Rica was a Presentation made by the Director of CINDE's New York office

THE PRESIDENCY

Direct involvement of the Presidency assured action from each government body

Ministry for Environment & Energy

I.C.E. (Costa Rican Electric Utility company)

Ministry for Public Works & Transport

Ministry of Finance

Ministry of Science & Technology

Ministry of Education

Technical Institute of Costa Rica

Ministry for Foreign Trade

CINDE (Investment Promotion Agency)

- Director of Investment Promotion (responsible for Free Zones)
- Investment Officer – Human Resources and Education
- Investment Officer – Real Estate, Construction, and Permits
- Director – New York office

As the process continued, the President assigned the Minister of Foreign Tade to coordinate all interactions with the Costa Rican government –Intel was given top priority.

The minister held weekly meetings with the President and CINDE to discuss progress

After the preliminary presentation, CINDE Costa Rica took over and assigned three full-time specialists to attend to Intel's requests and questions.

In the initial stages, CINDE coordinated government involvement.

Sources: Authors, based on Spar (1998); figure reprinted from Spar 1998, 29.

Chile: *ProChile* Export Promotion

In the past two decades, Chile has become a major export success, particularly beyond its traditional minerals sectors, encompassing the agricultural and agriprocessing sector, including salmon, wine, and horticulture. *ProChile*, Chile's export promotion agency, is widely acknowledged as having played a critical role in facilitating the country's export-oriented growth over this period, with its specific focus on the SME export sector (it focuses mainly on firms with a turnover range between US$50,000 and US$7.5 million). Two important components of its success—its sectorally oriented structure and approach, and its program to identify and support promising exporters—are summarized below.

ProChile has four operating divisions: a Sectoral Division (about 40 staff) manages the delivery of export promotion products and services to each exporting sector; an International Division (about 160 staff; 140 of which are based outside the country) manages the operation of the trade offices abroad; a Marketing Division (about 30 staff) manages all marketing activities, including trade missions; and an Information and Technology Division (about 15 staff) manages systems for providing information to clients, including websites and training modules. Key to the operations of *ProChile* is the targeting of priority sectors—the Sectoral Division is organized into seven separate business units, one for each key sector. Linked to this, *ProChile* maintains close financial and working relationships with the main industry associations representing these sectors. Asoex, the industry association representing 85 percent of Chile's fruit exporters, exemplifies the relationship between *ProChile* and sector organizations. Asoex has an annual export promotion budget of about US$5 million, of which $2 million comes from *ProChile*'s cofinancing fund. With assistance from

(continued on next page)

MODULE 3

Box 3.8. *(continued)*

ProChile, Asoex was able to set up an office in the United States, opening new opportunities for export of previously unknown Chilean fruits. Wines of Chile, an international marketing association representing 90 percent of all wine exporters, has an annual export promotion budget of about US$6 million of which $2 million comes from *ProChile.* With this assistance, Wines of Chile set up a European office in the United Kingdom in early 2000.

To improve the export skills of smaller existing exporters and to encourage new SME exporters, *ProChile* developed the *Internalization Plan* in 2001. One component, Interpac, is designed for SMEs in the agricultural sector; the other, Interpyme, is designed for SMEs in industrial sectors. These programs provide Chilean companies with systematic training in exporting issues faced by SMEs. They include training modules on production capabilities, market research, logistics, marketing plans, banking, international law, searching for partners, and the export process. Interpyme and Interpac are operated by a team of private sector consultants hired by *ProChile* and participants are provided with individual one-on-one counseling as part of the program. Participants complete one module at a time, and when they have completed the full program, they become eligible for *ProChile* cofinancing programs, provided that they have promising export plans. These programs take about one year to complete. *ProChile* covers up to 90 percent of the cost, provided that participants have an exportable product for which there is international demand and that they use labor-intensive production methods.

The results have been impressive. Since the early 1990s, the number of exporters in Chile has doubled. Diversification of sectors, products, and markets has been dramatic, with the number of new products doubling, the number of markets growing by more than 50 percent, and the relative concentration of the mining sector reducing significantly. Between 1996 and 2006, Chile's nontraditional exports (which account for 90 percent of SME exports from Chile) increased from US$6 billion to US$15 billion, an annual growth of 10 percent. Several impact evaluation studies have shown that ProChile has had a positive and significant impact on export participation, new product introduction, and firm-level technological and management improvements.

Source: Derived from Nathan Associates (2004).

Costa Rica: Linking Local Firms to FDI—the *Provee* Program
Until the mid-1990s, Costa Rica's economy was highly concentrated in the natural resources sector (mainly traditional agriculture). With the attraction of FDI, and of Intel in particular, in the 1990s, its export and economic structure changed dramatically. Recognizing that sustainability of growth would require the development of more innovative and value adding domestic firms, the country's government embarked on a program designed to develop enhanced linkages between local SMEs and MNC foreign investors. The aim was to support the growth of local SMEs and promote technology transfer to facilitate upgrading.

The *Supplier Development Project for High-Technology Multinational Companies,* a program inspired by Singapore's Local Industry Upgrading Program, was established in late 1999. Its aim was to enhance domestic value added in high-technology MNC production and improve domestic SME competitiveness. This project had three key components: a Pilot Procurement Program, a Comprehensive Information System, and Costa Rica *Provee* (a domestic supplier development office). From 2003 on, Costa Rica *Provee* operated out of the Foreign Trade Corporation of Costa Rica (PROCOMER), but in 2005 it became one more management unit of PROCOMER. This latter organization includes Costa Rica *Provee* in its strategic plan, as a key component of value added for domestic exports.

Costa Rica *Provee* engages in detecting the needs of MNCs, identifying business opportunities, and recommending registered suppliers who meet the production, technical, and quality specifications and characteristics required by the business at hand. The work of *Provee* with domestic suppliers focuses on ensuring their strategic role as MNC suppliers. For local suppliers, benefits include the following:

- Participation in a supplier network highly qualified by these foreign companies
- Reliance on a team made up of professionals from different fields including chemistry, electronics, materials, marketing, and business management
- No investment requirement
- Permanent project follow-up by Costa Rica *Provee*'s staff that ensures fulfillment of transnationals' requirements

Specific support provided by *Provee* includes technical support and diagnosis. *Technical support* focuses on analyzing goods to be offered to MNCs. This task is undertaken by *Provee*'s staff, made up of professionals with relevant experience in business development and majoring in engineering, industrial chemistry, and business management. *Diagnosis* applies evaluation tools aimed at ensuring long-term business relationships, including comprehensive diagnosis in finance, production, marketing, business management, and environmental and quality systems, among others. The mission consists of facilitating business deals between MNCs and domestic suppliers, thus contributing to enhance value added from Costa Rican industries as well as the country's global competitiveness.

More than 258 domestic suppliers have profited from the direct operation of Costa Rica *Provee* as well as from access to transnational companies (TNCs). This has led to improved supply of goods and services, technological specialization of suppliers' production processes, and increased social benefit resulting from additional daily business. Currently, more than 186 TNCs cooperate with PROCOMER and Costa Rica *Provee.*

Source: Spar 1998.

Czech Republic: Pilot Supplier Development Program
CzechInvest (CI, the investment promotion agency of the Czech Republic) learned from surveying investors that multinationals considered the local supplier network to be a key determinant in their investment decisions, in fact, second only to labor availability. Yet multinational investors operating in the Czech Republic imported 90 to 95 percent of their components to meet their production requirements, driven by world-class standards and global competition. CI's top management perceived a two-sided opportunity: address investors' supply demand and a willingness to source locally by strengthening the capabilities of Czech

(continued on next page)

Box 3.8. *(continued)*

suppliers. From CI's perspective, a robust, competitive Czech supplier base for key prominent sectors was a way to "embed" FDI into the economy and channel its benefits, helping to both retain and attract investors while supporting domestic suppliers. With these objectives in mind, CI launched the *Pilot Supplier Development Program* (also called the Twinning Programme) in the electronics sector, the Czech Republic's fastest growing and second-largest FDI sector after automotive.

The program's orientation was demand driven and practical; its overall objective was to equip participating suppliers with the information and skills to meet investors' requirements and win more and higher value-added contracts. The program consisted of three elements:

- *Collection and distribution of information* regarding the products and capabilities of potential Czech component suppliers to enable foreign manufacturers to shortlist and contact potential suppliers. The profiles of potential suppliers are available through CI's website. Approximately 1,000 firms were listed in 2001.
- *Matchmaking*, including three elements: (1) "Meet the Buyer" events between foreign investors and potential Czech suppliers. The sessions focus on identifying the type of components and services that foreign investors are considering subcontracting. (2) Seminars and exhibitions organized with and for Czech suppliers and foreign affiliates. (3) Taking forward concrete proposals to potential foreign investors, indicating potential suppliers in the Czech Republic.
- *Upgrading of selected Czech suppliers:* Suppliers are selected according to predefined criteria in high-technology industries, such as electronics, or for selected engineering firms supplying to a wide range of industries. The selected firms produce an upgrading plan, tailored to their individual capacities and requirements. The upgrading process usually includes consultancy and training support in such areas as the utilization of technology, general management operations, quality control, and organizational change. In the case of the electronics sector pilot, CI identified 45 companies as potential candidates to expand their businesses and supply foreign manufacturers based in the Czech Republic. These companies outlined the areas of support they needed and then were provided training by Czech and international experts in the first phase of the program. After seven months, the companies were reevaluated. The 20 suppliers that were found to have shown the most improvement in their performance were invited to participate in the program's second phase of individually tailored assistance. CI's researchers determined all but four of the initial 45 company participants demonstrated marked improvement in their capabilities.

CI's evaluation of the electronics sector pilot program 18 months after it ended in July 2002 showed promising results. Fifteen suppliers had landed new, renewable contracts, amounting to more than US$46 million for the period 2000–03. Participating suppliers especially valued improvements in their strategic management, management of customer relationships, and communications. The experience suggested that government assistance could help an important segment of Czech firms compete for contracts that otherwise might be won by new foreign suppliers or sourced abroad. On the basis of these results, CI subsequently rolled out Twinning II, extending the scheme to the aeronautics, automotive, pharmaceutical, and engineering sectors.

Source: Potter 2001.

Standards and Certification

Although the policy prescriptions in any one country will be context dependent, certain broad policy issues should be considered with regard to the standards environment. These issues are outlined below.

Promoting Awareness of Standards

It is incumbent on each government or supporting agency to ensure that the producers in their lead and emerging sectors are aware of the nature and changing portfolio of standards. The producers also should be aware of the consequences of achieving or not achieving these standards as well as the steps required to achieve them when this is a feasible and sensible objective. Are governments aware whether their economies possess the certification bodies and capabilities required to gainfully meet global standards requirements? To what extent do their standards align with global standards, and does this matter?

Ensure that Standards Do Not Rule Out Local Suppliers

In some sectors, lead firms specify standards that have the unintended consequence of ruling out local suppliers. This is, for example, a common case in Africa's mining sector, in which the mine-commissioning firms often specify the use of standards for items such as electrical fittings and piping that are used in their home market but not in the local market. For instance, in Tanzania, this has led to the exclusion of existing suppliers utilizing UK rather than Australian specifications. Particularly in large infrastructure and mining contracts (in which both have considerable potential for local linkages), governments need to be aware of the need for lead contractors to utilize those standards that are in use in the domestic economy.

Role of Lead Firms in Promoting Standards

In many sectors, lead firms in global value chains are the key drivers of standards. There are, however, two contrasting outcomes of the standards imposed in corporate-driven value chains. The first is reflected in the contributions made to metal- and plastics-working suppliers by global auto assemblers. Driven by the imperatives of lean production, auto assemblers have made it their business to upgrade their suppliers' performance through the systematic use of standards, setting a moving target of standards that suppliers need to meet. Attracting these firms to upgrade their supply chains (which also feed into other value chains and hence have spread effects) has been a core and successful component of government industrial policy in high-income and middle-income countries alike (for example, South Africa and the United Kingdom).

Government May Need to Assist Firms when Lead Firms Do Not

In cases in which lead firms do not upgrade their supply chains, a key challenge for policy makers is to ensure that a system of incentives is introduced to enhance both the demand for appropriate standards by firms wishing to participate gainfully in global value chains and the capacity of local providers to supply support for local firms seeking to achieve accreditation. Support for the business services sector is a key component of this agenda. In some cases, this may be provided by the relevant industry association. In other cases, specialized providers may address the needs of many industries, such as those offering to assist firms to introduce ISO 9000 and ISO 14000 standards.

Assisting Small-Scale Producers

Special problems arise for small firms, because achieving standards accreditation may be a relatively costly process (the costs tend to be fixed, irrespective of scale, and thus adversely affect small producers). One way to reduce these scale economies can be achieved by banding together a group of small producers to share the costs of certification, both in its initial and then annual recertification stages. But this will only diminish the disadvantage confronting small producers, not remove it. A strategic decision will have to be made about whether small producers have a place in standards-intensive global value chains or whether a subsidized scheme should be established to sustain their participation. This will require a country- and sector-specific set of judgments, balancing off distributional concerns and the upgrading benefits of standards against their fiscal and economic cost.

Targeting Low-Income Markets

Individual producers, or countries, may actively segment markets, depending on standards requirements. Some firms—perhaps small-scale producers—and some production lines may be dedicated to the low-income markets, whereas others develop the standards' capabilities to participate in high-income markets. This agenda is appropriate for firms and their industry associations as well as for governments engaged in industrial policy designed to maximize the gains from participating in the global economy.

MODULE 3

Harmonizing Standards and Developing Countries Participation in Standards-Setting Bodies

Many developing country firms are confronted with a bewildering variety of standards that their producers have to meet and at considerable cost. This is perhaps most evident with regard to labor standards, but it is not unique to labor standards. At the same time, some of the technical industry standards that are set reflect the operating conditions in high-income economies—predominantly temperate climates with

pervasive and reliable infrastructure. In these and other cases, low-income country governments need to participate actively in setting standards in those international fora that are relevant to local producers. Particularly for small economies, this process may be best undertaken through collaborative specialization and collective action.

Box 3.9 provides case study examples of good practice in developing standards programs that support export competitiveness.

Box 3.9. Case Examples of Good Policy Practice—Standards and Certification

Peru: Quality Standards Promote Asparagus Exports

Realizing that it was in the best interest of the country, the leaders of Peru's asparagus industry and government specialists worked together to bring Peruvian agricultural standards in line with international norms. Both the industry and Peru have greatly benefited as a result. Over the past decade, Peru has quickly risen to become one of the world's largest exporters of asparagus. This is particularly true for fresh green asparagus and, to a lesser extent, for fresh white asparagus and canned asparagus. In 2002, export revenue for all forms and presentations reached $187 million, representing nearly 25 percent of the value of Peru's agricultural exports. Peru is able to produce quality asparagus year-round; however, in certain seasons, high air and sea transportation costs prevent it from matching prices with inexpensive asparagus from Mexico. Nonetheless, the Peruvians have continued to increase exports and gain market share during their main season by growing asparagus of consistently higher quality that can be internationally certified with respect to good agricultural practices, good manufacturing practices, and HACCP.

In 1997, Spanish health authorities asserted that two cases of botulism had been caused by consumption of canned Peruvian asparagus. Despite assurances from the Peruvian government and companies, press coverage of the botulism scare left an unfavorable impression among consumers in European markets, causing sales to slump in Peru's leading market. The incident motivated the industry and government to take action by reinforcing the fact that one careless (usually artisanal) exporter could disrupt markets. Beginning in 1998, officials of the Peruvian Commission for Export Promotion (PROMPEX) convinced the asparagus industry to implement the Codex code of practice on food hygiene. PROMPEX specialists worked with industry leaders and production managers to ensure proper implementation. The industry soon saw improved production and processing methods, as well as better product quality and safety. In 2001, national fresh asparagus norms were published. They provided a quality and performance baseline for the industry that allowed many firms and farms to generate the skills and experience needed to be certified under stringent international standards. Many large exporters have reached the level at which they can now be certified under the even stricter Eurepgap protocol. Looking ahead, the Peruvian asparagus industry should be well positioned to adjust to new or more stringent requirements from its trade partners on the basis of continued strong leadership and public-private cooperation.

Source: World Bank 2005.

Spain: Using Standards to Develop a Quality Export Brand: *The Consorcio del Jamón Serrano*

In 1990, the producers and exporters of air-dried cured ham in Spain formed the *Consorcio del Jamón Serrano Español* to harmonize standards and create a quality brand. The Consorcio's seal, which is given only to hams that meet its standards, guarantees the high quality of the certified product. Under EU regulation, the "Serrano ham" denomination is protected as a Traditional Specialty Guaranteed (TSG). The TSG standard for Serrano ham specifies the method of processing the meat, although it does not refer to a specific processing area or to the origin of the raw material. Cured ham cannot be sold in the European Union with the words "Serrano ham" on the label unless it is duly certified as meeting the TSG standard for the product.

In addition to meeting the TSG requirements, the Consorcio also imposes its own standards, which in certain aspects are more demanding than the TSG standards. For a ham to earn the Consorcio seal of quality, it must—

- be "Serrano" ham (meeting TSG requirements), produced by a certified company
- use only Spanish raw material (Spanish pigs slaughtered in Spain)
- be processed exclusively in Spain
- be cured a minimum of nine months
- have a fat covering of at least 1 centimeter (to ensure the ham's texture and aroma)
- have shrunk 34 percent in relation to the weight of the original fresh ham
- pass an individual sensorial inspection (piece by piece)
- be produced by a company that has passed the quality inspections that the Consorcio constantly carries out

The inspections performed by the Consorcio are certified according to the Spanish national standards. The Consorcio strives to ensure that hygienic, temperature, and humidity conditions established in the TSG standard, as well as the boning, slicing, and packaging procedures, are respected during the different stages of the process. In addition, each piece of ham is subjected to visual inspection. A ham that meets all the standards will have a fire seal on the skin with the *Consorcio del Jamón Serrano Español* logo and will also have a numbered control label. Consumers who purchase the certified products pay a premium price in exchange for the quality assurance that the certification provides.

Source: Guasch et al. 2007.

Special Customs Regimes and SEZs

Policy areas and main issues	Remedies/Project components
Duty drawback and MUB	• Improving efficiency of reimbursement • Reducing documentation or other administrative requirements
EPZs/SEZs	• Reform of legal and regulatory framework • Addressing institutional design of zones authority • Infrastructure implementation or upgrades • Shifting from traditional EPZ to SEZ models • Establishing or improving "one-stop shop" services

Source: Authors.
Note: EPZ = export-process zone; MUB = manufacturing under bond; SEZ = special economic zone.

Box 3.10 provides some case study examples of good practice in developing special customs regimes and SEZs.

Box 3.10. Case Examples of Good Policy Practice—Special Customs Regimes and SEZs

Zambia: Duty-Drawback Regime
The refund of duty drawback works more efficiently in Zambia. To guarantee duty-drawback refunds, the Customs and Excise Division of Zambia has created a ring-fenced fund at the central bank. All import duties paid are deposited into that fund. The fund is then used to pay duty drawbacks within a period of six weeks, following claims. The remaining balance, after all pending drawback payments have been made, is then remitted on a monthly basis to the Treasury. A similar system is used for refunding value added tax.

Source: UNCTAD 2006.

Ghana's Tema Free Zone: The MPIP, A New Approach for Integrating Local Firms with FDI
As part of the relaunch of the Tema zone following the departure of the initial private developer, Business Focus of Malaysia, the Ghana Free Zones Board (GFZB) decided to commit part of the enclave to nonexport companies. The GFZB denominated about 70 hectares of Tema as Multipurpose Industrial Park (MPIP), with the support of the World Bank for the development of on-site infrastructure. The MPIP is designed to support the development of small-scale domestic industries and to create linkages with major exporters. Although companies within the MPIP will not have access to a special fiscal and customs regime, the plan for the industrial park is to facilitate competitiveness by establishing critical common infrastructure and cluster-based business support services. These services might include, for example, common packaging and labeling facilities, kiln drying, warehousing, and so on.

The creation of the MPIP represents an innovative shift in the enclave model in Ghana, becoming that of a hybrid EPZ, which combines free zone and non-free-zone investors in the same location. It should offer a substantial opportunity for local firms to become better integrated into the supply networks of exporters in Tema.

Source: Authors.

MODULE 3

Industry Coordination and Sector Support

Policy areas and main issues	Remedies/Project components
Clusters and industry bodies	• Ensuring cluster and sector targets in line with comparative advantage • Facilitating public-private dialogue • Provision of key public and coordinating infrastructure • Facilitating the building of networks among cluster participants
Subsidies and incentives to sectors and exporters	• Aligning incentives with comparative advantage

Source: Authors.

Box 3.11 provides some case study examples of good practices for industry coordination and sector support.

Box 3.11. Case Examples of Good Policy Practice—Industry Coordination and Sector Support

Italy: The Role of Trade Associations in Supporting SME Export Clusters

In Italy, the main trade associations representing small firms identify cooperation opportunities, suggest ways in which firms can link complementary skills, create contacts among potential partner firms, motivate firms to cooperate, and mediate critical phases in the establishment of a network.

In Bologna, one of the three major trade associations, the CAN (*Confederazione Nazionale Artiglianato*) has about 17,000 member firms, 41 local offices, and 500 employees. The CAN prepares 22,000 pay packets monthly for 5,000 firms. It keeps financial records for 10,000 firms, prepares income tax declarations for most of its members, and organizes 80 training courses a year on subjects ranging from management and business administration to computing and foreign languages.

In the 1950s, the CAN established a large assessment and guarantee consortium in Bologna, which now has 7,500 member firms and guarantees some US$12 million in loans. So far, it has promoted 41 other consortia dealing with production and joint buying and selling, which now have 8,000 member firms and 42 industrial parks, in which 1,030 small firms are located.

Sources: OECD 2001; Word Bank 2010b.

Chile: Growth of the Salmon Cluster

Chile has become a major export success beyond its traditional minerals sectors, most notably in the agricultural sector. Within this sector, the growth of the salmon industry exemplifies the success of Chile's cluster approach to developing export industries.

Very early on in the development of the cluster, many stakeholders formed collaborative associations that worked together to solve upstream and downstream challenges. The Chilean Farming Association (SalmonChile) for instance was the main group that represented producers and suppliers of the cluster. Other groups contributed to the development of the cluster, such as *Instituto Technologico del Salmon*, which was the technological arm of the association. Ship-owners, and Maritime Services, the Association of Diving Companies, and the Association of Veterinary Laboratories were other important associations that significantly supported the development of the industry. Together these associations launched initiatives to address issues and constraints faced by the sector, including the following:

• The development of a pioneer quality seal to face stringent quality market requirements
• The launching of a phytoplankton vigilance program
• The monitoring of a series of environment, market, and regulation variables
• The establishment of geographic and good management practices tools
• The development of a labor-competency certification system for various subsectors of the salmon cluster by SalmonChile
• The implementation of a "Clean Production Agreement" for the salmon industry and a Vigilance and Management Model that serves the principal producers and suppliers in the industry, both coordinated by SalmonChile and INTESAL

The government of Chile, through its public sector institutions, has played a significant role as a catalyst and facilitator in the development of the cluster. Working with respective associations, it actively sought to promote joint actions and to build trust among cluster participants. The government sought to enforce regulations related to coastal zones and to mitigate environmental impacts from projects. More recently, the government sought to promote research and development (R&D) among associations, particularly among producer-supply relations. Some of the initiatives include creation of an innovation and knowledge platform to coordinate public and private efforts on areas, such as fish health, genetics, animal feeding, environment, clean production, development of new technology and production management, and certification.

Chile's salmon industry grew from US$538 million in 1997, to US$2.2 billion in 2006, more than a threefold increase in 10 years. The sector now contributes 4 percent of total exports and more than 56 percent of total fisheries exports, and employs more than 53,000 persons (directly and indirectly).

Source: Ramsawak 2010.

(continued on next page)

Box 3.11. *(continued)*

Malaysia: Evolving Incentives

Like most developing countries, Malaysia has used a system of incentives to attract investments. The structure of incentives, however, has been revised continuously to meet the evolving national development objectives. By linking the incentives and the provision of specialized infrastructure facilities to skills development and technology upgrading, Malaysia was able to take advantage of the global changes to improve Malaysia's competitive position. The evolution of the system of incentives in Malaysia reflects a shift from general investment promotion to a focus on high-technology sectors and industrial clusters.

The Pioneer Industries Ordinance (PIO) was introduced in 1958 to provide incentives and tariff protection for the development of manufacturing industries. These firms enjoyed *tariff protection and tax relief* of two to five years depending on the level of investment. By the late 1960s, the need to shelter import substituting industries was overtaken by the need to export. Toward this end, the Malaysian government passed the Investment Incentive Act (IIA) in 1968 to encourage *employment creation, dispersal of industries, and investment of capital-intensive projects.* The incentives provided under the IIA (the Pioneer Status, Labor Utilization Relief, and locational incentives offer tax relief for 2–10 years, and the Investment Tax Credit offers tax credits ranging from 25 to 40 percent of capital expenditure) were oriented to attract more labor-intensive and export-oriented industries compared with those of the import substituting industries-oriented PIO.

In addition, to enhance the role of the manufacturing sector in the economy, several new policies and programs were introduced. The most notable was the Free Trade Zone Act of 1971 to allow for the formation of Free Trade Zones (FTZs). The main objective was to attract export-oriented MNCs to invest in Malaysia. Industries operating inside the FTZs would enjoy better (and subsidized) infrastructure, expedited customs formalities, and duty-free imports of raw materials, components, and machinery. This approach to promote export manufacturing was timely and successful in attracting the first major wave of export-oriented electronics manufacturing, concentrated initially in components, to Malaysia. To supplement the FTZ program as well as to promote dispersal of industries to the less developed regions of the country, in 1973, Malaysia introduced the Licensed Manufacturing Warehouse program, which extended similar treatment to individual factories set up outside the FTZs.

In 1985, the industrialization process took on a more cohesive program with the announcement of an Industrial Master Plan (IMP), which identified three policy instruments for increasing technology capability, namely, *research manpower; institutional arrangements,* such as industrial parks; and *incentives for R&D.* Twelve priority sector development plans were announced as part of a comprehensive strategy to lift Malaysia's industrial base. To further give the boost to the IMP, the Promotion of Investment Act (PIA) of 1986 was legislated to replace the IIA. Under the PIA, the Labor Utilization Relief incentive was abolished and the Pioneer Status incentives were modified. Promoted industries and projects would enjoy tax relief up to five years regardless of the size of the capital investment. In addition, an amendment to the Income Tax Act of 1967 provides tax incentives for training, R&D, and reinvestments, and complements the PIA. Other instruments including the exemption of import duty on raw materials, tariff protection for selected industries, and financial and credit assistance were used to promote industrial development. These incentives, along with other moves to create a more liberal investment environment, are the impetus behind the recovery of the Malaysian economy in the late 1980s and the rapid uptake of manufacturing investments.

The Second Industrial Master Plan, 1996–2005 (IMP2), extended its approach beyond export manufacturing operations toward more *locally integrated clusters* to encourage the growth of supporting industries, including the services sector. The IMP2 emphasized deepening integration of manufacturing operations along the value chain, including investments in R&D and design capability; development of integrated supporting industries; enhancement of industrial linkages through packaging, distribution, and marketing activities; and increased productivity and competitiveness.

Since the early 1990s, the investment incentives were increasingly tied to *technological deepening, exports,* and *domestic sourcing of inputs.* Beyond these incentives, R&D and *training incentives* were also introduced. In 1991, a broad reform of Malaysia's investment policy regime was carried out by phasing out tax incentives for exports and reducing the scope of the Pioneer Status. With these changes, ordinary Pioneer Status would qualify for only 60 percent exemption (instead of the previous full exemption), and the period would be for only three to six years (instead of 10 years). Full tax exemptions, however, were granted to investments in specific high-technology and strategic sectors. Furthermore, the Malaysian Investment Development Authority announced that it would screen applications for Pioneer Status more rigorously using four broad criteria: value added of 30 to 50 percent, local content levels of 20 to 50 percent, depth of technology, and linkage effects.

Source: Summarized from a background paper prepared for UNCTAD by Lim and Ong (2002).

Innovation

Policies to support innovation are diverse. *First*, developing countries still have huge unrealized benefits as they catch up to the frontier. Developing countries should prioritize diffusion, technological learning, and adaptation of existing technologies. All developing countries have more to gain in terms of growth and improved living standards from the adoption of existing global technologies than from riskier and costlier invention and commercialization of new technologies. *Second*, policies should promote appropriate technological learning by grassroots entrepreneurs. These entrepreneurs typically include farmers, artisans, and subsistence entrepreneurs who may have little or no formal education and who devise new solutions at the individual or collective level largely through improvisation and experimentation.

Third, policies should support the incremental adaptation of existing technologies across the range of informal and formal micro and small enterprises in developing countries. These enterprises are often in traditional clusters and typically are characterized by limited deployment of capital and by low technical and managerial capabilities. Their main challenge is usually not commercializing new technologies but rather upgrading quality and productivity by reverse engineering existing technologies. Any policy to incentivize innovation as a driver of trade competitiveness that is designed for broad-based development should take into account that exports usually are concentrated in relatively few firms that continuously export. A reduced number of firms persistently sell to international markets, however, which accounts for the majority of the export value. Therefore, policies that aim to develop a broader base of innovative exporting firms may need to create mechanisms to foster entrance, intensity, and permanence in international markets.

Finally, policies to facilitate integration of firms into global production networks can play a critical role in facilitating low-level innovation in low-income countries. Indeed, trade in tasks could provide a lifeline for countries yet to industrialize because it simplifies getting started. Starting to export by undertaking a single task is far less daunting than breaking into the global market for an entire product. In some manufacturing activities, a production process that eventually generates a finished product can be decomposed into a series of steps or tasks. Each task is distinct. It may (1) require distinct skills, (2) use labor and capital in different proportions, (3) require distinct inputs, and (4) have distinct consequences for the local environment (UNIDO 2009). And no evidence indicates that task-based production is less technologically sophisticated than production of final products. Instead of needing to acquire the entire range of skills necessary to produce a product all at once, manufacturing can start with specialization in tasks most suited to the skills available.

Box 3.12 provides some case study examples of good practices in innovation.

Box 3.12. Case Examples of Good Policy Practice—Innovation

Malaysia: National and Regional Incentives for Innovation
Malaysia is a model of an economy that, over a period of two decades, achieved dramatic export-oriented growth along with structural change from a reliance on natural resources toward manufacturing and services. The government of Malaysia, at both a national and a regional level, has played a significant role in supporting export-entry as well as firm-level innovation and upgrading, through a series of industrial policy programs. Among these are a number of financing and incentive schemes designed to support investment in innovation.

At the national level, the Ministry of Industry and Trade (MITI) operates a Commercialization of Research and Development Fund, which provides partial grants of 50 to 70 percent of R&D expenditures related to innovation. Activities covered through the grants include market research, product design and development, standard and regulatory compliance, intellectual property concerns, and demonstration costs. In addition, the Technology Acquisition Fund provides grants of up to 70 percent to purchase technology licenses and patent rights.

Specifically in the Penang region, a number of financing schemes are available to support innovation, some of which are targeted specifically to support the SME sector. Three of these include the following:

- The *Industrial Technical Assistance Fund (ITAF)* was set up in 1990 to prompt SMEs to upgrade their technical capabilities in areas such as product development, design, quality, and productivity enhancement. Assistance is given in the form of grants, with 50 percent of the project costs borne by the government and the remainder by the applicant.
- The *Modernization & Automation 2 Scheme (MAS)* is a soft loan scheme aimed at promoting the use of modern technology processes by Malaysian-owned SMEs. The scheme assists SMEs in the acquisition of new machinery and equipment. Loan amounts are up to RM 1 million and up to 75 percent of the machinery or equipment purchased, with an interest rate of 4 percent per year and loan periods of 5–10 years.

(continued on next page)

Box 3.12. *(continued)*

- The *Normal Loan Scheme* offers project loans, leasing, and share financing. The scheme offers lease financing of machinery and equipment for a minimum amount of RM 100,000, at 5 percent interest and for a maximum period of five years. With regard to share financing, the scheme offers to take up equity in companies for amounts ranging from RM 100,000 to RM 5 million, with an interest rate of 5 percent and a maximum period of five years.

Rapid growth in Malaysia's high-end manufacturing activities (especially electronics) has contributed to the country now having one of the most sophisticated export mixes in the world. More recently, patenting activity outside of Malaysia by Malaysian residents also increased. Between 1995 and 2008, US patents issued to residents of Malaysia rose 20-fold, from an average of less than 10 per year to nearly 200.

Sources: World Bank 2010c; UNCTAD 2011.

Ireland: Leveraging European Union Assistance to Support Innovation and Growth
As a relatively peripheral European economy, with a small population, an agricultural history, and a long-term problem of persistently high unemployment, the dramatic growth and structural change achieved by Ireland stands as a useful lesson for developing countries. Government policy stimulates innovation through research, education, and industry-specific measures. Resources of about €2 billion were applied for this purpose in the period 2001–06 under measures agreed with the European Commission in the Ireland National Plan.

Through the agency Enterprise Ireland, three types of programs are available to encourage the acquisition of technology:

- *Grants*: Enterprise Ireland has a number of grant schemes, which are designed to encourage and support research, development, and innovation by firms. They support projects, the acquisition of equipment, and various kinds of cooperation with third-level educational institutions. These include: (1) the *RTI Competitive Grant Scheme,* which supports commercially focused, industry-led projects in product and process development (expenditure is greater than €95,000); a grant of between 25 and 45 percent of eligible expenditure is available, depending on company size and its location in Ireland, up to a maximum of €440,000. The aim of this scheme is to increase the level of high-quality R&D in businesses in Ireland, with a focus on improving competitiveness; (2) *The Research and Development Capability Initiative,* which covers additional resources, such as R&D staff, equipment, and so on; it also provides a grant of between 25 and 45 percent of eligible expenditure is available; (3) *Innovation Partnerships*, which support collaboration on applied research projects, with commercial application, between industry and third-level colleges; (4) a *Basic Research Grant Scheme* for third-level institutions; and (5) *Regional Business Incubation Space,* which aims to strengthen regional innovation infrastructure by facilitating the provision of incubation and commercial R&D space for the establishment of high potential start-ups.
- *Equity schemes*: Enterprise Ireland also invests in some of its client companies, where it is satisfied that such investment is justified. Equity may be in the form of ordinary shares. Loans can be provided in the form of redeemable preference shares.
- *Venture capital*: With the support of the European Commission, Enterprise Ireland established a seed and venture capital initiative under the operational program for industrial development, 1994–99. The aim was to develop a venture capital market to fill an existing gap in equity for SMEs. Fifteen partnership funds were created between Enterprise Ireland and the private sector, offering not only funding for these companies but also badly needed skills to accelerate their growth.

From 2000 to 2007, Enterprise Ireland supported 430 high-performance start-ups, 40 percent of which were specifically R&D projects. This investment yielded sales of €638 million and exports of €344 million, and generated employment for 5,500 people. More broadly, business expenditure on R&D quadrupled between 1995 and 2008; similarly, spending by higher education institutions on R&D doubled over this period to reach EU average levels.

Sources: UNCTAD 2005; Department of Enterprise, Trade and Employment (Republic of Ireland) 2009.

References

Chauffour, J. P., and T. Farole. 2010. "Trade Finance in Crisis: Market Adjustment or Market Failure." In *Effective Crisis Response and Openness: Implications for the Trading System*, eds. Simon J. Evenett, Bernard M. Hoekman, and Olivier Cattaneo, 119–142. Washington, DC: World Bank and CEPR.

Department of Enterprise, Trade and Employment (Republic of Ireland). 2009. *Science, Technology & Innovation: Delivering the Smart Economy.* Dublin: Department of Enterprise, Trade and Employment. Dublin: Department of Enterprise, Trade and Employment.

Ffrench-Davis, R. 2010. Economic Reforms in Chile: From Dictatorship to Democracy. Second edition. Ann Arbar: University of Michigan Press.

Guasch, J. L., J. L. Racine, I. Sanchez, and M. Diop. 2007. *Quality Systems and Standards for a Competitive Edge.* Washington, DC: World Bank.

IFC (International Finance Corporation). 2006. Simplification of Business Regulations at the Sub-National Level: A Reform Implementation Toolkit for project Teams. Washington, DC: World Bank.

InvestPenang 2010. http://www.investpenang.gov.my.

IFC (International Finance Corporation). 2008b. "Regulatory Transformation in Mexico, 1988–2000." World Bank, Washington, DC.

IPC (*Instituto Politécnico Centroamericano*). 2009. IPC Company Brochure. San Pedro Sula, Honduras: IPC.

ITC (International Trade Commission). 2009. *How to Access Trade Finance: A Guide for Exporting SMEs.* Geneva: International Trade Commission.

Jayasekera, Douglas. 2004. "Bilateral and Regional Free Trade Agreements: Case Study of Sri Lanka." Background Paper, UNDP Asia Trade Initiative, Hanoi.

Lim, P. L., and C. I. Ong. 2002. "Malaysian Case Study of the Use and Impact of Performance Requirements." Paper prepared for UNCTAD, Geneva.

Nassif, C. 2010. "Promoting New Exports: Experience from Industry Case Studies." In *Trade Competitiveness of the Middle East and North Africa: Policies for Export Diversification*, eds. J. R. Lopez-Calix, P. Walkenhorst, and N. Diop, 47–62. Washington, DC: World Bank.

Nathan Associates. 2004. Best Practices in Export Promotion. Technical Report Submitted to USAID El Salvador/EGE. April 2004.

OECD (Organisation for Economic Co-operation and Development). 2001. *Innovative Clusters: Drivers of National Innovation Systems*. Paris: OECD.

OECD. 2008. OECD Review of Agricultural Policies: Chile. Paris: OECD.

Penang Skills Development Centre. 2010. http://www.psdc.org.my.

Potter, J. 2001. Embedding Foreign Direct investment. Paris: OECD.

Ramsawak, R. 2010. Cluster Best Practices: Lessons from the Field. Trinidad: Arthur Lok Jack Graduate School of Business, University of the West Indies.

Salas, Fernando. 2005. "Institution Building: Lessons from Mexico, Public Policy for the Private Sector." Washington, DC, World Bank.

Sovicheat, Penn. 2006. Cambodia Ministry of Commerce, speaking at the Consultative Meeting on Trade Facilitation and Regional Integration, Bangkok, August 17–18.

Spar, D. L. 1998. "Attracting High Technology Investment: Intel's Costa Rica Plant." FIAS Occasional Paper 11, World Bank, Washington, DC.

UNCTAD (United Nations Conference on Trade and Development). 2006. *Blue Book for Ghana*. Geneva: UNCTAD and Japan Bank for International Cooperation.

UNCTAD (United Nations Conference on Trade and Development). 2005. *Improving the Competitiveness of SMEs through Enhancing Productive Capacity*. Geneva: UNCTAD and Japan Bank for International Cooperation.

UNESCAP (United Nations Economic and Social Commission for Asia and the Pacific). 2003. Training Workshop on Trade Finance Infrastructure, Tblisi, Georgia, October 15–16.

UNIDO (United Nations Industrial Development Organization). 2009. "Industrial Development Report 2009: Breaking In and Moving Up: New Industrial Challenges for the Bottom Billion and the Middle-Income Countries." United Nations Industrial Development Organization, Vienna.

Weerakoon, D. 2010. "Implementing Preferential Trade Agreements for Development: A Case Study for Sri Lanka." World Bank, Washington, DC.

World Bank. 2011a. *Border Management Modernization,* eds. Gerard McLinden, Enrique Fanta, David Widdowson, and Tom Doyle. Washington, DC: The World Bank.

World Bank. 2011b. "The Russian Federation: Export Diversification through Competition and Innovation—A Policy Agenda." World Bank, Washington, DC.

Word Bank. 2010b. *Innovation Policy: A Guide for Developing Countries.* Washington, DC: World Bank.

World Bank. 2010c. *Malaysia Economic Monitor: Growth through Innovation.* Washington, DC: World Bank.

World Bank. 2010d. *Trade and Transport Facilitation Assessment: A Practical Toolkit.* Washington, DC: World Bank.

World Bank. 2009c. *Duty and Tax Relief Suspension Schemes: Improving Export Competitiveness, A Reference and Learning Toolkit.* Washington, DC: International Trade Department, World Bank.

World Bank. 2008. *Doing Business.* www.doingbusiness.org.

World Bank. 2006. "Expanding Access to Finance: Good Practices and Policies for Micro, Small, and Medium Enterprises." World Bank, Washington, DC.

World Bank. 2005. "Food Safety and Agricultural Health Standards: Challenges and Opportunities for Developing Country Exports." Poverty Reduction & Economic Management Trade Unit and Agriculture and Rural Development Department, World Bank Washington, DC.

World Bank. 2004. *Global Economic Prospects 2005: Trade, Regionalism, and Development.* Washington, DC: World Bank.

MODULE 3

APPENDIX A: SUMMARY OF RECENT PAPERS ON DETERMINANTS OF TRADE COMPETITIVENESS

This toolkit refers to an extensive body of literature related to trade competitiveness. This appendix presents a more detailed summary of four recent papers—two of which were commissioned as background to this project—that explore determinants of different dimensions of export performance and thus are closely related to the general objective of this toolkit. The first, Carrère, Strauss-Kahn, and Cadot (2011), identifies several drivers of export diversification as a base to prescribe policy recommendations in developing countries. The second, Hallaert, Cavazos, and Kang (2011), identifies and quantifies the severity of binding constraints to trade expansion in developing countries in general and in some categories of countries—landlocked countries (LLCs), small and vulnerable economies (SVEs), and commodity exporters—in particular. Finally, in the two papers commissioned for this report, Şeker (2011) investigates the possible reasons that prevent convergence of countries in export performance, and Cusolito (2010) sheds light on the relationship between export competitiveness and the extensive and intensive margins of international trade.

Olivier Cadot, Céline Carrère, and Vanessa Strauss-Kahn. 2011. "Trade Diversification: Drivers and Impacts." World Bank, Washington, DC.

This paper proposes a quantitative assessment of the main determinants of export diversification. The authors address the issue of how export diversification is measured and discuss the stylized facts about export diversification across time and countries. Then, the authors identify the potential determinants of export diversification. Finally, they tackle the relationship between export trade diversification, growth, and employment. This work is important because

it provides insight on policy prescriptions that aim to achieve export diversification by pointing out several drivers of diversification (for example, infrastructure, education, and governance).

The authors employ the Theil index to examine how concentration (diversification) has evolved over time on 134 countries. They take advantage on the decomposability property of this index to identify changes in diversification within groups (the intensive margin of trade) and between groups (the extensive margin of trade). They define two groups to be analyzed: group one includes active export lines for a country-year pair, and group zero includes inactive export lines (that is, export lines for which there are no exports). Results confirm previous findings of a U-shaped relationship between export concentration and income and, most important, indicate that most of the concentration in levels occurs at the intensive margin (in goods that are long-standing exports) whereas changes in concentration occur at the extensive margin (see figure A.1).

Next, the authors take account of the main variables used in the literature and propose a quantitative assessment of the main determinants of export diversification. Specifically, they regress the overall Theil index, the within-groups Theil, the between-groups Theil, and the number of exported products on 10 variables using a panel database including 87 countries during 1990–2004. Country and year fixed effects control for unobservable characteristics in all regressions. Table B.1 reports the results.

Results confirm the U-shaped tendency of income on export diversification. Once controlling for gross domestic product (GDP) per capita, the results show that infrastructure appears to be an important driver of diversification: A 10 percent increase in the infrastructure index decreases the Theil index by about 0.7 percent. Remoteness also has the expected sign: The more remote the country, the lower

Figure A.1. Contributions of within- and between-Groups to Overall Concentration, All Countries

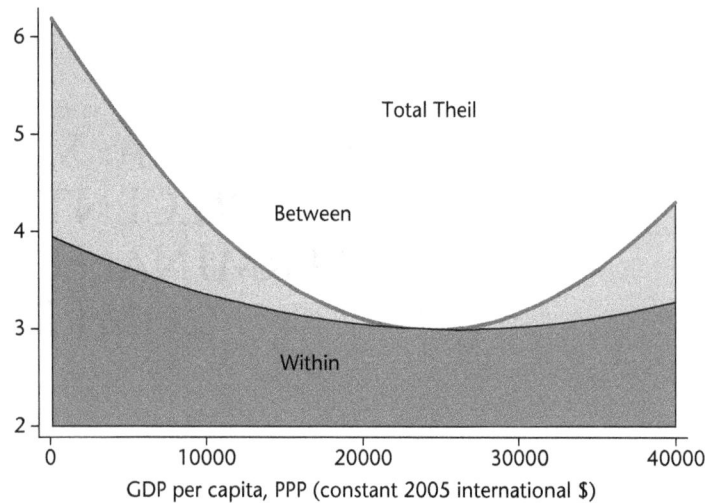

GDP per capita, PPP (constant 2005 international $)

Source: Authors.

Table A.1. Diversification Drivers in a Panel Data Set, 1990–2004, 87 Countries

	ln (Theil)		ln (Theil_within)		ln (Theil_between)		ln (Nber)	
	Coef.	Std. Err	Coef.	Std. Err	Coef.	Std. Err	Coef.	Std. Err
ln (per capita G-DP)	−0.505	0.09***	−0.193	0.13*	−1.054	0.32***	1.055	0.38***
ln (per capita G-DP) – squared	0.040	0.01***	0.009	0.01	0.054	0.02**	−0.106	0.02***
ln (Infrastructure)	−0.072	0.03***	−0.122	0.04***	−0.303	0.08***	0.119	0.07*
ln (Remoteness)	1.092	0.46**	−0.439	0.50	3.753	2.14*	−3.533	1.51**
Trade liberalization	−0.009	0.01	0.017	0.02	0.031	0.05	0.108	0.06*
Pref. Market Access	−0.179	0.04***	−0.244	0.05***	−1.031	0.21***	0.316	0.11***
FDI (% GDP)	0.001	0.00**	0.001	0.00*	0.002	0.00	0.000	0.00
ln (Years of Schooling)	−0.114	0.06*	0.017	0.07	−0.625	0.26**	0.619	0.21***
ICRG	−0.047	0.04*	0.086	0.04**	−0.584	0.14***	0.416	0.12***
Policy Score	−0.002	0.00*	0.002	0.00	−0.003	0.00	0.019	0.00***
ln (population)	−0.187	0.07***	0.041	0.08	−0.642	0.27**	1.582	0.27***
Country fixed effects	yes		yes		yes		yes	
Year fixed effects	yes		yes		yes		yes	
Observations	1195		1257		1257		1257	
Ajusted R-squared	0.97		0.92		0.98		0.95	

Source: Cadot, Carrère, and Strauss-Kahn (2011).
Note: Robust standard errors in italics.
*Significantly different from zero at 10 percent ;**significant at 5 percent ;***significant at 1 percent.

its export diversification (that is, the higher its Theil) essentially in terms of the extensive margin and number of products. The analysis thus confirms that high distance to importers increases the export fixed cost and consequently drastically reduces export diversification. Preferential market access is clearly an important factor of diversification at both margins. In contrast, net inflows of foreign direct investment (FDI; in percent of GDP) seems to concentrate exports value on some products and thereby increases concentration at the intensive margin. This result could be expected as multinationals specialize in specific products

that they produce in high volumes. They also find a significant impact of education on export diversification. A 10 percent increase in the years of schooling reduces the Theil index by 1.1 percent and increases the numbers of exported products by 6.2 percent. Similarly, the quality of institution appears clearly significant with a positive impact on diversification. Finally, as expected, the larger the population, the more diversified the economy.

As noted by the authors, these results should be seen with caution. The regressions are informative of the factors that have a significant impact on diversification and of the sign of this impact once controlled for others factors. It is difficult, however, to rank these factors and clearly isolate a single impact because of potential multicolinearity issues existing between these variables.

Next, the authors single out the role of trade liberalization as a driver of diversification. To do so, they combine the Theil index of export concentration computed at the HS six-digit level for 1988–2006 with the trade liberalization date of Wacziarg and Welch (2008). The sample used includes 100 countries, 62 middle-income and 38 low-income countries over 1988–2006, with respectively 68 percent and 49 percent of country-year observations occurring in liberalized regimes. The authors run fixed-effects regressions of the Theil index on a binary liberalization indicator defined by the dates of liberalization (equal to one when liberalized) to assess the within-country effect of trade liberalization on the diversification of exports. Specifically, they use a difference-in-difference approach given by the following:

$$Theil_{it} = \lambda_i + \delta_t + \phi LIB_{it} + \varepsilon_{it} \qquad (A.1)$$

where $Theil_{it}$ is the Theil index of country i exports in year t, LIB_{it} a dummy equals to one if t is greater than the year of liberalization (defined by Wacziarg and Welsh, 2008) and zero otherwise. λ_i and δ_t are respectively country and year fixed effects. The sample is not restricted to countries that underwent reforms. Results are reported in table A.2.

The regression shows a highly significant within-country difference in export diversification between a liberalized and a nonliberalized regime (reported in table A.2, column 1), with a coefficient twice as high for middle- than for low-income countries. They also regress equation A.1 using the Theil index's decomposition (within groups versus between groups). Results are reported in table A.2,

columns 3–6. Controlling for country and year effects, the results suggest that middle-income countries that undertook trade liberalization reforms have a significantly more diversified structure of exports along the intensive margin. By contrast, low-income countries diversify mostly along the extensive margin.

Overall, this work suggests that poor countries have, on average, undiversified exports. As they grow, they diversify, and then reconcentrate at high-income levels. The extensive margin (new products) dominates the action in terms of diversification, but the intensive margin (higher volumes) dominates the action in terms of export growth. Thus, if governments ultimately are interested in export (and employment) growth, then the intensive margin appears to be a better bet. Because of enormous churning, many of today's new products are tomorrow's failed products.

Jean-Jacques Hallaert, Ricardo Cavazos Cepeda, and Gimin Kang. 2011. "Estimating the Constraints to Developing Countries Trade." Organisation for Economic Co-operation and Development, Paris

This paper adds to the literature by identifying and quantifying the severity of binding constraints to trade expansion as well as by assessing the role of complementary policies in affecting trade reforms impact on economic growth. Although the authors acknowledge that constraints to trade expansion are largely country specific, they empirically test the role of these constraints in a cross-country exercise that is used as a benchmark against the specific needs of three country groupings: LLCs, SVEs, and commodity exporters. This analysis is complemented by two

Table A.2. Fixed-Effects Regressions of Diversification Index on Liberalization Status

	Theil		Theil-within		Theil-between	
Liberalization (LIB)	−0.190*		−0.075		−0.100*	
	(2.0)		(0.8)	(2.8)		
LIB - Middle Income		−0.241*		−0.271*		0.067
		(2.0)		(2.0)		(0.5)
LIB - Low Income		−0.138*		0.053		−0.209*
		(1.6)		(0.5)		(2.0)
Number of Obs.	1794		1394		1394	
Number of countries	100		100		100	
Period	1988–2006		1990–2004		1990–2004	
Country fixed effects	Yes		Yes		Yes	
Year fixed effects	Yes		Yes		Yes	
R^2 within	0.39	0.39	0.28	0.29	0.75	0.75

Source: Jean-Jacques Hallaert, Ricardo Cavazos Cepeda, and Gimin Kang (2011).
Note: Standard errors in parentheses; heteroskedasticity consistent and adjusted for country clustering.
* significant at the 10 percent level.

case studies (Azerbaijan and Uganda) that illustrate not only the mechanisms highlighted by the econometric work but also the importance of some variables the econometric work could not capture because of data limitations.

The empirical work to determine the impact of the variables identified as the binding constraints on trade and, subsequently, the impact of trade on growth is composed of two stages.[1] They employ a two-stage least squares estimator (2SLS) in which the first stage quantifies the magnitude and direction of the direct effect of the binding constraints on trade indicators (exports, imports, and openness),[2] and the second stage quantifies the magnitude and direction of the composite effect of the binding constraints on the economy's growth rate through their effect on trade indicators. The first stage is then given by the following:

$$Trade = W\partial + \tau GDP_{i,\,t-1} + \varepsilon_{i,t} \qquad (A.2)$$

where *Trade* is defined as above; W is a vector of exogenous variables in the model that determine the country's level of trade, including those related to the binding constraints and a constant; GDP represents initial $GDP_{i,\,t-1}$; τ is a parameter to be estimated; $\varepsilon_{i,t}$ represents the regression error term; and ∂ is also a parameter to be estimated. The second stage regression is given by the following:

$$\Delta GDP = \alpha_0 + \alpha_1 GDP_{t,0} + \alpha_2 \widehat{Trade}_{it}$$
$$+ \alpha_3 Investment + X\beta + \omega_{i,t} \qquad (A.3)$$

where ΔGDP is the change in real GDP, $GDP_{t,0}$ represents initial GDP, $\widehat{Trade}_{it}$ is the predicted value of the trade indicator in stage one (exports, imports, or openness), *Investment* is the amount of investment in the country as a share of GDP (investment is part of this equation because it is a key determinant of growth and because literature has shown that it is an important channel of the impact of trade on growth), X is a vector of other variables affecting GDP growth, $\omega_{i,t}$ represents the regression error term, and the α_k and β are parameters to be estimated.

This model is estimated on a database of 65 countries that are recipients of Official Development Assistance (ODA) covering the period from 1981 to 2009. These countries account for 57 percent of the aid for trade disbursed since the inception of the Aid for Trade initiative (2005–08) and 55 percent of 2008 aid-for-trade commitments. Results for the whole sample of countries are reported in table A.3.

The results for the unrestricted sample show five main findings: (1) In line with economic literature, both imports and exports boost economic growth, but the constraints to exports differ from the constraints to imports. (2) Despite recent trade liberalization, a cut in import tariffs can still boost exports and imports performance, but the impact is small compared with other constraints. (3) Electricity

appears to be the main constraint to trade expansion; this is less related to availability than to reliability. (4) Air transport, labor force, labor productivity, and rule of law are important factors affecting exports but not imports, whereas investment, access to domestic credit, and mismanagement of the real effective exchange rate appear to remarkably affect imports but not exports. (5) The results confirm the importance of complementary and compatible policies (education, governance, business environment, and macroeconomic stability) that are important for trade expansion and economic growth because they affect factors having a large impact on trade performance, such as investment, labor productivity, and labor participation.

How do the binding constraints differ from these general results for the various country groupings? The authors shed light on this question by looking at three different country groups (LLCs, SVEs, and commodity exporters) to identify the most binding constraints for each group. The highlights of the main results follow.

Landlocked Countries

LLCs face particular constraints that significantly diminish their trade integration. The openness ratio is reduced by 5 percent, just for the fact of being a landlocked country. Electricity is the main problem followed by tax rates, access to finance, and transportation. The growth effect of trade appears to be slightly larger in LLCs than in the benchmark scenario: An increase of 10 percent in the openness ratio will determine an increase of growth rate of 1.6 percent (compared with 0.8 percent/1.1 percent of the unrestricted sample). This result is valid both for imports and for exports.

Poor domestic policies are one of the factors responsible for the low trade performance of LLCs. Restrictive trade policies (measured by customs tariff) seem to have a greater impact on trade performance of LLCs than in other countries. A 10 percent appreciation of the real effective exchange rate would lead to a drop of about 1 percent of export, import, and openness ratios. Access to credit instead appears not to be a significant constraint to trade expansion in LLCs.

Small and Vulnerable Countries

The authors define SVEs as countries whose share in global market does not exceed 0.12 percent and whose population does not exceed 15 million. According to these criteria, and given the available data, 36 ODA-eligible countries are defined as SVEs. In these countries, the size of the state limits the diversification opportunities of production.

Table A.3. Results for the Unrestricted Sample

	(1)			(2)		
	Openness	Exports	Imports	Openness	Exports	Imports
Loggdp1	−0.287***	−0.413***	−0.192**	−0.277***	−0.401***	−0.183**
	(0.0906)	(0.106)	(0.0814)	(0.0852)	(0.0997)	(0.0766)
l_air_trans_carr_dep	0.101***	0.195***	0.039	0.119***	0.203***	0.067*
	(0.0388)	(0.0574)	(0.0343)	(0.0425)	(0.0598)	(0.0367)
l_roadkm2	0.097***	0.082**	0.111***	0.074**	0.064	0.083***
	(0.0280)	(0.0405)	(0.0238)	(0.0295)	(0.0392)	(0.0266)
l_electric_power_losses _p_out	−0.185***	−0.240**	−0.170***	−0.214***	−0.288***	−0.174***
	(0.0666)	(0.0984)	(0.0546)	(0.0644)	(0.0945)	(0.0546)
l_dom_credit	0.176**	0.004	0.290***	0.171*	0.011	0.271***
	(0.0866)	(0.117)	(0.0733)	(0.0907)	(0.121)	(0.0758)
Simple_average3_mfn	−0.013**	−0.014**	−0.011**	−0.012*	−0.013*	−0.010*
	(0.00561)	(0.00670)	(0.00506)	(0.00602)	(0.00703)	(0.00549)
l_gfcf1	0.423*	0.218	0.507**	0.480*	0.257	0.582**
	(0.254)	(0.294)	(0.228)	(0.273)	(0.313)	(0.242)
l_property_rights	0.229	0.496**	0.159	0.127	0.458**	−0.015
	(0.167)	(0.219)	(0.149)	(0.156)	(0.202)	(0.139)
l_l_force	0.138**	0.263***	0.055	0.154**	0.290***	0.057
	(0.0674)	(0.0857)	(0.0594)	(0.0770)	(0.0916)	(0.0700)
l_productivity_per _worker	0.122*	0.309***	−0.027	0.110	0.287***	−0.026
	(0.0736)	(0.0942)	(0.0664)	(0.0681)	(0.0869)	(0.0625)
l_reer	−0.678*	−0.696	−0.572**	−0.557*	−0.580	−0.450
	(0.367)	(0.440)	(0.332)	(0.319)	(0.395)	(0.284)
l_government_spending	−1.570***	−1.840***	−1.404***	−1.737***	−2.016***	−1.553***
	(0.510)	(0.571)	(0.479)	(0.608)	(0.682)	(0.562)
Landlocked	−0.501***	−0.709***	−0.359***	−0.633***	−0.852***	−0.470**
	(0.126)	(0 179)	(0.113)	(0.196)	(0.247)	(0.183)
Island	0.005	0.019	−0.033	−0.004	0.033	−0.053
	(0.137)	(0.163)	(0.129)	(0.137)	(0.161)	(0.132)
SVE				0.264	0.246	0.274
				(0.185)	(0.218)	(0.166)
Commodity exporters				−0.069	−0.040	−0.193***
				(0.0889)	(0.130)	(0.0730)
Constant	−2.972	−3.994	−4.095	−3.438	−4.582	−4.393
	(3.778)	(4.230)	(3.493)	(3.427)	(3.861)	(3.157)
Observations R–squared	175	176	176	175	176	176
	0.454	0.411	0.503	0.462	0.416	0.520
Trade variable in growth estimate	0.081	0.054	0.102	0.111	0.074	0.07
	(0.0885)	(0.0607)	(0.127)	(0.0801)	(0.0580)	(0.077)

Source: Jean-Jacques Hallaert, Ricardo Cavazos Cepeda, and Gimin Kang (2011).
Note: Robust standard errors in parentheses, ***$p < 0.01$, **$p < 0.05$, *$p < 0.1$.

This would result, other things being equal, in a larger import-to-GDP ratio. More in detail, SVEs are characterized by a physical isolation, geographic distance from the main markets, high transport and transit costs, minimal or no export product diversification, dependency on few export markets, low competitiveness, difficulties in attracting FDI, and susceptibility to natural disasters.

SVEs are open to trade by necessity. Export concentration reduces significantly their openness: the Herfindahl Index (HS four digits, SVEs export concentration, 2000–07) equals 0.176, which is much higher than the

index for non-SVEs (0.145) or LDCs (0.127). Furthermore, the small size of their labor force is an important statistical constraint: A 10 percent increase in the labor force would increase the openness ratio by more than 3 percent of GDP.

In SVEs, the relevance of the electricity problem appears larger than any other group. Transportation issues seem to be more severe than for the average country but less than for LLCs. According to the estimations, quality of road infrastructure largely affects trade openness in SVEs: A 10 percent increase in paved roads would augment openness by 3 to 5 percent of GDP. Similarly, a 10 percent increase in road density would increase openness by about 2 percent of GDP. Finally, the impact of roads on the whole economic growth would be substantial: A 10 percent increase in the quality of roads should increase the economic expansion by more than 0.4 percent, mainly through trade.

Electricity is the main constraint for SVEs' exporters. The problem is associated, in particular, with the reliability of electricity. Telecommunication infrastructure, given the remoteness, landlockedness, and insularity of most of these countries, also represents a major issue of constraints: Increasing the number of fixed telephone lines per 100 inhabitants would increase the trade openness ratio by 0.2 percent.

Supportive macroeconomic policies are essential for the sustainability of trade reforms. Although the impact of the mismanagement of the exchange rate appears more limited in the case of SVEs, the impact of government spending remains absolutely significant, much more than for the unrestricted sample. Estimation results show that focusing on tariff reforms would not affect SVEs significantly. The biggest impact would be given by the complementary policies, in particular, by addressing the export concentration issues. Access to credit is also a major impacting factor: A 10 percent increase in credit to the private sector would increase all trade ratios by 3 to 4 percent of GDP.

Commodity Exporters

The commodity exporters group is defined by countries for which raw materials account for more than 45 percent of goods exports. The impact of trade on the whole economic growth appears to be smaller in magnitude than for any other country group: A 10 percent increase of openness ratio would increase the economic growth to between 0.09 percent and 0.17 percent. In short, it seems that their high export concentration makes them more vulnerable to world commodity prices.

The tariff regime appears to be a more important constraint for commodity exporters than for other country groups: A 10 percent cut in tariffs would augment the export-to-GDP ratio by 0.2 to 0.6 percent and the import-to-GDP ratio by 0.2 to 0.3 percent. Electricity also appears to be a major constraint (more in terms of availability rather than in terms of reliability): A 10 percent increase in electricity consumption is associated with an increase of 4 percent of the export-to-GDP ratio and of 1.6 percent of the openness ratio.

Complementary policies to boost investment have a positive impact on trade openness for commodity exporters. According to the results, an increase in investment would have a significant impact mainly for imports (although it had remarkable significance for both importers and exporters, in the case of SVEs and LLCs). This may be due to the specificities of the investment in commodity countries and to the impact of a Dutch disease.

Interestingly, in the case of commodity exporters, property rights are a significant statistical variable. Specifically, property rights are highly significant (and negative) for imports and basically insignificant for exports. A 10 percent increase in the property right variable will determine an increase of between 2.3 percent and 2.5 percent of GDP of the openness ratio for the unrestricted sample but will cause a reduction of 1.2 percent of GDP in the commodity exporter group.

Murat Şeker. 2010. "Trade Policies, Investment Climate, and Exports across Countries." World Bank Policy Research Working Paper No. 5654, World Bank, Washington, DC.

This study investigates the possible reasons that countries fail to converge in export performance. The study's data set comprises countries with various income levels and from different regions of the world to shows how trade policies, trade facilitation, and investment climate (IC) variables affect export performance.

To accomplish this goal, the author uses two indexes to measure the restrictiveness of tariff policies. The first is the Trade Tariff Restrictiveness Index (TTRI), which shows the restrictiveness of domestic trade policies on imports. The second is the Market Access Trade Tariff Restrictiveness Index (MATTRI), which shows the ease of foreign market access of the country. Unlike simple or weighted average tariff rates, these indexes are well grounded in trade theory and provide sound aggregate measures of trade restrictiveness.

The author focuses on six indicators, each representing a different aspect of the IC. These indicators are regulatory quality, trade facilitation, entry regulations, access to finance, infrastructure, and property rights. Although a number of studies analyze how some of these indicators affect export performance, none have looked at the interaction of these indicators with the restrictiveness of foreign market access.

Regulatory quality—obtained from Worldwide Governance Indicators (WGI)—captures the capability that a government has to carry out sound policies that facilitate private sector development. It fluctuates between -2.5 and 2.5 (high scores correspond to better outcomes). Access to finance measures financial development. It corresponds to the log of money divided by quasi-money (M2) to

GDP collected by World Bank's *World Development Indicators*. The entry regulations measure is an index that tells how many procedures are needed to start a business. Trade facilitation is measured by a country's customs efficiency. Time to export is counted as the log of the number of days needed to export a good. Infrastructure represents the quality of overall infrastructure (for example, transport, telephone, and energy). It varies between one and seven, where one corresponds to very low rating. Finally, property rights is an index obtained from Heritage Foundation's Economic Freedom database and ranges from one to seven as well.

The data set covers three years of observations between 2005 and 2007 for 137 countries. It is not balanced because some variables have missing observations for some of the countries. The data include countries from six regions of the world and five income groups. The primary estimation method is pooled ordinary least squares (OLS) method. The estimation equation is presented as follows:

$$\log(Export_{it}) = \beta_0 + \beta_1 \log(GDP_{it-1}) + \beta_2 \log(Area_i)$$
$$+\beta_3 \log(remote_i)$$
$$+\beta_4 \log(ExpGrowth)_{it-1,t-2}$$
$$+ \beta_5 \log(TTRI_{it-1})$$
$$+ \beta_6 \log(MATTRI_{it-1}) + \beta_7 Indicators_{it-1}$$
$$+ \beta_8 \log(MATTRI_{it-1})*Indicator_{it-1}$$
$$+ \beta_9 d_{2006} + \beta_{10} d_{2007} + \varepsilon_{it}. \qquad (A.4)$$

The results of estimating this equation are presented in table A.4. GDP is a strong correlate of high export performance, which is a common finding in gravity models. Conversely, large and remote countries export less. A 10 percent increase in the remoteness of the country decreases export sales by 4 to 5 percentage points. Past export growth also contributes significantly to the current export performance. Lastly, the trade restrictiveness index, which measures the stringency of domestic trade policies on imports, negatively affects exports. This index shows that there is complementarity between importing and exporting activities, which could be caused by exporters' extensive usage of imported intermediate goods.

The author uses the MATTRI as a proxy for foreign market access. Table A.4 shows that difficulties in market access significantly decrease export performance. In four of the six specifications, its coefficient is negative and significant. A 10 percent increase in market access leads to a 2 to 8 percentage point increase in exports. Among the IC indicators, the significant indictors are in accordance with the empirical findings in the literature. Better regulatory quality, quality of infrastructure, and protection of property rights lead to higher export sales, whereas inefficiencies in trade facilities decrease exports. The interaction terms between market access and IC indicators are significant with the expected signs in all specifications. This shows that improvements in IC would make larger contributions

Table A.4. Estimation Results with Pooled OLS Method

	Regulations	Finance	Entry	Time to Export	Infrastructure	Property
RealGDP(PPP)	0.989	1.006	1.064	0.976	0.978	0.994
	(0.031)***	(0.045)***	(0.034)***	(0.032)***	(0.030)***	(0.034)***
Log(Area)	–0.082	–0.081	–0.129	–0.060	–0.079	–0.091
	(0.035)**	(0.043)*	(0.043)***	(0.037)	(0.040)**	(0.041)**
Remoteness	–0.384	–0.470	–0.422	–0.474	–0.504	–0.533
	(0.155)**	(0.188)**	(0.182)**	(0.157)***	(0.163)***	(0.175)***
Export Growth$_{t,t-1}$	0.094	0.094	0.077	0.101	0.134	0.121
	(0.046)**	(0.060)	(0.049)	(0.047)**	(0.048)***	(0.047)**
log(TTRI)	–0.265	–0.498	–0.458	–0.432	–0.397	–0.411
	(0.094)***	(0.111)***	(0.109)***	(0.085)***	(0.084)***	(0.096)***
log(MATTRI)	–0.185	–0.805	0.202	0.269	–0.526	–0.536
	(0.046)***	(0.318)**	(0.131)	(0.257)	(0.170)***	(0.167)***
log(MATTRI)*Indicator	0.124	0.173	–0.037	–0.141	0.299	0.058
	(0.055)**	(0.089)*	(0.011)***	(0.077)*	(0.117)**	(0.025)**
Indicator	0.281	–0.028	0.004	–0.345	0.599	0.114
	(0.076)***	(0.139)	(0.021)	(0.134)**	(0.195)***	(0.039)***
Constant	3.493	4.357	2.915	5.761	4.321	4.457
	(1.612)**	(1.959)**	(1.843)	(1.671)***	(1.591)***	(1.833)**
Observations	205	175	204	203	193	189
R^2	0.953	0.933	0.944	0.952	0.954	0.954

Source: Seker (2010).
Note: Robust standard errors clustered by country are in parentheses. All regressions control for year fixed effects.
***$p < 0.01$, **$p < 0.05$, *$p < 0.1$.

to increasing export performance of countries with low foreign market access relative to those with high foreign market access. Firms in a country with low foreign market access have to be more competitive and efficient in export markets to be able to compete with those firms in more open countries. Hence, the marginal contribution of improvements in IC to export sales will be relatively greater in countries with low foreign market access.

Using the estimation results reported in this table, the author computes the total impact of one standard deviation change in IC indicator on growth rates of export sales. To show how countries with different levels of foreign market access benefit from this improvement, the author compares 25th and 75th percentiles of a foreign market access restrictiveness index, which corresponds to 2 and 5.5 percent tariff rates, respectively. The difference between growth rates of export sales generated by the change in each IC indicator for the two values of the foreign market access index are given in table A.5. The table shows that a country in the 75th percentile of market access index distribution benefits from a one standard deviation improvement of regulatory quality by 10 percentage points more than a country in the 25th percentile of the distribution. The impacts of the other IC indicators are of similar magnitude. This finding shows that IC improvements are important in reducing the barriers to trade and leading to the convergence of export performance of countries.

After controlling the effects of size, remoteness, and past export growth performance of countries, this analysis indicates that restrictions in foreign market access and domestic tariff policies reduce export performance. Another important result is that improvements in the IC indicators (regulatory quality, trade facilitation, entry regulations, access to finance, infrastructure, and property rights) not only increase export volumes but also reduce the distortions caused by restrictive foreign market access.

Ana Paula Cusolito. 2010. "Export Competitiveness and the Intensive and the Extensive Margins of Trade." World Bank, Washington, DC.

This note studies the impact of export competitiveness determinants, such as market access, institutional environment,

labor market regulations, and business environment on both the extensive and intensive margins of international trade. It identifies constraints that prevent countries from increasing trade along these margins. Variations in the intensive margin capture changes in the value of already exported and imported goods. By contrast, variations in the extensive margin account for changes in the number of exported and imported products.

The author uses a version of the standards gravity equation that controls for selection, firm heterogeneity, remoteness, and endogeneity. The methodology has two steps. In the first step, a probit model is estimated where the dependent variable, Y_{ij}, is a dummy that takes value one if country i exports to country j. In the second step, the standard gravity equation is estimated, controlling for selection, remoteness, and firm heterogeneity. Specifically, the model is as follows:

$$
\begin{aligned}
X_{ij} = {} & \beta_1 + \beta_2 LPI_i + \beta_3(MKT\ Access_i) + \beta_4(ICT_i) \\
& + \beta_5(Institutional\ Index_i) + \beta_6(Labor\ mkt\ inst.i) \\
& + \beta_7(Knowledge\ economy\ index_i) \\
& + \beta_8(Av.\ Tariffs_i) + \beta_9(GDP_i) + \beta_{10}(GDP_j) \\
& + \beta_{11}(Remoteness_i) + \beta_{12}(Distance_{ij}) \\
& + \beta_{13} Z_{ij} + \beta_{14}(Heterogeneity_i) + I_j + \mu_{ij}, \quad \text{(A.5)}
\end{aligned}
$$

$$
\begin{aligned}
Y_{ij} = {} & 1[\alpha_1 + \alpha_2 LPI + \alpha_3(MKT\ Access_i) + \alpha_4(ICT_i) \\
& + \alpha_5(Institutional\ Index_i) + \alpha_6(Labor\ mkt\ inst.i) \\
& + \alpha_7(Knowledge\ economy\ index_i) \\
& + \alpha_8(Av.\ Tariffs_i) + \alpha_9(GDP_i) + \alpha_{10}(GDP_j) \\
& + \alpha_{11}(Remoteness_i) + \alpha_{12}(Distance_{ij}) + \alpha_{13} Z_{ij} \\
& + \alpha_{14} Entry\ Costs_i + I_j + v_{ij} > 0], \quad \text{(A.6)}
\end{aligned}
$$

where $v_{ij} \sim N(0,1)$ and (μ_{ij}, v_{ij}) is independent of X with zero mean.

The variables are as follows:

- X_{ij} is the volume of exports from country i to country j
- LPI_i is the logistic performance index of country i
- $MKT\ Access_i$ is a variable related to the difficulties to have access to foreign markets
- ICT_i is the information and communications technology index of country i
- $Institutional\ Index_i$ is an index related to the quality of institutions in country i

Table A.5. Impacts of Improvements in Investment Climate Indicators on Exports (in Percentage Points)

Indicator	Regulations	Finance	Entry	Time to Export	Infrastructure	Property
Total Impact	10.1	9.9	12.4	7.9	10	9.6

Source: Cusolito (2010).
Note: Improvements in IC indicators indicate an increase for regulations, finance, infrastructure, and property indicators, and indicate a decrease in entry time and time to export.

Table A.6. Impact of Export Competitiveness Determinants on the Extensive and Intensive Margins of Trade

Extensive margin	I	II	III	IV	V	VI	VII	VIII	IX
Competitiveness index	0.0018792*** [0.0002393]***								0.0009922 [0.0000305]***
Starting a business	0.004545 [0.0000705]***	0.0044718 [0.0000627]***	0.0048344 [0.0000503]***	0.0092452 [0.0001409]***	0.0029094 [0.0001069]***	0.0051268 [0.000068]***	0.0022697 [0.0000554]***	0.0997738 [0.001161]***	0.0009409 [0.0001568]***
Logistic performance index		0.0031626 [0.0003799]***							
Input costs index			−0.0007365 [0.0000105]***						−0.0002196 [7.93e−06]***
Institutional index				0.0477447 [0.0007383]***					0.0018187 [0.0001293]***
Labor market institutions index					0.0170846 [0.0005755]***				0.0048798 [0.0001332]***
Innovation index						0.0022063 [0.0000996]***			0.0008842 [0.0000541]***
Trade restrictions							0.003139 [0.0000615]**		0.0010258 [0.0000384]**
Market access								−0.0934245 [0.0027671]***	−0.0008957 [0.0000349]***
Num. of obs.	511567	590253	512682	246361	246361	512682	512682	512682	511567

Intensive margin	I	II	III	IV	V	VI	VII	VIII	IX
Competitiveness index	671273.8 [786408.4]								
Logistic performance index		19174.39 [1811.708]***							33200.4 [9638.709]***
Input costs index			31259.08 [120344.9]						−1007.211 [2213.621]
Institutional index				18320.78 [1447.257]***					−12206.62 [18334]
Labor market institutions index					2580.366 [2640.032]				18302.31 [49116.03]
Innovation index						−1649529 [682173.6]***			5869.807 [8924.48]
Trade restrictions							−1030.634 [180.3156]***		4291.595 [10346.13]
Market access								3737039 [1.29e+07]	−3282.468 [9049.59]
Num. of obs.	511567	590253	512682	246361	246361	512682	512682	512682	511567

Source: Cusolito (2010).
Note: ***p < 0.01, **p < 0.05, *p < 0.1.

- *Labor mkt inst.i* is an index related to the rigidities in labor regulations
- *Knowledge economy indexi* is an index related to the intensity of the R&D activity in country *i*
- *Av. Tariffsi* is the mean of the tariffs imposed by country *i*
- *GDP* refers to gross domestic product
- *Remotenessi* is a measure of how far country *i* is from the rest of the world
- *Distanceij* refers to the distance between country *i* and country *j*
- *Zij* is a vector of variables that includes dummies capturing the landlocked condition of country *i*, the existence of a common border between country *i* and *j*, a common language between country *i* and *j*, a colonial relationship between country *i* and *j*, and a common colonizer between country *i* and *j*
- *Entry Costs* is a measure of the number of procedures a country has to complete to operate legally in the markets

The data are at the Industry level (SITC revision 3 three-digit classification) from the World Integrated Trade Solution (WITS) database. Data on competitiveness come mainly from the World Bank. The TTRI and the MATTRI are used to measure trade policy barriers. The author constructs an index of export competitiveness by applying principal component analysis (PCA) to the main determinants of export competitiveness: *TTRI, MATTRI, LPI, ICT, KEI, II,* and *LMR*. The new indicator is defined as the predicted value of the first component. Higher values indicate better performances. Table A.6 shows the result of estimating these equations.[3]

The estimated coefficient is positive for the extensive and intensive margins. It is statistically significant at the first one, however. A 1 percent change in the Export Competitiveness Index increases the probability of exporting by 0.018 percent. To analyze how different determinants of export competitiveness affect the intensive and the extensive margins of exports, columns II–VII report results using the determinants of competitiveness separately. The last column displays the estimation outcome when we include all the variables.

The Logistic Performance Index is statistically significant and positive to explain both the probability that two countries engage in trade and the value of their trade relation. A change of one unit in the index increases the probability of trade by 0.09 percent. The same variation raises the volume of exports by US$33,200.

The quality of the institutional environment is another important factor that affects trade. A 1 percent change in regulatory and rule of law quality increases the probability of trade by 0.0018 percent. No evidence indicates, however, that institutional quality affects the volume of exports.

Innovation has a positive and significant impact on trade. This is the result that innovation increases total factor productivity, reduces production costs, and allows firms to cover the fixed cost of exporting. A change of one unit in the innovation index increases the probability of exporting by 0.088 percent. No evidence indicates, however, that innovation affects the intensive margin.

Tariffs and other trade policy barriers to trade limit the access to foreign markets and reduce the probability that two countries engage in trade. By contrast, expanded policy-induced export opportunities can have a positive effect on firm performance, which in turn affect trade. In the estimation, a 1 percent change in the uniform tariff of trading partners increases the probability that two countries engage in trade by 0.0009 percent.

In sum, the signs of the coefficients for trade logistics, institutions, innovation, and market access are according to the theory. The signs of the coefficients for starting a business, labor market rigidities, and tariffs are different from those expected. Unfortunately, the author cannot rationalize these findings.

Notes

1. The motive for using a two-stage procedure is the presence of an endogenously determined variable in the growth regression, the level of trade. Previous literature has shown the reverse causality between trade levels and GDP growth.

2. The reason behind the idea of splitting the impact of binding constraints on openness into impact on exports and impact on imports hinges on the political-economic developments of the Aid for Trade initiative. In the Hong Kong, China, declaration (WTO, 2005), the stated objective of the initiative was actually to "expand trade." The role of imports, however, in explaining growth and in trade policy analyses is largely underestimated and not well understood. Part of the difficulty in explaining the role of imports in growth probably comes from limited data availability. Theory suggests that imports may foster growth by more efficiently reallocating resources, ameliorating domestic manufacturing by lowering the cost of inputs and of capital goods, allowing better access to foreign technologies, and so on. Most of these gains are dynamic; for instance, imports increase productivity, which is a major determinant of economic growth and in per capita income. The impact of imports on economic expansion is not limited, then, to the technology embedded into imports but also arises from competition from cheaper imports.

3. To satisfy the exclusion restriction, the author introduces the number of legal procedures needed to start a business (*SB*) as an explanatory variable in the first step.